GET THE MOST FROM YOUR BOOK

SPRINGER PUBLISHING
CONNECT™

VOUCHER CODE:

2BA0HUSP

Online Access

Your print purchase of *An Innovative Approach to Career Counseling* includes **online access via Springer Publishing Connect**™ to increase accessibility, portability, and searchability.

Insert the code at https://connect.springerpub.com/content/book/978-0-8261-5073-8 today!

Having trouble? Contact our customer service department at cs@springerpub.com

Instructor Resource Access for Adopters

Let us do some of the heavy lifting to create an engaging classroom experience with a variety of instructor resources included in most textbooks SUCH AS:

INSTRUCTOR MANUAL

POWERPOINTS

TEST BANK

Visit **https://connect.springerpub.com/** and look for the **"Show Supplementary"** button on your **book homepage** to see what is available to instructors! First time using Springer Publishing Connect?

Email **textbook@springerpub.com** to create an account and start unlocking valuable resources.

AN INNOVATIVE
APPROACH
TO CAREER
COUNSELING

Angie C. Smith, PhD, LCMHC-S, ACS, NCC, embraces multiple roles as a partner, mother, associate teaching professor, program coordinator at North Carolina State University, and licensed clinical mental health counselor-supervisor (NC). She has been teaching online and on campus at NC State University for 13 years, and before joining NC State she worked in corporate environments, in college counseling academia, and in private practice.

Angie holds a doctorate degree in counseling and counselor education with a minor in psychology, is a licensed clinical mental health counselor (LCMHC) and supervisor (LCMHC-S) in North Carolina, an approved clinical supervisor (ACS), and nationally certified counselor (NCC). Angie is an alumna of the National Career Development Association (NCDA) Counselor Education Academy and currently serves on the Ethics Committee.

Angie is dedicated to the counseling profession, advocating with her clients and students, and teaching counseling skills to counselors-in-training and within the community. She has served as president of the North Carolina Career Development Association (NCCDA) and on the Executive Board on the Awards Committee. For the past decade, she was on the review board for the *Journal of Employment Counseling* and is a recipient of the Roy N. Anderson Award for outstanding contributions to the career field. Since 2020, Angie has been awarded the Provost's Award for Excellence in Teaching, the Alumni Outstanding Teaching Award, and the North Carolina State University (NCSU): Outstanding Teacher Award.

She has authored and coauthored several articles for the NCDA *Career Convergence* magazine, and in 2018 she directed a book project titled *Developing Online Learning in the Helping Professions: Online, Blended, and Hybrid Models*.

Katie Peterssen, MEd, NCC, LCMHC-A, has been helping people explore career and academic pathways and strategies to meet their life goals for 15 years. Currently, Katie serves as an associate director for Career Management Services at Duke University's Fuqua School of Business and is the cofounder of Ignite Career and Leadership Development, LLC. Katie has broad experience serving clients at all levels across higher education, government, and corporate settings.

Katie earned her bachelor of science in information design and corporate communication from Bentley University and an MEd in counselor education at North Carolina State University. She is a National Certified Counselor under the National Board for Certified Counselors (NCC) and a Licensed Clinical Mental Health Counselor Associate in North Carolina (LCMHCA). As an expert in career and professional development, she has honed the skill of recognizing and cultivating strengths in individuals and teams.

Katie has delivered tech-savvy presentations on career and professional development to Fortune 500 companies, national nonprofit organizations, and higher education groups. She has also served in leadership roles on the board of the North Carolina Career Development Association, including as president from 2020 to 2021.

While she has lived up and down the East Coast, Katie currently resides in Raleigh, North Carolina, with her partner and young son.

AN INNOVATIVE APPROACH TO CAREER COUNSELING

Theory and Practical Application

Angie C. Smith, PhD, LCMHC-S, ACS, NCC

Katie Peterssen, MEd, NCC, LCMHC-A

 SPRINGER PUBLISHING

Springer Publishing Company, LLC
11 West 42nd Street, New York, NY 10036
www.springerpub.com
connect.springerpub.com/

Acquisitions Editor: Mindy Okura-Marszycki
Compositor: S4Carlisle Publishing Services

ISBN: 978-0-8261-5072-1
ebook ISBN: 978-0-8261-5073-8
DOI: 10.1891/9780826150738

SUPPLEMENTS

A robust set of instructor resources designed to supplement this text is located at http://connect.springerpub.com/content/book/978-0-8261-5073-8. Qualifying instructors may request access by emailing textbook@springerpub.com.

Instructor Manual: 978-0-8261-5074-5
Instructor Test Bank: 978-0-8261-5075-2
Instructor Chapter PowerPoints: 978-0-8261-5076-9

Student Materials:
Student Resources: 978-0-8261-5077-6

23 24 25 26 27 / 5 4 3 2 1

The author and the publisher of this Work have made every effort to use sources believed to be reliable to provide information that is accurate and compatible with the standards generally accepted at the time of publication. The author and publisher shall not be liable for any special, consequential, or exemplary damages resulting, in whole or in part, from the readers' use of, or reliance on, the information contained in this book. The publisher has no responsibility for the persistence or accuracy of URLs for external or third-party Internet websites referred to in this publication and does not guarantee that any content on such websites is, or will remain, accurate or appropriate.

Library of Congress Cataloging-in-Publication Data

Names: Smith, Angie C., author. | Peterssen, Katie, author.
Title: An innovative approach to career counseling : theory and practical application /
    Angie C. Smith, PhD, LCMHC-S, ACS, NCC, Katie Peterssen, MEd, NCC, LCMHC-A.
Identifiers: LCCN 2022060027 (print) | LCCN 2022060028 (ebook) | ISBN
    9780826150721 (cloth) | ISBN 9780826150738 (ebook)
Subjects: LCSH: Vocational guidance. | Vocational guidance—Vocational
    guidance. | Career development. | Counseling—Practice.
Classification: LCC HF5381 .S6228 2024 (print) | LCC HF5381 (ebook) | DDC
    331.702—dc23/eng/20221215
LC record available at https://lccn.loc.gov/2022060027
LC ebook record available at https://lccn.loc.gov/2022060028

Contact sales@springerpub.com to receive discount rates on bulk purchases.

Publisher's Note: **New and used products purchased from third-party sellers are not guaranteed for quality, authenticity, or access to any included digital components.**

Printed in the United States of America by Hatteras, Inc.

"In a world where you can be anything, be kind."
—**(unknown author)**

I dedicate this book in kindness and appreciation to my family, friends, mentors, and support system who have demonstrated and modeled kindness to me throughout my personal and professional career. The love and gratitude I have for my immediate family—my husband, Jeff; three children, Hannah, Ella, and Colton; and sweet pug, Pete Waffles—is indescribable. Thank you all for believing in me and reminding me that life is precious and anything is possible with faith, love, and a caring support system. Thank you also to my grandparents, Rocco and Teresa Ferrone, for setting the tone for my career exploration by reinventing their own career identity in their 50s, demonstrating career changes are always possible. I am eternally grateful for the support and love of my aunt Carla and in-laws, Steve and Emma Lou Smith, for encouraging me to strive for my career goals and aspirations.
I also want to thank Katie, my amazing copilot in writing this book. I am grateful for the privilege to work with you and develop this project together. Thank you for being a shining beacon of light in this journey and always reminding us that we are "in this together" and offering your generosity, sense of humor, and caring nature each day.
—*Angie Smith*

For my staunchest supporter, biggest cheerleader, and partner, Bob. My dreams are possible because of you. To my son George: may your curiosity never wane and your career journey be filled with joy. Thank you to my parents, Jeff and Sue McIntyre, for supporting my love of learning and fostering my dedication to helping others. My village is strong; I am forever grateful to my friends who supported me and my family through this process. To Angie: from faculty, to mentor, coauthor, and dear friend, thank you for your undying encouragement, positivity, and leadership. You are a highlight in my career story.
—*Katie Peterssen*

CONTENTS

CONTRIBUTORS

Foreword Author

Lakeisha Mathews, EdD, CPCC, University of Baltimore

Chapter Authors

Christopher T. Belser, PhD, NCC, University of New Orleans

Seth C. W. Hayden, PhD, LCMHC, NCC, CCMHC, ACS, Wake Forest University

Terah L. Henderson, PhD, LPC, NCC, Yorkville University

Carolyn D. Jones, MEd, CCSP, CMCS, CDJ Consulting, LLC

Thommi Odom Lawson, PhD, LCMHCS, LPC (GA&SC), ACS, NCC, BC-TMH, Yorkville University

Raychelle Cassada Lohmann, PhD, NCC, LCMHCS, ACS, GCDF, University of Mount Olive

Helen Lupton-Smith, PhD, LCMHCA, North Carolina Central University

Erik Messinger, PhD, LCMHCA, NCC, Hood College

Helen Morgan, Student, Wake Forest University

Katie Peterssen, MEd, NCC, LCMHCA, Duke University Fuqua School of Business

Samara Reynolds, MEd, Virginia Commonwealth University

Angie C. Smith, PhD, LCMHCS, ACS, NCC, North Carolina State University

Terri L. Tilford, EdD, LCMHCS, North Carolina State University

Stacy M. Van Horn, PhD, University of Central Florida

Melissa A. Venable, PhD, Red Ventures Education and National Career Development Association

Regina Gavin Williams, PhD, NCC, LCMHC, North Carolina Central University

Ethical Corner

Sharon K. Anderson, PhD, Colorado State University

Azra Karajic Siwiec, PhD, LPC, Capella University

Scholar's Perspectives

Sylvia C. Nassar, PhD, LPC, NCC, ACS, CSP-T, MHF-T, CDF-I, North Carolina State University

Practitioner's Perspectives

Jonathan Adams, MA, Duke University

Steven Allman, LCMHC, Retired

Katy Breitenbach, Catalyst
Cindy Broderius, MEd, NCC, Duke University, Retired
Marcy L. Bullock, MS, North Carolina State University
Sara Concini, MS, LCMHC, North Carolina State University
Stephen DeWitt, Association for Career and Technical Education
Christy Dunston, MEd, North Carolina Agricultural and Technical State
    University
Barbara Efird, MEd, North Carolina State University
Amanda Friday, PhD, LPC, NCC, Georgetown University
Lori Nero Ghosal, EdD, PCC, Inner Quest Coaching
Emily Gomez, MS, CCC, Hire Heroes USA
Megan Guidi Kadrmas, MEd, NCC, George Mason University
Cindy Haeck, LCMHC, NCC, CCC, Wilmington Career Counseling
Laura Inscoe, PhD, NBCT, Wake County Public Schools, North Carolina
Devan Lane, EdS, The University of Tennessee, Knoxville
Jane Matthews, MEd, NCC, Meredith College
Teri Mills, MS, Duke University, Retired
Megan Collins Myers, MS, LCMHCA, NCC, Myers Career Coaching
Ashley Pelham, MEd, NCC, University of California, Davis
Trinka Polite, MA, LPC, NCC, Zeiders Enterprises, Inc.
Damarcus Smith, EdD, CWDP, Zeiders Enterprises, Inc.
Megan Tajlili, PhD, NCC, PMH-C, LCMHCS, New York University & North
    Carolina State University
Christin Taylor, MEd, North Carolina State University
Wesley J. Wade, MA, NCC, CCMHC, LCMHC, LCAS, Forward Counseling &
    Consulting, PLLC
Christy Walker, EdD, Durham Technical Community College
Linda Whited, MS, NCC, CCC, Time to Be Career Savvy

Student Voices

Connor Brady, MEd, North Carolina State University
Brittany Coles, MA, NCC., Argosy University and The Chicago School of
    Professional Psychology
Lian Currie, MEd, LPC-R., Virginia Commonwealth University
Gloria Vann Debnam, MSM, MEd, NCC, Wake Technical Community College
Byron J. Dickey, MA, North Carolina Central University
Kevin Eason, North Carolina Central University
Ciandra Gaston, MEd, North Carolina State University
Angela Richardson Hathaway, MEd, North Carolina Central University
Erica M. Jimenez, MEd, North Carolina State University
Derek Jeffrey Just, MEd, North Carolina State University
Sheena Kelly, MS, APC, NCC, Walden University
Amber Lovell, MEd, NCC, University of California, Irvine
Shamikia McGhee, MS, NCC, Alabama State University
Patrick Stephenson, MEd, North Carolina State University
Anne Sylla, MEd, MBA, PMP, North Carolina State University
Nicholas Vogel, NCC, LCMHCA, William Peace University

FOREWORD

I was thrilled to hear that Angie Smith and Katie Peterssen were writing an innovative textbook on career development—such a book is desperately needed. I am familiar with their unique style and contribution to the field, and I knew that this book would be interesting, engaging, thorough, and thoughtful. It is a pleasure for me to introduce you to *An Innovative Approach to Career Counseling*. I'm sure that you will enjoy reading this gem as much as I did.

Chapter 9 of this exciting new publication affirms that *"[t]he link between career and mental health is evident in our own lives as well as those of our students and clients."* Now, more than ever, as the world recovers from a global pandemic and high unemployment rates, the impact of these challenges on career development and mental health and wellness is undeniable. Finally, there is a resource that merges both academics and practice, seamlessly integrating career development and mental health. Whether you are a career development practitioner, licensed counselor, graduate student, counselor educator, or researcher, this book is for you.

As a career development practitioner who has worked in three career centers over the course of 15 years helping traditional students and nontraditional students engage in career development, I am appreciative of Smith and Peterssen's ability to provide a holistic approach to career development. In Chapters 1 and 2, the reader is given a definition of career development and provided with a historical perspective of the field, starting with Frank Parsons. Most impressive is Smith and Peterssen's decision to feature a discussion on diversity, equity, and inclusion at the beginning of book in Chapter 3, which acknowledges the "possible barriers faced by marginalized groups" and stresses the importance of multicultural competence for career development professionals.

Chapters 4 and 5 provide the reader with an overview of career development theories that align with the Council for Accreditation of Counseling and Related Educational Programs (CACREP) standards. Classical theories are covered, including life-span, vocational personality, and social learning theory. In addition, postmodern career theories and approaches are also covered, including chaos theory of careers and kaleidoscope. Both experienced and new professionals will find the theoretical overviews helpful and relevant to administering career development to diverse populations in various settings. Most impressively, to ensure that readers are equipped to integrate both classical and postmodern theories into their daily practice, Chapter 6 is dedicated to "Thinking and Doing." Here, readers have the opportunity to "experience the career development job search process themselves" as Smith and Peterssen ask them to consider hallmark career development questions such as Who am I? Where am I going? How do I get there? How can I stand out?

If you are not convinced that this book is an essential addition to your bookshelf, I am happy to share that Chapter 9 focuses on total wellness. Here, Smith and Peterssen focus on the interconnection of career development and mental health, citing the centrality of work across the life span. Both counselors and career specialists will appreciate the review of mental health concerns, including trauma, anxiety and depression, stress, identity development, and more. I was especially thrilled to see attention given to counselor self-care. Knowing how to care for others and oneself is an essential skill for today's career counselors and specialists.

In the final chapters, Smith and Peterssen give attention to teaching and planning career development, career-counseling settings, and career-counseling skills. Of note is the care given to explain the various environments in which career counselors work, including K–12 schools, higher education, private practice, nonprofit organizations, government agencies, and corporations/businesses, as well as the various roles in each of those environments, including corporate roles within an employee assistance program, talent development, human resources, or outplacement services. The final chapter of the book provides a glimpse into the future, focusing on trends in career counseling. Smith and Peterssen reflect on current environmental crises, including public health and diversity and inclusion, discussing the impact of this on employment and career readiness. No stone is left unturned, with readers being provided with a robust discussion on disaster mental health counseling, grief counseling, and telecounseling—all trends in career development that have touched practitioners around the world.

Finally, readers will be pleased to see the impressive list of experts who contributed to the book and lent their voices and experience to the content covered. This book is undoubtedly an essential guide for all professionals interested in exploring the field of career counseling and development from a holistic perspective, including the interconnection of mental health and wellness.

Lakeisha Mathews, EdD, CPCC
Director of the Career and Professional
Development Center, University of Baltimore
President, National Career Development Association (NCDA)

PREFACE

Dear Reader,

We designed this book to appeal to a wide audience, including counselors-in-training, novice career counselors, seasoned career professionals, career explorers, helping professionals, and anyone who is learning about careers, career development, and career exploration across the life span. One of the key hallmarks in the counseling profession is "know thyself," and in this book, we strike a balance of empirically based research and personal reflection prompts inviting you to deeper levels of self-awareness and exploration.

Regardless of your rationale for selecting the book, we hope that you will gain clarity and a deeper understanding of who you are in relationship to the world around you. We invite you to immerse yourself in the exercises, activities, and intentional reflection questions. By doing so, you will support your own personal growth and also learn ways to make the connection as you translate the skills into professional practice with your current and/or future clients.

Career counseling should not be a mystery in theory or practice. Our hope is to unveil the process to demonstrate a variety of ways practitioners engage with their students, clients, and in the community.

THE CAREER JOURNEY: GOALS AND PURPOSE OF THE BOOK

Our desire in creating an innovative career text is to meet readers where they are in this moment. The intent of the structure is to provide practical, easily "digestible" portions of text that you can read and review at your own pace. It can be read in its entirety or explored separately based on topics and specific interest in individual chapters.

THE STRUCTURE

As counselors, we are enthralled with story and narrative, and we do not want to make this book a mystery for you. We structured the content extremely purposefully to create an easy-to-read text to aid career professionals in training.

The image that came to mind when we first began mapping out the project is that of a mosaic that includes all sorts of shapes, sizes, and colors. Much like a mosaic, the book was envisioned as bringing together a variety of "parts" that may not make much sense as individual pieces, but when carefully fitted together, they create a magnificent, beautiful, and holistic picture for the reader. The metaphor speaks to our process as our intent from the beginning has been to identify and amplify a multitude of voices in our community who can speak about career development and related topics in a practical, accessible, and realistic manner. This image is also insightful because career professionals see a career as a mosaic of a person's life, weaving together various jobs, experiences, life choices, relationships, and time.

Another image that came to mind as we envisioned this project was that of a puzzle. The goal in building a puzzle is to use individual puzzle pieces to create a concrete picture made up of 100, 500, or even 1,000 pieces. The final outcome is an exquisite picture of individual pieces perfectly fitted together revealing a comprehensive and seamless image. This book and the process of developing it mirrors the creation of a puzzle in that in each chapter there are many topics from unique voices collectively collaborating to contribute their beautifully personalized perspectives, backgrounds, and experiences that weave together each subject area into a final picture that is purposeful, rich, and full of life.

INTRODUCTION TO KEY FEATURES

The book is organized in an easy to navigate, structured format to aid the reader in understanding professional career development. Each chapter incorporates key features that are related to the topic at hand. In every chapter, you can expect to find the following features.

LEARNING OBJECTIVES

The authors provide a few key bullet points covered in the chapter to help the reader set a framework for the content before reviewing it. These learning objectives may also serve as a chapter summary to help jog your memory in the future after you've finished the book.

WARM-UP EXERCISE

You are about to stretch the muscles of your mind, and to help you prepare, we offer a quick warm-up exercise that will tone and focus your thoughts to help you enjoy and process the content and journey.

CONTENT EXPERTS

One or two content experts contribute their knowledge and perspective based on their background, career expertise, and practical application of career development techniques. Our content experts also spotlight the various ways career professionals explore and navigate their areas and specialties. Some content experts are faculty, others are theory experts, while others are administrators in the field. Each content expert shares not only their time but also their personal and professional experience related to the career field as they offer their authentic and unique perspective to the text. We are grateful for their contributions and for sharing their "voice" with all of us.

ETHICAL CORNER

Ethical Corner is authored by two career professionals and ethics experts, Azra Karajic Siwiec and Sharon K. Anderson. Azra Karajic Siwiec PhD, LPC, is a counselor educator employed by Capella University. She has been working in the counselor education field for over 14 years and has served as a committee member of the Ethics Committee of NCDA since 2015, and served as the chair of the Ethics Committee since 2017. Sharon K. Anderson, PhD, is Professor of Counseling and Career Development at Colorado State University. Sharon has taught the master's level ethics course for counseling students for over 20 years, teaching and mentoring a multitude of students. She has coauthored or coedited four professional ethics books used by practitioners in counseling and coaching.

In this section, Azra and Sharon lead the reader through topical scenarios to surface common ethics questions and dilemmas faced by career professionals. They ask pertinent and personal questions to encourage reader reflection and insight into personal and professional ethics.

PRACTITIONER'S PERSPECTIVES

Each chapter includes one or two perspectives from practitioners who currently work or have previously worked in the career field. These practitioner essays help us learn from their knowledge and experience and from the relationships they have developed with clients and students. Career counseling is an applied profession, and our practitioners share how they go about doing the work and honing the craft as they meet with clients every day. They offer personal insight into the counseling practice from a realistic perspective.

STUDENT VOICES

In our Student Voices sections, students offer their learner viewpoint as they begin in the career-counseling field. These students share their thoughts and reflections about the career-counseling profession and offer personal takeaways.

COUNSELING SKILLS CONNECTION

In this section, the authors link the content from the chapter to additional material based on the Council for Accreditation of Counseling and Related Educational Programs (CACREP) standards, including theories of counseling, human development, multicultural counseling, and assessments. We also share related concepts based on CACREP standards.

MINDFUL MOMENTS

How often do we pause to rest and rejuvenate? The mindful moment is exactly this: an intentional "pause" in each chapter to serve as a reminder for us to rest. The authors share a resource, practice, activity, or exercise as a prompt to be mindful and to introduce and incorporate mindfulness into our daily practice.

We invite you to continue current mindfulness practices that you may have employed throughout your life as well. Define mindfulness in your own way, and emulate this practice in whatever way allows you to maximize the benefits. For some this may look like doing nothing, which is something. For others, mindfulness may mean being quiet, calm, peaceful, and silent. Yet for others of us, it may mean engaging our mind, spirit, and body and taking on a more active stance. Our world is a busy and hurried space. Let's all take a breath and a moment to recharge.

TECH TOOLS

Technology will continue to press limits and expand beyond what we could ever imagine. We offer specific and concrete technology tips in the book that connect with and go beyond that of the content and links concepts with outside resources and technological advancements in the world around us.

REFLECTION ACTIVITY

After reading the content expert, practitioners, and student perspectives, we invite you to reflect on prompts and questions to expand your thinking about a particular topic. The reader is encouraged to journal responses and thoughts in response to the questions so that you may look back upon them throughout your career journey.

Journaling can look different for everyone. For some, journaling can mean writing your thoughts in the book beside each question or creating a separate journal to record your thoughts. Auditory learners may prefer to share or record the reflections verbally on their phone or other device, whereas other more visually oriented readers may enjoy creating and responding to the prompts with colors, images, and pictures. We invite you to slow down, pause, and reflect at the pace and cadence that works best for you and your learning style.

SUMMARY

As we wrap up each chapter, we will provide a summary of the key features and points to take away from the content. The summary may also include additional food for thought and next steps to explore in practice or in your own life.

RESOURCES

We, along with our content experts, practitioners, and students, collected a list of chapter-related educational resources, tools, organizations, and associations to help the reader dig deeper into the chapter topics. We encourage you to take the time to explore the many resources available to you that will help move you forward in your career.

We hope you enjoy this book and find it a helpful resource in your career services journey. We offer additional resources, worksheets, and ancillary material, as seen on p. xxiii.

Angie C. Smith
Katie Peterssen

ACKNOWLEDGMENTS

We were approached about writing this book in 2020 during a time of extreme challenges and strife in our country and world as we all collectively experienced multiple pandemics amidst COVID-19, social unrest, and much more. Honestly, this may have been one of the most difficult times to take on a project like this one, as we were navigating personal and professional roles ourselves, including raising children during a time of uncertainty. However, we knew that all of our careers and world of work would forever be changed, and this may be the perfect time to delve into career discussions and organize a book like this one. With this in mind, we want to acknowledge and express our deepest appreciation for our partners, children, and extended family and friends who have sustained and encouraged us, despite all the chaos, to pursue this project and share information about careers during a pivotal time in our history. We remain eternally grateful for your unwavering love and support.

The book would not be possible without the extraordinary contributors who selflessly carved out time among all their other tasks and life events. We are so thankful to our content experts, practitioners, and students across the nation for sharing their expertise and telling their stories. Thank you for giving of your time, creativity, and positive spirit, even as you and your families may have been struggling and moving forward. We value you and thank you for trusting us throughout the inception and creation of the project.

Katie and I would like to acknowledge and thank our employers, North Carolina State University and Duke University, respectively, for believing in us and providing space to complete the book. There are many contributors who are affiliated with the National Career Development Association (NCDA), and we thank the NCDA for representing the career profession, offering standards and credentials that prepare career professionals to support and uplift clients worldwide. Special thanks to our state division, North Carolina Career Development Association (NCCDA) and its many leaders for fostering our careers and providing opportunities for leadership development, connections, and lifelong friendships. NCCDA leaders and members have continuously demonstrated innovation, commitment to clients, and dedication to positive change within our communities that we admire and aspire to emulate.

We offer a special thank you to the ethics committee spearheaded by Dr. Azra Karajic Siwiec and Dr. Sharon K. Anderson, who contributed to the ethical corner for each chapter by adding a common theme and thread of ethical topics for all of us to be mindful of as we practice within the profession. Thank you to Dr. Sylvia Nassar for sharing your scholarly research, tools, and insight. All of your voices and expertise are valued and appreciated.

We would also like to extend our appreciation to Dr. Lakeisha Mathews, NCDA president, for championing this collective work, trailblazing for other career leaders, and modeling excellence in career practice. We thank Rhonda Dearborn at Springer Publishing for seeing the possibility, being persistent, and sparking the creation of this text.

We are grateful for our students past and present. You have shared your hopes, dreams, and challenges with us, and we are thankful to have been a part of your journey. Thank you to our mentors and supervisors who have modeled excellence in career development, leadership, and building relationships, particularly, Dana Sumner, David Solloway, Emily Gomez, Dr. John Lee, Dr. Paola Sztajn, Dr. Marc Grimmett, Dr. Kimberly Allen, Dr. Diane Chapman, Dr. Marie Sumerel, Angela January, and Dr. Maria Gallardo-Williams. Thank you to Dr. Mark Savickas, Dr. Rich Feller, Dr. Janet Lenz, and Dr. Spencer Niles for tirelessly sharing your words of wisdom and contributions to the field.

The book is intended for multiple audiences, including counselors-in-training, practitioners, instructors, and anyone seeking to explore career topics. With this in mind, we want to acknowledge you, the reader, and thank you for taking the time to explore and unpack your own career story. Examining who we are and how we show up in the world is not for the faint of heart. As you do so, we sincerely hope you give yourself grace and extend compassion to yourself as you would do for your clients and students. We wish you joy, love, and healing today and always.

AVAILABLE RESOURCES

INSTRUCTOR RESOURCES

 A robust set of instructor resources designed to supplement this text is located at http://connect.springerpub.com/content/book/978-0-8261-5073-8. Qualifying instructors may request access by emailing textbook@springerpub.com.

- **Instructor Manual** containing discussion questions, activities and exercises, out-of-class assignments and/or activities, and practice-based resources for each chapter, as well as sample syllabi.
- **Test Bank** with 140 multiple-choice, true/false, and short answer questions. All questions include answers with full rationales and are available on Respondus®.
- **Instructor Chapter PowerPoints**

STUDENT RESOURCES

Links to websites, podcasts, My Storyboard Activities, suggested readings, worksheets, and more.

VIDEOS

An Innovative Approach to Career Counseling features 5 videos hosted by the book's authors featuring interviews with some of the book's content experts who help the reader contextualize the chapters and "bring the content to life." To access the videos and their transcripts, see the list of videos on p. xxv, or go right to http://connect.springerpub.com/content/book/978-0-8261-5073-8 and enter the voucher code on the first page of this book.

LIST OF VIDEOS

Videos are available to help readers contextualize some of the chapters. Each video features Dr. Angie Smith and Katie Peterssen interviewing contributing authors from the book. These authors provide background and in-depth discussion of the concepts discussed in their chapters. Transcripts are also available for each video. To access the videos, use the QR codes provided and enter the voucher code found on the first page of this book.

Chapter 3
Diversity, Equity, and Inclusion in Career Counseling
Guests: Thommi Odom Lawson and Terah L. Henderson

Chapter 6
Thinking to Doing: An Exploration of Your Own Career Story
Katie Peterssen and Angie C. Smith

Chapter 7
Assessments in Career Counseling
Guest: Christopher T. Belser

Chapter 9
Career and Mental Health: Total Wellness
Guest: Erik Messinger

Chapter 12
The Nuts and Bolts of Career Counseling: Skills for Practitioners
Guest: Samara Reynolds

CHAPTER 1

CAREER: DEFINING AND HIGHLIGHTING THE JOURNEY

Angie C. Smith and Katie Peterssen

LEARNING OBJECTIVES

By the end of this chapter, you will be able to:

- Define career, career counseling, and the role of work.
- Describe a variety of **career pathways** for individuals to explore across the life span.
- Examine the role of work in your own life and your current career goals.
- Identify transformative recent events that have impacted work and career.

WARM-UP EXERCISE

As we embark on this journey through **career** topics, we invite you to consider and reflect on the following: What, where, or with whom do you find sanctuary, joy, fun, beauty, and peace? When do you find yourself in the calmest place? When do you naturally know the steps to be taken? What is the best time of day for you when you feel your best? At peace? Morning, midday, evening, late evening? In what activities do you find yourself so engrossed or engaged that you lose track of time?

INTRODUCTION

Congratulations on beginning your journey of self-discovery! We are excited to engage with you on this adventure through career exploration. This introductory chapter defines the concept of career and provides an overview of the career field—past, present, and future.

Through every season of life, the evolutionary process of career development offers ways to explore, recycle, adapt, and change the trajectory along one's path. It's never too late to examine or reexamine where you are now and consider where you hope to be in the future. Our hope is that this book will serve as a resource, reference, and even a guide to discovery. Perhaps it will precipitate "ah ha" moments in your own career path.

CAREER DEFINITIONS

Within the career field, there are a variety of popular phrases and keywords that relate to the world of work. Throughout the book, the reader will encounter these specific terms as well as references to recent occurrences that have impacted careers and career development. These key terms are defined here to lend context to the specific concepts and topics discussed later in the book.

Career

There are many **definitions** from various professional organizations for the word *career*, although it is usually understood to be an occupation in a field with opportunities for promotion for the duration of a person's working life. Yet, today, it isn't unusual for some people to have multiple careers over a lifetime, while others remain focused on one or two careers. Some people remain in their one function or industry for the duration of their lives, whereas others change careers spanning various fields.

Job, Occupation, and Vocation

The key terms *job* and *occupation* are often used interchangeably to describe the skills, tasks, and daily work routines related to a particular position or function. They may be temporary, and they may be sought out of necessity for financial needs or security. They may also be lifelong and deeply fulfilling. Often, temporary jobs spark an interest and lead you to your desired career path.

Historically, vocation is associated with a deep, personal inclination or calling toward a particular occupation. For example, one may feel a calling to the priesthood, to nursing, or to serve one's country in the military. A vocation may also be a calling to a nonpaying occupation, such as years of service as a Boy or Girl Scout leader or parenthood, which requires the person to have a job or career for financial support. However, today the term *vocation* is often used synonymously with job and occupation.

One resource that can be used for identifying potential occupations is called O*NET OnLine (onetonline.org). For job seekers, the resource notes projected trends for job demand within individual occupations. Job seekers can apply this data to make informed decisions about the occupations they pursue. For example, if a job seeker values security and wants to have many job opportunities, a strategy aligned with those values may focus on those occupations projecting rapid growth. O*NET provides extensive occupational data related to abilities, interests, knowledge, and skills typical of that occupation.

Few workers will have one lifetime job, and it is increasingly unlikely that anyone will have a decade-plus tenure within a single organization. A Bureau of Labor Statistics (BLS) national longitudinal survey published in August 2021 found that people born in the years 1957 to 1964 held an average of 12.4 jobs from age 18 to 54 (BLS, 2021). As of 2020, the average job tenure of workers was 4.1 years, consistent with the 2018 finding of 4.2 years (BLS, 2020). Tenure trends vary by occupation, with food service workers, who are often

TABLE 1.1 AVERAGE JOB TENURE BY AGE

AGE	AVERAGE JOB TENURE (YEARS)
25–34	2.8
35–44	4.9
45–54	7.5
55–64	9.9
65+	10.3

Source: Adapted from Bureau of Labor Statistics. (2020, September 22). *Employee tenure in 2020*. https://www.bls.gov/news.release/pdf/tenure.pdf

younger, having the lowest media tenure at just 1.9 years, and workers in management and legal occupations having among the longest tenures at 5.8 years (Table 1.1; BLS, 2020).

Career Development

Career development is the process of self-discovery leading to career choices over a lifetime that are financially viable and fulfilling. The process includes exploring skills, values, interests, abilities, and talents combined with education and experiences, to arrive at an actionable plan to start or progress in a career.

Career Counseling

The National Career Development Association (NCDA) differentiates career planning services from career counseling services within the principles of the Code of Ethics (2015). "Career planning services include an active provision of information designed to help a client with a specific need" (NCDA, 2015, p. 3). These services span the career development and job search processes and could include resume review, selection of occupations, development of job seeking skills, and career assessments. The NCDA defines career counseling as being inclusive of and going beyond career planning by "provid[ing] the opportunity for a deeper level of involvement with the client, based on the establishment of a professional counseling relationship and the potential for assisting clients with career and personal development concerns" (NCDA, 2015, p. 3).

Career Development Professional

A career professional offers support to people in their lifelong process of discovering career abilities and aspirations, pursuing those aspirations, progressing in their chosen career path, and seeking skills, satisfaction, stability, and balance in work–life. Credentials and required training vary based on professional identity or orientation. All career professionals are responsible for protecting client privacy and actively seeking to increase cultural competencies to better understand and serve clients with diverse cultural identities and backgrounds (NCDA, 2015).

The professions in career development include the following NCDA roles and credentials:

- Certified Career Counselor (CCC)
- Certified Master of Career Services (CMCS)
- Certified Career Services Provider (CCSP)
- Certified School Career Development Advisor (CSCDA)
- Certified Career Counselor Educator (CCCE)
- Certified Clinical Supervisor of Career Counseling (CCSCC)

Role of Work

The role of work in our lives evolves over time based on each person's lifeline and the context of what is happening in the world around us. For many, the role of work plays a central part in their daily lives and is tightly connected with their identity. Occupational wellness, including career satisfaction, is one of eight core dimensions of wellness, along with emotional, social, financial, spiritual, physical, intellectual, and environmental wellness. All eight dimensions are interconnected, and holistic well-being requires a delicate balance across each area. Career counselors serve clients as they seek integration across these dimensions, often when an imbalance is experienced and dissatisfaction with one or multiple domains is present. The role as worker is one of many roles among our other life roles, such as parent, student, friend, caretaker, and so forth. Even though the role of worker can take up significant portions of our time, we cannot neglect the various additional roles that are as important, or more important, to us. Life events often clarify and challenge the notion that the role of work is the primary focus, and this causes us to recalibrate based on our core values and priorities.

COVID-19 Pandemic

It may seem odd to include an entry about a virus in a book on careers, yet its influence on career, industry, the human psyche, families, everyday life, and societies worldwide can hardly be overstated. On January 9, 2020, the World Health Organization announced a coronavirus-like respiratory disease spreading quickly in China. The SARS-CoV-2 virus (COVID-19) quickly spread across the world and proved to be dangerous and deadly, especially for those with compromised health and the elderly. In the United States alone, over 1 million people died of the virus. Countries made policy choices to close their borders and issued lockdown or stay at home orders, schools were closed, and all but "essential" businesses were shuttered. In the United States, governors and state legislators issued public health guidance that varied from state to state. Jobs and revenue were lost, and hospitals and healthcare workers were overburdened with treating COVID cases as non-COVID–related needs were delayed. In some states, children and their parents were forced to conduct school and work via online apps from home. As of August 2022, there are ongoing disruptions to international and local economies, supply chains, workforce stability, and business revenue stemming from COVID.

The Great Resignation

You will come across the phrase "the Great Resignation" frequently as you read this book, as it has significantly impacted the role of career counselors and how we think about work. The phrase was coined by Professor Anthony Klotz of Texas A&M University, and he predicted that high numbers of people would leave the workforce after COVID and not return, even after life regains normalcy (World Economic Forum, 2021). In late 2020 through the first half of 2021, waves of people chose to resign from their jobs or the workforce entirely. Businesses small and large experienced, and continue to experience workforce shortages as former employees reevaluate career and work. The number of people leaving their jobs was well above the average; according to *Fortune* magazine, the number was well over 4 million (Bove, 2022). The COVID-19 pandemic was one factor, yet even before the coronavirus arrived in the United States, workers were leaving their jobs in record numbers in search of better pay, more flexibility, and more fulfilling work. Now, after the pandemic, many members of the workforce are thinking outside the box and getting creative with their careers and sources of income, and this is how career professionals are meeting the moment and serving the American workforce.

REAL-LIFE CAREER STORIES

We have collected a few real-life career stories to share with you. In sharing these stories, we hope that you will connect with the humanity in and the variety of these work **narratives**. We also aim to showcase different orientations to work (calling, career, job), different career mosaics, and different career and vocation experiences. Some people feel called to a particular profession early in life; others select a career and move steadily along that path; while yet others find work or a job based on necessity and access. These stories highlight just a few of the ways that career and life intersect and how we create meaning in our work and our lives. Career is highly personal, and in many ways it is very fragile as so many of us are tied into the deep connection between our identity and our work.

When you think about careers, whose do you admire most? What do you admire about their path?

Toni Morrison

Toni Morrison, the acclaimed American novelist, didn't publish her first story, *The Bluest Eye*, until she was 39 years old. As a single mom, she woke up at 4 o'clock in the morning to carve out time to write while her children were still asleep. Then, after seeing her sons off to school, she went to work at her day job. Morrison taught English at Howard University, her alma mater, and later worked as an editor for LW Singer and Random House. She retired to write full time in 1983 at 52 years old.

Myron Rolle

Myron Rolle received 80 football scholarship offers before committing to Florida State University in 1994, where he played safety. Two and a half years later, he left

FSU with a bachelor's degree to attend Oxford University as a Rhodes Scholar, where he earned a master of science degree in medical anthropology. Afterward, Rolle returned to the United States to foster his dream of playing professional football. In 2010, he was drafted by the Tennessee Titans in the sixth round, and by 2012 he was on the roster of the Pittsburg Steelers. Rolle never got as much playing time as he'd hoped for, so he left the NFL in 2013 to attend medical school. Dr. Myron Rolle is now a Global Neurosurgery Fellow at Harvard Medical School. He recently authored a book, *The 2% Way*, on his philosophy of small improvements and how he wove two seemingly opposite dreams—that of football player and doctor—into one life span.

Jeannette Rankin

Jeannette Rankin was born June 11, 1880, the first of six siblings, in a small town near Missoula when Montana was still a U.S. territory. She graduated from Montana State University in 1902 with a degree in biology and soon thereafter developed an interest in social work. With the goal of becoming a social reformer, she attended the New York School of Philanthropy (now known as Columbia University School of Social Work) and then moved to Washington state to serve needy children. In Washington, she joined a local women's suffrage group to prepare for an upcoming referendum on voting rights, and in 1910, Washington became the fifth state to adopt women's suffrage (Hardaway, 1980).

When Rankin learned that her home state's legislature would soon be debating a women's suffrage resolution, she returned to Montana to bolster the effort. Working through her contacts with the National American Woman Suffrage Association, Rankin became the first woman invited to address the Montana state legislature, and her efforts convinced a majority of the Montana House of Representatives to support the measure (Hardaway, 1980). And thus began Raskin's political career.

Three years before the 19th Amendment was ratified granting all U.S. women the right to vote, Rankin declared her candidacy as a Republican for one of Montana's two at-large seats in the U.S. House of Representatives. Her campaign platform focused mostly on domestic issues such as women's suffrage and child welfare, but she also spoke out against the United States involving itself in the war being waged in Europe at the time. Although the Montana newspapers largely ignored her campaign, she actively canvassed the women of Montana, both Republicans and Democrats, and in November of 1916, after winning the election by almost 7,000 votes, Jeannette Rankin became the first woman to serve in the United States Congress (Hardaway, 1980).

In a post-election statement, Rankin said, "I am deeply conscious of the responsibility, and it is wonderful to have the opportunity to be the first woman to sit in Congress. I will not only represent the women of Montana, but also the women of the country, and I have plenty of work cut out for me" (Hardaway, 1980, p. 63).

Charles Clinton Spaulding

You may not know his name, but if you're familiar with Black Wall Street in Durham, North Carolina, then you know Charles Clinton Spaulding.

According to family oral tradition, Spaulding's great grandfather was an emancipated slave who moved to a community of free Black farmers in Columbus County, North Carolina, where Spaulding was eventually born in 1874. When Spaulding turned 20 years old, he moved to Durham where he finished high school and worked in lowskill jobs—dishwasher, bellhop, and errand boy—for a few years until he landed a position as manager of a Black-owned and operated cooperative grocery store (Powell, 1994).

Spaulding's success in managing the store led him to a bigger, better position 4 years later as the manager of the North Carolina Mutual Life Insurance Company, which was another all-Black business that provided life insurance to Black residents. In a short 10 years, Spaulding transformed North Carolina Mutual into a thriving, successful business. The company claimed they were the "black captains of industry" (Powell, 1994, p. 408). North Carolina Mutual was so successful and made so much money that Parrish Street in Durham, where the company was headquartered, was dubbed Black Wall Street. It was in this setting that Durham became the "capitol of the Black middle class" (Powell, 1994, p. 408).

In 1923, Spaulding became president of North Carolina Mutual and then added a variety of financial institutions to his business portfolio. His reputation and leadership in the community gave him important influence in Durham, and his influence eventually extended to the rest of the South and then to Washington, DC, as a respected voice in education, philanthropy, politics, and race relations (Powell, 1994). When Spaulding passed away in 1952, North Carolina Mutual was reportedly worth $40 million (Weller, 2020).

John H. Glenn, Jr.

John H. Glenn, Jr., is known as the first astronaut to complete three orbits around Earth. Yet, his career and life as an American hero is so much more than that.

Glenn was born and raised a proud son of the state of Ohio, and he graduated from high school in 1939 and went on to study chemistry at Muskingham College. When the United States entered World War II in 1942, Glenn left school without graduating to enlist in the U.S. Army Air Corps, and when the Army failed to call him into active duty, he enlisted in the Navy as an aviation cadet. Glenn's love affair with flying began early in his life as he accompanied his father, who was a pilot, on flights, and Glenn himself had earned a pilot's license while in college (Editors of Encyclopedia Britannica, 2022).

After Navy flight school, Glenn joined the Marines and had a distinguished career; he flew 57 combat missions in the South Pacific in World War II and 90 missions in the Korean War (Editors of Encyclopedia Britannica, 2022), and he earned 10 Air Medals and two Distinguished Flying Crosses (Wikipedia, n.d.).

In 1954, after the wars, Glenn attended the Naval Test Pilot School to become a test pilot for emerging aviation technology. He was involved in test piloting the Vought F-8 Crusader, and in 1957, he set a transcontinental speed record of 725.55 miles per hour as he flew the F-8 from California to New York in just 3 hours and 23 minutes (Editors of Encyclopedia Britannica, 2022).

In 1959, Glenn's career changed trajectory after he was selected to be one of the first Americans to pilot a flight into space on the *Friendship 7* space capsule. Glenn became a celebrated American hero after circling Earth three times and surviving a tricky reentry and ocean landing (Editors of Encyclopedia Britannica, 2022). Astronaut John Glenn was given a ticker tape parade in New York City with 4 million citizens attending (Heichelbech, n.d.).

He retired from the space program to begin a political career in 1964 at 43 years old. Yet 1 month after announcing his candidacy for a U.S. Senate seat for Ohio, Glenn fell and hit his head on a bathtub and had to withdraw to convalesce (Editors of Encyclopedia Britannica, 2022). Later that year, he set aside his political aspirations to accept the position of Working Director of Royal Crown (RC) Cola and a year later became president of the company (Editors of Encyclopedia Britannica, 2022). Yet his public spirit and desire to serve his country resurfaced in 1970, and he put himself forward as a candidate for a Senate seat for Ohio but lost in the Democratic primary to Howard Metzenbaum (Wikipedia, n.d.). He ran again, successfully this time, in the 1974 election, and served three terms in the U.S. Senate.

With his sights set beyond the Senate, and banking on name recognition, Senator Glenn entered the Democratic primary race for the 1984 presidential election. But by the New Hampshire primary vote on February 28, his campaign was already running out of steam as former vice president, Walter Mondale, was the clear front runner (Wilkinson, 2020, para. 13). One month later, he called it quits on the campaign trail, but he continued to represent Ohio in the U.S. Senate until his retirement in 1999.

Glenn's career wasn't over, though. In 1998, at 77 years old, John Glenn returned to space aboard the space shuttle *Discovery*. He was, of course, the oldest person to go into space, and on this 9-day mission, Glenn was studied regarding the effects of aging on the body's response to weightlessness (Editors of Encyclopedia Britannica, 2022). He also founded the Ohio State University John Glenn School of Public Affairs, where he was an adjunct professor. In 2012, he was awarded the Presidential Medal of Freedom by President Barack Obama (Pearlman, 2012).

Joni Eareckson Tada

When Joni was 17 years old, she dove into a shallow pool of the Chesapeake Bay and hit her head on the bottom, fracturing her fourth vertebrae and breaking her spinal cord. Since that tragic accident in 1967, she has been quadriplegic, paralyzed from the shoulders down. At first she sank into a deep depression, but her firm Christian faith rallied her and gave her a renewed sense of purpose. She is now an acclaimed artist, a global ally for families impacted by disability, and a source of information, hope, and inspiration for Christian and Christian ministries worldwide.

After the accident, Joni learned to paint using a mouth stick in occupational therapy, and she began to sell her paintings. Her art and methodology caught the attention of the local TV station in 1974, and they ran a feature on her and her paintings. A producer at the *Today Show* on NBC saw the show, and Joni was invited to New York City to be interviewed by Barbara Walters. The interview went well, and soon after a publisher asked her to write her story. In 1976, *Joni: An Unforgettable Story* was released. The book led to a film, in which Joni played herself, that was produced by the Billy Graham Evangelistic Association. And that is when the letters from people with disabilities started pouring in asking for her help and support.

Heeding the advice of friends, Joni used her newfound fame to start a Christian ministry for people with disabilities called Joni & Friends, which was formed to provide spiritual support and resources to families affected by disability. Since then, Joni & Friends' mission has expanded to include a 4-minute daily radio show and podcast, accessible family retreats, and Wheels for the World, which provides used wheelchairs, refurbished by the incarcerated, to those in need worldwide.

In the 1980s, under Presidents Reagan and Bush, Joni served on the National Council on Disability, which authored the Americans with Disabilities Act, which prohibits disability-based discrimination. In 2006, she was appointed to the U.S. State Department's Disability Advisory Committee, which offers guidance and shares communication with the department on issues pertaining to the disabled community.

Joni, her husband Ken Tada, and her colleagues later founded the Christian Institute for Disabilities (CID), headquartered in California, with 17 offices across the United States. CID addresses issues "pertaining to life, dignity, justice, and equality" for people with disabilities by advising public institutions and helping individual disabled people find resources, such as accessible transportation, assistance dogs, and spiritual guidance (Joni & Friends, n.d., para. 1).

Now in her 70s, Joni is still a popular conference speaker and contributor to publications such as *Christianity Today*, *Today's Christian Woman*, and *The War Cry*. In her career, she has also authored 48 books on Christianity and disability, and in 2019 she celebrated 40 years of ministry.

All of the given biographical information on Joni and her work, as well as further resources for people with disabilities can be found on the website of JoniAndFriends.org.

Michael Jordan

Michael Jordan is equal parts man and brand, and in every way he is a superstar. It is easy to make the case that he is the NBA's greatest basketball player, with six NBA championships in 15 seasons in which he earned a long list of accolades— and a lot of money. He was also a basketball star in college. As a freshman at the University of North Carolina (UNC), he made the game-winning shot in the 1982 NCAA basketball championship game, and later he described it as the shot that made him "Michael Jordan," and not just another basketball player (ESPN, 2016).

Jordan was drafted by the Chicago Bulls after his junior season at UNC, although 2 years later he finished his Bachelor of Arts degree with a major in geography (NESN Staff, 2014). In this season of his life, Jordan the professional basketball player also became a businessman and cultural icon, forming a relationship with Nike to make his signature brand of basketball shoes, the Air Jordan, which also set the sports shoe company on the path to world success. In the 1980s and 1990s, MJ also signed a host of endorsement deals with Coca Cola, Wheaties, McDonalds, Hanes, and many others, including Gatorade's famous "Be Like Mike" ad campaign (watch the original ad at www.youtube.com/watch?v=b0AGiq9j_Ak).

Jordan was also a member of the 1992 U.S. Olympic basketball team, nicknamed the Dream Team, which was lauded as "the greatest team ever assembled in any sport" (ESPN, 2010, para. 4). The Dream Team won every game, including the gold medal, and they were the first Olympic team to score at least 100 points in every game. Jordan was on top of the world. Yet in 1993, tragedy struck when James R. Jordan, Sr., Michael's dad, was murdered. A few months later, Jordan stunned the sports world when he announced his retirement from professional basketball, stating that he'd lost the desire to play after his father's death (Berkow, 1994).

Weeks later, Jordan again shocked the sports world with a radical career change: He joined the White Sox organization to try his hand at professional *baseball*. "It began as my father's idea," Jordan said (Berkow, 1994, para. 11). "My father used to say that it's never too late to do anything you wanted to do" (Berkow, 1994, para. 14). Jordan's dad was a baseball fan, and he had once mentioned to young Michael that he thought he could make it in professional baseball too, and so Jordan decided to give it a shot.

Like most professionals, he had to start at the bottom, in the minor leagues. Jordan moved to Alabama to play with the Birmingham Barons and try to earn his way to the majors, the big league. As a 31-year-old rookie, he was 12 years older than most of his new teammates, and it wasn't an auspicious career for Jordan. His play was described as "adequate" (Berkow, 1994). Jordan said, "It's been embarrassing, it's been frustrating—it can make you mad. . . . And I've been working too hard at this to make myself look like a fool" (Berkow, 1994, para. 8). In 1994, Jordan retired from baseball after one season.

"I'm back." With those two simple words, Jordan announced his return to the NBA and to the Chicago Bulls after an 18-month absence from the sport (Collier, 2020). Jordan played four more seasons with the Bulls, from 1995 to 1998, and won two NBA championships with the team. Faced with a retiring coach and the departure of a few teammates, Jordan decided again to retire as a player in January 1999, and then returned to the NBA just 1 year later as president of basketball operations for the Washington Wizards, beginning yet another career (Sandomir, 2000).

At 38 years old, Jordan was "99.9%" sure he was finished playing ball, and so was everyone else (Schwartz, 2002). Yet his team, the Wizards, just weren't that good, at least not according to MJ's standards. So, in 2001, Jordan made another comeback—this time as a player for the Wizards—and generously donated his salary to the victims of the September 11th attacks (CNN.com, 2001). Jordan's abilities on the court hadn't waned, yet they weren't enough to pull the Wizards out of mediocrity, and he retired, for good this time, after the 2002 to 2003 season.

After retiring as a player, Jordan expected to return to his former position in operations for the Wizards, but in May 2003, the owner of the team fired him (ESPN, 2003). Since then, Jordan stays busy playing golf, spending time with his family, which now includes a grandchild, and building his brand. Jordan co-owns a car dealership franchise, including Michael Jordan Nissan in Durham, NC. He has a controlling interest as an owner of the Charlotte Hornets, is part owner of the Miami Marlins, is an investor in the sports betting company, the DraftKings, and invests in a variety of philanthropic organizations. In 2020, Jordan was the focus of the Emmy-winning documentary *The Last Dance* (Wikipedia, n.d.). He has also authored four books on life, basketball, and his personal journey (Wikipedia, n.d.).

These stories are a small sampling of the fascinating and complex pathways that careers can take over a lifetime, and, of course, people who aren't famous can have interesting career stories, too. In that category, we submit to you our own career stories and how we arrived to the field of career development.

AUTHOR CAREER STORIES

Angie Smith

I was just laid off, and I was devastated.

The tragic events of September 11th occurred just as I was moving along in my career and up the corporate ladder. At the time, I was recruiting students from colleges across the United States to work at IBM, and then working with IBM departmental managers to onboard these new hires. But after 9/11, everything changed in our country and in my life, too. Suddenly, everyone around me was being laid off, and I was one of the last in my department to be let go. I assumed it was coming, but I was stunned and devastated nonetheless.

As I look back now, it was one of the most pivotal times in my career and life. This event created some space for me to pause to explore and reflect on my values and where I was headed. I asked myself questions like "what do you want to do next," "what aspects of your job do you care about and want to continue in my next role," "what would you change in your next role," and "how are you living your life in concert with your values?"

As far back as I can remember I loved a good story. As a child, I spent many days creating "stories" as I immersed myself in play and teaching my stuffed animals, dolls, and brother math, English, art, and more. One of my earliest childhood memories is "dressing up" with a red cape draped across my neck, long, black boots, and gold bracelets tightly woven around my wrists. I transformed myself into Wonder Woman and clearly remember attempting to "fly" like she could down the stairs to save the day. I was woefully unsuccessful with the flying, and I'm thankful that I didn't break a bone. Wonder Woman, and all she represented, was intriguing to me: her energy, ability to "save the world," and help people in distress was appealing and admirable. Reality eventually set in, and I realized the dream of transforming into a superhero would not be attainable for me.

One's career is extremely personal, and my career is no different. My family strongly influenced my choices and career direction. As a child of a single parent, the message to me about employment was "you better think about how you are going to make enough money to support yourself, as you never know what will happen in life." I also witnessed family members struggle as they attempted to find jobs that would provide enough money to put food on the table.

I got my first job when I was in high school working at a grocery store bagging groceries, and then I became a cashier. I enjoyed meeting new people and developing relationships with the customers and their families. A "job" wasn't enough though. My wise grandfather would tell me that education is something that "no one could take away from me." Words are powerful, and I took this to heart. I pursued educational opportunities as if it were my "job." Education was my way out.

In college, I became a peer health educator with the Student Health Center and presented workshops to fellow students on alcohol use, HIV/AIDs, relationship issues, and so on, and they would often stay after the session to ask questions and seek advice, resources, and support. I would tell them that I wasn't a counselor, but I would gladly refer them to professionals and helpful contacts at the university and in the community. As I reflect back, that role set the foundation for learning about my interest in serving and supporting people in my community.

After college, I got married, moved to Minnesota, and took my first position at the Mayo Clinic in Human Resources. I knew I wanted to go back to school eventually, but not right away. I stayed in HR for about 8 years in a variety of companies in recruitment, benefits administration, mediation, training and development, and other HR functions. I loved connecting with employees and helping to improve their working conditions and personal lives with raises, promotions, and increased benefits.

After I was laid off, I started thinking about what was important to me and recognized that the best part of my job at IBM was working with students, hearing their stories, and helping them identify options and pathways. I knew I'd have to go to graduate school to pursue working with students at the college level, and after multiple informational interviews with professors in master's programs and people in corporate and counseling roles, I decided that a counseling degree would afford me the opportunity to holistically support students in the way I had wanted to in my role at IBM. I did not have the training or experience to support students, and obtaining a master's degree in counseling would give me the tools I would need.

The period I spent in graduate school was a learning experience, literally and figuratively. I worked full time and even had two of my three children while a graduate student. I completed my masters degree in counseling and immediately applied to the doctorate program in counselor education. Interweaving the roles of student, partner, and parent was extremely challenging but also rewarding. I would not change a thing, as through these experiences juggling the responsibilities of multiple life roles I developed more compassion and understanding as a person and instructor. When it comes to organizing childcare, caring for sick children at home, balancing work and school priorities, struggling to be on time to class due to traffic and commuting from work to school, I understand the struggle.

I have shared my story with graduate students, especially students who are also parents, seeking suggestions for integrating all of their roles. It can be a source of comfort to them in validating that it is not easy, and at times they will feel like giving up. For example, during COVID, I shared with students my own journey, including the challenges of working and integrating online schooling for my children who were in three different schools and grade levels (elementary, middle, and high school), all different with schedules, expectations, and support systems. Remaining "real," human, and transparent is how I show up in my classroom both on campus and online. Relationships are important, and developing rapport through connection, kindness, and compassion has been an essential part of my life, including my work with my students, colleagues, and administrators. As counselors, we learn from our very first class that the hallmark of the counseling profession is building trust and offering a nonjudgmental space to develop the therapeutic alliance and counseling relationship.

I have been teaching at the university for 13 years, and I enjoy school so much that I have decided to stay in academia, at least for this chapter of my life. I find it ironic and serendipitous how life works out; I never would have imagined in my wildest dreams that I would be serving as a program coordinator and teaching in the very same classrooms where I once was a master's level graduate student.

Counselors often notice patterns in people's stories, and a common thread in my own story is that I have always desired connection and enjoyed meeting interesting new people. I value all people and their experiences—no one is perfect, and finding beauty amid the imperfections can be one of life's greatest gifts. Learning that life "happens," and seeing how we respond to it can be telling about ourselves and the students and clients we serve. My hope is that we can be a more compassionate people and society whereby we give more grace and less judgment. As the saying goes, everyone has a story. If we stop, pause, and listen long enough to truly be present and "hear" the story, we may be giving the author of the story an opportunity to be heard, maybe for the first time, and deeply valued. At our core, we all want connection and to be valued, cared for, and heard. My hope for you is that you can experience all of these areas in your own career and life.

Katie Peterssen

I went to college to study business, but I didn't know what I wanted to do career-wise. My best friend was studying business, and we had similar strengths, so it seemed like a good enough idea to me to study business too.

Many people imagine that they will wake up one day and know what they want to do or who it is that they are meant to be. Sometimes this happens, yet I never had an epiphany moment. In my experience many more people, like me, are still figuring it out.

Career development is a journey and a lifelong iterative process; as our life roles and priorities evolve, our career choices do too. One of my favorite quotes is from Rainer Maria Rilke: "Live the questions now. Perhaps you will then gradually, without noticing it, live along some distant day into the answer" (Goodreads, n.d., para. 1). For me, "living the questions" means following my curiosity and interests, bolstered by a love for learning and belief in education.

Education, work ethic, and curiosity were cultivated early in my life. My mother and grandparents were teachers, and my dad to this day starts most of his sentences with, "I wonder. . . ." My mom took an early exit out of education for many of the same reasons we see educators leaving the field today. After that, I watched her work long, unsteady hours in retail at a Sears store at our local mall. My parents worked hard to provide for our large family, and we lived paycheck to paycheck.

I absorbed from my family an inexhaustible work ethic and a deep commitment to the people with whom I work. As an undergraduate, I quickly took a job working for the service-learning program on campus, teaching and assisting in the computer lab at a local elementary school. Later, I took a second job working in the admissions office, where I connected with prospective students and families.

Four years later, while most of my peers pursued full-time roles in accounting, finance, or marketing, I still had little idea what I wanted to do. I was excited about corporate social responsibility, but in 2007 entry-level roles in this area did not exist. I explored opportunities from big financial firms to local nonprofits, and when my mentor in the admissions office prompted me to explore roles in college admission, I was intrigued. These opportunities were new to me, but soon I was referred to a few openings and interviewing for college admissions counselor roles.

As an admissions counselor and recruiter, I loved working with prospective students and families. Helping students discover pathways toward their academic and career goals energized me. I really enjoyed the exploratory conversations of "what do I want to do" and "how can I get there?" Yet, I wanted to be part of these students' discovery process, and as my life roles shifted, the excitement I got from the demanding admissions travel schedule waned. I was eager to advance my career, so I took my first graduate class as a non–degree-seeking student in career development with Dr. Angie Smith. My eagerness to complete assignments and curiosity to learn more indicated to me that I was on the right track, and I went on to complete the master's program with a focus on college counseling and a driving interest in careers.

Unlike many of my classmates, I worked full time and completed the program part time until it was time to start my practicum and internship. It took 4 years to finish the degree, and my work experience combined with the relationships I developed in my internship experience made my job search easier. I soon landed in a career counseling role at a women's college, Meredith College, in Raleigh, North Carolina.

My mentor in college played a pivotal role in my life and sparked my career in higher education. My mentor in my first job after college showed me what it is to be a colleague and a professional. She also helped me with the challenges and possibilities of balancing leadership at work with being a partner and mother. I saw in her much of what I aspired to; she was a smart, compassionate, and influential leader while also being a great mom. In my first career counseling role at Meredith College, I was fortunate to have an equally exceptional supervisor who quickly became a mentor and friend.

Our careers are often shaped by our relationships, and our communities help expose us to new occupations, work interests, and opportunities. For me, strong relationships with my supervisors and mentors became the catalyst to board appointments for regional and statewide professional associations. And in these leadership roles, I developed relationships with thought leaders and professionals who help me to grow as a professional career counselor and serve my clients more effectively.

The exceptional team that I worked with in the Office of Career Planning at Meredith College kept me in that role through the first 9 months of the coronavirus pandemic. Yet, in February 2021, I became part of the "Great Resignation" and left Meredith to work on a Department of Defense contract as a career and education counselor serving military spouses worldwide through the Spouse Education and Career Opportunities (SECO) program. This new, part-time role was fully remote and gave me the space and time to write this book and set up a private practice while making more time for my family. After a year of working completely remotely and pouring countless hours into my business, I found that I missed working on a team, and I still felt drawn to education.

Before my latest career transition to my current role at Duke University, I took some time to reassess my own career values. I love the tactile activity of the Knowdell Career Values Card Sort, so I made myself do what I so often had clients do—sort the cards. Among my top career values are family, fun and humor, working with others, creativity, exercising competence, and helping others. (Perhaps you have seen some of these themes arise as you have read my story.) Grounding my career decisions in my values defines the qualities and characteristics of work that will be satisfying and engaging to me, and those are good indicators of future career success.

I'm midcareer and still figuring out what I want to be when I grow up. Currently, I love the work that I do and who I do it with. In the years ahead, my life will change, my priorities may shift, and opportunities that I cannot yet foresee may present themselves, and I know that rightly integrating the life roles that are most important to me—partner, mother, counselor, sister, friend, and so forth—will continue to challenge me as it does for so many of my clients. My life is a journey.

CURRENT STATE OF CAREER AND COUNSELING PROFESSION

Careers are a focal point and central in our lives. The career counseling field continues to evolve and change based on the economy, impacts of COVID and its multiple social impacts, climate change, fast-paced technological advances, and more. Career counselors must be steadfast in keeping current with the times and understanding the varied needs of students and clients who they will be serving.

Given the changes within the context of work, including increased opportunities for remote work, the expertise offered by career counselors will continue to be needed by all who seek to explore new career options, transition to new jobs or careers, or seek opportunities to live a holistic life that includes work that doesn't encompasses one's life. Even in popular culture, resources, books, and topics for career discovery are offered to help people seeking to transform their life. For example, Jonathan Fields, the renowned author and host of *The Good Life Project,* offers a method to uncover a person's "imprint" as it relates to work and career options. This method is called SPARKED: Discover your unique imprint for work that makes you come alive. In it, the author posits that we all have a "spark" that ignites us to "come alive" in our work that is rooted in who we are in and is imprinted in our DNA. It offers a methodology to identify a person's preferred Sparktypes and the creation of a Sparktype profile. Resources, such as this one, can provide career counselors and professionals ways to discuss career exploration and development across the life span with their students and clients.

Professional organizations, such as NCDA lead the way in providing credentialing for career professionals who seek to gain professional development opportunities, skills, and connections to like-minded professionals related to career counseling, coaching, and career development topics. Career resources, seminars, research, podcasts, and virtual and in-person conferences are offered to members, and the website provides general information for the community about career-related information and even links to a network of providers for people seeking professional career assistance from a career counselor or coach.

Diversity, Equality, and Inclusion Work

The brutal deaths of George Floyd, Ahmaud Arbery, and Breonna Taylor at the hands of law enforcement and vigilantes sparked a national social justice movement and renewed demand for economic and social equality. Career counseling is social justice work, and career professionals are called to advocate for and empower Black, Indigenous, and people of color (BIPOC) clients. One way career professionals might advocate for equity is by bringing attention to structural inequalities that may exist within a company based on race, gender, and other protected classes. The American Psychological Association defines equity as "providing resources according to the need to help diverse populations achieve their highest state of health and other functioning" (American Psychological Association, 2021, para. 47). This is an ongoing process.

Career professionals may also provide counsel to clients navigating bias in the workplace and hiring process. NCDA curates a list of resources for career professionals to explore social justice issues and apply them within the context of their work. Visit https://ncda.org/aws/NCDA/pt/sp/social_justice to learn more about racism and systemic oppression, explore and adopt anti-racist actions, and apply culturally competent career development practices. Opportunities for career professionals to pursue roles focused on diversity, equality, and inclusion (DEI) work increased by more than 56% from 2019 to 2020 in response to social pressures and demand for companies to do more to foster and maintain safe, inclusive workspaces where all people have opportunity to thrive (Murray, 2020). These roles might include titles such as employment equity manager, diversity program manager, inclusion specialist, diversity trainer, and so forth.

VALUES

Career counselors offer support to clients by assisting them to identify, clarify, and connect values with their preferred work environment or setting. Exploring personal and professional values can be revealing and offer opportunities for clients to explore options within industries and fields that correspond to their values. For example, if clients share their interest in spending time outdoors and with nature, they may be prompted to explore occupations that allow them to be outdoors, focus on the environment and sustaining natural resources, or are located near nature preserves. Career professionals may use assessment tools to assist students and clients to dig deeper into questions pertaining to their values. We invite you to begin to consider your own values as we segue into reflecting on your own journey and career.

Consider what you want most in your career: What does a good life look like to you? Complete the Work Values Matcher on CareerOneStop at www.careeronestop.org/Toolkit/Careers/work-values-matcher.aspx. What values rose to the top for you? How do your work values match your current career goals? Discuss your insights, questions, and any concerns with trusted mentors, faculty, and supervisors.

When our work values are aligned and present in our work and career, our well-being improves. Occupational wellness is one dimension of overall wellness and is interconnected with seven other dimensions of wellness: physical, environmental, spiritual, intellectual, emotional, financial, and social (Swarbrick, 2006). As you learn about career development throughout this book, you will see many ways in which occupational choices and work experiences have dramatic impacts on other areas of wellness, such as social, financial, and emotional wellness. The dimensions are described as being in a wheel, a wellness wheel, illustrating that balance is key to living a healthy, satisfying, and fulfilling life. Assess your current status of wellness with the wellness wheel activity as you envision your future and chart your pathway forward (Exhibit 1.1).

EXHIBIT 1.1 WELLNESS WHEEL ACTIVITY

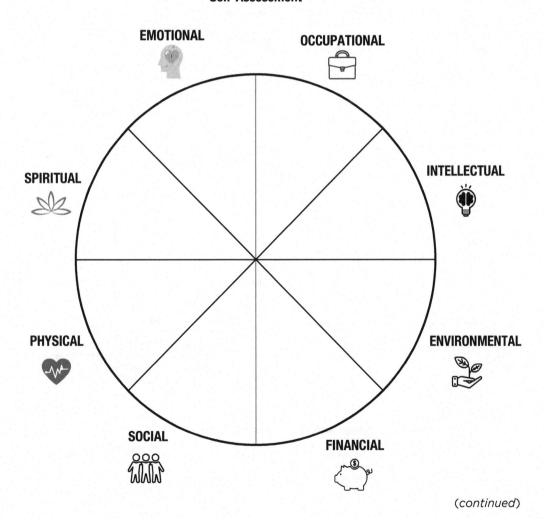

YOUR WELLNESS WHEEL
Self-Assessment

EMOTIONAL

OCCUPATIONAL

INTELLECTUAL

SPIRITUAL

PHYSICAL

ENVIRONMENTAL

SOCIAL

FINANCIAL

(continued)

EXHIBIT 1.1 WELLNESS WHEEL ACTIVITY (*CONTINUED*)

Directions & Guiding Questions

Directions:

Analyze your well-being in each dimension. Use the dimension definitions and question prompts to guide you. Using a crayon or writing tool of your choice, start at the center of the wheel and color the area that illustrates your satisfaction with each area of wellness.

SAMHSA definitions of the 8 dimensions of wellness are used across this resource (SAMHSA's Wellness Initiative: Wellness Community Power Point Presentation, 2016).

OCCUPATIONAL

Fulfillment, satisfaction and enrichment derived from your work

Think About:

- Do you find your work satisfying, stimulating, or fulfilling?
- Are you able to use your strengths, skills, and knowledge each day?
- How do you feel about your communication and relationships with your co-workers?
- Are you advancing toward your career goals?

INTELLECTUAL

Recognizing creating abilities and finding ways to expand knowledge and skills

Think About:

- Are you able to learn about current regional, national, or international affairs regularly?
- Do you often take part in discussions, conversations, or debates which enhance your knowledge and broaden your perspectives?
- How are you learning new skills and developing your talents?
- How often do you take time to invest in your own personal or professional development?

FINANCIAL

Satisfaction with current and future financial situations

Think About:

- Are you able to save toward your priorities and long term goals such as vacations, home ownership, or retirement?
- How do you budget your spending across regular expenses?
- Do you have resources to do things that you enjoy?

SPIRITUAL

Expanding our sense of purpose and meaning in life

Think About:

- How often do you have a feeling of inner peace?
- Are there core values or beliefs which guide your thoughts, feelings, and behaviors?
- To what extent do you feel a sense of purpose or meaning in life?
- How often do you take time to meditate, pray, or reflect on your spirituality?

ENVIRONMENTAL

Good health by occupying pleasant, stimulating environments that support well-being

Think About:

- Do you regularly find time to be outdoors, in nature or other spaces that stimulate you?
- Do your work and home spaces make you happy?
- How often do you recycle, conserve energy, and have awareness of other natural resources which you are consuming?
- Do you have access to clean air, food, and water?

SOCIAL

Developing a sense of connection, belonging, and a well-developed support system

Think About:

- How often do you set aside time to spend with family, friends, and other loved ones?
- How often do you visit new places and meet new people?
- How often do you keep in touch with family and friends?
- Are you able to set reasonable boundaries and resolve conflicts in your life?

PHYSICAL

Recognizing the need for physical activity, diet, sleep, nutrition

Think About:

- How often do you exercise or get physical activity?
- Are you able to eat nutritious food and balance your diet?
- How often do you get 7–8 hours of sleep and feel well rested?
- Do you use medications, alcohol, and other substances safely?

EMOTIONAL

Coping effectively with life and creating satisfying relationships

Think About:

- How well do you adapt to change?
- Are you involved in safe relationships where you can express your feelings and thoughts?
- How often do you engage in activities to help you remain calm and centered, or reflect on your feelings?
- How well do you recognize triggers and manage stress?

REFLECTION PROMPTS:

After completing your wellness wheel, consider the following questions.

1. Reflecting on your wheel, what surprised you?
2. Which area or areas of wellness would be important for you to work on?
3. What steps will you take to improve your wellness in those areas?
4. What resources or support do you need to take those steps? Who can be your partner as you seek to make these changes in your life?

Source: Author generated using SAMHSA's Wellness Initiative: Wellness Community Power Point Presentation, 2016.

ETHICAL CORNER

In this section, the authors lead the reader through topical scenarios to surface common ethics questions and dilemmas faced by career professionals. They ask pertinent and personal questions to encourage reader reflection and insight into personal and professional ethics.

Azra Karajic Siwiec, PhD, LPC, is a counselor educator employed by Capella University. She has been working in the counselor education field for over 14 years and has served as a committee member of the Ethics Committee of NCDA since 2015 and served as the chair of the Ethics Committee since 2017.

Sharon K. Anderson, PhD, is Professor of Counseling and Career Development at Colorado State University. Sharon has taught the master's level ethics course for counseling students for over 20 years, teaching and mentoring a multitude of students. She has coauthored or coedited four professional ethics books used by practitioners in counseling and coaching

VIGNETTE

Sandi is new to the counseling profession and is taking initial courses in counseling. In the ethics course, she learns about the unethical practice of some counselors and wonders why she has to take the course as she feels that some of the ethical dilemmas she is learning about don't apply to her as they are no-nonsense types of dilemmas where ethical issues were bad judgment calls made by counselors. She swears that this is not something she would ever deal with.

DIGGING INTO ETHICS

What assumptions are you making about the counseling profession right now? How can you allow space in your learning for compassion and understanding of the scaffolding in which all learning takes place (e.g., you did not learn to walk without learning to sit, crawl, stand, etc.)? How will you know that you are reaching premature conclusions about the profession or "catch yourself" so that you don't rush to judgment?

Consider doing the following role-play with a peer. You become friendly with counselors next to your office and you start chatting about their practice as you are so eager to learn how experienced counselors manage their lives. As you are chatting with them, you recognize that they are dissatisfied with their career and share with you how overwhelming the work in the agency is as well as how overwhelming the clientele is. How do you respond back to them?

1.1 PRACTITIONER'S PERSPECTIVE

Dr. Christy Walker currently serves as the Director of Career Services at Durham Technical Community College in Durham, North Carolina. Dr. Walker has over 15 years of experience in academic advising and career services at the undergraduate and graduate levels.

I am a career changer.

I am a former chemist and engineer with a bachelor of science degree in chemical engineering from North Carolina A&T State University. I worked as a chemist for 3 years after graduation and briefly as an engineer before being laid off due to restructuring. Through sheer networking, I landed a position as a chemistry instructor at Norfolk State University. Teaching at the college level made me realize that I truly enjoyed working with college students, and I enjoyed helping them navigate such a pivotal time in their lives. This led me to earn a master of arts degree in higher education administration from Old Dominion University (ODU), where I completed a graduate internship in academic advising. In 2018, I earned a doctorate in Higher Education Administration from Northeastern University.

After graduating from ODU, I accepted a position as an academic and career advisor at James Madison University. At the time, they were one of the few universities with a fully integrated academic advising and career services department, so all employees who were hired were trained to do both academic advising and career counseling. After 3 years of working at James Madison University, I accepted a role as an academic advisor for science, technology, engineering, and math (STEM) students at the University of North Carolina (UNC) at Chapel Hill, where I also worked for 3 years.

My next role was as assistant director at UNC's University Career Services (UCS), where I worked for 6 years. At UCS, I counseled everyone from first-year students to doctoral students. I also served as the liaison to the Eshelman School of Pharmacy, where I created specialized programming for pharmacy students, including workshops on interviewing, resume preparation, and salary negotiation.

In 2016, I accepted a role as the Director of Career Services/Quality Enhancement Plan at Durham Technical Community College, where I am currently employed. In my work at a community college, I have worked with students from ages 16 to 70. Durham Technical Community College serves students in Durham and Orange counties in North Carolina and has the following student enrollment demographics:

- 34.6% African American
- 31.9% White
- 18.6% Hispanic or Latino
- 5.19% Asian
- 3.32% Two or more races
- 0.547% American Indian or Alaska Native
- 0.146% Native American or other Pacific Islanders
- 5.7% Did not report their race

The college has a total enrollment of 5,556 students, and 25.7% are enrolled full time. The most popular majors are liberal arts and sciences, Registered nursing, information technology, and early childhood education (Data USA, 2022). Durham Tech offers more than 100 credential programs under its newly implemented Guided Careers Pathway structure, combining curriculum and continuing education programs to help students more efficiently stay on track in earning their degree, certificate, or diploma and allowing them to enter their careers sooner. The college did not have a career services department until I was hired. Every department did its own career programming at different levels. I was hired to build the Career Services Department from scratch, and therefore the entire student population is my population.

Getting to build a career services department from the ground up is a unique experience. It has included everything from creating a mission statement to doing strategic planning, hiring counselors, and setting up infrastructure, such as choosing a career management system. One of the first areas I addressed upon arrival on campus was figuring out a career management system that would fit our needs and budget. Previously, all job openings were posted by the college's webmaster. Having a career management system allowed the employers to post their position openings, thus reducing strain on the webmaster and pointing students to a central spot to apply to jobs and store their resumes.

Another facet involved meeting and creating relationships with the stakeholders surrounding a community college. I previously worked in 4-year institutions, and I had to acclimate myself to the terminology and the community college way of doing things. There was a bit of a learning curve involved, and I had to shift my way of thinking in some areas. I created all documentation and published materials for the department, including the contents of a career guide and presentations on career-related topics. I also created social media channels for publicity.

The largest responsibility I had in planning the office was getting the word out about my services to the student population. This involved getting to know the instructors, directors, and deans of the many programs the college offers. I felt that it was my duty to cultivate a culture of career services at the college. Career services were previously decentralized, so I needed to work to inform the students of our resources.

On a typical day, I counsel students, work with employers to set up opportunities for students to get hired, plan events such as career fairs and panels, and facilitate career-related presentations in classrooms. I attend meetings representing the college in local and regional Economic and Workforce Development boards. For the most part, I am a one-person office, with the exception of graduate student interns who volunteer as part of their master's degree requirements, and whom I also supervise. They have been lifesavers, and free up time for me to complete director-level tasks as they counsel students.

I am also the director of the college's Quality Enhancement Plan (QEP), which is a 5-year plan to improve this aspect of the college. Since the college's QEP dealt with improving academic advising and career services, and since I had experience in both areas, I was hired to direct the plan. This involves managing an implementation team composed of deans, directors, and vice presidents to ensure the QEP is carried out as a part of the college's reaffirmation of its accreditation. Right now, I am in the process of completing the Fifth-Year Impact Report, which lists the goals, changes, and outcomes of the QEP.

TRAITS OF CAREER COUNSELORS

A person who is interested in my role must be knowledgeable in career services, particularly someone who has been exposed to different career services settings. I have had the opportunity to work in large and small departments, and this has given me a wide perspective on what a typical counselor does. You also need to be able to work independently and have the drive to get projects completed. Resourcefulness is a good trait, too, because there is generally not a lot of funding focused on community colleges. Although there are opportunities for smaller grants offered by the college and professional organizations, such as the North Carolina Career Development Association, funding is still minimal compared to most 4-year universities.

Being an advocate for your students is a vital part of the position. A balanced experience of counseling students and working with employers is necessary, and you must have the ability to build relationships with stakeholders at all levels. I feel that I'm really helping the students change their lives, whether it is getting a promotion at their current job or helping them to change careers. Our students come from so many different backgrounds and have fascinating stories to tell. Many of them rise up from dark circumstances to improve their own lives and the lives of their families. They are grateful, and I am honored to have the opportunity to work with them. I also feel proud to help make a positive impact in my community.

PROFESSIONAL ETHICS

Ethics are important, and I use the National Association of Colleges and Employers' Principles for Ethical Professional Practice (www.naceweb.org/career-development/organizational-structure/principles-for-ethical-professional-practice/) as a guide. I keep all student appointments confidential, as some of them share personal information with me. I also try to ensure equitable hiring standards for the employers I work with. For example, when employers call me to ask for my "best five students," I reply that Career Services' role is to give *all* students an opportunity to apply for the position.

DEFINITION OF CAREER COUNSELING AND DEVELOPMENT

Career development is the lifelong process of cultivating one's career goals. It involves setting goals and objectives based on one's work values, interests, and skills. Career development also involves creating strategies to help a person meet their career goals. A career counselor helps clients to better understand themselves and the world of work in order to make clear and constructive career and life decisions.

CAREER IMPACT OVER THE LIFE SPAN

I once worked with an international student who had earned a doctorate of pharmacy in his home country, but the degree was not recognized in the United States. He came to me because he needed guidance on a career that he could pursue in the United States. I helped him confirm that he wanted to stay in the health industry, yet he was unaware of all of his options within healthcare. I helped to clarify some of them. Through determining his work values and interests, we both determined that a career in clinical trials research was a good fit. He completed our Clinical Trials Research Assistant program and is well on his way.

Student Voices

In Student Voices, students offer their learner viewpoint as they begin in the career counseling field. These students share their thoughts and reflections about the career counseling profession and offer personal takeaways.

ANNE SYLLA

I received a MEd in college counseling and completed an internship at the Counseling Center at NC State University. I was 25 years into my career when I applied to the counseling master's program. The catalyst was an advertisement that I saw that led me to explore the field and then to join the online program. It also led to a major career change. That advertisement is an instance of Pasteur's observation that "chance favors the prepared mind." I had been contemplating a career adjustment for many years as I thought about what I enjoyed, what I valued, and what I was good at.

After college and a summer publishing program, I started full-time work as a low-paid editorial assistant at a university press. My fiscally concerned father who saw my low pay encouraged me to attend business school. My undergraduate concentration in management included career assessments, and it was in those classes that I learned the concept that career satisfaction may correlate with personality. However, instead of using this knowledge, I decided to try management consulting, which was lucrative and a great learning experience, but very stressful. Fortunately, I was able to segue into a job as an instructor for the company that made the software I had been implementing.

I loved teaching the classes, but my excitement faded as I taught the same class repeatedly; I also felt I needed to stop traveling after having a baby. So, when some of my students offered me a job at their company, I accepted. I ended up spending the next 20 years at that company in a variety of IT and business roles. I received raises and promotions, but I often felt like something meaningful was missing in my career. To figure that out, I participated actively in HR-sponsored workshops on strengths, personality, social style, and interests, and I gathered knowledge through informational interviews.

These workshops resulted in a list of careers that I thought would be a better fit for me. Because I am analytical, I put all the details of those possibilities into spreadsheets and did calculations, but I was stuck for a long time and made only small changes in my career. During that time, I also got divorced and remarried, had more children, lost loved ones, moved a number of times, and accumulated a lot of life experience.

After noticing the advertisement, I entered the field of counseling lightly, joining with online night classes so I could keep working. I wasn't sure where I was going on this new path, but I really enjoyed what I was learning. However, a series of coincidences helped me to commit to a career change: I was offered a voluntary separation package, the pandemic interrupted a lateral career move, and, amazingly, I found the meaning and satisfaction I had been looking for in my counseling practicum and internship.

That educational journey led me to where I am now: planning to obtain a Clinical Mental Health Counselor Associate's license and to find work using it. I also have a vision for the next few years of growth in the profession. After years of contemplation, suddenly, I'm ready to start a new chapter.

COUNSELING SKILLS CONNECTION

Courses offered within counseling and training programs focus on topics across the life span. For example, courses such as theories of counseling and human development cover specific milestones, issues, and challenges experienced by children, adolescents, and adults. Counselors, including career counselors, may work with clients to support them in their goals pertaining to total wellness and to develop a solid foundation of coping and self-care strategies.

The wellness wheel, presented earlier in this chapter, is a tool used by counselors with their clients and students to explore and identify areas in which the client is thriving and areas of growth. Clients can create a pictorial representation of the eight dimensions to develop a visual representation of their current wellness. The wellness wheel may reveal presenting issues that the counselor and client can work on together during the therapeutic process.

MINDFUL MOMENT

The career exploration process can induce stress for anyone. A mindful tip for reducing stress can include creative and tactile activities. For example, at any age, coloring and creating as a way of expression and relaxation can be beneficial. For example, there are adult coloring activities called mandalas that invite you to create a beautiful picture of your choosing. After finishing it, we suggest putting it in a place to induce calm and peace in your workspace or home setting. Visit Monday Mandala to try your hand at coloring a mandala of your own at https://mondaymandala.com.

TECH TOOLS

CareerOneStop is a U.S. Department of Labor program that provides a comprehensive resource for "career exploration, training, and jobs" (CareerOneStop, n.d., p. 1). This tool is a strong starting place for clients and has extensive information for diverse audiences. CareerOneStop also links clients to local community career and work support resources, including unemployment benefits, community colleges, employment networks, and credentialing requirements. For a career counselor, the toolkits provided by CareerOneStop may be particularly useful for interest, values, and skill assessments; salary research; and industry trends.

REFLECTION ACTIVITY

A useful exercise for self-reflection is to consider your life as a timeline. As you reflect on your experiences, background, life events, transition points, and so forth, up to this point in your life, we invite you to plot your journey from your birthday to today, at this current moment in time. Begin this exercise by creating a list, including your date of birth and significant times, dates, and events during your life. Brainstorm events related to your family, career, education, relationships, turning points, and so on. Draw a line on a piece of paper and plot each event for review. After creating your timeline, what do you notice? Are there any patterns? What feelings come up for you as you review your life up to this point? Can you envision using this activity with your current or future clients or students? If so, in what way?

END-OF-CHAPTER RESOURCES

SUMMARY

Counselors love a story, and in this chapter the reader has enjoyed the stories of the authors' own personal career stories as well as those of a few well-known people who have experienced incredible career journeys, all of which were nonlinear, unexpected, and unplanned. In reading these real-life stories, we hope that you will take the time to consider your own story and explore where you are and how you arrived at this point in time. As you embark on your own personal journey, our hope is for you to engage in the wellness wheel activity to learn areas where you have optimal health and other areas where there may be gaps. For the reader's convenience, we have offered definitions of key terms and specific concepts related to career, career development, and the world of work. We are thrilled you are taking this next step to take this personal journey with us!

REFERENCES

American Psychological Association. (2021). *Inclusive language guidelines.* https://www.apa.org/about/apa/equity-diversity-inclusion/language-guidelines.pdf

Berkow, I. (1994, April 11). A humbled Jordan learns new truths. *The New York Times.* https://archive.nytimes.com/www.nytimes.com/library/sports/basketball/041194bkn-jordan.html

Bove, T. (2022, July 21). Great Resignation shows no signs of slowing down: 40% of U.S. workers are considering quitting their jobs—Here's where they're going. *Fortune* magazine. https://fortune.com/2022/07/21/great-resignation-40-percent-want-to-quit-where-are-they-going/

Bureau of Labor Statistics. (2020, September 22). *Employee tenure in 2020.* https://www.bls.gov/news.release/pdf/tenure.pdf

Bureau of Labor Statistics. (2021, August 31). *Number of jobs, labor market experience, marital status, and health: Results from a national longitudinal survey.* https://www.bls.gov/news.release/pdf/nlsoy.pdf

CareerOneStop. (n.d.). https://www.careeronestop.org/

CNN.com. (2001, October 17). *Jordan donates his salary to relief efforts.* CNN. https://edition.cnn.com/2001/US/10/17/rec.jordan.salary/

Collier, J. (May 10, 2020). 'I'm back.' Everything you need to know about Michael Jordan's 1995 return to the Chicago Bulls—and the famous 2-word fax that preceded it. *Chicago Tribune.* https://www.chicagotribune.com/sports/bulls/ct-chicago-bulls-jordan-im-back-last-dance-20200509-xzmp2t63xnfkbcpnawec2tc7cq-story.html

DataUSA. (2022). *Durham Technical Community College.* https://datausa.io/profile/university/durham-technical-community-college

Editors of Encyclopedia Britannica. (2022, July 14). John Glenn: American Astronaut and US Senator. *Britannica online.* https://www.britannica.com/biography/John-Glenn

ESPN.com. (2003, May 9). *Pollin's decision to cut ties leaves Jordan livid.* ESPN. https://www.espn.com/espn/print?id=1550445

ESPN.com. (2010, August 8). *This day in sports: The dream team takes gold in Barcelona.* https://www.espn.com/blog/sportscenter/post/_/id/71610/this-day-in-sports -the-dream-team-takes-gold-in-barcelona

ESPN.com (2016, April 4). *Michael Jordan says his title-winning shot in 1982 was 'the birth of Michael Jordan.'* https://www.espn.com/mens-college-basketball/story/_/ id/15136507/title-winning-shot-1982-was-birth-michael-jordan

Forbes. (2022, August 15). Profile: Michael Jordan. https://www.forbes.com/profile/ michael-jordan/?sh=597dff232d83

Goodreads. (n.d.). *Rainer Maria Rilke quotes.* https://www.goodreads.com/ quotes/717-be-patient-toward-all-that-is-unsolved-in-your-heart#:~:text= Do%20not%20now%20seek%20the,distant%20day%20into%20the%20 answer.%E2%80%9D

Hardaway, R. D. (1980). Jeannette Rankin: The early years. *North Dakota Quarterly,* 48, 63.

Heichelbech, R. (n.d.). *This American hero gets a warm NYC welcome home with a giant ticker tape parade in 1962!* Dusty Old Thing. https://dustyoldthing.com/john -glenn-ticker-tape-parade/

Joni & Friends. (n.d.). *About the CID.* https://www.joniandfriends.org/ministries/ christian-institute-on-disability/

Murray, J. K. (2020, March). *Jobs in diversity, inclusion and belonging have risen 123% since May—Here's how to get one.* Indeed. https://www.indeed.com/career -advice/finding-a-job/diversity-inclusion-and-belonging-jobs-rise

National Career Development Association. (2015). *NCDA 2015 code of ethics.* https:// ncda.org/aws/NCDA/asset_manager/get_file/3395?ver=738700

NESN Staff. (2014, January 10). *Michael Jordan's College transcript reveals he took beginning tennis, majored in geography.* NESN.com. https://nesn.com/2014/01/ michael-jordans-college-transcript-reveals-he-took-beginning-tennis-majored -in-geography-now-up-for-auction/

Pearlman, R. Z. (2012, May 29). *President Obama awards John Glenn with medal of freedom.* Space.com. https://www.space.com/15908-john-glenn-medal-freedom -award.html

Powell, W. S. (Ed.). (1994). *Dictionary of North Carolina biography* (Vol. 5, p. 408). University of North Carolina Press.

SAMHSA Publications and Digital Products. (2016, April). *SAMHSA's wellness initiative: Wellness community power point presentation.* Retrieved August 20, 2022, from https://store.samhsa.gov/product/SAMHSA-s-Wellness-Initiative -Wellness-Community-Power-Point-Presentation/sma16-4955

Sandomir, R. (2000, January 20). Jordan sheds uniform for suit as a wizards owner. *The New York Times.* https://www.nytimes.com/2000/01/20/sports/pro -basketball-jordan-sheds-uniform-for-suit-as-a-wizards-owner.html

Schwartz, L. (2002). *Michael Jordan transcends hoops.* ESPN Classic. https//www.espn .com/classic/biography/s/Jordan_Michael.html

Substance Abuse and Mental Health Services Administration. (2016, April). *Creating a healthier life: A step-by-step guide to wellness.* Author.

Swarbrick, M. (2006). A wellness approach. *Psychiatric Rehabilitation Journal, 29*(4), 311–314. https://doi.org/10.2975/29.2006.311.314

Weller, F. (2020, February 20). *Black history month spotlight: CC Spaulding.* WECT News. https://www.wect.com/2020/02/20/black-history-month-cc-spaulding -man-columbus-county-who-ran-richest-black-owned-company-america/ #:~:text=he%20should%20be.-,C.C.,pursue%20big%20dreams%20in%20Durham

Wikipedia. (n.d.). *Michael Jordan.* https://en.wikipedia.org/wiki/Michael_Jordan #Business_ventures

Wilkinson, H. (2020, January 18). *John Glenn's big disappointment: Running for president.* WVXU. https://www.wvxu.org/politics/2020-01-17/john-glenns -big-disappointment-running-for-president

World Economic Forum. (2021, November 29). *What is 'The Great Resignation'? An expert explains.* https://www.weforum.org/agenda/2021/11/what-is -the-great-resignation-and-what-can-we-learn-from-it/

CHAPTER 2

STARTING FROM THE BEGINNING: AN EXPLORATION THROUGH CAREER COUNSELING

Seth C. W. Hayden, Helen Morgan, Katie Peterssen, and Angie C. Smith

LEARNING OBJECTIVES

By the end of this chapter, you will be able to:

- Describe the origins of career counseling.
- Compare and contrast approaches to career counseling services for special populations.
- Assess your own career lifeline and the factors that have shaped it.

WARM-UP EXERCISE

As you reflect on your life and your own history, what is your earliest memory? How old were you in this memory? What is significant about this memory? Are you alone, or are there people with you in this memory? What feeling(s) are evoked as you reflect on this early memory? What have been a few key milestones or turning points in your life? How has your historical context impacted your current career choices?

INTRODUCTION

This chapter describes a brief **history** of career counseling, starting from the beginning of the profession. Throughout the chapter, there will be a focus on a variety of career-counseling populations, including creative ways career professionals provide **career-counseling** services within the community and specific to **populations** of interest. **Resources** are provided to assist counselors-in-training, practitioners, and counselor educators in their work with their students and clients. Readers are invited to reflect on their own journeys, build the context for where we are today in the field, and pay attention to where the trends are leading future counselors.

PIVOTAL MOMENTS IN TIME

It All Begins With Frank Parsons

There are several key moments in history that influenced the development of the career-counseling field, and many of them trace back to Frank Parsons, who is often known as the founder of guidance (Gladding, 2018; Herr, 2001). Parsons' methodology emphasized a clear understanding of yourself and your abilities, accessibility to **resources**, and opportunities for growth. His method also includes that a person should understand the benefits and drawbacks, financial compensation, growth opportunities, and outlook for various careers (Parsons, 1909). One of Parsons' most notable accomplishments was the founding of the Vocational Bureau of Boston in 1908, a step that revolutionized the practice of career guidance.

The Vocational Bureau of Boston provided a resource for vocational exploration, and it emphasized the importance of exploring one's personal interests and strengths and matching them with job factors or characteristics to create a meaningful life (Parsons, 1909). This led to the institutionalization of career counseling and development, as well as the establishment of vocational development departments in organizations for both men and women, such as the Young Men's Christian Association (YMCA), Women's Educational and Industrial Union, and the Twentieth Century Club (Parsons, 1909). The goals of these programs and the Vocational Bureau were to partner with people to help them determine the right career path on their *own*, thereby empowering the individual (Parsons, 1909).

Parsons developed three key steps that would aid a person in choosing a career (Parsons, 1909):

1. A clear understanding of self, abilities, and resources
2. An understanding of the job or career requirements to achieve success, of the pros and cons of the opportunity, of the compensation, and an understanding of a comparative analysis of other fields
3. An understanding of the relationship between one's *traits* and self-understanding and the *factors* outlined in step two around the job

To use these steps, it became necessary to train vocational counselors to work in organizations, schools, colleges, universities, and businesses, and this set the foundation for modern-day career counseling (Parsons, 1909).

Much like professions and work evolve in response to social, political, economic, and other driving forces, so do terms and organizations. The roots of the counseling profession and today's American Counseling Association (ACA) grew out of the American Personnel and Guidance Association (APGA). With a focus on occupations and work, the National Vocational Guidance Association (NVGA) was one of the four founding subdivisions of the APGA. Founded in 1913, NVGA was renamed to the National Career Development Association (NCDA) and continues to be the recognized leader in setting professional standards and ethical guidance for career development professionals (NCDA, n.d.).

TABLE 2.1 HISTORICAL EVENTS IN CAREER DEVELOPMENT

STAGE	TIMEFRAME	NOTABLE EVENTS
One	1890–1914	Post-Civil War, Urbanization, Beginning of Vocational Guidance
Two	1914–1929	Focus on Measurement, Vocational Education and Organization, Post WWI Vocational Support
Three	1929–1939	The Great Depression, Widespread Economic Depression, Vocational Legislation
Four	1940–1957	Post WWII, Increase in Vocational Instruments, Shift From Vocational Guidance to Career Counseling and Development
Five	1958–1970	Space Race, Increase Focus on Science and Technology, Civil Rights Movement, The Great Society
Six	1970–1979	Enhance Attention on Career Needs of Ethnic Minorities and People with Disabilities, Career Development Theory Focused on Social Learning
Seven	1980–1989	Second Largest Wave of Immigration, Increase Attention on the Needs of Diverse Populations, Shift to Holistic Models of Career Development
Eight	1990–2005	Enhanced Focus on School-to-Work Transition, Attention to Inclusivity Within Career Development Theories, Career Counseling Outcome Research, Rise of Postmodern Career Theories
Nine	2005–Present	Information Age, Globalization, Automation of Labor, Pandemic, Social Justice Movement, Standards and Credentialing in Career Services

Source: Adapted from Shen-Miller, D. S., McWhirter, E. H., & Bartone, A. S. (2012). Historical influence on the evolution of vocational counseling. In D. Capuzzi & M. D. Stauffer (Eds.), *Career counseling: Foundations, perspectives, and applications* (pp. 3–42). Routledge.

Table 2.1 provides an overview of important events in career development in the United States. This is by no means exhaustive, but it highlights a general timeline of movements that have impacted careers and work.

Lifeline for the Career Field: Brief Overview

TRAIT-AND-FACTOR APPROACHES

Parsons' work led to the use of **trait-and-factor** approaches that assume that people have different traits, occupations require a particular combination of worker characteristics, and effective vocational counseling matches a person's traits with job requirements (Kosciulek et al., 2015). This perspective was continued by other career development influencers, such as John Holland, who emphasized the importance of considering one's unique traits, gifts, and interests along with skills and activities relevant to a particular occupation or career field. Holland's work has been frequently cited, evidenced by 2,318 references to the RIASEC approach and its application to practice from 1953 to 2016 (Kennelly et al., 2018).

In his work, Holland (1959, 1997) asserted that personalities tend to fall into six key categories, which he coded by letter:

R—Realistic

I—Investigative

A—Artistic

S—Social

E—Enterprising

C—Conventional

This became known as the RIASEC theory (see Figure 4.3 in Chapter 4). Each category encapsulated various personality styles and the occupational environments that are likely to match the personality style to create congruence and occupational satisfaction. He theorized that people sought work environments that allow them to thrive by capitalizing on their skills, matching their attitudes and values, and engaging in activities that they enjoy or are good at (Holland). Holland's theory continues to be used and serves as the basis for several career assessments used today (e.g., Strong Interest Inventory, Self-Directed Search).

Career Counseling in the 20th Century

Throughout the 20th century and into the 21st century, career counseling continued to develop and adapt to the needs of our society. With U.S. commerce transitioning from manufacturing and production to services and technology in today's postindustrial age, career counselors have needed to adapt to shifting trends and adopt new practices to best serve those in need. Some of these include the assessment procedures used to classify and place army recruits in World War I via the alpha and beta tests and the Army General Classification Test (AGCT), opening career service centers for returning veterans at the Veterans Administration during World War II, creating career education programs in schools, and developing numerous professional associations, such as the NCDA, to discuss and implement these changes and movements (Zunker, 2016). These adaptations also led to the development of several postmodern theories, including Savickas' Career Constructivism, Blustein's Psychology of Working, and Krumboltz's Social Cognitive Career Theory (Zunker, 2016).

Career Development 2020–Present

The coronavirus pandemic that began in 2020 dramatically impacted health, economic, and social systems across the world. The onset of COVID-19 sent many workers home, shuttered schools, stalled logistics hubs, and created confusion for businesses and business owners. It also exposed dramatic health, economic, and opportunity disparities. While many workers with professional roles were able to work remotely and exercise some control over their health risks, many workers in service industries, manufacturing, and healthcare continued to report to their workplace and had little control over health risks. Service industry employees, including restaurants, retail, and hospitality, were sent home and laid off in mass. Closure of schools and childcare facilities drove many working parents, particularly women, to reduce work hours or leave the workforce altogether as they juggled personal and professional roles.

Even as world economies rebounded and most of the jobs lost in the early pandemic were recovered, by January of 2022, 4.5 million Americans had voluntarily left their jobs, and this has been dubbed the "Great Resignation" or "Great Realignment" (CGT Staffing, 2022). Workers are increasingly focused on the intersection of their life and career and are seeking roles and environments that better align with their values, including increased flexibility through remote work.

In 2014, the ACA declared that promoting social justice is a core value of the profession, and it states that its mission "promotes human dignity and diversity, respect, the attainment of a quality of life for all, empowerment, integrity, social justice advocacy, equity and inclusion" (Lee, 2020, para. 4). The term *social justice* in this context is defined as an inquiry into and promotion of the fair distribution of opportunity, wealth, and status in society. Then, in May 2020, amid the COVID lockdowns, the ideology of social justice erupted into mainstream American awareness and gained momentum after the tragic death of George Floyd at the hands of police, which ignited nationwide demands for the equal protection of civil liberties that are due to all Americans.

The social justice movement directly impacts career professionals as the movement is also driving employers to enact change as demands from employees grow for inclusive spaces and systems where all have opportunity to thrive. As workers and employers evolve to meet the current era and studies emerge highlighting overarching trends, it is likely that we will see 2020 as a new demarcation in the timeline of the career development profession.

A HISTORICAL SNAPSHOT OF CAREER THEORY

Table 2.2 offers a brief snapshot of key career theories from the early 1900s to today. It is an overview of career theory and approaches and is not intended to serve as a comprehensive review of all career theories, approaches, and models to date. Key concepts, limitations, and sample interventions are included to make it easy to compare and contrast theories across history.

A BRIEF HISTORY OF CAREER IN VARIOUS COUNSELING CONCENTRATIONS

School Counseling

Career-focused counseling resonates across the developmental landscape, requiring counselors in all settings to consider career development in their work. The American School Counselor Association (ASCA) has a long history of embedding

TABLE 2.2A HISTORICAL SNAPSHOT OF CAREER THEORY

THEORY/ FRAMEWORK/ APPROACH	TRAIT-AND-FACTOR	PERSON-ENVIRONMENT-CORRESPONDENCE THEORY OF WORK ADJUSTMENT (TWA)	TIEDEMAN'S DECISION-MAKING APPROACH	LIFE SPAN, LIFE SPACE
Theorist	Parson's (1909) Williamson (1939, 1965)	Lofquist and Dawis (1991)	Tiedeman and O'Hara (1963)	Donald Super (1972)
Key concepts/terms	Matching a person's traits to the requirements of a job	Individual and work environment congruent, i.e., correspondence. Individual needs key for environmental fit; Individual and work environment demonstrate some degree of flexibility or adjustment. A matching process assessing individual worker traits and correspondence to the work environment part of this process of determining satisfaction or dissatisfaction: ■ Personality structure ■ Personality style ■ Ability dimensions ■ Values ■ Environmental structure.	Self-development Decision-making Cognitive development Ego-identity Ego-development Career development parallels Erikson's (1950) stages of development, Erikson's eight psychosocial crises.	Self-concept, life span, development, cycling (i.e., minicycle), recycling, life-career rainbow, career life stages, life theatres, career maturity, career adaptability, life roles, archway model (i.e., biographic, psychologic, and socioeconomic considerations), career rainbow model Vocational developmental tasks: Crystallization (14–18) Specification (18–21) Implementation (21–24) Stabilization (24–35) Consolidation (35+) Stages of vocational development: growth, exploration, establishment, maintenance, disengagement
Assessments	Assessment not the only data point used in the career counseling	Minnesota Classification Index III (Dawis et al., 1987): finding a connection between work skills and occupations and ASVAB (U.S. Department of Defense, 2023): abilities Minnesota Importance Questionnaire (MIQ) (Rounds et al., 1981): values	One of the first attempts at creating a computer-based guidance system titled Information System for Vocational Decisions (ISVD) (Tiedeman & O'Hara, 1963)	C-DAC: career development assessment and counseling model, Salience Inventory (Nevill & Super, 1986), Adult Career Concerns Inventory (ACCI) (Super et al., 1988), Values Inventory (Nevill & Super, 1986), and Work Value Inventory (Super, 1970)

Population of Interest				
Thing to note about the theory (limitations or cautions: things to watch out for in practice and application)	Narrow in scope, posits that an individual has one career goal with a single decision point. Approach directly links career direction to ability. (Herr & Cramer, 1996)	Lack of relevant research to support alignment evaluation with new and emerging occupations. Satisfaction in one job may be challenging, May need to find multiple jobs to achieve satisfaction.	Limited research to support reliability due to key terms being challenging and lacking clear, discrete definitions. Pays little attention to external environmental factors that may be particularly salient for historically marginalized populations.	The most researched career theory to date.
Activity or Intervention Idea	Identify a client's personality traits and list the requirements of a specific occupation. Review any similarities between the two.	Brainstorm a list of potential skills, values, or needs an individual client may determine as being essential to fulfilling job satisfaction. Utilize O*Net to identify occupations which correspond to those identified needs.	Review Erickson's eight stages of psychosocial development and evaluate where the client is on the development model. Identify the psychosocial crisis impacting decision-making for the client and develop related interventions.	Utilize the career–life rainbow; have clients/students review the image and identify the roles where they spend most of their time. Students or clients can review the following life roles (child, student, "leisurite," citizen, worker, spouse, homemaker, parent, and pensioner) and shade or highlight all roles that apply for a visual representation or current snapshot of the client's time.

Note: The chart is an overview of career theory and approaches and is not intended to serve as a comprehensive review of all career theories and approaches to date.

TABLE 2.2B

	CIRCUMSCRIPTION AND COMPROMISE	ROE'S NEEDS APPROACH	HOLLAND'S TYPOLOGY	LEARNING THEORY OF CAREER COUNSELING
	Gottfredson (1981)	Roe (1956)	Holland (1959)	Krumboltz (1979)
	Occupational aspirations, social space, images of occupations, cognitive maps of occupations, self-concept, circumscription, compromise, four stages of development: orientation to size and power (ages 3–5), orientation to sex roles (ages 6–8), orientation to social valuation (ages 9–13), orientation to the internal, unique self (age 14+) (Gottfredson, 1981)	Experiences in early childhood; needs structure; early personality development; family relationships may lead to career choice; draws heavily from Maslow's hierarchy of needs; person-oriented; non-person-oriented; needs-theory approach to career choice	Vocational personalities and work environments, Trait-factor, career choice, RIASEC, congruence, consistency, differentiation, vocational identity; six types of work environments and six types of personalities: realistic, investigative, artistic, social, enterprising, conventional	Social learning, happenstance, learning experience, self-observation, generalizations, worldview generalizations, task approach skills, actions, genetic endowment, environmental conditions, unplanned events/chance occurrences
	Mapping Vocational Choice, Position Classification Inventory	Roe's Classification System	Vocational Preference Inventory, My Vocational Situation, Self-Directed Search Form-R, Strong Interest Inventory, You and Your Career	Career Beliefs Inventory (CBI)
	Youth and adolescents	Early childhood and school-aged adolescents	Ages 11–70	Young adults–Adults

Challenging to research due to nature of the constructs and developmental stages of the population	Relevant application may be challenging.	It is particularly important to support clients who had an inconsistent or incongruent profile, as these occupations can be harder to identify. Similarly, clients with a profile that lacks differentiation may struggle with decision-making, and so forth. Clients with limited experience or exposure to differentiated work environments may require support to understand their interests, skills, and abilities.	Research varies in support and depth, depending on which component of Krumboltz's theory being discussed: LTCC, SLCTDM, planned happenstance.
Mapping Vocational Choice activity for high school or middle school students: Gottfredson, L. S., & Lapan, R. T. (1997). Assessing gender-based circumscription of occupational aspirations. *Journal of Career Assessment, 5*(4), 419–441. https://doi .org/10.1177/106907279 700500404 Additional resources for occupation information include: O*Net and CareerOneStop	School counselors may inquire about early parent–child relationships as they explore career options with youth.	See the RIASEC Party Game Example from the University of California, Berkeley: https://career.berkeley. edu/sites/default/fi les/pdf/Plan/ PartyGame2.pdf.	Learning happens throughout development. One of the ways we learn is through watching and observing behavior in videos and other media. Instruct your clients or students to select two to three movies or shows that depict different types of careers or roles. Use a worksheet to note any key differences or observations among the roles or careers selected. Students or clients then may research and validate observations with occupational information available via onetonline.org or careeronestop.org.

TABLE 2.2C

THEORY/ FRAMEWORK/ APPROACH	COGNITIVE INFORMATION PROCESSING PERSPECTIVE (CIP)	BROWN'S VALUES-BASED HOLISTIC MODEL	GINZBERG ET AL.	SOCIAL COGNITIVE CAREER THEORY (SCCT)
Theorist	Reardon et al. (2004)	Brown (1996)	Ginzberg et al. (1951)	Lent et al. (1994)
Key concepts/ terms	CASVE cycle: communication, analysis, synthesis, valuing, execution; career problems, career problem-solving, career decision-making, career development; Knowledge domains, Decision-Making Skills Domain, Executive Processing Domain, meta cognitions	Value orientation, life-role decision-making, genetic and environmental influences, life satisfaction	Stages of development (age 11–17): fantasy, tentative, realistic Individual values, emotional factors, educational considerations, and tension or pressure from the external world Considered first to approach a theory of occupational choice from a developmental standpoint (Zunker, 2002, p. 80)	SCCT uses cognitive mediators, personal agency, triadic reciprocal interactions, self-efficacy, outcome expectations, interest, intentions/goals for activity involvement, activity selection and practice, performance attainments, "overcoming barriers to choice" (Zunker, 2002, p. 105)
Assessments	Career Thoughts Inventory, Decision Space Worksheet	Card sorts, checklists, Rokeach's Values Survey, Values Scale, Life Values Inventory (LVI)		
Population of interest	Young adult–adult	Young adult–adult	Focus on adolescent timeframe ages 11–17	Young adult–adult

Thing to note about the theory (limitations or cautions: things to watch out for in practice and application)	The instruments used in CIP have been adapted globally and are available in multiple languages. Depending upon the client's needs and access to resources, the process laid out in this framework could be time consuming and cost-prohibitive for a client needing support throughout a comprehensive career development cycle. Florida State University pioneered and continues to provide information about the theory, research, and practice.	Values-based approaches may address many contextual factors influencing career decision-making but may not fully consider other constructs such as interests or abilities.	Limited scope of career interests challenges in defining key terms and constructs related to "choice," adjustment, and process of compromise	Research support for the self-efficacy construct is strong. The complexity of the model could be overwhelming for practitioners to follow.
Activity or intervention idea	Walk through the CASVE cycle role-playing client and counselor roles. A prompt to offer a career concern such as indecision between pursuing military enlistment, enrolling in a 2-year college, or going to work in the local manufacturing facility. As the counselor, reflect on walking through the cycle what was easy for you and what parts were more challenging?	Ask the client to complete a values inventory or card sort. Challenge your client to deepen their understanding of their values by asking, "why" questions to expand on how they arrived at their core values. For example, "Why do you think X career is well-aligned with your values?"	Classroom Career Activity (K–12): Awareness of occupations Resource: Explore occupations through tactile play and imagination with My Future (2021)	Evaluate the experiences and beliefs that may have shaped a client's decision-making. Ask the client to discuss how they determined which roles or paths they were not going to pursue. Focus on assessing inaccuracies within their self-efficacy beliefs or knowledge of careers.

Note: The chart is an overview of career theory and approaches and is not intended to serve as a comprehensive review of all career theories and approaches to date.

TABLE 2.2D

CAREER CONSTRUCTION	INTEGRATIVE LIFE PLANNING (ILP)	TRANSITION THEORY	CHAOS	KALEIDOSCOPE CAREER MODEL (KCM)
Savickas (2002)	Hansen (1996)	Schlossberg (1984)	Bright and Pryor (2011)	Mainiero and Sullivan (2006)
Career construction, narrative, story, life theme, vocational personality, career adaptability, meaning-making, life design, Career Style Interview (CSI, 1998)	ILP emphasizes finding work that needs doing, attending to our health, connecting family and work, valuing pluralism and diversity, exploring spirituality and life purpose, managing transitions and organizational change; holistic perspective; quilts and their pieces; connectedness, wholeness, and community.	Transition theory emphasizes transition as an event or nonevent, perception, anticipated transition, unanticipated transition, context, impact, situation, self, social support, strategies, coping responses.	Chaos theory emphasizes anticipating changes, creating back-up plans, constants: personality, skills; reality is unpredictable, systems, unplanned events, shiftwork, 11phase shifts.	ABCs of KCM are authenticity, balance, challenge; mirrors, alpha and beta careers.
My Career Story, Student Career Construction Inventory				Kaleidoscope Career Self-Inventory (KCSI)
Adolescents–Adults	Adults	Adolescents–Adults	Adults	Adults

Marginalized populations may have limitations due to access, social capital, knowledge of opportunities, and so forth. Youth may have difficulty articulating a narrative due to limited work experience. Constructing a positive narrative and future may be challenging for clients with a history of trauma.	The holistic viewpoint of life and career supported by this theory make it applicable when working with clients from historically marginalized groups. ILP is one of a small number of theories that address spirituality's influence on career development.	Resources include Retire Smart, Retire Happy, Finding Your True Path in Life (Schlossberg, 2003), Revitalizing Retirement, Reshaping your Identity, Relationships, and Purpose (Schlossberg, 2009) transitionsthroughlife. com	Origins of chaos theory stem from studies of economics, mathematics, physics, and biology.	KCM is particularly useful for clients who are struggling to find balance between work and family lives. KCM may be less applicable across cultural contexts outside the United States.
Use the free My Career Story workbook available in multiple formats. Examples: www.vocopher .com/CSI/CCI_workbook .pdf and www.vocopher .com/mcsu/MCS_26_ GIUGNO%20(1).pdf. This tool may be used with individuals or groups.	Review the ILPs critical life tasks related to the model. In society, our actions impact each other. The "global context" in relation to one's work is an important concept. How does your current or future work role connect to global contexts in your own community and in a larger context around the world?	Pinpoint a time in your life when you navigated a transition. Make parallels to Schlossberg's transition theory to your own lived experience. What were your reactions to the transition? What did you learn from the transition?	Help students explore options and preferences by creating a wandering map. See Dr. Katharine Brook's Wise Wanderings activity in her 2009 book, *You Majored in What? Mapping your Path from Chaos to Career.*	Use a wheel or pie of life activity to support your client in evaluating satisfaction with different areas of their life and overall well-being. Examples: www .mindtools.com/ pages/article/ newHTE_93.htm and positivepsychology .com/wheel-of-life -coaching/

career development within the focus of the profession, and school counseling as a profession began as vocational guidance in the early 1900s, with a shift to more personal attention in the 1920s (Gysbers, 2010). While the focus of school counseling expanded, the career development of students has remained intertwined with the work of school counselors. This is evidenced by the ASCA model (2019) that identifies career development, academic development, and social-emotional development as areas of growth impacted by the work of school counselors. The concept of career readiness for K–12 students also falls within the purview of professional school counselors, indicating the importance of preparing students for the world of work (ASCA, 2014).

Career Counseling in Higher Education

Two- and 4-year institutions of higher education began providing career services in the mid-20th century. In the post–World War II era of the 1940s through the 1960s, the GI bill was incredibly influential in the creation of career centers on college campuses to provide career support to veterans within higher education (Day & Cruzvergara, 2014). In the 1970s and 1980s, colleges and universities shifted to a developmental model, with students taking on responsibility for aspects of their career development, such as the job search (Kretovicks et al., 1999). This evolution has continued as college and university career centers serve as hubs of career exploration, networking, and interviewing (Day & Cruvergara, 2014). The integration of career development into higher education continues to be more pronounced as institutions of higher education attempt to ensure a return on investment in terms of occupational opportunities for students.

Career Counseling in Clinical Mental Health

Career counseling and clinical mental health are deeply connected. Frank Parson's (1909) work related to "true reasoning" positioned the career as the central feature of career counseling. This is considered by some to be the genesis of the profession of counseling. Career and mental health have been established as interacting aspects of human functioning (e.g., Blustein, 2013; Hayden & Osborn, 2020; Lenz et al., 2010; Sampson et al., 2020), with a direct connection to counselors working in clinical mental health settings. Career development exercised within clinical mental health has waxed and waned over time, while rehabilitation counseling has long held the tenet that career and work are critical to supporting those with varying degrees of capability and in recovery from an array of ailments. Career development within the profession of counseling has diminished over the years, evidenced by only six Council for Accreditation of Counseling and Related Educational Programs (CACREP)-accredited programs offering career development as a specialty. Despite this, career development continues to be a focus area in the CACREP counseling curriculum (CACREP, 2016).

Whether in private practice, in employee assistance programs, or other mental health–focused settings, elements of career development will manifest within presenting concerns. The connection between career and mental health may become apparent quite early in intake evaluations and in assessing daily functioning, which often includes the ability to perform work. The COVID pandemic further highlighted the impact of career concerns on people's mental health. The ongoing consideration of career in clinical mental health will continue to evolve over time.

Career Development With Military Veterans

One population of interest in career development is military veterans. While veterans' career concerns are similar to their civilian counterparts, there are unique considerations such as frequent transitions and translation of military experience to civilian employment. Successfully transitioning out of the military into the civilian workforce can have a significant impact on veterans' civilian employment potential and viability as candidates within the job search process (Minnis, 2017).

In the history of career development, providing career support for U.S. military service members and their successful transition has been instrumental in the establishment of career support. The Vocational Rehabilitation Act of 1918 initiated vocational rehabilitation training for honorably discharged disabled World War I veterans, and supportive funding was provided to veterans who struggled with maintaining gainful employment (U.S. Department of Veterans Affairs, 2020). Subsequent initiatives focused on the concept of transition readiness. Each branch of the military allocates resources to assist those reentering the civilian workforce with successfully securing employment. This speaks to the long-standing consideration of career as instrumental to the successful reintegration of veterans into civilian life.

Recently, strategies have been proposed to serve veterans with differentiated status postseparation from the military (Robertson & Hayden, 2019). For example, Hayden (2018) initiated a career development group for veterans experiencing homelessness, and that group was grounded in Holland's RIASEC framework (1959, 1997) and cognitive information processing theory (Sampson et al., 2020, 2004). Participants in that career development group reported that it offered improved strategies for addressing career development, and it help them understand what the next steps were in their career development. This speaks to the potential benefits of a theoretically grounded counseling intervention designed to support military veterans' career development.

Career Development With First-Generation College Students

First-generation college students, which make up about 50% of the total college population and about 34% of the population at 4-year institutions, are an additional area of career development work and a particularly relevant demographic to consider (Tate et al., 2015). Also, first-generation students are disproportionately students of color (Malott et al., 2019). These students may need more guidance in the college and career process given that their parents have not had an American college experience, may not know what resources to point them to, or be able to share personal anecdotes about choosing a major, writing a resume or cover letter, or attending networking and career fairs. Many first-generation students feel pressure to perform, feel a greater desire to make their families proud, and understand that they may have less of a "fallback cushion" than their peers with college-educated parents (Tate et al., 2015).

First-generation students may potentially lack a professional network. While career coaches and counselors may advise students to first look to their closest ties, such as parents and parents' friends, for opportunities, first -generation college students may not have contacts in their fields of interest, making the power of the college or university alumni network and support programming all the more valuable and important (Tate et al., 2015). Because these students sometimes start with fewer resources, they may feel that they need to work harder, while lacking the support. And, like other undergraduate students, they may discount or undersell their experience. (For all students, it is important to view each one as a unique individual and not assume they have strong professional networks in place.) As career counselors, we must be aware of this and provide our students with concrete steps to showcase their skills, and when possible, create programming specifically for this population so that they feel valued and welcomed by us and as though college career centers are a place for them.

Using or finding resources tailored to this group of students may be helpful, and this may be done in conjunction with other offices, such as scholarship departments, academic advising, academic success centers, and through affinity groups or clubs on campus. It may also prove helpful to bring career services *to* these students. For example, should there be an association of first-generation college students or an organization involving a significant number of these students, consider partnering with the association to bring professional development workshops to their spaces on campus to build a bridge. There even may be opportunities to partner with employers, particularly those seeking diverse candidates, to create networking opportunities specifically for this population and to work toward democratizing opportunity. Bringing services *to* these students may help students see the career development process and see the counselors as more manageable and approachable, and thus they are more likely to enter the counseling office.

Finally, opportunities exist for career centers to work toward training small groups of first-generation students as career ambassadors and peer leaders, which could lead to increasing first-generation career engagement and help students know that the career center is a safe and welcoming space regardless of where they are in their career journey.

Career Development for International and Immigrant Populations

In 2019, there were over a million international students in the United States, though enrollment declined by 15% in the 2020 to 2021 school year due to the coronavirus pandemic (Institute of International Education, 2020; Silver, 2021). If a job search in the United States is difficult for U.S. citizens, it is exponentially more challenging for noncitizens to successfully secure and maintain legal, long-term employment. Furthermore, career counselors in higher education and community-based settings frequently support students and clients without permanent legal work authorization, and they support the development of international students on F, J, or M student visas, students with nonpermanent work authorization such as Temporary Protected Status (TPS), young undocumented immigrants (aka "Dreamers"), refugees and asylees, and unauthorized immigrants. Similarly, community-based career professionals are likely to serve clients with the same variety of work authorization statuses.

Many international students seek higher education in the United States with the goal of working in the United States after graduation for a few years before returning to their home country, and it is helpful to first understand the many costly, complex steps international students and their families manage in the college application process. In addition to the application requirements of domestic students, international students often will have to take a language assessment (e.g., TOEFL, IELTS) and provide certified bank or investment statements with account balances of liquid assets in excess of the cost of attendance for at least 1 full academic year or proof of scholarship support from a sponsoring agency. Add application, testing, and other fees, and you begin to get a picture of the investment that international students make when they enroll in a U.S. college or university.

Internship and work opportunities for international students vary based on the student's visa status. F-1 international students can apply for Curricular Practical Training (CPT) that authorizes full or part-time training opportunities, such as internships, during the school year or summer vacation. International students can also participate in Optional Practical Training (OPT), which allows students to work in a field related to their degree for up to 12 months after completion of their academic program. Students completing degrees in a STEM field have the option of staying for an additional 24 months of OPT, though there are additional requirements that sponsoring employers must meet. It is important to note that these work authorizations all require that work be directly related to or integral to the major field of study (U.S. Department of Homeland Security, n.d.).

Since the H-1B specialty worker visa was created in 1990, international students and foreign professionals have competed annually for a capped number of these visas that provide temporary work authorization for professionals in specialty occupations that require at least a bachelor's degree (American Immigration Council, 2022). A lottery system is used to determine which workers can file an H-1B petition. The annual statutory cap stood at 65,000 visas in the early 1990s before increasing to its highest peak at 195,000 from 2001 to 2003 (American Immigration Council, 2022). Today, visa numbers regularly fall far short of demand, and the cap remains at 65,000, with an additional allowance of up to 20,000 visas for international students graduating with a master's or doctoral degree from a U.S. college or university (American Immigration Council, 2022). The COVID-19 pandemic reduced the number of H-1B visa holders in 2020 to 2021, and their families by nearly 39% or 233,000 people, as the Trump administration restricted travel, visas, and admission into the United States (American Immigration Council, 2022).

The job search process is very complex before adding in the paperwork and guidelines that international students and foreign workers face, and they may also need support in managing expectations and timelines, ensuring compliance with training programs, exploring the career options that align with their major with the best opportunities for employment, and connecting with employers open to sponsorship. Career counselors should be knowledgeable about the systems and structures that international students and foreign professionals must navigate.

Cultural competency is also an essential skill in building rapport and trust and ethically serving international students and professionals. A good first step is to practice pronouncing a client's name; when approached with a genuine desire and interest in the client, this can be a strong way to set a foundation for trust.

In 2012, the Deferred Action for Childhood Arrivals (DACA) gave hope to a particularly vulnerable group of young adults residing in the United States without authorization. Since its inception, "DACA has allowed hundreds of thousands of eligible young people whose immigrant parents brought them to the United States to get benefits such as a Social Security card, driver's license, and 2-year work permit. It also opened the door for many to go to college" (Douglas-Gabriel & Svrluga, 2022, para. 3). Dreamers are eligible for work authorizations renewable 1 year at a time. More than 616,000 people are currently protected under DACA, though new DACA approvals have been halted since July 2021 when a district court judge ruled that the protections are unlawful (TheDream.us, 2021).

The DACA program, however, remains controversial, and it has left those young adults in limbo for years. The program has long been scrutinized and threatened, resulting in uncertainty for the Dreamers. You don't have to search far to find stories of Dreamers and their families. Douglas-Gabriel and Syrluga highlighted four DACA recipients and their journeys in their June 2022 article, "A Decade Ago, DACA Gave 'Dreamers' Hope. Since Trump, It's Been in Limbo."

Counselors may benefit from employing a trauma-informed approach, feminist approach, or other frameworks that empower clients while recognizing that systems that have impacted them in substantive ways. It is not hard to imagine that many of these clients may have histories of trauma, anxiety, and other mental health concerns. DACA recipients often face steep financial challenges as a result of having no access to federal aid and limited access to state- or college-based aid, and as a result, many balance school with work to provide support for their education and families (TheDream.us, 2021).

When working with Dreamers, career counselors might be mindful of the client's prior knowledge of career and occupational options. For example, if a client's parent has an unauthorized immigration status, the job opportunities available to the parent in the United States would be quite limited. Knowledge of occupation and career options is constructed beginning at an early age as children observe their parent(s) and community members engage in work. With this lens, a career counselor would ensure that no assumptions about prior knowledge were made and aim to remove financial barriers to accessing quality career resources. It is important to note that unlike international students, active DACA and TPS holders do not require visa sponsorship to work in the United States (TheDream.us, n.d.).

A study of international students conducted in 2015 found that 85% of respondents had no knowledge or limited knowledge of career services prior to coming to the United States, though nearly the same percentage expressed a desire to secure employment in the United States after graduating (Balin et al., 2015). These results reinforce the importance of proactive career services programming, early networking, and facilitating the development of peer support systems (Balin et al., 2015).

U.S. populations of international students, foreign workers, and immigrants are large and diverse. There are many groups within these populations, such as migrant and seasonal workers, that require similar considerations for support. Counselors with foreign language skills may invite clients to communicate in the language that they feel most comfortable. Clients having difficulty expressing themselves or finding the right words to use to say what they want may benefit from sharing first in their preferred language, later translating for the counselor. The incredible diversity of these populations demands that counselors are continuously thoughtful about assumptions, biases, and cultural impacts.

Career Development for Rural Populations

Approximately one-fifth of Americans live in rural areas, and though areas are thriving, deep poverty, high unemployment and underemployment persists across many rural communities (Ajilore & Willingham, 2019). Agriculture, manufacturing, mining, and service sectors form much of the employment opportunity for non-metro workers. Globalization and automation left deep impacts on the manufacturing industry, while regulations of fossil fuels and emissions had similar effects on mining (Ajilore & Willingham, 2019). According to the U.S. Department of Agriculture (USDA), during the Great Recession of 2007 to 2009, 1.4 million jobs across non-metro or rural counties were lost, and this had dramatic impacts on workers, families, and communities (USDA, 2022). Rural employment rates grew slowly after the Great Recession, and did not return to prerecession levels until 2019 (USDA, 2022).

During the pandemic, employment recovery was limited, particularly in rural communities that lack reliable high-speed internet connections and adequate healthcare services. In these rural areas, the gap between prime-age (25–54) unemployment rates widened between Whites and Blacks or African Americans and Hispanics or Latinos (USDA, 2022).

While rural America is home to many diverse communities, there are challenges. "Rural African American populations are concentrated in the Southeast, where the legacy of Jim Crow laws has had lasting effects on economic mobility and where poverty persists at rates far higher than for the rest of the U.S. rural population" (Ajilore & Willingham, 2019, para. 17). Immigrants have become a vital part of many rural communities, although immigration policies threaten families and negatively impact access to education. Examples of families and communities devastated by immigration policies abound; Ajilore and Willingham (2019) note the example of a 2018 raid on a meatpacking plant in rural Tennessee where nearly 100 workers were arrested. LGBTQIA+ individuals in non-metro areas are more vulnerable to employment discrimination, have limited access to specialized healthcare, and face higher poverty rates than do non-LGBTQIA+ people (Ajilore & Willingham, 2019). Healthcare access and less-skilled support services also present barriers for disabled people in rural America. Also, mental health and well-being is a significant concern for marginalized communities, with many reporting a lower quality of life, increased feelings of loneliness or isolation, compounded by reduced healthcare resources and increased structural barriers (Ajilore & Willingham, 2019).

Career counselors might consider a non-metro client's level of access to external resources, job information, social supports, and education. Rural Americans are more likely to access career development support and resources through public services, including schools, libraries, and American Job Centers or non-profit affiliated services. Though broadband and high-speed internet are increasingly available in rural areas, many areas of the country remain unconnected, limiting opportunities for career and work.

Career Development for Retirees

Retirement is a modern concept. Until the late 19th century, most people worked until they could not physically work any longer. Spurred by the Industrial Revolution and the growth of manufacturing, the labor movement in the late 1800s paved the way for worker's rights, such as time off, employer-sponsored healthcare, and the right to retire. Changes to financial support systems and savings vehicles developed as the economy shifted, and banking, railroads, and manufacturing industries grew (*Seattle Times* Staff, 2013). The Social Security Act was passed in 1935 in the wake of the Great Depression, and it created the framework for the modern Social Security system designed to provide some protection against poverty in old age. Through this system, American workers contribute to a federal fund via taxes taken out of each paycheck and receive an income from the fund during retirement. A scarcity of workers during WWII drove the growth of pension plans, and these plans were available to 25% of the private-sector workforce by 1950. This figure would grow to 50% in the following 10 years (Phipps, 2021). These defined-benefit plans offered workers guarantees so that they could plan their futures; they were to receive defined dollar amounts or percentages of their salary in retirement. Today, defined-contribution plans such as 401(k) plans, where employers may or may not match employee contributions, are the leading source of retirement income.

Retirement research often focuses on the history and behavior of men as through the early 1940s women generally exited the labor force while young as they married and did not return to work (Goldin, 1990). There are other systemic or structural factors that shape retirement decisions across the workforce, including education level and income. Workers with a college education continue in the workforce longer than those with lower levels of education. Unsurprisingly, income and expected income replacement (e.g., Social Security, investments, savings, pensions), play an important role in retirement decisions as workers plan for their financial future (Career Research, n.d.).

The U.S. Bureau of Labor Statistics cited that 35.5% of people aged 65 and older were working at least part-time in 2020 and projected that the figure will grow to a whopping 43.7% in 2030 (U.S. Bureau of Labor Statistics, 2021). Currently, Social Security does not pay full benefits until the age of 67. The government has adjusted age limits upward to encourage people to work longer and increase their savings prior to retirement, and it is anticipated that additional benefit reductions or age restrictions will be passed as the federal fund struggles to keep up with payouts. Millions of older workers left the labor force for retirement as a result of COVID-19, though recent studies show that many are unretiring due to inflation, plummeting retirement account balances due to stock market fluctuations, loneliness, and increased flexibility available across today's workforce (Fuscaldo, 2022).

Longer life expectancies and innovations in health care that increase the quality of life beyond working years gave rise to additional years of leisure. Retirement for many is an opportunity for a new career phase and to reimagine work and life rather than being the endpoint of career development. Lankford (2022) offers persuasive reasons to consider working after retirement, such as cushioning savings to improve retirement security, cognitive exercise and other health benefits, sense of purpose, community, and a chance to give back. Career counselors who support workers seeking encore careers may encounter clients who are redefining or in search of a new sense of purpose as well as experiencing feelings of loneliness and depression, navigating changes in physical health, and feeling financial stress. Counselors can facilitate client interventions that enable clients to build better connections, improve holistic well-being, and reimagine what it means to lead a good life.

Career-focused counseling has a long history and is a cornerstone of the counseling profession. In response to societal trends, a body of knowledge has evolved that accounts for the complex career development needs of those receiving services, and specific theories have been developed to inform this career counseling. Almost everyone has a career and may need support, and specific populations such as military veterans, first-generation students, international students and foreign professionals, immigrants, rural workers, and retirees present unique considerations for those supporting them. Integrating theory, research, and practice provides a sophisticated response to these complex needs. There are multiple resources that can be used to support career practitioners in their important work.

MY STORYBOARD ACTIVITY

As we review the history of the counseling profession, it is essential to pause and develop our own lifeline, to take note of formative and pivotal moments that shaped our lives. These moments may evoke an array of memories: happiness, sadness, remorse, calm, and more. Some points in time that may come to mind for you may include birth, transitioning from a child to a teenager, education transitions, changes within your home or family, and other significant events in your life that impacted who you are today. We encourage you to think about this activity as a brainstorming session rather than trying to perfectly remember in sequence the events that happened throughout your life thus far.

Directions

We invite you to be as creative and innovative as you would like. You can draw, use words, pictures, phrases, or quotes to depict your life. You are the author and it's truly your story.

Let's begin by reflecting on your earliest memories. Generate a bulleted list of events you remember and periods of time in your life that you would want to include on your storyboard that impact who you are and influenced your career decisions, negatively or positively. This activity is meant to be visual and tactile.

Using the My Storyboard worksheet, give your story or "production" a title. Add your name as the artist/director, as you are the creator and lead in your story. Beginning with early memories, plot different points, or scenes, in different boxes across your storyboard. Continue adding important events through today. These may or may not be directly related to your career; life events may broadly impact our interests, values, opportunities, etc. "Scene" might be the name of the key point or period of your life and "timing" will be the dates or age ranges when those events occurred. Next, draw, add pictures, or use words to describe each of your experiences. Under each event, note the transition point to mark the movement, change, or growth to the next scene in your story. What was the catalyst or turning point that led you to the next stage?

Once you have reached present day, think about your "sequel." Where do you hope your future will lead? Plot any specific future events, goals, hopes, dreams, and aspirations that you look forward to working toward. Who else do you want to be in your story? Add extra pages to your storyboard as needed.

Every production has a crew to support the artist or director. In the first credits frame, include the names of all the people who have been your cheerleaders and support and who serve on your "production team" as you move through your life. They may be family members, guardians, friends, teachers, mentors, coworkers, or partners. Next, in the "acknowledgments," write the first several values that come to mind that are most important in your life. For example, some values may be family, freedom, or stability.

We encourage you to use as many pages or scene frames as you need to depict who you are, including your core values and support system

Here are a few examples to support your thinking and reflection:

- Date of birth
- Turning 13
- First job
- Sibling's birth
- Loss (loss of a relationship or someone who may have been important to you)
- Achievements and celebrations
- Turning 16 years old
- Turning 21 years old
- Graduation: all levels throughout the lifespan
- Birth of your first child
- Career highlights and lowlights
- Transitional periods: 20s to 30s, 30s to 40s, 40s to 50s, 50s to 60s, and so on

EXHIBIT 2.1 MY STORYBOARD

My Storyboard

Production Title: _____   Date: _____

Artist/Director: _____   Page: ____ of ____

SCENE:	TIMING:
TRANSITION:	

SCENE:	TIMING:
TRANSITION:	

SCENE:	TIMING:
TRANSITION:	

SCENE:	TIMING:
TRANSITION:	

SCENE:	TIMING:
TRANSITION:	

SCENE:	TIMING:
TRANSITION:	

(continued)

EXHIBIT 2.1 MY STORYBOARD (*CONTINUED*)
My Storyboard

Production Title:		Date:
Artist/Director:		Page:_____ of _____

SCENE:	TIMING:	SCENE:	TIMING:	SCENE:	TIMING:
TRANSITION:		TRANSITION:		TRANSITION:	

SCENE:	TIMING:	CREDITS		CREDITS	
TRANSITION:					

Here are some questions for you to consider as you tell your story:

1. What words of wisdom would you tell a younger version of yourself?
2. How have the life events and experiences you noted impacted your career path? Is there anything that you would have done differently?

Reflecting on the activity:

1. What was completing this activity like for you?
2. What memories came back easily for you and that you recalled quickly? Why?
3. What memories were more challenging to recall and recollect for you? Why?
4. How could you envision using and adapting this activity with your clients/ students in your current or future practice?

ETHICAL CORNER

In this section, the authors lead the reader through topical scenarios to surface common ethics questions and dilemmas faced by career professionals. They ask pertinent and personal questions to encourage reader reflection and insight into personal and professional ethics.

Azra Karajic Siwiec PhD, LPC is a counselor educator employed by Capella University. She has been working in the counselor education field for over 14 years and has served as a committee member of the Ethics Committee of NCDA since 2015 and served as the chair of the Ethics Committee since 2017.

Sharon K. Anderson, PhD, is professor of counseling and career development at Colorado State University. Sharon has taught the master's level ethics course for counseling students for over 20 years, teaching and mentoring a multitude of students. She has coauthored or coedited four professional ethics books used by practitioners in counseling and coaching.

When Frank Parsons was envisioning this profession he certainly did not know that it would later be called counseling and not "vocophy." Just as we have grown and developed and continue to progress as a profession, we don't know what we don't know or have not discovered. In that vein, let's take a look at our counselor in practice, Sandi.

VIGNETTE

Sandi is currently in an internship and working hard to tally up hours and have meaningful experiences. Another counselor tells Sandi to share information about a client with another colleague from another agency. Sandi feels torn because the client information is private, and while a supervision and consultation perspective would be wonderful, the privacy belongs to the client.

Role-play that you are Sandi and respond to the counselor who is waiting for your next words and ready to hear what you will share about your client. How do you share your concern about client confidentiality and privacy? How do you communicate the concern to maintain the profession's importance of client's rights to confidentiality that took time to build within the profession?

DIGGING INTO ETHICS

Ethics deal with three important levels: virtues, principles, and codes. Ethical virtues relate to the moral character of a person and focus on the question, "Who will I be?" Ethical principles deal with the question, "What will I do," and relate to the teachings of Karen Strohm Kitchener. She identifies five ethical principles: autonomy (the right to choose), beneficence (doing well for others), non maleficent (not doing harm), justice (being fair), fidelity (being loyal), and the most recent addition, veracity (being truthful; Kitchener, 1984; Forester-Miller & Davis, 1996).

Ethical virtues are more focused on the professional's inner guide, whereas ethical principles prompt broader thinking about what is good, right, and best for the client and the profession. Ethical codes are developed to help us identify ethical and unethical behaviors, and these have changed over the years as different concerns become visible and necessary for the profession to address. Ethical codes may be more prescriptive and reflective of the professional guide of work.

Examine your ethical values and moral strengths and weaknesses. Make a chart of your values and moral strengths and weaknesses as they currently stand. Consider what values you may want to add to your list and how you want to bolster your weaknesses. A good way to get started is to reflect on previous ethical and moral challenges. As those come to mind, think about the times you were able to identify the ethical concern and move to make the ethical decision. Also think about the times where you identified the ethical concern, but for various reasons, you didn't do the right thing. We all have these moments. When you think back to those moments, what value or virtue was missing or what ethical principle was ignored? What would have helped you make the right choice? What do you need to bolster so that the next time a different outcome is manifested?

2.1 PRACTITIONER'S PERSPECTIVE

Steven Allman has been licensed as a professional counselor for more than 20 years including certification as a Master Career Counselor through NCDA. He has engaged in career development and management since the late 1970s, including executive search work, outplacement, direct placement, and occupational selection. He works as a vocational rehabilitation counselor for Vocational Rehabilitation Services in North Carolina.

I've been asked how I chose career counseling as my occupation, but this work chose me! I experienced a couple of eureka moments, and one such moment was entering the exhibit hall at the National Career Development Association Annual Conference in San Francisco in 1995. This was my first NCDA conference, and I was overwhelmed! I had been in the personnel consulting industry doing recruiting for 15 years and had been searching for a way to expand my practice, and the "Hall" was jammed with activities associated with occupational selection and career management. It was a candy store for me!

For 16 years, I've managed a mental health caseload for Vocational Rehabilitation Services, and the population is largely without health insurance, other than possibly Medicare/Medicaid. Most clients are unemployed when we meet, and some are homeless or residing in temporary housing that may be classified as a shelter or halfway house. Many have active substance use issues or are "clean" as measured by days or weeks. Some have recently been treated as an inpatient or released after a period of incarceration. Indeed, active substance abuse and unmanaged mental health conditions often lead to recurring bouts with the legal system. Many clients have physical disabilities, including missing limbs or chronic progressive conditions such as cerebral palsy. To be a Vocational Rehabilitation Services client, the only requirement is that the client has an interest in going to work. If they already have a job, they want to hold onto it and may be able to do so with on-the-job accommodation.

It was a multistep process for me to begin working with this population. The NCDA event led to a midcareer graduate degree and to getting licensed as a professional counselor. Then I added career counseling to my existing personnel consulting business, yet many of my clients were unemployed, and those needing the most help had the least ability to pay, so I did as much pro bono work as fee-for-service.

Career counseling is generally not third-party (insurance) reimbursable, so my objective of transitioning away from recruiting was problematic. I knew in the early 2000s that the recruiting business would change as the internet evolved. I had an arrangement with an outplacement services provider to manage a large account, but the amount of work was unpredictable. I was asked to travel nationally for other outplacement projects, but travel was problematic due to family responsibilities. At the time, I also wrote a weekly career column for my local paper that led to a chance meeting with Vocational Rehabilitation Services, and I became intrigued by the challenge associated with supporting clients with such severe needs and with few resources.

The work setting with Vocational Rehabilitation (VR) Services is unique as it is a government agency that never charges for services. VR Services also has a budget to pay for services that are necessary for employment that are not offered in-house. For example, the agency can sponsor the cost of transportation for clients who don't have a means of transportation to get to a job interview or to begin work.

The work with this population is endlessly challenging, and every client presents a unique profile. I never had two identical workdays! The clients I worked with in my recruiting business often had graduate level training and the necessary resources to be successful; those without resources require the most creativity and commitment, sometimes years to support their success.

North Carolina's Mental Health Reform Act in 2003 was a historical moment that changed how our population was served by the public mental health system. After the state mental health centers were replaced with private providers compensated through state-managed care, people without private or public insurance were underserved as the transition to managed care evolved. During that period, it was not unusual to meet new clients with undiagnosed, and therefore untreated, mental health disorders. Fortunately, VRS was able to address the gap and support folks in exploring, creating, and executing a career plan.

PROFESSIONAL ETHICS

All counselors listen and respond to their clients while honoring their choices, to whatever extent possible. With that said, informed choice is the hallmark in career counseling. For example, ethical standards prohibit telling a client what occupation to choose. It is the counselor's responsibility to support the client's informed choice with appropriate information to make that choice.

Another important ethical standard is to constantly mentor practicum students, interns, and new counselors. Mentoring is both a professional privilege and responsibility integral to being a licensed counselor!

2.2 PRACTITIONER'S PERSPECTIVE

Barbara Efird has a MEd in Counselor Education from North Carolina State University and a BS from Canisus College, Buffalo, New York. She has been a private practitioner for 30 years—concurrently as a school counselor for 8 years, director of career services in higher education for 21 years, and career coach for the NCSU alumni association for 2 years.

I graduated with a degree in business management, and I always knew that I was more interested in psychology and human development than the economics and accounting side of the major. I worked briefly in a few administrative settings and found myself encouraging other women to go to college or finish degrees and helping them find programs and financial aid.

When I had a few moments of contemplation in the midst of having a family and attempting a few available positions, I realized that I was happiest professionally when I was assisting high school students make college and career decisions.

Traveling would not fit with my lifestyle as a mom, so I considered the possibility of going to graduate school to become a school counselor. We were moving to Raleigh, North Carolina, and there was a graduate degree program in Raleigh where I could get the credentials needed to enter the profession.

I was thrilled to be accepted and start grad school in my mid- to late-thirties. I loved the classes, my professors, and my classmates. I was introduced to the NC Career Development Association and found my niche, my kindred spirits, and my passion. I was a bit conflicted as I chose secondary school counseling because I also was considering a position in higher education. But I had to choose as they were separate programs. I chose the secondary school counseling track as I thought there would be more positions available to me than in higher education.

During my studies in counselor education, it was evident that career counseling was my passion. I structured my projects and course work in that area whenever possible. My hope was to help young people with career decision-making as well as college choice at the secondary level. I did a practicum and internship at local high schools and learned about the real life of a school counselor. When I completed my degree and was job searching, I found a position at a large inner city high school as a career-development coordinator. I loved it! It had its challenges yet was very fulfilling.

I stayed in that position for 8 years and became active in the NC Career Development Association, which had a membership of professionals from all areas of career development from cradle to grave! I met college career counselors and found their work also to be exciting, and I was ready for the next challenge. It took several attempts to market myself at the postsecondary level, and each position I sought was highly competitive. I was almost ready to give up and take it as a sign to stay put when an opportunity arose. I tried one more time, and yes! I finally got a chance to work with college students as a director of career services at a local private college. I was their first director, and I poured my heart and soul into that position and that college. I created their first career center and developed an experiential learning program (internship) that every student was required to complete. I expanded my office to have an assistant director and eventually a graduate student along with adjunct faculty to teach career-related courses.

As director of career services at a small liberal arts coeducational university, the position calls for one to wear many hats. You must do the career planning and curriculum development along with the employer development, job search coaching, and everything in between. At the university where I spent most of my years, we also had a required internship program that was implemented by career services. Preparing students for this requirement, along with teaching career-planning courses, coordinating career fairs, and developing relationships with faculty and employers, requires a spirit of partnership with internal and external constituents.

During this time, I also began a private practice in career counseling. A mentor of mine was a private practitioner and allowed me to use her office to see clients. After 20 years, I retired as the director of career services and continued in my private practice. Also, I had the opportunity to work for another university as a career counselor while the director of Alumni Career Services was on maternity leave. This was an awesome position, and I loved working with alumni and concentrating solely on career counseling for that time. In my private practice, and as a temporary career counselor for an alumni office, my client population was adults, mostly with college degrees.

We know that there are career development needs from birth to grave, and I've enjoyed working with people in many of those stages. I noticed that in secondary education, the focus is often on college admissions without adequate discussion or reflection on what a student wanted to do with the education. Undergraduate college students are making a huge transition from academics to the workplace, and their focus shifts to immediate needs within the next 4 years to discover, design, and implement their knowledge and skills in a workplace. I found this exciting and rewarding.

I also enjoyed working with adults, including the alumni, as they had some years of experience. I tested their values, interests, and skills in the workplace to help them continue to grow in their careers. At times, the job changes that the alumni/ adults were facing were not their choice, and it took all the tools in our counseling toolkit to assist them in rediscovering their self-esteem and moving forward in their next steps in their careers. That work is equally challenging and rewarding.

What kept me in this field was the diversity of each day and each academic year. You have to be able to keep up to date with the needs of the economy along with creating new and innovative ways to reach students. It is challenging and rewarding.

TRAITS OF CAREER COUNSELORS

People who thrive in this profession have many qualities, values, skills, and interests in human development. One must be able to stay up to date with the labor market and economic trends and keep the lines of communication open to create partnerships with employers and faculty members. They also have to have superb counseling and listening skills.

This career path draws professionals with graduate degrees in counseling and/ or student development. People who have worked in the private sector in business or social sciences often can bring those elements to the career-counseling field. Also, the field requires technical skills and being able to present topics and information in various formats.

PROFESSIONAL ETHICS

As a licensed professional counselor, one may not share information about clients, in this case, students, and yet, as a career counselor, you want to connect students with alumni, employers, and your network. I used a few methods to handle this balancing act and to maintain the ethical standards of the profession. When I was teaching career-planning courses, students in the class were asked to sign a waiver stating that I could discuss their grades and conduct with the administration if needed. If I wanted to connect a student or alumnus with a colleague or someone in my network, I could ask the student/alumnus permission to discuss their career goals and skills with the person. Mostly, we teach students and alumni how to network and, when appropriate, give them suggestions of who they can connect with about their career. I would then give students permission to connect with my network via LinkedIn or by email, and they could use my name as an introduction.

Any time a student was working on personal or academic issues with the college counseling center, if it was in the best interest of the student, we asked permission to discuss the student's case.

In career-counseling private practice, when clients were working with a therapist, I would encourage them to let the therapist know about the work we were doing. If it was in their best interest to have a professional conversation with the therapist, the client would need to grant us permission in writing.

CHANGES IN CAREER COUNSELING

Technology has been the most prominent change in the field over the last 2 decades; it especially helps manage the workload of a career services department with efficiency. Also, our students are technologically savvy, so staff members must stay up to date technologically to reach students where they are, communicate with them, and reach their level of attention and motivation. More recently, I am fascinated about this current trend of "the Great Resignation." I look forward to reading and learning more after more extensive research has been done.

Student Voices

In Student Voices, students offer a unique viewpoint as they begin in the career-counseling field. Here, students share their thoughts and reflections about the career-counseling profession and offer personal takeaways.

DEREK JUST

Derek Just is a U.S. Navy combat veteran who received his MEd in College Counseling and Student Development from North Carolina State University in 2022. His professional background includes work with justice-involved youth, treatment foster care youth, veterans, and college students.

My first formal experience as a career counselor started during the practicum portion of my graduate degree program. While it wasn't my original intention to become a career counselor, I quickly found out that it was an area I excelled in and enjoyed.

Career counseling differs from other types of counseling in that there are generally fewer sessions with a client whose expectations may be of a more transactional nature; perhaps clients are looking for guidance about how to write a cover letter, to have their resume reviewed, or their LinkedIn profile enhanced. However, even while working within this more straightforward framework, I found that the clients I was meeting with would sometimes become comfortable enough in a session to bring up deeper feelings such as anxiety or imposter syndrome. I believe one can be a fairly successful career counselor by simply assisting the client in typical functions such as job searching and resume improvement, but I also believe a career counselor has an opportunity to form a deeper connection with their clients by using a holistic approach. Asking clients an exploration question, such as what their confidence level is about finding meaningful employment, gives them a chance to open up about how difficult the job search process has been for them. Some clients may simply want help

(continued)

Student Voices (*continued*)

editing a document, while others may be experiencing a professional or academic crisis that led them your way.

My advice to students new to career counseling is to try to focus on one or two counseling theories to structure their sessions. I found a lot of success with solution-focused brief therapy, as its strengths-based approach lent itself to the task-oriented nature of career counseling. Basing my techniques on a theoretical framework made it easier to improve my effectiveness and gave me direction when I got stuck with a client.

Another piece of advice is to not be afraid to reach out to colleagues for resources and best practices. It isn't possible to memorize the intricacies of every available job market, but knowing which job search site, resume template, or mock interview question set that works well for others can help you provide the best service to your clients.

My final suggestion would be to try to enjoy the career-counseling journey. As a new counselor, there are inevitably going to be times where you feel lost or frustrated. Try to think of those occasional bumps in the road as opportunities for improvement. I found career counseling to be a gratifying experience that allowed me to make a positive impact on the professional lives of a lot of wonderful people.

COUNSELING SKILLS CONNECTION

The history of the counseling profession intersects with the origins of the career counseling and vocational guidance movement. Dr. Frank Parsons, often referred to as the "father of vocational guidance," is referenced in counseling programs across the country in the introduction to counseling courses, among others. At the time, Parsons' trait and factor approach to working with clients was pivotal. He used somewhat of a matching process as he critically examined the traits and skills of a person while simultaneously considering the environmental tasks and skills required to perform the job (Parsons, 1909). *Choosing a Vocation* (1909) is his seminal and foundational book, and it is still referenced today.

MINDFUL MOMENTS

Instructors can use this activity as homework assignment or in-class activity.

Guided imagery exercises encourage you to immerse yourself in sensory details and may be used to reduce stress, increase relaxation, and build a more positive mindset. The University of Houston Clear Lake has curated a wonderful set of visualization activities in audio, visual, and pdf transcript formats. Visit www.uhcl .edu/counseling-services/resources/visualization.

Examples of imagery exercises include: abdominal breathing, "leaves on a stream" mindfulness, beach visualization, managing math anxiety, and much more.

TECH TOOLS

There are a multitude of podcasts available to support counseling and career development work. Whether you listen as you navigate your own career journey or when seeking insight for your professional role as a counselor, podcasts can offer new perspectives and are well positioned to discuss the effects of current events on work.

Here are a few career development–related podcasts you might enjoy:

- Career Talk: https://podcasts.apple.com/us/podcast/career-talk-learn-grow-thrive/id1141754534
- Pivot: https://podcasts.apple.com/us/podcast/pivot-with-jenny-blake/id1054817076
- Squiggly Careers: https://podcasts.apple.com/us/podcast/squiggly-careers/id1202842065
- The Good Life Project: https://podcasts.apple.com/us/podcast/good-life-project/id647826736
- The Voice of Counseling (sponsored by the ACA): https://podcasts.apple.com/us/podcast/the-voice-of-counseling/id1581474035

REFLECTION ACTIVITY

Let's take a moment to reflect on your own historical roots. Construct a family career genogram based on your personal family constellation. This is an opportunity to be creative! Bring out your colored pencils and markers. Identify family members or guardians within your family unit. List all the people you wish to include and write down their career or job. Notice any particular patterns or professions that continue to be noted in each generation in your immediate and extended family or community. At your comfort level, share with a partner noting any specific career highlights. For reference, check out Virginia Commonwealth University's genogram sample: https://careers.vcu.edu/media/vcu-careers/docs/CareerGenogram.pdf.

END-OF-CHAPTER RESOURCES

SUMMARY

Though the functions of work and careers have changed over the years, the fundamentals of career counseling remain. The origins of career counseling begin with the vocational guidance movement led by Dr. Frank Parsons. The introduction of the trait and factor theory brought about a new way of thinking about the world of work through the lens of the person and environment perspective. Like all theories, the trait and factor theory possesses limitations as well. The trait and factor theory offered a starting point for future theorists and researchers to develop and adapt innovative approaches related to the context at the time. An historical timeline was presented to depict and provide a context for the pivotal events that impacted the career profession. Career-counseling services are offered in a variety of spaces and settings, including schools, clinical mental health agencies, and higher education. The chapter provides strategies for working with populations, such as first-generation college students and military veterans. Counselors-in-training and seasoned counselors alike can review, reflect, and draw upon the historical framework and build upon it within their own practice to best benefit and serve their clients and population of interest.

REFERENCES

Ajilore, O., & Willingham, C. (2019, July 17). *Redefining rural America*. Center for American Progress. https://www.americanprogress.org/article/redefining -rural-america/

American Counseling Association. (2021). *ACA response to the Derek Chauvin trial*. https://www.counseling.org/news/updates/news-detail/2021/04/20/aca -response-to-the-derek-chauvin-trial

American Immigration Council. (2022, July 15). *The H-1B visa program and its impact on the U.S. economy*. https://www.americanimmigrationcouncil.org/research/ h1b-visa-program-fact-sheet

American School Counselor Association. (2014). *Mindsets and behaviors for student success: K–12 college- and career-readiness standards for every student*. Author.

American School Counselor Association. (2019). *ASCA national model: A framework for school counseling programs* (4th ed.). Author.

Balin, E., Yaji Chudasama, S., & Knapp, E. (2015). *Understanding the career development needs of international students*. International Issues in Career Development: A Global Perspective. National Career Development Association. https://www .ncda.org/aws/NCDA/asset_manager/get_file/700060?ver=1

Blustein, D. L. (2013). The psychology of working: A new perspective for a new era. In D. L. Blustein (Ed.), *Oxford handbooks online*. http://www.oxfordhandbooks .com/view; https://academic.oup.com/edited-volume/34468

Bright, J. E. H., & Pryor, R. G. L., (2011). The chaos theory of careers. *Journal of Employment Counseling, 48*, 163–166. https://doi.org/10.1002/j.2161-1920.2011 .tb01104.x

Brown, D., & Crace, R. K., 1996. Values in life role choices and outcomes: A conceptual model. *Career Development Quarterly, 44,* 211– 223.

Career Research. (n.d.). *Retirement.* https://career.iresearchnet.com/career-deve lopment/retirement/

CGT Staffing. (2022, March 8). *"The Great Resignation" and workforce trends.* PR Newsire. https://www.prnewswire.com/news-releases/the-great-resignation -and-workforce-trends-301497693.html

Council for Accreditation of Counseling and Related Educational Programs. (2016). *2016 CACREP standards.* http://www.cacrep.org/wp-content/uploads/ 2017/08/2016-Standards-with-citations.pdf

Dawis, Rene V., Dohm Thomas E,. Lofquist, Lloyd H., Chartrand, Judy M., & Due, Allan M. (1987). *Minnesota occupational classification system III a psycholosical taxonomy of work.* University of Minnesota. https://vpr.psych.umn.edu/sites/vpr .umn.edu/files/files/mocsiii_1987.pdf

Department of Defense. (2023, February 10). ASVAB career exploration program. *ASVAB career exploration program.* https://www.asvabprogram.com/media-center -article/130

Dey, F., & Cruzvergara, C. Y. (2014, Winter). Evolution of career services in higher education. *New Directions for Student Services, 148,* 5–18.

Douglas-Gabriel, D., & Svrluga, S. (2022, June 30). A decade ago, DACA gave "dreamers" hope. Since Trump, it's been in limbo. *The Washington Post.* https://www .washingtonpost.com/education/2022/06/30/daca-students-college-education/

Erikson, E. H. (1950). *Childhood and society.* W W Norton & Co.

Fuscaldo, D. (2022, May 31). *5 unexpected reasons retirees are returning to work.* American Association of Retired Persons. https://www.aarp.org/retirement/ planning-for-retirement/info-2022/returning-to-work.html

Forester-Miller, H., & Davis, T. (1996). A practitioner's guide to ethical decision making. *American Counseling Association.* https://www.counseling.org/docs/ ethics/practitioners_guide.pdf?sfvrsn=2

Ginzberg E., Ginsburg S. W., Axelrad S., Herma J. L. (1951). *Occupational choice: An approach to a general theory.* Columbia University Press.

Gladding, S. T. (2018). *Counseling: A comprehensive profession* (8th ed.). Pearson.

Goldin, C. (1990). *Understanding the gender gap: An economic history of American women.* Oxford University Press.

Gottfredson, L. S. 1981. Circumscription and compromise: A developmental theory of occupational aspirations [Monograph]. *Journal of Counseling Psychology, 28,* 545–579.

Gysbers, N. C. (2010). *Remembering the past, shaping the future: A history of school counseling.* American School Counselor Association.

Hansen, L. Sunny, (1996). *Integrative life planning: Critical tasks for career development and changing life patterns.* Jossey-Bass. https://www.wiley.com/en-us/ search?pq=%7Crelevance%7Cauthor%3AL.+Sunny+Hansen

Hayden, S. C. W. (2018). Supporting veterans experiencing homelessness through a theoretically-based career development group. *Journal of Military and Government Counseling, 6*(4), 215–225. https://mgcaonline.org/wp-content/ uploads/2019/10/JMGC-Vol-6-Is-4.pdf

Hayden, S. C. W., & Osborn, D. S. (2020). Impact of worry on career thoughts, career decision state, and cognitive information processing skills. *Journal of Employment Counseling, 57*(4), 163–177. https://doi.org/10.1002/joec.12152

Herr E. L. & Cramer S. H. (1996). *Career guidance and counseling through the life span: Systematic approaches* (5th ed.). HarperCollins College.

Herr, E. L. (2001). Career development and its practice: A historical perspective. *The Career Development Quarterly, 49*(3), 196–211. https://doi.org/10.1002/j.2161-0045.2001.tb00562.x

Holland, J. L. (1959). A theory of occupational choice. *Journal of Counseling Psychology, 6*, 35–45. https://psycnet.apa.org/record/1960-06165-001

Holland, J. L. (1997). *Making vocational choices: A theory of vocational personalities and work environments* (3rd ed.). Psychological Assessment Resources.

Institute of International Education. (2020). *United States hosts over 1 million international students for the fifth consecutive year*. https://www.iie.org/Why-IIE/Announcements/2020/11/2020-Open-Doors-Report#:~:text=WASHINGTON%2C%20D.C.%2C%20Nov.,the%202019%2F2020%20academic%20year

Kennelly, E., Sargent, A., & Reardon, R. (2018). *RIASEC literature from 1953-2016: Bibliographic references to Holland's theory, research, and applications* (Technical Report No. 58).

Kitchener, K.S. 1984. Intuition, critical thinking, and ethical principles: The foundation of ethical decisions in counseling psychology. *The Counseling Psychologist, 12*, 43–55.

Kosciulek, J. F., Phillips, B. N., & Lizotte, M. C. (2015). Trait–factor theory and counseling process. In F. Chan, N. L. Berven, & K. R. Thomas (Eds.), *Counseling theories and techniques for rehabilitation and mental health professionals*. Springer Publishing Company. https://doi.org/10.1891/9780826198686.0008

Kretovicks, M., Honaker, S., & Kraning, J. (1999). Career centers: Changing needs require changing paradigms. *Journal of Student Affairs at Colorado State University, 8*, 77–84. https://sahe.colostate.edu/wp-content/uploads/sites/10/2016/03/The-Journal-1999.pdf

Krumboltz, J. D. (1979). A social learning theory of career decision making. In A. M. Mitchell, G. B. Jones, & J. D. Krumboltz (Eds.), *Social learning and career decision making* (pp. 19–49). Carroll Press.

Lankford, K. (2022, June 17). *Why you should keep working after retirement*. American Association of Retired Persons. https://www.aarp.org/work/careers/working-after-retirement/

Lee, K. (June 22, 2020). *ACA Anti-racism statement*. American Counseling Association. https://www.counseling.org/news/updates/2020/06/22/aca-anti-racism-statement

Lent R. W., Brown S. D., & Hackett G. (1994). Toward a unifying social cognitive theory of career and academic interest, choice, and performance [Monograph]. *Journal of Vocational Behavior, 45*, 79–122.

Lenz, J. G., Peterson, G. W., Reardon, R. C., & Saunders, D. E. (2010). *Connecting career and mental health counseling: Integrating theory and practice*. Vistas: Online. http://counselingoutfitters.com/vistas/vistas10/Article_01.pdf

Mainiero, L. A., & Sullivan, S. E. (2006), *The opt-out revolt: How people are creating kaleidoscope careers outside of companies*. Davies-Black.

Malott, K. M., Havlik, S., Gosai, S., Diaz Davila, J., & Steen, S. (2019). College readiness and first-generation college goers: Group impacts with students from an urban, predominantly African American population. *Journal of Child and Adolescent Counseling, 5*(3), 256–274. https://doi.org/10.1080/23727810.2019.1672241

Minnis, S. E. (2017). Preface: Veterans in career transition and employment. *Advances in Developing Human Resources, 19*(1), 3–5. https://doi.org/10.1177/1523422316682951

My Future. (2021, June 1). *9 activities to help children understand careers.* https://myfuture.edu.au/career-articles/details/9-activities-to-help-children-understand-careers

National Career Development Association. (n.d.). *NCDA history.* https://ncda.org/aws/NCDA/pt/sp/about_history#:~:text=The%20National%20Vocational%20Guidance%20Association,development%20association%20in%20the%20world

Nevill, D. D., & Super, D. E. (1986). *The Salience Inventory: Theory, application, and research* (Research ed.). Consulting Psychologists Press .

Parsons, F. (1909). *Choosing a vocation.* Houghton Mifflin.

Phipps, M. (2021, October 14). *The history of pension plans in the U.S.* The Balance. https://www.thebalancemoney.com/the-history-of-the-pension-plan-2894374

Reardon, R. C., Sampson, J. P., Jr., Peterson, G. W., & Lenz, J. G. (2004). *Career counseling and services: A cognitive information processing approach.* Brooks/Cole.

Robertson, H. C., & Hayden, S. C. W. (2019). Serving all that served: Career development among at-risk veterans. *Career Planning and Adult Development Journal, 34*(4), 54–65. https://web.p.ebscohost.com/abstract?direct=true&profile=ehost&scope=site&authtype=crawler&jrnl=07361920&AN=137594216&h=ypFrvUL2nRBLHFdK%2fcC35WIrxBVZOeN1xU%2bZpFon2TfsV2YeBld1AnH9YrTpNxb5bSsMpV%2f2ReHy65QNdHV%2fmw%3d%3d&crl=f&resultNs=AdminWebAuth&resultLocal=ErrCrlNotAuth&crlhashurl=login.aspx%3fdirect%3dtrue%26profile%3dehost%26scope%3dsite%26authtype%3dcrawler%26jrnl%3d07361920%26AN%3d137594216

Roe, A. (1956). *The psychology of occupations.* Wiley.

Rounds, J. B., Henly, G. A., Dawis, R. V., Lofquist, L. H., & Weiss, D. J. (1981). *Manual for the Minnesota importance questionnaire: A measure of needs and values.* University of Minnesota Department of Psychology.

Sampson, J. P., Osborn, D. S., Bullock-Yowell, E., Lenz, J. G., Peterson, G. W., Reardon, R. C., Dozier, V. C., Leierer, S. J., Hayden, S. C. W., & Saunders, D. E. (2020). *An introduction to CIP theory, research, and practice* (Technical Report No.62). Florida State University, Center for the Study of Technology in Counseling and Career Development.

Sampson, J. P., Reardon, R. C., Peterson, G. W., & Lenz, J. G. (2004). *Career counseling and services: A cognitive information processing approach.* Brooks/Cole.

Savickas, M. L. (1998). Career style assessment and counseling. In T. Sweeney (Ed.), *Adlerian counseling: A practitioner's approach* (4th ed., pp. 329–359). Accelerated Development.

Savickas, M. L. (2005). The theory and practice of career construction. In S. D. Brown & R. W. Lent (Eds.), *Career development and counseling: Putting theory and research to work* (pp. 42–70). John Wiley & Sons, Inc.

Schlossberg, N. K. (1984). Exploring the adult years. In A. M. Rogers & C. J. Scheirer (Eds.), *The G. Stanley Hall lecture series,* (Vol. 4, pp. 105–154). American Psychological Association. https://doi.org/10.1037/10089-003

Schlossberg , N. K. (2003). *Retire smart, retire happy: Finding your true path in life.* American Psychological Association (APA); 1st edition. https://www.amazon.com/Nancy-K-Schlossberg/e/B001H6MTX2/ref=dp_byline_cont_book_1

Schlossberg , N. K., (2009). *Revitalizing retirement: Reshaping your identity, relationships, and purpose.* Lifetools; 1st edition. https://www.amazon.com/Nancy-K-Schlossberg/e/B001H6MTX2/ref=dp_byline_cont_book_1

Seattle Times Staff. (2013, December 31). A brief history of retirement: It's a modern idea. *The Seattle Times.* https://www.seattletimes.com/nation-world/a-brief-history-of-retirement-its-a-modern-idea/

Silver, L. (2021). *Amid pandemic, international student enrollment at U.S. universities fell 15% in the 2020–21 school year.* Pew Research Center. https://www.pewresearch.org/fact-tank/2021/12/06/amid-pandemic-international-student-enrollment-at-u-s-universities-fell-15-in-the-2020-21-school-year/

Super, D. E. (1970). *The work values inventory.* Houghton Mifflin. https://bpb-us-e1.wpmucdn.com/sites.psu.edu/dist/b/37738/files/2016/01/Work-Values-Inventory.pdf

Super, D. E. (1972). Vocational development theory: Persons, positions and processes. In J.M. Whiteley & A. Resnikoff (Eds.) *Perspectives on vocational development,* (pp. 13–33). American Personnel and Guidance Association.

Super, D. E., Thompson, A. S., & Lindeman, R. H. (1988). *Adult career concerns inventory: Manual for research and exploratory use in counseling.* Consulting Psychologists Press.

Tate, K. A., Caperton, W., Kaiser, D., Pruitt, N. T., White, H., & Hall, E. (2015). An exploration of first-generation college students' career development beliefs and experiences. *Journal of Career Development, 42*(4), 294–310. https://doi.org/10.1177/0894845314565025

TheDream.us. (n.d.). *DACA and TPS holders: What you need to know as a job seeker.* https://www.thedream.us/wp-content/uploads/2021/08/TheDream.US-DACA-and-TPS-Holders-Job-Seeker-Fact-Sheet.pdf

Tiedeman, D. V., & O'Hara, R. (1963). *Career development: Choice and adjustment.* College Entrance Examination Board.

U.S. Bureau of Labor Statistics Employment Projections. (2021). *Civilian labor force participation rate by age, sex, race, and ethnicity.* https://www.bls.gov/emp/tables/civilian-labor-force-participation-rate.htm

U.S. Department of Agriculture Economic Research Service. (2022, May 10). *Rural employment and unemployment.* https://www.ers.usda.gov/topics/rural-economy-population/employment-education/rural-employment-and-unemployment/

U.S. Department of Homeland Security. (n.d.). *Training opportunities in the United States.* https://studyinthestates.dhs.gov/students/training-opportunities-in-the-united-states

U.S. Department of Veterans Affairs. (2020). *World War I created millions of conscripted veterans, improved benefits.* https://blogs.va.gov/VAntage/73270/world-war-created-millions-conscripted-veterans-improved-benefits/#:~:text=The%20Vocational%20Rehabilitation%20Act%20of,carry%20on%20a%20gainful%20occupation

Williamson, E. G. (1939). *How to counsel students: A manual of techniques for clinical counselors.* McGraw-Hill.

Williamson, E. G. (1965). *Vocational counseling: Some historical, philosophical, and theoretical perspectives.* McGraw-Hill.

Zunker, V. G. (2002). *Career counseling: Applied concepts of life planning* (6th ed.). Brooks/Cole.

Zunker, V. G. (2016). *Career counseling: A holistic approach* (9th ed.). Cengage Learning.

CHAPTER 3

DIVERSITY, EQUITY, AND INCLUSION IN CAREER COUNSELING

Thommi Odom Lawson, Terah L. Henderson, Angie C. Smith, and Katie Peterssen

LEARNING OBJECTIVES

By the end of this chapter, you will be able to:

- Explore the importance of diversity in work and career.
- Review intentional considerations for working with marginalized populations.
- Define ethics and diversity.
- Summarize employment law and relate them to protected classes.
- Describe age discrimination and ways to respond to illegal questions.

WARM-UP EXERCISE

What is your name? What is your preferred name? How do you prefer to be identified? As you consider who you are and how you show up in spaces around you, what identities are most salient for you? As you consider the questions, reflect on aspects of your identities related to ethnicity, gender, race, birth order, spirituality, abilities, and more. What parts of your identity do you share with the world around you? What parts of your identity remain private?

INTRODUCTION

This chapter will focus on the importance of counselors becoming culturally competent. As we consider career opportunities and possible barriers related to marginalized groups, a focus on **diversity**, **equity**, and **inclusion** is paramount. A diverse array of populations is spotlighted in the chapter, including, but not limited to, women; Black, Indigenous, and people of color (BIPOC); veterans; individuals with disabilities; lesbian, gay, bisexual, transgender, and questioning (LGBTQIA+); **international** students; older adults; and people who have been incarcerated. Advocacy and **social justice** efforts are essential within career counseling and the world of work, and counselors-in-training, career coaches, and related professionals must be mindful of ways they can use their voices to support clients, students, and the community. Helping professionals need a knowledge of ethics related to employment, discrimination, and illegal questions in the workplace, and employment law provides a context for supporting clients and students.

THE IMPORTANCE OF DIVERSITY IN WORK AND CAREER

For this chapter, historically marginalized populations include BIPOC and LGBTQIA+ communities, people with disabilities both visible and invisible, internationals within the United States, and the formerly incarcerated. Individuals who identify as people of color are challenged to find meaningful work in labor markets and environments that enact systems of power, privilege, and oppression (Blustein & Guarino, 2020). Research posits that individuals who have been historically underserved typically experience higher rates of employment difficulties because of negative stereotypes and portrayals established and perpetrated by long-standing systematic hierarchies of power (Blustein & Guarino, 2020; Fortuna et al., 2020; Guan et al., 2020; Kantamneni, 2020).

One of the largest groups of internationals living within the United States is international students. International students are typically English-speaking students who have entered the United States from their home country, initially to pursue higher education within the American higher educational school system. In addition to being intellectual and innovative assets across influential industries and fields, they bring a significant estimated economic impact of $38.7 billion and support more than 415,000 U.S. jobs (NAFSA, 2022). For every eight international students, three U.S. jobs are created and supported by spending within the higher education, accommodation, dining, retail, transportation, telecommunications, and health insurance sectors (NAFSA, 2022).

For over 15 years, there has been a deep focus in the literature on the challenges faced by international students, specifically during the initial phases of recruitment and settling in America, yet little to none of the literature examined or addressed life after graduation (Davis, 2017). As current and future international students transition from university to employment within the United States, inclusive career counseling will be increasingly important and essential to the longevity and life satisfaction of internationals within the United States.

Employment Law and Protected Classes

Title 7 of the Civil Rights Act of 1964 prohibits employers from discriminating in their hiring practices based on origin, race, color, sex, or religion. The term *protected class* identifies a group of people who have legal protection against workplace discrimination based on these specified traits. Since 1964, people with other traits have been added to the protected class so that term now includes traits such as age, gender, race, pregnancy, religion, national origin, physical or mental disability, and whistleblowers. The list is not all-inclusive, and state laws and local ordinances may offer additional protections. The U.S. Equal Employment Opportunity Commission (EEOC) enforces many federal laws prohibiting employment discrimination.

It is important to note that these laws do not cover all employers, and not all employees are protected. Certain limitations, such as the type of employer, the number of employees, and the type of discrimination alleged, could impact one's status as a member of the protected class. Additionally, anti-discrimination laws do not protect certain groups, including undocumented immigrants and those with criminal records.

Age Discrimination

The Harvard Business Review states that nearly two out of three workers aged 45 and older say they have experienced age discrimination (Zucker, 2019). When it comes to answering the question of "What does age discrimination look like?", a recent American Association of Retired People (AARP) article cites that age discrimination can take the form of (a) hearing negative remarks related to being older than other colleagues; (b) not getting hired for a job (overtly and covertly) due to age; or (c) being passed up for a promotion. In a value of experience study by AARP, only 3% of participants made an official complaint concerning age discrimination in the workplace (Perron, 2018).

Career professionals working with a client who is faced with age discrimination and illegal questions during an interview may advise the client to take the following approaches:

- Reframe any inappropriate comments or questions.
- Lead with energy instead of experience.
- Adopt a consulting mindset.
- Demonstrate humility and a nonhierarchical approach.
- Connect with the interviewer.
- Show your ability to work well with diverse groups of people (Zucker, 2019).

One of the most powerful strategy combinations can be to engage with curiosity and reframe inappropriate comments or questions (Gonzalez, 2022). Take, for example, this statement: "We at (organization's name) are looking for younger minds." One may reframe this by addressing the age bias by responding with, "it sounds like you are seeking innovative thinkers, and I would be happy to share how I envision helping (insert organization's name) increase its impact in the field."

AARP and many other advocates have committed to targeting ageism in the workplace by adopting the Employer Pledge Program that focuses on a commitment to recruit and hire from all age groups (Terrell, 2018). Programs such as the Employee Pledge Program provide a starting place, a foundation, for inclusive hiring practices across industries.

POPULATIONS: CAREER COUNSELING STUDENTS/CLIENTS, CONSIDERATIONS, PROJECTIONS, AND TRENDS

Career counselors that assist diverse and marginalized populations must not take a one-size-fits-all approach. It is essential to consider the population, projections, and current trends relative to historical factors, current context, individual preferences, and within and between-group differences. Some populations to spotlight include BIPOC, LGBTQIA+, veterans, persons with disabilities, women, and the elderly.

BIPOC

BIPOC stands for Black, Indigenous, and people of color. Pronounced "bye-pock," this is a term specific to the United States that highlights the "unique relationship to Whiteness that Indigenous and Black people have," acknowledging that not all people of color face equal levels of injustice (The BIPOC Project, n.d., para. 2). For example, Black workers are far more likely to be unemployed than White workers at every level of education (Economic Policy Institute, *State of Working America Data Library*, Unemployment by race and education, 2019). There exists no singular definition of Whiteness, rather the meaning changes over time. The criteria for who is considered "White" and who is not vary with context. In the United States, White is often used to describe a racial and skin color classification primarily composed of people of European descent (Irvin Painter, 2020).

American Indian and Alaska Natives (AIANs) in the prime working ages of 25 to 54 are more likely to be working or looking for work than people in older age groups. However, AIANs also were more likely to have a disability and to have lower educational attainment; both of these characteristics are associated with lower labor force participation (Allard & Brundage, 2019).

Hispanics are projected to account for 78% of net new workers between 2020 and 2030. Despite the U.S. labor force growth rate decreasing over the past few decades, the growth that has occurred is largely due to the increasing number of Hispanic workers (Dubina, 2021).

Asian Americans tend to have the lowest unemployment rates among any ethnic group. They are highly represented in high-paying occupations, but also in low-paying personal care service roles (USA Facts, 2021).

LGBTQIA+

LGBTQIA+ is an acronym for lesbian, gay, bisexual, transgender, queer, intersex, asexual, and more. This term is used to describe sexual and gender minorities (American Psychological Association, 2021). When working with this community, it is essential to not only create a space that is safe for the client but also builds trust and understanding by "initiating the discussion of the client's experiences related to their intersectional identity and having less power than members of mainstream society" (Speciale & Scholl, 2019, p. 30). Intersectionality is a framework for understanding how a person's identity includes multiple intersecting factors (e.g., race, gender identity, gender expression, socioeconomic status, religion, ethnicity; Ramos & Brassel, 2020).

Regarding workforce participation, LGBTQIA+ representation across various roles is low, particularly at senior executive levels. Transgender workers face greater barriers in the workplace, from job offers to career advancement.

Veterans

The shift from military service to civilian life is often referred to as transitioning. Transitioning from the military to civilian life is comparable to the culture shock experienced by immigrants first arriving in the United States, as military service has its distinct subculture governed by its own set of rules, traditions, values, and laws (Coll et al., 2011; Rausch, 2014). The severity of such culture shock varies among veterans based on length of service, the branch of service, rank/title held, types of deployments, and experiences during combat.

Because military experience impacts the worldview of veterans, Rausch (2014, p. 92) encourages counselors to view the "wholeness of the military experience" when conceptualizing veterans. This includes gaining an understanding of military culture, the importance of rank and branch of service, terminology, jargon, and how this translates to the civilian world. Counselors should also become familiar with the military discharge form, formally referred to as Certificate of Release or Discharge from Active Duty—DD Form 214. This form lists military education and military job specialties, which may help translate to skills gained while in service when preparing the resume. Employing theories such as The Career Construction Theory (Savickas, 2002) provides a holistic perspective that may help veterans process their military service experience.

Regarding barriers to entering the workforce, veterans may hesitate to seek counseling because of the associated stigma (Bonar & Domenici, 2011). Expressing mental health concerns is discouraged for fear it might impact one's career path while enlisted (Westwood et al., 2002). Career counselors can inquire about service-connected disabilities that may impact a veteran client's career path, such as posttraumatic stress, traumatic brain injury, physical limitations, depression, and so forth, and then assess the veteran's readiness to proceed with career decision-making. Miles (2014) suggests using a cognitive information processing framework

Individuals With Disabilities

The Americans with Disabilities Act (ADA) is a civil rights law that prohibits discrimination against individuals with disabilities in all areas of public life, including jobs. Within the context of the ADA, *disability* is a legal, not medical, term. The ADA defines a person with a disability as a person who has a physical or mental impairment that substantially limits one or more major life activities (ADA National Network, n.d.).

When assisting a person with a disability, career counselors should be aware of their own biases and reactions to disability and understand the intersectionality of the cultural component of disabilities. For example, the client might also be a member of the BIPOC community or a queer woman. Then, assess how the client's limitations may impact their psychological well-being (Bureau of Labor Statistics News Release, 2022).

Regarding workforce barriers, workers with a disability were more likely to be employed part-time than those with no disability. Persons with a disability were also less likely than those with no disability to have completed a bachelor's degree or higher (Bureau of Labor Statistics, 2015).

Women

Notable challenges and considerations exist when addressing diversity, equity, and inclusion (DEI) initiatives for women in the workplace. According to McKinsey & Company (2022), women who experience microaggressions can be more prone to stress, burnout, lack of focus, and work dissatisfaction. They might experience professional undermining in the form of being interrupted in meetings and by having their professional judgment questioned. "Microaggressions—those subtle messages that demean, insult and invalidate a person—are routine occurrences for many diverse groups" (Wilson, 2016, para. 1). These subtle messages are harmful and can negatively impact people in the workplace.

Parker and Funk (2007) report that about 4 in 10 U.S. women have experienced discrimination at work because of their gender. A recent study outlines the following examples of gender discrimination and considerations for individual and organizational impact (Exhibit 3.1).

Women in the Workplace, the largest study of women in corporate America, analyzes the representation of women and provides an overview of human resources policies and programs (e.g., the most effective **diversity**, **equity**, and **inclusion** practices), among others (McKinsey & Company, 2022).

The most recent data set reflects 423 participating organizations employing 12 million people, and over 65,000 people were surveyed on their unique workplace experiences. The in-depth interviews conducted included women with diverse identities, i.e., women of color, LGBTQIA+ women, and women with disabilities (McKinsey & Company, 2022).

From this research, the following results were highlighted.

EXHIBIT 3.1 CAREER AND WORK BARRIERS FOR WOMEN

EXAMPLES OF GENDER DISCRIMINATION
1. Misjudgment of competence and leadership suitability due to biased patriarchal assumptions
2. Paid less than men despite having similar job responsibilities
3. Evaluated or held to a different standard due to gender
4. Excluded from important meetings and assignments
5. Subjected to unwanted sexual advances
6. Fired or demoted due to a pregnancy
7. Less support from senior leadership than peers

INTRAPERSONAL IMPACT
8. Burnout
9. Lack of focus
10. Work dissatisfaction
11. Psychological stress
12. Reduced sense of self-efficacy
13. Lack of desire for fellowship, collegiality, collaboration, and teamwork

ORGANIZATIONAL IMPACT
14. Toxic work environment
15. Success of the organization at stake
16. Loss productivity
17. Increased absenteeism
18. Increased turnover rates
19. The erosion of fellowship, collegiality, collaboration, and teamwork

Sources: Parker, K. & Funk, C. (December 14, 2017). *Gender discrimination comes in many forms for today's working women.* Pew Research Center. https://www.pewresearch.org/fact-tank/2017/12/14/gender-discrimination-comes-in-many-forms-for-todays-working-women/; McKinsey & Company. (2022). *Women in the workplace 2022.* https://www.mckinsey.com/featured-insights/diversity-and-inclusion/women-in-the-workplace

LEADERSHIP AND PROMOTION

The representation of women in leadership has gradually increased since 2016; however, women of color remain markedly underrepresented. Reports reflected that women continue to face structural challenges when it comes to corporate promotions. Statistically, for every 100 men promoted to the position of manager, only 86 women are promoted. This is important to note from a cyclical and homeostatic perspective. If men outnumber women drastically at the manager level, this in turn means that there are fewer women within the role of manager to consider for promotion—and the hierarchical cycle keeps its homeostatic functioning.

ADVOCACY AND ALLYSHIP

Outside formal job responsibilities, women leaders reported spending more time than men on DEI work. Senior-level women were twice as likely as senior-level men to devote time toward addressing DEI tasks on a weekly basis. Women leaders are indeed showing up as more active allies to women of color. They are more likely than men to seek the necessary education to understand the unique challenges women of color face at work; to recognize and speak out against discrimination; and to also mentor or sponsor women of color.

However, in comparison to the results of the previous year, the reports show that although more White employees saw themselves as allies to women of color, they were no more likely to speak out against discrimination, mentor, or sponsor women of color, neither were they more inclined to take other actions to advocate for them (McKinsey & Company, 2022).

DEI programs that focus on creating a transformational impact on the company's culture is efficacious. Such transformational impact can include targeting microaggressions and gender discrimination; evaluating current recruitment/hiring practices; and updating retention procedures. There is also a critical need for businesses to equip employees at every level to challenge bias and commit to engaging in the work of active allyship for women in the workplace. See Student Resources for links and other helpful information (available by accessing Springer Publishing Connect™ via the instructions on the opening page of this book and clicking on the drop down Show Supplementary, Student Materials).

Elderly and Retirees

The workforce population is getting older (Zacher et al., 2018) and more age diverse (Truxillo et al., 2015). The labor force of people ages 16 to 24 is projected to shrink by 7.5% from 2020 to 2030. According to the Society for Human Resource Management (SHRM), while the 55 to 74 age group is expected to grow by 7.7%, the number of workers 75 years and older is expected to grow by 96.5% over that same decade (SHRM, 2022). The U.S. Bureau of Labor Statistics (BLS) proposes that by 2026 there will be approximately 42.1 million older workers, representing a quarter of the workforce (U.S. Senate Special Committee on Aging, 2017).

For workers who are older than age 65, it is expected that they will remain in the labor market at even higher rates, while prime-age workers (ages 25 to 54), are predicted to remain at current levels (U.S. Senate Special Committee on Aging, 2017; Van Horn & Heidkamp, 2019). Changing workforce demographics due to economic, health, social, and psychological factors have resulted in a higher proportion of workers remaining at work until later ages than in the past (Fisher et al., 2016, 2017). Discussions on the economic and social impacts of aging at work and the importance of lengthening working life (Zacher et al., 2018) have led to an increased interest in exploring aging at work and supporting successful aging (Truxillo et al., 2015).

It is important to consider how older workers ascribe meaning to retirement. For instance, retiring from a job can mean the likelihood of the retiree beginning another career. In this sense, retirement can also be viewed as just another type of career transition (Kim & Hall, 2013). Although many organizations recognize that their workers are aging, few have actually taken the necessary steps to adequately prepare for issues associated with older workers remaining on the job, leaving the workforce, or seeking new employment opportunities (SHRM, 2022).

Exhibit 3.2 is a chart that outlines the career challenges and considerations faced by older workers and retirees.

EXHIBIT 3.2 CAREER CONSIDERATIONS AND CHALLENGES FACED BY OLDER WORKERS AND RETIREES

CONSIDERATIONS	CHALLENGES
The number of workers older than 60 growing from 12% to 20% between 2015 and 2050 (World Health Organization, 2018)	Person–environment fit
Societal needs, worker financial needs, and psychological benefits of work (Fisher et al., 2016; Wang & Shultz, 2010)	Age-related ability changes
Keeping workers healthy and engaged in productive work to positively impact mental, physical, and cognitive health (Fisher et al., 2017)	Lack of employer support in successful retirement
Worker health and retirement intentions (Zacher et al., 2014)	Demand-ability fit and retirement
Elderly workers' self-assessment of their financial situation (Kuznetsova, 2019)	Varied country-specific circumstances of foreign workers returning to home countries, i.e., gender, marital status, lack of job opportunities, low savings, broken family ties, reintegration into society issues (Rowson & Gonzalez-White, 2019)
Household composition and discussing potential housing-related deprivation associated with financial well-being (Kuznetsova, 2019)	Inadequate income for employees with low salaries considering retirement
Sense of loneliness	Medical coverage postretirement
Social and economic factors influencing time of retirement (Mishra, 2019)	Retirees transitioning from role of provider to dependent (Mishra, 2019)

(continued)

EXHIBIT 3.2 CAREER CHALLENGES FACED BY OLDER WORKERS AND RETIREES (*CONTINUED*)

CONSIDERATIONS	CHALLENGES
The main problems of retirees: fear of being physically weak, psychological tension, fear of social negligence, shortage of friend circles and peer groups, empty time, and fear of widowhood (Mishra, 2019)	Forced retirements, long-term unemployment, precarious work, decreased access to retirement benefits (Van Horn & Heidkamp, 2019)
Change in life satisfaction not immediately reported (on average), but decreases after 2 years, compared to the beginning of the retirement (Sohier et al., 2021)	Employers' hesitancy to hire older workers (Johnson & Gosselin, 2018)
Desire to explore types of retirement, i.e., partial versus full retirement (Sohier et al., 2021)	Outdated job-seeking strategies and little public workforce programs assistance (Heidkamp et al., 2012)

Exhibit 3.3 offers a few recommendations to address potential challenges.

EXHIBIT 3.3 ADDRESSING WORKPLACE AND RETIREMENT CHALLENGES FOR OLDER WORKERS

KEYS TO ADDRESSING WORKPLACE AND RETIREMENT CHALLENGES FOR OLDER WORKERS
Hiring Practices

Hiring Practices

- Take inventory of current hiring policies to reduce age discrimination in hiring.
- Use targeted recruitment messaging for older workers.
- Analyze job qualifications (e.g., choosing not to use the term *overqualified*).

Supporting Current Employees

- Consider job redesign.
- Revise scheduling options.
- Analyze employment data for retirement eligibility.
- Conduct stay interviews.
- Focus on succession planning.

Supporting Retirement + Postretirement Connection

- Consider and engage in discussions on phased retirement (e.g., fewer hours, etc.).
- Expand access to transition assistance and lifelong learning.
- Conduct exit interviews.
- Consider postretirement consulting services with retired employees.

Sources: Society for Human Resource Management. (2022). *Employing older workers*. https://www.shrm.org/resourcesandtools/tools-and-samples/toolkits/pages/employing olderworkers.aspx; Van Horn, C. E., & Heidkamp, M. (2019). Older workers, precarious jobs, and unemployment: Challenges and policy recommendations. *Generations: Journal of the American Society on Aging, 43*(3), 21–28. https://www.jstor.org/stable/26841728

International Students

Although the United States is still listed as the top host destination for international students for almost two decades, it is notable to mention that there have been drastic declines in international student enrollments according to the Institute for International Education (IIE; 2020), current mobility, and academic trends. Other countries (e.g., Canada and the United Kingdom) are intentionally seeking to attract more international students by creating long-term responsive strategies that address gaps between university and employment with one major goal of appearing more attractive than the United States for academic study and life after graduation.

Here are a few notable enrollment trends:

■ In 2020 to 2021, the total number of international students at U.S. universities declined by 15% from 1,075,496 to 914,095.

■ There was also a reported 45.6% decrease in new international student enrollment from 267,712 in the 2019/2020 school year to 145,526 in 2020/2021.

■ Leading states for hosting international student enrollment experienced a decrease. For example, California had a 17.3% change and New York had a 15.8% change (IIE, 2022).

Academic trends:

■ Undergraduate studies shifted from a 2.9% decrease in 2019/2020 to a 14.2% decrease.

■ On the graduate level, there was a shift from 0.9% in 2019/2020 to a 12.2% decrease.

■ Most shockingly, for nondegree international students, there was a 63.7% decrease from a total of 58,201 students to 21,151 (IIE, 2022).

It is important for career professionals to support international students. There are a few key questions to be asked that can best assist them individually and as community.

■ In addition to robust initial-phase overseas recruitment plans, how can we adopt healthy full-cycle recruitment strategies?

■ What are the current job-seeking knowledge patterns of international students?

■ How have we identified and addressed current international office biases, myths, and assumptions of international students? What can we do differently?

■ Have we asked if our current international students desire to return to their home country or remain in their host country before providing resources?

■ How can we go beyond public awareness for equal services?

■ How will the future predictions of the world of work impact current and incoming international students?

■ How do we support internationals with reluctant employers? Is there anything we can improve on to be better advocates?

Formerly Incarcerated

The stigma of a criminal record can be devastating and pervasive. The unemployment rate for formerly incarcerated people is nearly five times higher than the unemployment rate for the general U. S. population. Black Americans and Hispanics are the two largest represented ethnic groups in prison (Couloute & Kopf, 2018). Research finds conclusive evidence that while a higher-than-average percentage of formerly incarcerated people are looking for work, having a criminal record has a significant negative impact on hiring decisions. When formerly incarcerated people do secure work, they are frequently part-time, low-paying, and less secure (Couloute & Kopf, 2018).

Career counselors should also be aware of licensing requirements that create additional barriers to work for people with a criminal record. Professional licenses (e.g., nursing, medical assistants, childcare providers, teachers, construction) are administered by states and frequently involve passing a criminal background check.

DEFINING COMPETENCE AND CAPABILITY: CLINICIAN CONSIDERATIONS

Career professionals should develop skills related to cultural competence and capabilities. Sue et al. (2019) assert cultural competence at the provider level consists of three components. First, the clinician is aware of their personal values and biases and how those might influence the perceptions of the client, the client's problem, and the counseling relationship. Second, the clinician has some knowledge of the client's culture, worldview, and expectations of the counseling relationship. This is obtained during the initial intake and throughout the therapeutic process. Third, the clinician has the skills and ability to utilize interventions that are culturally sensitive and relevant.

There are considerations that a culturally competent clinician may consider when working with marginalized populations. Talking about marginalized identities is complex and can be emotionally draining, so be sure to embrace and include restorative practices. (Resource recommendation: *From Self-Care to Soul-Care: Restorative AF Practices for Clinicians* by M. Boyd and T. Lawson)

Be mindful of your language and ask questions that may elicit responses that reflect cultural beliefs and attitudes. For example, "What are some wrong assumptions people have made about you or your family that have caused problems?" Be mindful of terminology that perpetuates oppression. Borgen (2005) purports that professionalism, when viewed as a structural set of practices, behaviors, and beliefs, perpetuates oppression in all professional communities. Small (2021) posits that professionalism is "born out of racism, washed in anti-Blackness, and rooted in oppression" (p. 130). Jaunarajs and McGarry (2018) believe that education around professionalism reinforces rules that exclude marginalized individuals. An example of such legislation that aims to dismantle such practices within work and educational settings is the CROWN Act. CROWN, which stands for Creating a Respectful and Open World for Natural Hair, is a law that prohibits race-based hair discrimination, which is the denial of employment and educational opportunities because of hair texture or protective hairstyles including braids, locs, twists, or Bantu knots.

When working with a person with a visible disability, it is okay to use words or phrases such as "disabled," "disability," or "people with disabilities" when talking about disability issues. Ask the people you are with which term they prefer if they have a disability. When talking about people without disabilities, it is okay to say "people without disabilities." But do not refer to them as "normal" or "healthy." These terms can make people with disabilities feel as though they are "abnormal" or less than.

Become a trauma-informed therapist. Trauma-informed care is an approach that assumes an individual is more likely than not to have a history of trauma, identifies trauma symptoms in others, and is aware of the role(s) trauma may play in one's life, according to the Substance Abuse and Mental Health Services Administration (SAMHSA; 2014). Research has demonstrated that exposure to adverse childhood experiences may undermine people's ability to attain employment (Topitzes et al., 2016; Zyromski et al., 2018). Trauma-informed practices will inform empathy, integrate culturally responsive approaches, and facilitate overlapping processes of the job search, career exploration, and mental health resources (Wright & Chan, 2022). SAMHSA's (2014) four R's framework for trauma-informed approaches is helpful for career counselors to examine their approach through a trauma-informed lens (Powers & Duys, 2020).

If you identify as a marginalized counselor, see Student Resources for additional information (available by accessing Springer Publishing Connect™ via the instructions on the opening page of this book and clicking on the drop down Show Supplementary, Student Materials). If you identify as a member of a nonmarginalized community, learn more about your racial identity and privilege. (See the Intrapersonal Advocacy section in Exhibit 3.5.)

UNDERSTANDING BIAS AND IMPLICATIONS FOR DIVERSE CLIENTS

There are a few theoretical models that can be used to inform clinicians on embracing and including racial, ethnic, and cultural concerns. A good place to start is with the Multidimensional Model of Broaching Behavior developed by Day-Vines et al. (2020) as it includes humanistic skills that allow counselors to broach clients' racial, ethnic, and cultural concerns in an effort to develop strong therapeutic alliances and alleviate distress. Day-Vines et al. (2007) coined the term *broaching* to refer to the counselor's deliberate and intentional efforts to discuss those racial, ethnic, and cultural concerns that may impact the client's presenting concerns. An example of this heuristic applied in career counseling may be to invite clients to share their experience using a question such as "What is it like to be an international student from Turkey at NC State?"

Using the life design model and narrative approaches, Savickas (2016) proposed that trauma-informed career counselors help clients view their stories through the lens that many of their present problems are indicators of adverse childhood experiences. The clinician could help the client reconstruct their narratives as they re-author and design their lives. A narrative approach promotes insight into how a single narrative details their traumatic experiences and encourages clients to create a narrative involving their strengths, cultural values, and goals (Wright & Chan, 2022). The clients' narrative includes factors such as family, culture, and support systems.

The culture-infused career counseling model (Arthur, 2018) is premised on the belief that cultural influences are inextricably woven into people's career development and cannot be dismissed (Arthur, 2008; Leong, 2010). The model emphasizes cultural self-awareness, awareness of client cultural identities, and the development of a culturally sensitive working alliance. The framework calls for social justice action.

BARRIERS FOR MARGINALIZED POPULATIONS

Historically, marginalized populations experience multidimensional career and work-related barriers. Exhibit 3.4 is a list of some of the most common operational, cultural, educational, mental, and emotional barriers.

EXHIBIT 3.4 CAREER AND WORK BARRIERS THAT MIGHT EXIST FOR MARGINALIZED POPULATIONS

OPERATIONAL BARRIERS

K12 schools lack early intervention services that introduce expansive career opportunities beyond traditional career roles.
Lack of access to senior leadership within their respective work environments

Government
*Visa and sponsorship issues
*Restrictive immigration laws and visas varying from state to state (e.g., stipulations designed to protect American jobs).
Lack of employment suitable to qualifications
Short grace period and/or restrictive procedures in finding gainful employment.

College Career Services/Support Team
Lack of guidance from career services
Lack of (and disregard for) full-cycle recruitment strategies (e.g., failure to follow up on career-related goals postgraduation).

Prospective Employers
Biased company hiring restrictions
*Employers categorizing nonimmigrants as immigrants and not understanding the differences when it comes to legal work authorizations.
Lack of desire, interest, and education of employers on how to legally and ethically hire marginalized populations.
Decrease in the number of companies/organizations willing to hire marginalized populations.

CULTURAL + EDUCATIONAL BARRIERS

*Level of sociolinguistic competence in the host country
Level of job-seeking knowledge, for example, international students not knowing the details of work allowance while pursuing higher education (Davis, 2017) or formerly incarcerated not having access to career counselors.
Acculturative stress (see Student Resources, available by accessing Springer Publishing Connect™ via the instructions on the opening page of this book and clicking on the drop down Show Supplementary, Student Materials)
*Little to no understanding of regulatory procedures for U.S. work eligibility and U.S. employment
Inability to communicate transferable skills to potential employers
Little to no understanding of Equal Employment Opportunity Commission (EEOC) procedures
Access to specialized education and training (e.g., marginalized professionals are often excluded from obtaining information about learning opportunities)

(continued)

EXHIBIT 3.4 CAREER AND WORK BARRIERS THAT MIGHT EXIST FOR MARGINALIZED POPULATIONS (*CONTINUED*)

MENTAL + EMOTIONAL BARRIERS

The collective impact of impostor syndrome, code-switching, White saviorism, tokenism, microaggressions, microinsults, microinvalidations, microassaults, and the emotional labor of educating nonmarginalized communities may leave a member of a marginalized community feeling mentally and emotionally drained. Unfortunately, marginalized communities are less likely to have access to affordable health care to obtain services such as mental health counseling to address the multilevel stress experienced.

*Internalization of "my worth is connected to my immigration status" (Davis, 2017, p. 83).

Decision fatigue (e.g., do I stay in my host country or go back to my home country for employment? Do I stay at this job and endure the microaggressions or leave?)

*Reference to internationals in the United States.

ADVOCACY

It is paramount that career counselors and professionals who are in direct and indirect contact with marginalized populations be aware of and have a clear understanding of current multilevel intrapersonal, interpersonal, and sociopolitical barriers faced: more specifically, employability needs. In proactively doing so, the individuals are working toward understanding additional needs of the marginalized population beyond finding a job to defining a career. This level of awareness is also a form of advocacy, social justice, and equity. Following are a few key considerations for career counselors who are dedicated to working from a social justice, advocacy, and equity lens or framework (Exhibit 3.5).

EXHIBIT 3.5 A CAREER PROFESSIONAL GUIDE TO SOCIOPOLITICAL, INTRAPERSONAL, AND INTERPERSONAL ADVOCACY FOR MARGINALIZED POPULATIONS

SOCIOPOLITICAL ADVOCACY

The American Civil Liberties Union (ACLU) is considered the nation's premier defender and protector of the rights outlined in the U.S. Constitution. It is composed of 500 staff attorneys and thousands of volunteer attorneys with offices throughout the nation. Much of their work focuses on equality for people of color, gay and transgender people, prisoners, immigrants, and people with disabilities (ACLU, 2022). www.aclu.org/

The NAFSA Association of International Educators is the world's largest nonprofit association dedicated to international education and exchange. It services the needs of more than 10,000 members and international educators worldwide at more than 3,500 institutions, in over 150 countries (NAFSA, 2022). www.nafsa.org/policy-and-advocacy/take-action

When it comes to sociopolitical advocacy, consider the following:

Ask lawmakers to support legislation that directly impacts marginalized populations (e.g., The Pregnant Workers Fairness Act and inclusion of **international** education and exchange in the U.S. Innovation and Competitiveness Bill).

(*continued*)

EXHIBIT 3.5 A CAREER PROFESSIONAL GUIDE TO SOCIOPOLITICAL, INTRAPERSONAL, AND INTERPERSONAL ADVOCACY FOR MARGINALIZED POPULATIONS (*CONTINUED*)

Ask lawmakers to *support funding* for international education and exchange programs and student loan debt relief.

Urge the White House to adopt a *national strategy* for international education and the educational needs of high school students in state prisons.

*Share with lawmakers the *economic value* of international students.

INTRAPERSONAL ADVOCACY

As a starting point for advocating the career needs of marginalized communities, consider connecting and collaborating with these organizations:

The National Career Development Association (NCDA) ncda.org
*NCDA-International Student Services Committee (NCDA-ISSC) https://ncda.org/aws/NCDA/pt/sp/about_committees
The American Council of Education (ACE) www.acenet.edu/Pages/default.aspx
NAFSA: Association of International Educators (NAFSA) www.nafsa.org
National Association of Colleges and Employers (NACE) www.naceweb.org
*The Institute of International Education (IIE), among others (NCDA, 2020). www.iie.org
American Counseling Association (ACA) www.counseling.org/government-affairs/advocacy-tips-tools
Human Rights Campaign (gay and lesbian issues) www.hrc.org/
NAACP (National Association for the Advancement of Colored People) https://naacp.org/
National Association of Social Workers www.socialworkers.org/About/Diversity-Equity-and-Inclusion
NOW (National Organization for Women) https://now.org/
TASH (people with disabilities) https://tash.org/
Also, revisit and integrate the Multicultural Career Counseling Competencies (NCDA, 2022) and review the updated Multicultural and Social Justice Counseling Competencies (AMCD, 2022), as well as the American Counseling Association's (ACA) Advocacy Competencies (ACA, 2020).

INTERPERSONAL ADVOCACY + ALLYSHIP RESOURCES

Educate yourself. Take time to read, listen, watch, and deepen understanding first before asking a marginalized person their experiences with inequity. This question may be triggering, or they may be exhausted from the burden of retelling their experiences.

Enjoy this 2019 Ted Talk: I'm Tired of Talking About Race with Jasmine Roberts at Ted X Ohio State University. https://youtu.be/ii4W9Y9pExk

BIPOC
An antiracist reading list: Ibram X. Kendi on books to help America transcend its racist heritage. *NY Times*, May 29, 2019. www.nytimes.com/2019/05/29/books/review/antiracist-reading-list-ibram-x-kendi.html

LGBTQIA+
Being an LGBTQ Ally
https://hrc-prod-requests.s3-us-west-2.amazonaws.com/ComingOut-Ally-Resource-2020.pdf

(continued)

EXHIBIT 3.5 A CAREER PROFESSIONAL GUIDE TO SOCIOPOLITICAL, INTRAPERSONAL, AND INTERPERSONAL ADVOCACY FOR MARGINALIZED POPULATIONS (*CONTINUED*)

Disability
Become a Disability A.L.L.Y in your Community and Promote Inclusion for All
https://www.cdc.gov/ncbddd/humandevelopment/become-a-disability-ALLY.html

Formerly Incarcerated
The National Council for Incarcerated and Formerly Incarcerated Women and Girls
    www.nationalcouncil.us/
A new way of life https://anewwayoflife.org/
See Resoures for a suggested list of media to learn more about *equity*. The list
    contains items that may be triggering. Use discretion.

Internationals
Review the *Resources for Partnering with International Students* guide. This guide
is normally updated every 2 years and is available to all NCDA members on the
NCDA website under members-only resources.

*Reference to internationals in the United States.

CASE STUDIES

CASE 1

Gloria is a 35-year-old Latina married mother of two children. She has a successful career as an assistant professor at an R1 University—a private, predominantly White university located in the Bible Belt. She has been employed for approximately 2 years.

Gloria recently completed writing an article that has been accepted in a well-known academic journal. Though Gloria feels confident in her work, she has ruminated about being considered a fraud, making statements like, "Maybe I am not as smart as I think I am?" and "Maybe I should consider a different career."

During her first session, she shared some of the thoughts that she constantly agonizes over. Some are "What if I unintentionally plagiarized?" "What if my peers consider me a fraud?" "What if the article is dismissed or torn apart by my peers?" This rumination has been going on for the past 6 months, and the article is scheduled to be published in less than a month. As the date gets closer, the rumination has increased. She is tense, easily irritated, and has trouble sleeping. This has impacted how she shows up as a mother and a wife.

Gloria has shared that she has experienced many microaggressions in the workplace but "just shrugs them off" considering it "par for the course." She shared that she feels like she works under a microscope and feels this publication comes with the pressure to prove her worth to keep her position.

At night, she finds herself rehearsing all the worst-case scenarios that may happen once the article is published, including public ridicule, losing her job, and the end of a career that she worked hard for.

Discussion Questions
1. What additional information would you want to learn during the initial intake?
2. What are some salient parts of her narrative?

(continued)

3. How do you conceptualize the client's situation?
4. Would the clients' gender, racial, and/or ethnic background make any difference in your case conceptualization?
5. What would be your intervention goals and strategies for Gloria? How would you present them to the client?

CASE 2

Andy is a 21-year-old male who identifies as biracial of Asian and Black descent. He was adopted at the age of 3 by a White family. Due to a birth defect, his right arm was amputated. He stated that he feels lucky to be adopted by an amazing family but feels that parts of his cultural identity were dismissed. "I feel like my mom hyperfocused on me being Asian and dismissed or ignored the other half of me—the Black side of me." There was an unspoken expectation that I should be "very smart academically." He shared he felt pressured to bring home perfect grades and attend college. While he did not struggle academically, he felt more drawn toward the arts.

Regarding his disability, he shared that his parents "fought to ensure I had every experience." While he appreciates this, he felt that he was often allowed to be in some places and spaces, but he did not feel included. He stated, "I really felt as though my attendance was a checked box on a diversity checklist."

Andy recently graduated from college with a degree in electrical engineering but is struggling to find a career path that supports the life he really wants. He stated he feels guilt as he wants to make his adoptive parents proud, but he feels like pursuing a career path as an electrical engineer would leave him emotionally drained and detached and ultimately unhappy long-term.

Discussion Questions
1. What additional information would you want to learn during the initial intake?
2. What are some salient parts of his narrative?
3. How do you conceptualize the client's situation?
4. Would the clients' gender, racial, and/or ethnic background make any difference in your case conceptualization?
5. What would be your intervention goals and strategies for Andy? How would you present them to the client?

CASE 3

Charlie is 21 years old and identifies as nonbinary. Charlie is White and of Italian descent. Their father raised them in a home that they describe as a "semi-strict Catholic." Their mother abandoned the family when they were approximately 2 years of age. They have no other siblings.

Charlie stated that their father relied on them to do everything. "I felt like I was his personal assistant. He was not a father to me. We did not have a bond. We were isolated from his family because of family drama. My life was hell. I hated every moment of it. He was so demeaning." They felt the only way to escape was via the military.

Charlie has been enlisted for 2 years, and while they do not enjoy it, they do enjoy the freedom from their father. Since enlisting, Charlie has started

(continued)

CASE STUDIES (*CONTINUED*)

expressing and exploring their identity as they knew they could not do that while living with their father. They stated, "He would have killed me for sure."

Charlie's position in the military is very physically demanding, and they have experienced two injuries, resulting in medical leave. Charlie is unhappy in their position and wants to do something that can translate into a civilian job once they leave the military. Their highest education is high school. It is important to note they were homeschooled by their dad, as they always felt socially awkward. Additionally, because of their father's verbal and emotional abuse, they struggle with feeling like they are not enough—not smart enough, good enough, and so forth. As such, Charlie struggles with major depression and uses alcohol to cope. They have been prescribed Wellbutrin to manage the depression, but Charlie admits to being noncompliant and thinks "nothing can cure what I have."

Discussion Questions
1. What additional information would you want to learn during the initial intake?
2. What are some salient parts of their narrative?
3. How do you conceptualize the client's situation?
4. Would the clients' gender, racial, and/or ethnic background make any difference in your case conceptualization?
5. What would be your intervention goals and strategies for Charlie? How would you present them to the client?

CASE 4

Ayofemi is a 32-year-old female. She is Nigerian and first-generation American. She is the oldest of four siblings and recently graduated from medical school.

Ayofemi identifies as a lesbian, but her family is unaware of her sexuality as she worries about being disowned as she is financially dependent on them. She presents feminine while at work and with family, but she feels more comfortable wearing more nonfeminine attire privately.

She is in the process of completing her residency and preparing for board exams. She has failed one exam and has high test anxiety. Additionally, she has come to the decision that she disagrees with Western medicine and philosophies and fears she has made an incorrect career choice. She shares she felt pressured by her parents and close family friends to be a doctor. She stated, "I never really thought about what I really wanted."

Ayofemi presents with high anxiety, including lack of appetite, intense and extensive crying spells, heart racing, sleep disturbance, lack of energy, and physiological reactivity. She diagnosed herself with attention deficit/hyperactivity disorder and is convinced that this is why she has been unsuccessful at passing the exam and struggled through medical school. She is seeking medical accommodations with her psychiatrist to support this diagnosis. There is pressure to pass the exam soon, or she could face termination in her residency.

In a session, Ayofemi expressed that she has an "internal tug-of-war raging in my head." She wants the credentials to practice medicine, but she also doesn't want to practice Western medicine.

(*continued*)

CASE STUDIES (*CONTINUED*)

Discussion Questions
1. What additional information would you want to learn during the initial intake?
2. What are some salient parts of her narrative?
3. How do you conceptualize the client's situation?
4. Would the clients' gender, racial, and/or ethnic background make any difference in your case conceptualization?
5. What would be your intervention goals and strategies for Ayofemi? How would you present them to the client?

ETHICAL CORNER

In this section, the authors lead the reader through topical scenarios to surface common ethics questions and dilemmas faced by career professionals. They ask pertinent and personal questions to encourage reader reflection and insight into personal and professional ethics.

Azra Karajic Siwiec, PhD, LPC, is a counselor educator employed by Capella University. She has been working in the counselor education field for over 14 years and has served as a committee member of the Ethics Committee of NCDA since 2015 and served as the chair of the Ethics Committee since 2017.

Sharon K. Anderson, PhD, is professor of counseling and career development at Colorado State University. Sharon has taught the master's-degree level ethics course for counseling students for over 20 years, teaching and mentoring a multitude of students. She also coauthored or coedited four professional ethics books used by practitioners in counseling and coaching.

It is important to know theory as you deliver your service; we call this competence. Competence includes knowledge, skill, diligence, and ability. As you review theories and think about their relationship to multicultural competence, you may feel overwhelmed and like there is a lot to learn. You may be concerned about impostor syndrome. Yet, no one starts off as an expert. Competence is meant to be a journey. The goal is to continue to grow and be challenged so that you deliver a service that honors the ethical principle of beneficence.

Reflect on when you encountered something you didn't know how to do, but it was important for you to start to learn it with the goal of mastery. How did you handle it? In these instances, it can be like learning how to ride a bike, learning how to drive a car, or like any developmental milestone. Think about how you approached the milestone. What was your developmental process?

VIGNETTE

Sandi loves the career constructivist theory (CCT) as it is well connected to her work as a mental health counselor with low-income families. She really wants to use this theory with her client, so she refreshed her memory by reviewing the material from the past as well as reviewing videos of Dr. Mark Savickas on YouTube.

When she and her supervisor discuss the session, Sandi addresses how she used the theory. The supervisor didn't know the theory and shrugged it off, stating that she should not have used it but rather the Holland theory instead, since it is most widely used. The supervisor asks Sandi not to use the CCT anymore. Sandi feels her knowledge is ignored and she wants to have a discussion with the supervisor, recognizing that the supervisor holds the power.

Role-play how to communicate with this supervisor if you were in Sandi's place.

DIGGING INTO ETHICS

How will you use the developmental approach and the process set out earlier to address how you will master knowing all of the career development theories? How could you make it a discussion with your supervisor addressing beneficence, nonmaleficence, autonomy, and justice when discussing the use of CCT and Holland theory? What ethical virtues do you see as being drawn on when you work with low-income families? How can you advocate for a cultural group or client if you were to chat with someone in power who decides whether this group gets treatment by your agency or school for example?

3.1 SCHOLAR'S PERSPECTIVE

Dr. Sylvia C. Nassar has enjoyed a long and satisfying history as a career counselor as well as an educator and supervisor of counselors and other helping professionals. You can learn more about her at www.drsylvianassar.com/.

After earning a master's degree in counseling and college student personnel, I held various positions as a career counselor. I started in the corporate sector, then worked in several university career center settings. I found myself often creating special services by collaborating with other entities, such as collaborating with community agencies to provide sign language interpreters for hearing-impaired people in automotive plants, collaborating with women's service centers to assist women entering or re-entering the workforce, and working with international student services offices. Eventually, I realized that the common denominator in this work was the intersections of ethnic, gender, and career-development processes. Later, this passion evolved into research projects with the National Science Foundation, NASA, the Research Triangle Institute-International, and other organizations.

The populations I'm interested in are marginalized in various ways, including first-generation and other underrepresented college student groups. At the same time, I've developed a deep commitment to addressing the global challenge of unemployment, particularly among youth. I've operationalized this latter commitment through research efforts and the dissemination of my findings and results.

As a scholar in a helping field, I have both an opportunity and an obligation to discover ways that can make the world a better place. One way I've tackled this is to figure out how research, practice, and policy can (and ideally should), interact. For years, we've talked about the importance of using empirically based practices—in essence, taking a research-practitioner approach to creating effective interventions. I believe that one hallmark of being a professional within career and counseling fields is the integration of policy work. For example, I recently held a position as a visiting scholar with the Research Triangle Institute (RTI) International. While there, I conducted a Delphi study, surveying career-service professionals globally across research, practice, and policy domains regarding the characteristics they deem essential to developing effective career interventions. Since then, I published the findings in a *Career Builders Toolkit* and have trained multiple constituent groups on best practices for developing and evaluating effective career services. These practices include collaborating across research, practice, and policy.

The *Career Builders Toolkit* is a free guide, so organizations and people with limited resources can easily access it and benefit from the expertise of the participants in the RTI/North Carolina State University–supported Delphi study. (To pique your interest, the six key considerations include holistic approaches, needs assessment, trainer curricula, participant curricula, delivery, and program evaluation.) While it is a resource that is potentially helpful to any career professional (practitioners, scholars, and policymakers), my intent was to help the most marginalized communities across the globe. My collaborators and I have applied it to various career services internationally and have disseminated the results of our applications and inquiries. For example, in Turkey, we applied the *Toolkit* as an evaluation tool to a new career-development curriculum that had just been rolled out nationally that identifies areas for growth within the structure as being a "train the trainer curricula" and "program evaluation." We also published an article in an international journal, providing this application as an example of how the *Toolkit* can be used for career program development and evaluation and also how practitioners, researchers, and policymakers need to take complementary responsibilities for a positive and synergistic end result.

Moreover, the first and second of the six key components in the *Toolkit* are focused on taking a holistic approach, along with conducting needs assessments within this holistic context. My coauthors and I stress the importance of ensuring that all stakeholder groups are included in this way, reflecting the commitment to ensuring that every voice is heard, particularly those most in need of accessible and effective career services.

Some of my recent researcher–practitioner projects as a career educator and project evaluator have involved serving undergraduate college students who are underrepresented in their particular majors. In that work, I have integrated assessments based on my earlier NSF and NASA projects. Applying those assessments helped identify gaps in career knowledge of student-participants, both before and after their program participation in summer discipline-specific immersion programs. The impact was positive for them as evidenced by gains in relevant career information and knowledge. It was also positive for future program participants due to the continuous improvements we made following these assessments and research. Most importantly, and perhaps in the most satisfying ways for me, I was able to see and hear how students grew in their respective career development.

PROFESSIONAL TRAINING

I have always been drawn to working with marginalized groups, particularly relative to interactions between ethnic, gender, and career development. Some of this commitment is connected with my own early (and ongoing!) ethnic, gender, and career-development processes, and the awareness I have attained on my own path.

I have worked with some wonderful mentors and collaborators within organizations such as the National Career Development and the International Association for Education and Vocational Development. It has been through those relationships and activities that I began to learn more about the importance of policy work. Most recently, I had the opportunity to help develop the Multicultural and Social Justice Counseling Competencies (MSJCCs), where I further developed the idea of policy-based interventions beginning with the intrapersonal and interpersonal, then community and institutional, and finally, policy and global levels. These MSJCCs now continue to inform my research and practice.

There is always room for improvement as there will always be marginalization in society. And, relatedly, we can always improve our career services and delivery. The whole notion of program evaluation is about continuous and systematic improvement. One thing that really hit home as I worked on the MSJCC with my colleagues is how our competence, particularly within DEI, is aspirational. In other words, we can never fully master multicultural and social justice competencies. We can only humbly seek to improve. Most of my recent publications, including my work with NASA and NSF, can be found on my website: www.drsylvianassar .com/career--workforce-development.html. The *Toolkit* can be found at https:// ced.ncsu.edu/news/2020/06/17/professor-sylvia-nassar-addresses-global -unemployment-issues-through-career-builders-toolkit-project/. Please feel free to contact me if you would like more information or need help accessing or applying the *Toolkit*!

3.2 PRACTITIONER PERSPECTIVE

Katy Breitenbach has a bachelor's degree in political science from Purdue University. She is currently the vice president of U.S. Corporate Engagement and Global Revenue Operations at Catalyst.

I worked in consultative sales across different industry sectors for most of my career, but always with a Fortune 1,000 client focus. As I continued to advance, I felt like I was missing out on working for a mission that I was passionate about. It was getting hard to feel pride in my career because it didn't feel grounded in my values or as though I was having any kind of impact that was not tied to revenue.

A family member pointed out a role with my current company that married my experience with work focused on DEI and was specifically focused on women in the workforce. It was a perfect fit of being able to take my skill set and apply it to a role that filled my need to be more deeply tied to my work. I'm still with that organization 11 years later and continuing to advance and grow my career.

In my role, I connect with DEI leaders at some of the largest corporations in the world. Within our client organizations, I can work with corporate employees from the C-suite to the summer interns and everyone in between. Our work is mostly focused on women, but as with most work in diversity and inclusion, we find we are most effective when we bring all leaders to the table. My role touches senior leadership, human resources, learning and development, talent management, and often, employee resource groups (also known as affinity groups or business resource groups), across client organizations.

As a young woman starting my career, I didn't grasp what it takes to build and grow a career. College and MBA courses may educate you on organizational communication, but a deep understanding of how to navigate an organization's culture, unwritten rules, bias, and sponsorship for advancement really comes through time-in-seat and great mentors. Having come from the academic world where gender disparities have made more progress than in the corporate world was not jarring initially. But after about 5 years in, it became clear who was being selected for fast-track roles and who wasn't. I wanted to be a part of understanding and changing the way talent grows within organizations, yet I wasn't sure how to go about it. My role with my organization really did just pop up at the right time and right place for me to shift careers.

Externally, my role is to understand how to meet an organization where they are on their DEI journey rather than trying to be overly prescriptive in what we think would be most helpful. I spend my day asking lots of questions and doing lots of listening. I have found that a collaborative and informative approach makes it easier to build trust and break down the necessary barriers for the work to be successful.

Internally, I lead two large teams, which makes people management and talent development the core of my role. I believe in overcommunicating, consistent and frequent feedback, and high degrees of transparency. Being remotely based, as is my entire team, I work hard to have social calls with my colleagues to feel more connected to the work we do and the passion side of our work. DEI work is tough and can be frustrating, so building a reliable sounding board of colleagues who "get it" is critical to navigating burnout and building what I like to call *cathartic camaraderie*. I am in this work because I see progress. DEI work is a slow process, but I know we are contributing to small pockets of change and creating more inclusive work environments.

For anyone working in DEI, these traits are important: curiosity, comfort with ambiguity, humility, exceptional communication, negotiation skills, and a quest for continued skill-building and improvement.

In the past decade, I have started a family, relocated several times, gone through some significant personal paths and trauma, and at no time did I feel anything but supported by my employer. Moreover, while navigating those things, my performance allowed me to continue to grow my career within the organization. I was promoted and nudged into stretching into roles that I didn't feel ready for, but leaders knew I could do. They challenged me, but they supported me every step of the way. My organization is an incredibly lean, global nonprofit, and occasionally the magnitude of the work we do can cause bandwidth strains. But the level of flexibility, autonomy, and trust keeps me inspired to keep growing here.

PROFESSIONAL ETHICS

We work on tough topics, so providing a safe space and a sounding board, and always demonstrating confidentiality, transparency, and honesty are all core to our organizational approach in the work we do.

Student Voices

In Student Voices, students offer a unique viewpoint as they begin in the career counseling field. Here, students share their thoughts and reflections about the career counseling profession and offer personal takeaways.

CIANDRA GASTON

Ciandra Gaston is a recent graduate of the Counselor Education Program at North Carolina State University. Ciandra is a student success coach and academic advisor for an online graduate program.

Diversity, equity, and inclusion are central to my work with students, and as a counselor in training I have engaged with students from diverse backgrounds. During my practicum, I worked with Chinese students in China as they were preparing to study at North Carolina State University. All of my students were male, and most of them had never lived outside of China. I am a Black woman from Maryland, and I have lived in two different countries. Our experiences were nearly polar opposites. My students would ask about my experience with race, share their traditions, and discuss their upcoming transition to campus. The relationship was characterized by acceptance and curiosity because we acknowledged our differences.

In my internship experience, I coached students on academic probation, and it was a lesson on equity in real time. The students that I worked with often had multiple challenges and minimal support. The challenges included caretaker responsibilities for siblings, learning disabilities, full- or part-time jobs, and athletic responsibilities, all during a pandemic. So many things felt out of control for these students and there was only so much I could offer as their coach. When we met and how we met were within my control, and I offered them multiple meeting times and options for how to meet via phone or video call. On a larger scale, I revised the program and spoke with the dean of academic affairs about the challenges that students faced that were not addressed by the current program. Identifying the inequity was not enough; I had to advocate for and with my students and take action steps to increase their level of access to success.

COUNSELING SKILLS CONNECTION

Identity development, such as racial, ethnic, sexual orientation, ability status, and career development frequently intersect and impact each other at varying stages throughout the life span. Career counselors must consider the development of their clients' multiple identities as they select appropriate interventions, theoretical frameworks, and techniques. For example, Gottfredson's theory of compromise and circumscription can be employed at younger ages as youth differentiate between roles and career paths that align with their interests, personality, and goals (Gottfredson, 1981, 2002). Counselors, specifically school counselors, working in the school setting may employ the theory to ask prompting questions about the skills and interests of today's youth.

MINDFUL MOMENT

It's time to relax and bring awareness to distinct parts of your body through a body scan activity. Body scans bring focus to the present moment and invite you to train your attention on individual body parts, from your toes to your head. Body scan activities can be completed in as little as a few minutes or may be adapted to train attention over 30+ minutes (Mindful, 2012).

Try one of these body scan activities available on YouTube or discover your own:

- https://youtu.be/15q-N-_kkrU
- https://youtu.be/zsCVqFr6j1g
- www.mindful.org/beginners-body-scan-meditation/

TECH TOOLS

LinkedIn.com is arguably the largest global professional network, and it's not just for job seekers. In fact, LinkedIn is much more powerful and productive if you use the platform regularly to build connections and manage your professional relationships. With more than 830 million members across 200+ countries and territories, LinkedIn can help you connect with colleagues across the globe (LinkedIn, n.d.)

Get started by creating your profile, including your education and experience, and uploading a headshot. Begin connecting with those who know you best right now, your friends, classmates, faculty, and mentors. Then, use search tools to join groups and follow professional organizations aligned with your areas of interest (e.g., National Career Development Association, American Counseling Association). Look to join and follow national, state, and local thought leaders and organizations. Each new organization you follow and connection you make will further hone the algorithm that determines the news you will see on your LinkedIn homepage. With some effort, your LinkedIn page will soon be a treasure trove of the latest and greatest in counseling and your specialty interests!

REFLECTION ACTIVITY

The 1967 film *Guess Who's Coming to Dinner* showcases the story of a newly engaged biracial couple played by Katherine Houghton and Sidney Poitier. Katherine's character, Joanna Drayton, is a liberal White woman, and Poiter's character, John Prentice, is a Black doctor. The movie centers around the dinner table where the couple's parents meet for the first time and must confront racism associated with being a biracial couple.

Purpose

Our personal and professional identities are often initially formed based on stories that we were told, observations, or our lived experiences. These stories sometimes lead to limiting beliefs that may prevent one from choosing a particular career. This activity aims to call to the table and examine all of the narratives the client may have heard, observed, or lived that shape how they view themselves in the world of work.

Materials Needed

Paper and pencil

Procedure

- Draw a rectangle in the middle of the sheet of paper.
- Identify the names or titles of people that influenced how they envision the world of work.
- Write those names around the rectangle, placing the two most influential at the head of the table—one on each end of the rectangle.
- Ask the client to write down the dominant narrative shared directly, overheard, or witnessed next to each name. For example: "My father said as a Black person I must work twice as hard as the White man to get the minimum" or "Abled differently individuals are not given the same opportunities as able-bodied individuals."

Process Questions

- What dominant narratives do you believe are true? Why?
- What limiting belief(s) do you hold about yourself due to those dominant narratives?
- How valid is the limited belief? What facts/experiences do you have to support it?
- How has the limiting belief impacted your career choices thus far?
- How would your life be different if this limited belief were extinguished?
- Imagine the limited belief(s) on a plate sitting before you at the dinner table. If you could flip the table on all of the dominant limiting narratives, what alternative beliefs would you replace the limiting beliefs with?

END-OF-CHAPTER RESOURCES

SUMMARY

The world of work continues to evolve and shift as the workforce propels forward focusing on the importance of DEI in all settings. Populations such as women, BIPOC, LGBTQIA+, elderly, retirees, and individuals who have been incarcerated clearly need a voice and recognition, not only in the literature but also within research and practice. It is hoped that creating safe working spaces that encourage inclusive practices will remain a trend in the mainstream of the U.S. and international workforces. The chapter lists an array of resources, links, and more to explore to become even more familiar with potential students and clients you may find yourself working with now and in the future. Becoming a culturally competent counselor is a lifelong process and does not have an end point or final destination, but rather is a continuous evolution of exploration and self-discovery.

REFERENCES

ADA National Network. (n.d.). *What is the Americans with Disabilities Act (ADA)?* https://adata.org/learn-about-ada

Allard, M. D., & Brundage Jr., V. (2019, November). American Indians and Alaska Natives in the U.S. labor force. *Monthly Labor Review, U.S. Bureau of Labor Statistics.* https://doi.org/10.21916/mlr.2019.24

American Counseling Association. (2020, May). *ACA advocacy competencies.* https://www.counseling.org/knowledge-center/competencies

American Multicultural Counseling Development. (2022). *Multicultural social justice counseling competencies.* https://www.multiculturalcounselingdevelopment.org/competencies

American Psychological Association. (2021). *Inclusive language guidelines.* https://www.apa.org/about/apa/equity-diversity-inclusion/language-guidelines.pdf

Arthur, M. B. (2008). Examining contemporary careers: A call for interdisciplinary inquiry. *Human Relations, 61*(2), 163–186. https://doi.org/10.1177/0018726707087783

Arthur, N. (2018). Culture-infused counselling: Contexts, identities, and social justice. In: Arthur, N. (Eds.), *Counselling in cultural contexts. International and cultural psychology.* (pp. 29–62). Springer, Cham. https://doi.org/10.1007/978-3-030-00090-5_2

Blustein, D. L., & Guarino, P. A. (2020). Work and unemployment in the time of COVID-19: The existential experience of loss and fear. *Journal of Humanistic Psychology, 60*(5), 702–709. https://doi.org/10.1177/0022167820934229

Bonar, T. C., & Domenici, P. L. (2011). Counseling and connecting with the military undergraduate: The intersection of military service and university life. *Journal of College Student Psychotherapy, 25*(3), 204–219. https://doi.org/10.1080/87568225.2011.581925

Borgen, F. H. (2005). Advancing social justice in vocational theory, research, and practice: comment. *The Counseling Psychologist, 33*(2), 197–206. https://doi.org/10.1177/0011000004272722

Brandeis University Prevention Advocacy and Resource Center. (n.d.). *Suggested language list.* https://sites.google.com/brandeis.edu/parcsuggestedlanguagelist/

Bureau of Labor Statistics, U.S. Department of Labor. (2015, July 20). *People with a disability less likely to have completed a bachelor's degree. The Economics Daily.* https://www.bls.gov/opub/ted/2015/people-with-a-disability-less-likely-to-have-completed-a-bachelors-degree.htm

Bureau of Labor Statistics News Release, U.S. Department of Labor. (2022, February 24). *Persons with a disability: Labor force characteristics—2021.* https://www.bls.gov/news.release/pdf/disabl.pdf

Coll, J. E., Weiss, E. L., & Yarvis, J. S. (2011). No one leaves unchanged: Insights for civilian mental health care professionals into the military experience and culture. *Social Work in Health Care, 50,* 487–500. https://doi.org/10.1080/00981389.2010.528727

Couloute, L., & Kopf, D. (2018, July). *Out of prison & out of work.* Prison Policy Initiative. https://www.prisonpolicy.org/reports/outofwork.html

Davis, T. (2017). *From university to employment: An exploration of employment barriers and perceived stress levels of internationals living in the United States* [Doctoral dissertation, Mercer University]. ProQuest Dissertations & Theses Global. Publication No. 10598560.

Day-Vines, N. L., Cluxton-Keller, F., Agorsor, C., Gubara, S., & Otabil, N. A. A. (2020). The multidimensional model of broaching behavior. *Journal of Counseling & Development, 98*(1), 107–118. https://doi.org/10.1002/jcad.12304

Day-Vines, N. L., Wood, S. M., Grothaus, T., Craigen, L., Holman, A., Dotson-Blake, K., & Douglass, M. J. (2007). Broaching the subjects of race, ethnicity, and culture during the counseling process. *Journal of Counseling & Development, 85*(4), 401–409. https://doi.org/10.1002/j.1556-6678.2007.tb00608.x

Dubina, K. (2021, September 15). Hispanics in the labor force: 5 facts. U.S. Department of Labor Blog. https://blog.dol.gov/2021/09/15/hispanics-in-the-labor-force-5-facts

Fisher, G. G., Chaffee, D. S., & Sonnega, A. (2016). Retirement timing: A review and recommendations for future research. *Work, Aging and Retirement, 2,* 230–261. https://doi.org/10.1093/workar/waw001

Fisher, G. G., Chaffee, D. S., Tetrick, L. E., Davalos, D. B., & Potter, G. G. (2017). Cognitive functioning, aging, and work: A review and recommendations for research and practice. *Journal of Occupational Health Psychology, 22,* 314–336. https://doi.org/10.1037/ocp0000086

Fortuna, L. R., Tolou-Shams, M., Robles-Ramamurthy, B., & Porche, M. V. (2020). Inequity and the disproportionate impact of COVID-19 on communities of color in the United States: The need for a trauma-informed social justice response. *Psychological Trauma: Theory, Research, Practice, and Policy, 12*(5), 443. https://doi.org/10.1037/tra0000889

Gonzalez, M. (2022). *How to keep hiring managers from asking inappropriate interview questions.* https://www.shrm.org/resourcesandtools/hr-topics/behavioral-competencies/global-and-cultural-effectiveness/pages/former-tech-lead-told-women-'go-have-some-kids'.aspx

Guan, Y., Deng, H., & Zhou, X. (2020). Understanding the impact of the COVID-19 pandemic on career development: Insights from cultural psychology. *Journal of Vocational Behavior, 119,* 1. https://doi.org/10.1016/j.jvb.2020.103438

Gottfredson, L. S. (1981). Circumscription and compromise: A developmental theory of occupational aspirations. *Journal of Counseling Psychology, 28,* 545–579. https://doi.org/10.1037/0022-0167.28.6.545

Gottfredson, L. S. (2002). Gottfredson's theory of circumscription, compromise, and self-creation. In D. Brown & Associates (Eds.), *Career choice and development* (4th ed., pp. 85–148). Jossey-Bass.

Heidkamp, M., Mabe, W., & DeGraff, B. (2012). *The public workforce system: Serving older job seekers and the disability implications of an aging workforce.* John J. Heldrich Center for Workforce Development, Rutgers University.

Institute for International Education. (2020). *Project Atlas: A quick look at global mobility trends.* https://iie.widen.net/s/g2bqxwkwqv/project-atlas-infographics-2020

Institute for International Education. (2022). *Open doors 2021 fast fact sheet.* http://www.iie.org/Research-and-Publications/Open-Doors/Data/Fact-Sheets-by-US-State/2015#.VyerKaPD_cs

Irvin Painter, N. (2020, June 27) White identity in America is ideology, not biology. The history of 'whiteness' proves it. *NBC News.* https://www.nbcnews.com/think/opinion/white-identity-america-ideology-not-biology-history-whiteness-proves-it-ncna1232200

Jaunarajs, I., & McGarry, E. (2018). Organizational alignment to promote leadership development for career readiness in college settings. *New Directions for Student Leadership, 2018*(157), 101–113. https://doi.org/10.1002/yd.20282

Johnson, R. W., & Gosselin, P. (2018). *How secure is employment at older ages?* Urban Institute. tinyurl.com/y43zwj8d

Kantamneni, N. (2020). The impact of the COVID-19 pandemic on marginalized populations in the United States: A research agenda. *Journal of Vocational Behavior, 119,* 103439. https://doi.org/10.1016/j.jvb.2020.103439

Kim, N. & Hall, D. T., (2013). Protean career model and retirement. In M. Wang (Ed.), *The Oxford handbook of retirement* (pp. 102–116). Oxford University Press.

Kuznetsova, P. (2019). Non-income poverty among the elderly. *Problems of Economic Transition, 61*(1–3), 192–210. https://doi.org/10.1080/10611991.2019.1691888

Leong, F. T. (2010). A cultural formulation approach to career assessment and career counseling: Guest editor's introduction. *Journal of Career Development, 37*(1), 375–390. https://doi.org/10.1177/0894845310363708

LinkedIn. (n.d.) *About.* https://about.linkedin.com

McKinsey & Company. (2022). *Women in the workplace 2022.* https://www.mckinsey.com/featured-insights/diversity-and-inclusion/women-in-the-workplace

Miles, R. A. (2014). Career counseling strategies and challenges for transitioning veterans. *Career Planning & Adult Development Journal, 30*(3), 123–135. https://www.careernetwork.org/Journals/Vol%2030%20Nr%203%20Fall%20'14%20VETERANS%20J..pdf

Mindful. (2012, November 7). *The body scan practice.* https://www.mindful.org/the-body-scan-practice/

Mishra, N. (2019). The nature of retirement: Factors responsible for affecting retirement decision. *Indian Journal of Gerontology, 33*(2), 205–215. http://gerontologyindia.com/pdf/vol-33-2.pdf

NAFSA Association of International Educators. (2022). *Policy and advocacy: Take action.* https://www.nafsa.org/policy-and-advocacy/take-action

National Career Development Association. (2022). *Multicultural career counseling competencies.* https://ncda.org/aws/NCDA/pt/sp/compentencies_multi_cultural

National Career Development Association. (2020). *NCDA supports international students.* https://ncda.org/aws/NCDA/asset_manager/get_file/510839?ver=0

Parker, K. & Funk, C. (December 14, 2017). *Gender discrimination comes in many forms for today's working women.* Pew Research Center. https://www.pewresearch.org/fact-tank/2017/12/14/gender-discrimination-comes-in-many-forms-for-todays-working-women/

Perron, R. (2018). *The value of experience study AARP's multicultural work and jobs study.* https://www.aarp.org/research/topics/economics/info-2018/multicultural-work-jobs/?CMP=RDR CT-PRI-OTHER-WORKJOBS-052118.html

Powers, J. J., & Duys, D. (2020). Toward trauma-informed career counseling. *The Career Development Quarterly, 68*(2), 173–185. https://doi.org/10.1002/cdq.12221

Ramos, C., & Brassel, S. (2020). *Intersectionality: When identities converge* (Report). Catalyst.

Ratts, M. J., Singh, A. A., Nassar-McMillan, S., Butler, K., & McCullough, J. R. (2015). *Multicultural and social justice counseling competencies.* https://www.counseling.org/docs/default-source/competencies/multicultural-and-social-justice-counseling-competencies.pdf?sfvrsn=20

Rausch, M. A. (2014). Contextual career counseling for transitioning military veterans. *Journal of Employment Counseling, 51*(2), 89–96. https://doi.org/10.1002/j.2161-1920.2014.00044.x

Rowson, T. S., & Gonzalez-White, M. D. C. (2019). "I'm older but I can still do this job": The experiences of mature women in an age-sensitive occupation. *Educational Gerontology, 45*(4), 248–258. https://doi.org/10.1080/03601277.2019.1611223

Savickas, M. L. (2002). Career construction: A developmental theory of vocational behavior. In D. Brown (Eds.), *Career choice and development* (4th ed., pp. 149–205). Jossey-Bass. http://www.borbelytiborbors.extra.hu/ZSKF/CareerDevelopment.pdf#page=170

Savickas, M. L. (2016). Reflection and reflexivity during life-design interventions: Comments on career construction counseling. *Journal of Vocational Behavior, 97,* 84–89. https://doi.org/10.1016/j.jvb.2016.09.001

Small, J. (2021). Reimagining an antiracist career center based on the professional identity development model for Black students and students of color. *The Vermont Connection, 41*(1). https://Scholarworks.uvm.edu/tvc/vol41/iss1/14

Society for Human Resource Management. (2022). *Employing older workers.* https://www.shrm.org/hr-today/news/all-things-work/pages/employing-older-workers.aspx

Sohier, L., Van Ootegem, L., & Verhofstadt, E. (2021). Well-being during the transition from work to retirement. *Journal of Happiness Studies, 22*(1), 263–286. https://doi.org/10.1007/s10902-020-00228-6

Speciale, M., & Scholl, M. B. (2019). LGBTQ-Affirmative Career Counseling: An Intersectional Perspective. *Career Planning & Adult Development Journal, 35*(1). https://www.researchgate.net/publication/333456514_LGBTQ-Affirmative_Career_Counseling_An_Intersectional_Perspective

State of Vermont. (n.d.). *Action and Allyship: An on-ramp towards equity.* vermont.gov. https://racialequity.vermont.gov/sites/reap/files/doc_library/Action%20and%20Allyship%20Guide.pdf

Substance Abuse and Mental Health Services Administration. (2014). *SAMHSA's concept of trauma and guidance for a trauma-informed approach* (HHS Publication No. SMA14-4884). Author.

Sue, D. W., Sue, D., Neville, H. A., & Smith, L. (2019). *Counseling the culturally diverse: Theory and practice.* John Wiley & Sons.

Terrell, K. (2018). *Age discrimination common in workplace, survey says.* https://www.aarp.org/work/age-discrimination/common-at-work/

The BIPOC Project. (n.d.) *About us.* https://www.thebipocproject.org/about-us

Topitzes, J., Pate, D. J., Berman, N. D., & Medina-Kirchner, C. (2016). Adverse child-hood experiences, health, and employment: A study of men seeking job services. *Child Abuse & Neglect, 61,* 23–34. https://doi.org/10.1016/j.chiabu.2016.09.012

Truxillo, D. M., Cadiz, D. M., & Hammer, L. B. (2015). Supporting the aging work-force: A research review and recommendations for workplace intervention re-search. *Annual Review of Organizational Psychology and Organizational Behavior, 2,* 351–381. https://doi.org/10.1146/annurev-orgpsych-032414-111435

USA Facts. (2021, May 12). *Which jobs have the highest representation of Asian Americans?* https://usafacts.org/articles/which-jobs-have-the-highest-representation-of-asian-americans/

U.S. Senate Special Committee on Aging. (2017). *America's aging workforce: Opportuni-ties and challenges.* tinyurl.com/yb8muac6

Van Horn, C. E., & Heidkamp, M. (2019). Older workers, precarious jobs, and un-employment: Challenges and policy recommendations. *Generations: Journal of the American Society on Aging, 43*(3), 21–28. https://www.jstor.org/stable/26841728

Wang, M., & Shultz, K. S. (2010). Employee retirement: A review and recommenda-tions for future investigation. *Journal of Management, 36,* 172–206. https://doi.org/10.1177/0149206309347957

Westwood, M. J., Black, T. G., & McLean, H. B. (2002). A re-entry program for peace-keeping soldiers: Promoting personal and career transition. *Canadian Journal of Counselling and Psychotherapy, 36*(3). https://files.eric.ed.gov/fulltext/EJ651687.pdf

Wilson, P. G. (2016, June 1). *Raising counselors' awareness of microaggressions. Counseling Today.* https://ct.counseling.org/2016/06/raising-counselors-awareness-microaggressions/

World Health Organization. (2018). *World health statistics 2018: Monitoring health for the SDGs.* http://apps.who.int/iris/bitstream/handle/10665/272596/9789241565585-eng.pdf?ua=1

Wright, G. G., & Chan, C. D. (2022). Integrating trauma-informed care into career counseling: A response to COVID-19 job loss for Black, indigenous, and people of color. *Journal of Employment Counseling,* 1–9. https://doi.org/10.1002/joec.12186

Wright, G. G., & Chan, C. D. (2022). Applications of intersectionality theory to enhance career development interventions in response to COVID-19. *Professional School Counseling,* 26: 2156759X2211068. https://doi.org/10.1177/2156759X221106807

Zacher, H., Feldman, D. C., & Schulz, H. (2014). Age, occupational strain, and well-being: A person-environment fit perspective. In P. L. Perrewé, C. C. Rosen, & J. R. B. Halbesleben (Eds.), *The role of demographics in occupational stress and well being* (Vol. 12, pp. 83–111). Emerald Group Publishing Limited. https://doi.org/10.1108/S1479-355520140000012002

Zacher, H., Kooij, D., Beier, M., & Wang, M. (2018). Successful aging at work: Empiri-cal and methodological advancements. *Work, Aging and Retirement, 4*(2), 123–128. https://doi.org/10.1093/workar/way002

Zucker, R. (2019). 5 ways to respond to ageism in a job interview. *Harvard Business Re-view Digital Articles,* 2–5. https://hbr.org/2019/08/5-ways-to-respond-to-ageism-in-a-job-interview

Zyromski, B., Dollarhide, C. T., Aras, Y., Geiger, S., Oehrtman, J. P., & Clarke, H. (2018). Beyond complex trauma: An existential view of adverse childhood experiences. *The Journal of Humanistic Counseling, 57*(3), 156–172. https://doi.org/10.1002/johc.12080Solor aces sum faciass imaiore ribus.

CHAPTER 4

THEORIES, FRAMEWORKS, AND APPROACHES IN CAREER COUNSELING PART ONE

Regina Gavin Williams, Angie C. Smith, and Katie Peterssen

LEARNING OBJECTIVES

By the end of this chapter, you will be able to:

- Examine classical theories, frameworks, and approaches to use in career-counseling sessions.
- Describe key elements of each theory presented.
- Explore theories to be applied within multiple settings and with diverse populations.

WARM-UP EXERCISE

What life roles are most salient to you right now (student, partner, friend, etc.)? Reflect back 5 years, then 10 years. What life roles were most salient at those times? How did they change over time? Now, consider how your early thoughts about work, vocation, or career may have been shaped by your environment and the people around you. As a child, what did work look like in your family and community? When you engaged in pretend play, what roles did you gravitate toward or away from? Think about early signals you received from role models, community, family, media, etc. about work.

INTRODUCTION

This chapter examines key classical theories, frameworks, and approaches to career development. The theories offered in this chapter offer counselors-in-training and seasoned professionals ways to meet students and clients where they are at in the moment. Practical applications and cultural considerations are also presented, highlighting research studies that use the theories presented in this chapter. The theories we cover will align with the Council for the Accreditation of Counseling and

Related Educational Programs standards in connection with the career-counseling course and assist in preparation for the National Counselor Exam (NCE). This will cover developmental, learning, and narrative theories. The author's professional cases are offered as examples of classic career theories in practice.

CAREER DEVELOPMENT THEORIES

In psychology, a theory is an idea backed by facts that both describes and predicts human behavior. Over time, as a theory develops, it gains practical application methods that can be used in a variety of professional settings, including career services. There are a few important classical theories in career development, and we present them here to assist career counselors and counselors-in-training.

Work Adjustment Theory

Developed from over 35 years of research from René V. Dawis, Lloyd Lofquist, and their affiliates, **work adjustment** is a theory that helps adults make career decisions or those who may be experiencing issues with work adjustment (Sharf, 2013). Work adjustment theory is concerned with job tenure (i.e., length of time) and job performance and includes 18 propositions and corollaries, each with the goal of a prediction of work adjustment (Sharf, 2013). The two major components of work adjustment are satisfaction and satisfactoriness (Lofquist & Dawis, 1984). *Satisfaction* refers to a person feeling fulfilled with the various aspects of one's work (e.g., work tasks, salary range), and *satisfactoriness* refers to employers feeling content with their employee's performance (Sharf, 2013).

Work adjustment theory consists of assessing personal abilities, values, personality styles, and interests. Lofquist and Dawis (1984) conceptualized that abilities encompass predicted skills or aptitude, and these can be measured through abilities tests. Values refer to a grouping of needs (Sharf, 2013), and the Minnesota Importance Questionnaire (MIQ) was developed "as a measure of vocational needs, [which] may be used in vocational counseling, career planning, and job placement." (Rounds et al., 1981, p. 3).

Personality styles refer to how people, keeping their values and abilities in mind, interact with their work situations (Lofquist & Dawis, 1984; Sharf, 2013). They identified four characteristics of personality style: celerity, pace, rhythm, and endurance. Celerity is the speed one uses to approach a task. Pace is the effort a person spends in working. Rhythm is the power of a person's effort or pace. Endurance can be described as how long a person continues to work on a task (Sharf, 2013). In addition to the four characteristics of personality style, interests also play a role in how people interact with their work situations. Interests refers to one's expression of ability-value relationships; for example, one's interest in becoming a teacher or a mechanic comes from the abilities and values the person has (Sharf, 2013).

PRACTICAL APPLICATIONS

Work adjustment theory can be used to provide career counseling to retired individuals who desire to explore career choices before settling on a new career

(Harper & Shoffner, 2004). Career counselors can take the opportunity to assess a client's preretirement work satisfaction and preretirement work satisfactoriness levels (Harper & Shoffner, 2004). Then, using that information, match the client to an environment that is in concert with the preferred job traits so that their satisfaction and satisfactoriness levels are increased (Harper & Shoffner, 2004).

Work adjustment theory has also been applied to adolescents who were identified as gifted. For example, the theory has been used to promote the educational achievement and adjustment of 13-year-old gifted students (Achter & Lubinski, 2003; Lubinski & Benbow, 2000; Sharf, 2013).

CULTURAL CONSIDERATIONS

Work adjustment theory has been used in work and research to provide pertinent insight into the career experiences of people from diverse populations. The theory can be applied to the discrimination that is experienced by LGBTQIA+ populations (Sharf, 2013). For instance, one study indicated that career counselors who are working with clients who identify as lesbian should have an awareness of the barriers lesbians may face in their career development and in employment settings (Degges-White & Shoffner, 2002). Researchers also noted that the work adjustment theory has been used to predict the job satisfaction of individuals who identify as lesbian, gay, and bisexual regarding workplace discrimination (Lyons et al., 2005; Sharf, 2013).

In issues related to women, research noted how work adjustment theory can be used to address issues related to women and family and sexual harassment (Fitzgerald & Rounds, 1993; Sharf, 2013). For instance, Velez et al. (2018) tested both the indirect and direct associations of workplace racist and sexist discrimination with poor work and mental health outcomes among some employees who were women of color. The findings directly and indirectly associated workplace discrimination with higher psychological distress and indirectly associated workplace discrimination with poor work outcomes (Velez et al., 2018).

Life Span, Life Space

Donald Super's **life-span**, life-space career theory (Savickas, 2002; Super, 1990), evolved from over 40 years of work by Super and his collaborators (Savickas, 1997; Super et al., 1996). Super's theoretical approach has three segments: career-development theory, developmental self-concept theory, and life-role theory (Savickas, 1997). The theory conceptualizes career choice and development in three ways:

1. A movement through developmental stages and developmental tasks over time within one's life span.
2. A compilation of an individual's social roles and the context where these roles are displayed, otherwise known as life space.
3. An execution of self-perception and situational perception, known as self-concept (Hartung, 2020).

The life-span, life-space theory uses the archway model of career determinants to depict an interrelationship that occurs among multiple career determinants and self-concept. Super noted that an individual's self-perception and how the person interacts "is a reflection of personality, needs, and interests"

(Sharf, 2013, p. 178). Therefore, in the archway model, there are a variety of self-concepts or life roles that one could have, such as student, worker, citizen, etc. (Figure 4.1; Scholl & Cascone, 2010).

Super also conceptualized five developmental stages of a career (Figure 4.2). Career stage 1 is growth, which is generally defined as ages 4 to 14 years old. This stage is where children and adolescents develop vocational self-concept, as well as the development of attitudes and needs in the general world of work.

Career stage 2 is exploration, generally including ages 15 to 24 years old. In this stage, people engage in educational commitments in an effort to make career choices and selections (Sharf, 2013). Likewise, they engage in vocational exploration in an effort to acquire information about occupations and about self to make informed career decisions (Savickas, 2002).

Career stage 3 is establishment, which includes ages 25 to 44 years old, and this stage involves implementing one's vocational self-concept. This stage involves three tasks: career stabilization, demonstrating a positive attitude and productivity at work, and work advancement to different or new responsibilities (Savickas, 2002).

Career stage 4 is maintenance or management, which generally includes 45 to 64 year olds who are reevaluating their work experiences, examining whether to remain on their chosen career path, or make changes. If this re-evaluation process

FIGURE 4.1 Archway of career determinants.

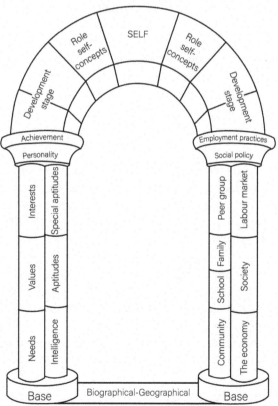

Source: Provided with permission from Brown, D., & Brooks, L. (1990). *Career choice and development: Applying contemporary theories to practice.* John Wiley & Sons.

FIGURE 4.2 Life-career rainbow: six life roles in schematic life space.

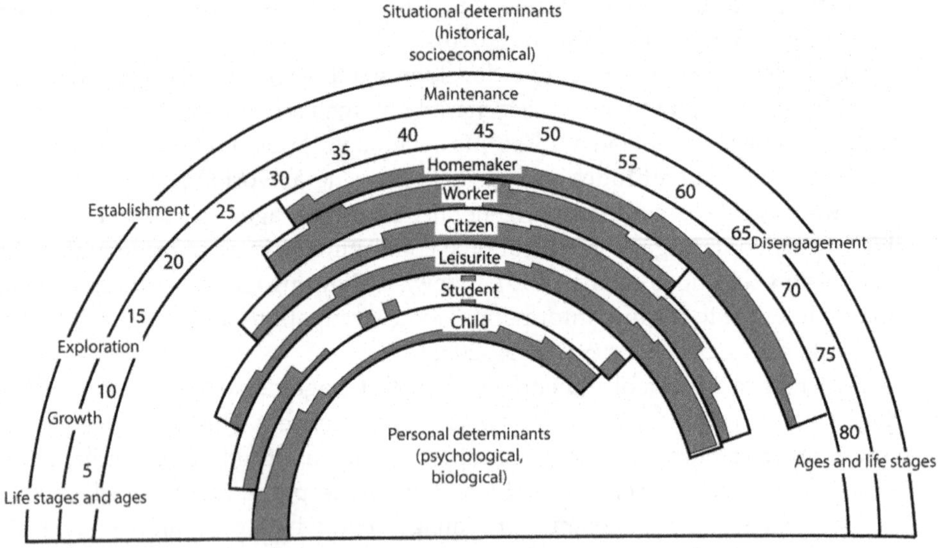

Source: Provided with permission from Brown, D., & Brooks, L. (1990). *Career choice and development: Applying contemporary theories to practice.* John Wiley & Sons.

leads them to a career change, one must reengage in the exploration and establishment stages. If they remain in their chosen career, they then enter the career maintenance stage from midlife to retirement, known as self-concept preservation (Savickas, 2002).

Career stage 5 is disengagement, which generally includes 65-year-olds and older, and it involves the deceleration of vocational development, planning for retirement, and retirement living. Retirement planning is a central activity in separating from an occupation and engaging the challenges of restructuring one's lifestyle postretirement (Savickas, 2002).

PRACTICAL APPLICATION

Super's (1990) model of childhood career development illustrates how children acquire a concept of themselves as it relates to career planning and career decision-making (Sharf, 2013). In using this model, counselors can examine a child's development of career interests and discuss the child's exploratory behavior in the context of developing these interests. For example, if an elementary-aged student expresses to her school counselor that she has an interest in reading and writing stories, the school counselor can help the student explore the level of importance of her engaging in these activities. The school counselor may then emphasize how well the student engages in these activities, which reinforces her strengths in doing so (i.e., solidifying the student's self-concept). This might later connect to how the student might see herself engaging in these activities in the future and in future careers she might be able to explore based on these interests.

CULTURAL CONSIDERATIONS

In reviewing the life-span, life-space theory in the context of cultural considerations, one study by Bigler et al. (2003) examined the perceptions of first- and sixth-grade African American students regarding the workforce. Another research study conducted by Lahner et al. (2014) used the Adult Career Concerns Inventory (ACCI; Super et al., 1988), to explore the reactions of organizational downsizing among older and younger employees within the context of Super's theory of career development. The results of the study revealed that younger employers reported more job dissatisfaction and saw downsizing as less equitable when compared to older employees who experienced a layoff at work. These are just two pertinent examples of how Super's theory is conceptualized in the context of age and race as it is related to career development and career concerns.

Personality Theory of Career Choice

MYERS-BRIGGS TYPE THEORY

Although not originally designed to be a theory of career development, Myers-Briggs Type Theory is popular among career counselors in their work with clients (Sharf, 2013). In the context of career development, the Myers-Briggs type system can be seen as a trait and factor theory (Sharf, 2013). Based on Carl Jung's psychological types, Katharine Briggs and Isabel Myers developed their own categories of human behavior and classified individuals into Jungian types (Myers, 1962). They then developed the Myers-Briggs Type Indicator (MBTI; Myers, 1962). There are four bipolar dimensions of Myers-Briggs theory: judgment-perception, sensing-intuition, thinking-feeling, and introversion-extraversion (Sharf, 2013).

The two basic concepts of Myers-Briggs theory are perception-judgment and introversion-extraversion, and the typology yields 16 different types based on the various ways of judging and perceiving and the preference for introversion versus extroversion (Sharf, 2013). Perceiving and judging displays how individuals observe their world and engage in decision-making based on their perceptions (Myers, 1962; Sharf, 2013). The two ways of perceiving are sensing (i.e., information taken in via the auditory or visual process) and intuition (i.e., one's unconscious adding ideas to external perceptions). There are also two ways of judging: thinking (i.e., remaining objective and analyzing an event or idea) and feeling (i.e., a subjective reaction that is most likely related to an individual's values; Sharf, 2013).

Introversion and extraversion reveal how individuals use perception and judgment through introversion versus extraversion. Introversion refers to how people make perceptions and judgments based on their interests within their inner world, and extraversion refers to how people use perceptions and judgments in their outer world. For extroverts, the concern with other people and objects is pertinent. Extraverts tend to gain energy from their interactions with people, whereas introverts prefer alone time and more concentrated activities to restore their energy and recharge their batteries (Sharf, 2013).

PRACTICAL APPLICATIONS

In literature, the relationship between Myers-Brigg typologies and Holland's typologies is examined using the MBTI and Self-Directed Search (SDS), and the researchers discuss the practical applications for career counselors (Chauvin et al., 2010). Another study explored the use of MBTI in the career counseling process (Kennedy & Kennedy, 2004). One study explored personality type differences among band, orchestra, and choir high school students using MBTI results (MacLellan, 2011).

To illustrate the number of years that the MBTI has been used in various research studies, one study conducted in 1994 examined whether certain personality types of college students performed better in an introductory computer programming class than students who presented with opposite personality types (Bishop-Clark & Wheeler, 1994).

Cultural Considerations

The Myers-Briggs theory and MBTI have been translated into 21 languages and are used with diverse populations. One study used the MBTI to examine the personality characteristics of a sample of South Korean high school students with visual impairments (Bak, 2012). Another study used the MBTI in order to assess the psychological type of a sample of women engineering students from a university in South India. Researchers of the study also sought to examine the effects of birth order on personality type (Menon & Anurekha, 2019).

Vocational Personality and Work Environment: John Holland's Theory of Types

John Holland (1966, 1973, 1985, 1992, 1997) believed that career choice and adjustment are an extension of one's personality (Sharf, 2013). In his theory of personalities in work environments, Holland noted that individuals express interests and values through one's work experience and choices and stated that one's generalizations, or stereotypes, regarding work were accurate (Figure 4.3).

FIGURE 4.3 John Holland's RIASEC model.

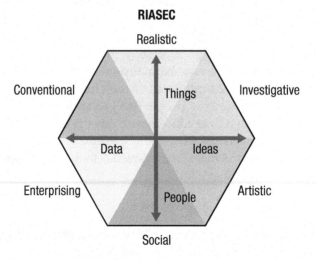

RIASEC

Holland assigned people and work environments into six specific categories based on these stereotypes (Sharf, 2013). These six types of work environments include realistic, investigative, artistic, social, enterprising, and conventional (RIASEC). Holland implied that individuals resemble more than one type or multiple Holland types and that these patterns are called subtypes (Spokane et al., 2002). However, the highest three letters, or summary code (e.g., SEC), are typically used in assessments (Spokane et al., 2002).

Here are the RIASEC categories:

Realistic (R): The Realistic environment career is physically demanding and includes an ability to work with objects. The work settings require people to have technical competencies, such as driving a car or truck, repairing equipment, roofing, or fixing a machine (Sharf, 2013). People who are realistic also approach issues in a practical manner and as a problem solver (Sharf, 2013).

Investigative (I): In the investigative environment, a person seeks solutions to problems by using their scientific and mathematical interests and abilities (Sharf, 2013). Investigative people enjoy using their intellect and are most likely to enjoy challenges. These individuals often use abstract thinking when solving problems. Occupations in this environment include physicians, mathematicians, veterinarians, and computer programmers (Sharf, 2013).

Artistic (A): Personal expression and creativity are encouraged in the artistic environment. Tools used by artistic people to express themselves (e.g., a saxophone or acrylic paint) rather than using tools to complete a task or solve a problem (Sharf, 2013). Some of the ideal careers in which individuals can express themselves in both creative and unconventional ways include artists, musicians, and freelance writers (Sharf, 2013).

Social (S): The social environment is full of people in the helping professions who understand and support others through personal or career-related issues. Social people are usually socially responsible and may impact others in a spiritual way (Sharf, 2013). They place an emphasis on human values such as generosity and kindness. Most social people find satisfying careers in the fields of education, counseling, and social services with positions as teachers, school counselors, social workers, and marriage and family therapists.

Enterprising (E): The enterprising environment includes persuaders who like to manage others in an effort to obtain either a personal or organizational goal (Sharf, 2013). Enterprising people are often assertive, sociable, and self-confident and tend to view economic and financial issues as being of primary importance (Sharf, 2013). Suitable enterprising environments that might give one power, status, and wealth include politics, business management, real estate, insurance, and sales (Sharf, 2013).

Conventional (C): The conventional environment typically includes planning and organization. Conventional people naturally organize reports, maintain records, duplicate materials, and keep accounting records (Sharf, 2013). People who are conventional tend to be dependable rule followers who also value money (Sharf, 2013). Examples of conventional positions include bank managers, tax experts, data processors, and accountants.

People may also have an appreciation for any one of the RIASEC codes due to their interests. For example, a student may score high on the "artistic" scale yet share with the career counselor that they are not artistic in any way. However, even if the student does not play a musical instrument or possess artistic talent, they may spend time listening and appreciating music in their free time or visit museums and appreciate the artwork demonstrated and created by others.

PRACTICAL APPLICATIONS

There are several studies that demonstrate the practical use of Holland's theory. One recent study highlighted the use of Holland's theory as a framework to examine if college students flourish in academic environments that were congruent with their personality type, as well as if student characteristics have an influence on person-environment fit (Rocconi et al., 2020).

Another recent study used Holland's code to identify the vocational preference of students who were studying to become paramedics (van Huizen et al., 2021). In a study that surveyed human service professionals from the National Organization for Human Services to determine and compare their Holland Codes, the results were subsequently used to advocate for *human services professional* to be included in the Standard Occupation Classification (SOC) system (Neukrug et al., 2017).

These examples illuminate the large number of approaches researchers have taken in using Holland's theory and the impact the theory has had on informing career and educational processes.

CULTURAL CONSIDERATIONS

When exploring the cultural considerations of Holland's theory, it appears to be applicable across diverse populations, both within the United States and internationally. For instance, one study used three self-efficacy inventories that incorporated the six Holland types to compare samples of African American and European American college students (Betz & Gwilliam, 2002).

Another study examined the usefulness and utility of Holland's theory in order to understand the connection between the personality of college students studying to become music teachers in Turkey and the appeal of music education (Cevik et al., 2013). One research study sought to examine the relationship between the vocational interests of Chinese college students and their career choices (Tang, 2009).

Research further showed that the Holland types of different cultural groups working in the United States provided useful insight into the employment of individuals from diverse populations (Sharf, 2013). These examples highlight just a few studies that have demonstrated the usefulness of Holland's theory and its affiliated instruments. Holland's theory is renowned and is arguably the most widely studied and researched theory both nationally and internationally.

Circumscription, Compromise, and Self-Creation

Linda Gottfredson's theory of circumscription, compromise, and self-creation (1981, 2002, 2005), focuses on childhood and adolescence and the idea of how people create themselves and intermingle with various environmental factors (e.g., gender and prestige; Sharf, 2013). Gottfredson (2002) suggested that occupational aspirations can begin in early childhood and should be seen as a fundamental part of social identity and development (Ettigi, 2017). In 1981, she proposed that children and adolescents progress through four career-development stages:

- Stage 1 (3–5 years old): Orientation to size and power
- Stage 2 (6–8 years old): Orientation to sex roles
- Stage 3 (9–13 years old): Orientation to social valuation
- Stage 4 (14 years and older): Orientation to internal unique self

Gottfredson's theory further noted that people hold occupational stereotypes (i.e., images of occupations) related to the kind of work that they do, the lives they are leading, the appropriateness of the work, and the condition and rewards of the work for different types of people (Gottfredson, 2002). In this regard, Gottfredson's theory holds the assumption that when individuals recognize and adopt occupational stereotypes, such as those related to one's gender identity (e.g., the notion that only women can pursue a career in nursing) in the environment, they will construct a cognitive map of occupations they might pursue (Ettigi, 2017). Gottfredson believes that selecting a career involves developing a cognitive map of occupations that are incorporated into one's self-concept (Savickas, 2002).

On this cognitive map, occupations are placed under three dimensions: masculinity-femininity (i.e., sex type), occupational prestige level (i.e., overall desirability), and field of work (Gottfredson, 2002). These dimensions are then presented in a two-dimensional map, sex type by prestige level (Gottfredson, 2002). Gottfredson further indicated that individuals develop an internal compass that serves as a guide as they make choices (Sharf, 2013).

In circumscription, youth eliminate unacceptable career alternatives, and compromise is the process by which youth start to relinquish most of their preferred alternatives in exchange for those that are less compatible than those they identify as more accessible (Gottfredson, 2002) and discover an inability to actualize their most preferred choice.

PRACTICAL APPLICATIONS

There are several studies that demonstrate the practical application of Gottfredson's theory of circumscription, compromise, and self-creation. For instance, one study applied Gottfredson's theory to investigate what personal aspirations children had for their adult lives (Bozzato, 2020). Another study by Forsman and Barth (2017) examined factors that might affect men's interests in occupations that were identified as female-dominated. The results of the study indicated that there was support for circumscription and compromise theory, among other theories (Forsman & Barth, 2017).

CULTURAL CONSIDERATIONS

In the context of cultural considerations, several studies reflect this theory's use with diverse populations. For instance, one research study examined the importance that South Asian Americans place on the three dimensions of sex type, prestige level, and interests, and the variation that might occur given potential societal and familial expectations related to their career development (Ettigi, 2017).

Another study using Gottfredson's theory examined the process and contextual variables that might influence the career development of African American male athletes and nonathletes (Bader, 2011).

Social Learning Theory of Career Decision-Making

John Krumboltz's social learning theory of career decision-making (SLTCDM; 1979) focused on how individuals make career decisions with an emphasis on the importance of behavior and cognition in career decision-making (Krumboltz, 1994, 2009; Mitchell & Krumboltz, 1996; Sharf, 2013). This theory teaches individuals career decision-making skills and assists them in how to effectively use and successfully handle unexpected events and select career alternatives (Sharf, 2013). His theory might attempt to answer questions such as why individuals choose certain occupations and why someone picks one academic major over another (Figure 4.4; Sharf, 2013).

SLTCDM consists of the four influencing factors of career decision-making:

1. genetic endowments and abilities
2. environmental conditions and events
3. instrumental and associative learning experiences
4. task-approach skills (Krumboltz, 1979)

These influencing factors are intended to explain career choice origins and their various interactions with one another (Datti, 2009; Krumboltz, 1979). These factors can also play a pertinent role in the eventual selection of a career alternative (Sharf, 2013).

FIGURE 4.4 How career interests evolve throughout time.

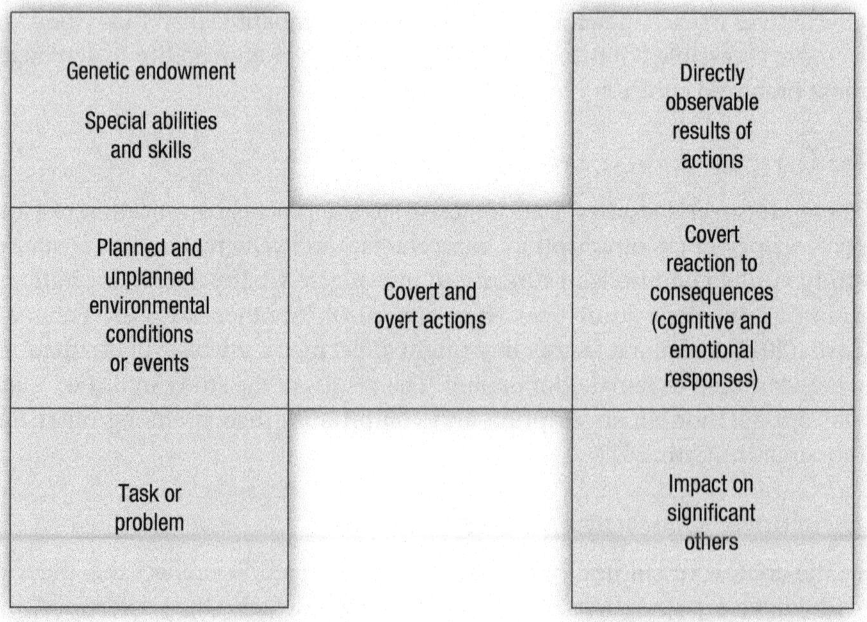

Source: Provided with permission from Brown, D., & Brooks, L. (1990). *Career choice and development: Applying contemporary theories to practice.* John Wiley & Sons.

Mitchell et al. (1999) also created a theory entitled *happenstance theory*. They posited that often the decisions we make create our own luck through a series of unplanned events that lead to a desired outcome. For example, if an individual seeking employment decides to make the decision to attend a networking event, a by-product of this event could include the high likelihood of meeting a potential employer or person who may lead to another opportunity or additional option. In turn, by attending this event, it could lead to a chance encounter or something unexpected and unplanned. In some ways, the saying "being at the right place at the right time" comes to mind. Situating ourselves in spaces that may involve a high probability of connection and opportunity for positive future outcomes can be indicative of happenstance theory; in essence, one might say we should take the time to create our own luck (Mitchell et al., 1999).

PRACTICAL APPLICATIONS

There are several studies that demonstrate the practical application of SLTCDM. For instance, one study used SLTCDM to examine the role-model influence on the career decidedness of undergraduate students (Perrone et al., 2002). A recent study used this theory to assess the self-efficacy of employees impacted by the virtual/remote work environments prompted by the COVID-19 pandemic (Yarberry & Sims 2021). Another study shared how using social learning theory can be used as a guide for career counselors working with college student-athletes (Shurts & Shoffner, 2004). It is clear the SLTCMD is an applicable framework in career counseling and development practice.

CULTURAL CONSIDERATIONS

There are several studies that point to the usability of the SLTCDM with diverse populations. Research noted that SLTCDM is one of the broader models with applicability across a variety of cultures (Datti, 2009; Herring, 2022). For instance, Datti (2009) used SLTCDM as a framework to explore the career development issues of LGBTQ adolescents and young adults. Another study used the theory as a framework to explore the career decisions of students at an urban historically Black college and university who identified as sexual minorities (Harris, 2014). Researchers in another study used Krumboltz's theory to examine the successful learning experiences of a sample of middle school students from urban, low-income, culturally diverse backgrounds to see if these experiences were affiliated with their occupational interests and aspirations (Jackson, 2006). These examples demonstrate the usability of the SLTCMD with individuals from culturally diverse backgrounds.

Social Cognitive Career Theory

Social cognitive career theory (SCCT) developed by Lent et al. (1994), focuses on the connection of outcome expectations, perceived barriers to success, self-efficacy, and goals that influence an individual's career choice. Grounded in Bandura's (1986) social cognitive theory (SCT), SCCT addresses the individual characteristics and perceived barriers related to contextual factors that may influence one's learning experiences and self-efficacy (Lent et al., 2004).

SCCT consists of three central building blocks to career development that interplay with one another in the self-regulation of behavior: self-efficacy, outcome expectations, and personal goals (Lent et al., 1994). In this theory, career interests and engagement in career-related activities are regulated by an individual's perceived personal competency. This, in turn, can reinforce one's belief in performing a specific behavior.

PRACTICAL APPLICATIONS

When exploring practical applications in career development, there are several notable studies that have used the SCCT framework. For instance, SCCT was used in a study to examine factors that affect the life satisfaction of university students (Mohd, Rasdi & Ahrari, 2020). Another researcher used horticultural therapy through the lens of SCCT as a vocational intervention for offenders (Ascencio, 2018). The career-development issues for women also have a prominent focus in SCCT (Sharf, 2013). Hackett and Betz (1981) purported that career self-efficacy belief plays a prominent role in the restriction of women's career choices.

CULTURAL CONSIDERATIONS

SCCT has been used as a model in multiple studies that examine or explore its use with diverse populations. For instance, SCCT has been used as a framework for the prediction of career decision-making self-efficacy within Asian American college students. Another research study sought to understand the relationship between constructs of SCCT as it related to science, technology, engineering, and math career interests and goal persistence in minority college students with disabilities (Dutta et al., 2015).

Researchers have frequently studied the use of SCCT with Black and Latin populations. For example, one researcher used SCCT to investigate the career development of ninth-grade Latino students residing in rural communities (Ali & Menke, 2014).

Cognitive Information-Processing Approach

The cognitive information-processing (CIP) approach is a career theory developed by Peterson et al. (2002) from the Florida State University Career Center for the Study of Technology in Counseling and Career Development. These researchers created the CIP approach to help individuals understand the *content* and *process* of career decision-making and problem-solving. In this regard, the researchers were concerned with helping individuals enhance their career problem-solving and decision-making skills that will persist throughout their lifetime.

The CIP framework consists of the following four key assumptions: (1) career problem-solving and decision-making involve the interaction of both affective and cognitive processes, (2) the capability for career problem-solving depends on the availability of cognitive operations and knowledge, (3) career development involves continual growth and change in knowledge structures, and (4) the goal of career counseling is the enhancement of information-processing skills (Peterson et al., 2002).

The CIP approach consists of two core constructs that serve as the building blocks of the framework. They are as follows: (a) the pyramid of information -processing domains and, (b) the CASVE (communication, analysis, synthesis, valuing, execution) cycle of information -processing skills used in career decision-making. The pyramid of information-processing domains involves the *content* of career problem-solving and decision-making represented by the knowledge domains (i.e., self-knowledge and occupational knowledge), decision-making skills domain (i.e., generic information-processing skills), and executive-processing domain (i.e., metacognitions). Within the decision-making skills domain lies the CASVE cycle, which involves the *process* of career problem-solving and decision-making and consists of the process of communication, analysis, synthesis, valuing, and execution (Peterson et al., 2002; Williams, 2016).

PRACTICAL APPLICATIONS

The CIP approach has been applied to a variety of settings such as middle and postsecondary schools, communities, and career centers. These settings have used CIP-derived interventions and strategies for service delivery. These interventions include career assessments, counseling, staff training, intervention planning, program development and evaluation, and employment problem-solving and decision-making (Peterson et al., 2002). For example, the CIP approach was used to help enlisted military service personnel transition into the civilian workforce (Clemens & Milsom, 2008). It was also used to assess the effectiveness of using the DISCOVER career guidance systems on college students who were unsure of their career paths (Hornyak, 2007). Moreover, it has contributed to the positive career outcomes of clients via offering resources, providing homework assignments, and encouraging clients to complete career-related self-research (Osborne, 2014).

CULTURAL CONSIDERATIONS

In the context of cultural considerations, there have been multiple studies reflecting the use of the CIP approach with diverse populations. For example, the theory was used to address barriers and provide suggestions for career counseling with women (McLennan & Arthur, 1999). Another study explored the career thoughts and spirituality of women diagnosed with breast cancer (Dames et al., 2019). One study investigated the relationships between racial identity development and the career thoughts of Black seniors at an urban high school (Williams, 2004). Additionally, the CIP framework has been used with the veteran population. For instance, a study used CIP to explore enlisted service members' transition into the civilian world of work (2008).

Career Constructivist Theory

The two ways that people construct their views of the world are through constructivism and social construction (Sharf, 2013). In this regard, constructivism is defined as how people think and process what they learn. Constructivism takes the stance that individuals create their own views of relationships and events happening in their lives (Sharf, 2013).

The constructivist approach to career counseling was derived from the observation that young people felt unmotivated or disempowered to put career information to use (Hoskins, 1995). Therefore, adopting a career constructivist approach allows for clients to feel empowered to take a proactive and mindful stance regarding their work life (Hoskins, 1995). Counselors who take a constructivist approach also help their clients give meaning to their problems as well as to assist them in viewing their problems as options that are not helpful anymore (Sharf, 2013).

Social construction is described as how interacting with others can affect one's worldview and actions as a result of these views (Sharf, 2013). In other words, the interactions a person has with other people can shape how they view the world and how they might engage within it. Counselors identifying as social constructivists examine how an individual fits into the work world as well as how individuals fit the work world into their lives (Sharf, 2013).

Two notable constructive approaches to career counseling are *career construction theory* and *narrative counseling*. Savickas's career construction theory (2002) holds a social construction point of view and examines four areas of client narratives: vocational personality, developmental tasks, dimensions of career adaptability, and life themes (Savickas, 2002; Sharf, 2013). Narrative career counseling is described as clients sharing their past career development, their career development of the present, and then constructing what they would like for their future career to look like (Sharf, 2013). Cochran's Narrative Career Counseling (1997) consists of a seven-episode counseling method that shows how clients can comprehend their career narratives and then apply this understanding to construct their future careers (Sharf, 2013).

PRACTICAL APPLICATIONS

Career development literature noted using a constructivist resume career -counseling approach as a career development exercise (Scholl & Cascone, 2010). This particular career-counseling approach consists of four sessions: the card sort, the future-oriented constructivist resume, co-constructing action plans and goals, and describing one's professional identity (Scholl & Cascone, 2010). For the future-oriented constructivist resume, the career counselor informs clients to use conventional resume heading (e.g., experience, skills) as well as encourages the use of unconventional resume headings (e.g., risks taken, networking activities, ideal lifestyle accomplishments; Scholl & Cascone, 2010). Although one does not actually submit this type of resume to a potential employer, this personal approach encourages clients to create a resume that is both future-oriented and allows them to reflect on what they would like to be doing in the next 5 to 7 years, while also including past and present activities and accomplishments (Scholl & Cascone, 2010).

CULTURAL CONSIDERATIONS

In the context of cultural considerations, career constructivist theory has been used with various diverse populations. For example, one research study used career constructionist theory to conceptualize the career decision-making process of people living with HIV/AIDS (Trujillo, 2010). In another study, a researcher applied a constructivist approach to career counseling as a framework for nurturing the development of gifted female adolescents (Maxwell, 2007). Furthermore, one study used a career constructivist application to working with African refugees (Pierce & Gibbons, 2012).

PROFESSIONAL EXPERIENCES

Counseling Children and Adolescents in Foster Care

I have professional experience as a licensed clinician providing counseling services to clients who were children and adolescents in the foster care system. They were required to have a counselor through their legal guardianship with their local department of social services. To get counseling services for the children, a social worker would contact the agency where I worked so that a counselor could complete an intake session with the child. The child would then be assigned a clinician based on the diagnoses and other needs.

Through my work, I found that many of the high school–aged clients in foster care had very little direction regarding what life might look like for them in the future after exiting the foster care system (i.e., aging-out). Research confirms my experience; while foster care youth aspire to pursue postsecondary education, they often succumb to multiple disruptions that impede their educational expectations (Kirk et al., 2013).

It is important to engage foster care adolescents in career exploration in a way that connects their interests to potential postsecondary education and career opportunities, and Holland's theory can be a useful approach for this. For example, in my research focused on the college and career readiness self-efficacy of adolescents in foster care, I engaged students in the career party interest game (see the section Integration Activities) where students discovered their Holland Code and explored potential careers related to these codes. From there, participants were able to examine helpful information, including educational requirements, wages, employment trends, etc., using O*NET Online.

Counseling High School Students

In my previous roles as a licensed school counselor and college access higher education professional, I facilitated the career, academic, and social-emotional development of high school students, and a critical part of ensuring the success of my students was enhancing their college and career readiness. Achieve, Inc. (n.d.) described the term "college ready" as being prepared for postsecondary educational training experiences that lead to obtaining postsecondary education credentials (e.g., bachelor's or associate's degree, license, or certificate). They described *college readiness* as high school graduates possessing the skills and knowledge needed to successfully complete entry-level college courses without having to engage in remedial coursework. They further defined the term *career ready* as a high school graduate that is able to acquire the skills and knowledge necessary to qualify and be successful in their postsecondary education or training for a career (Achieve, Inc., n.d.). In this role, I took a pragmatic approach to counsel and advise my students using the American School Counselor Association (ASCA) National Model as a framework for delivering services to students and engaging stakeholders (ASCA, 2019, 2012).

I also used tangible tools to support students' career development and postsecondary educational needs. The use of websites such as College Foundation of North Carolina (CFNC), BigFuture on Collegeboard.org, O*Net, and the Common

App helped me engage my students in career assessments, college and career exploration, and planning for their future post–high school. Using SCCT as a contextual framework, I was able to improve the college and career readiness self-efficacy of my students through these counseling and support services, while also enhancing their outcome expectations and encouraging their personal aspirations.

Academic and Career Development of College Students

In my previous experience in a university setting, I was a director of student engagement and diversity affairs within a college of education. In this role, I supported the academic and career development of preservice educators and engaged them in field service and professional development opportunities that enhanced their cultural competency and allowed them to gain further exposure to the K–12 education field.

For one of the field service opportunities, I facilitated a cultural and language domestic immersion experience in New Orleans. Preservice educators were able to learn about the K–12 educational system in a post–Hurricane Katrina era and were also introduced to rich cultural influences in New Orleans communities. From a theoretical perspective, my students were engaged in the second stage of Super's life-span, life-space approach to career development: exploration. Students engaged in an educational commitment that helped to inform their career selection of becoming a teacher. In a post-trip survey, participants felt they were more informed in techniques to learn about the communities that they will be teaching in. They also gained a greater awareness of their preconceptions and biases that may impact their careers as future educators.

In the ever-expanding field of career development, these theories are just a few of the many practical and helpful models used by career professionals. As a practitioner, the best tool you have is the one you are most comfortable with and the one that you think will resonate with the client. While it is important to know and understand existing and newly developing theories, it is more important that these tools are used appropriately, effectively, and compassionately with career clients.

INTEGRATION ACTIVITIES

Career Exploration and Postsecondary Exploration: Career Interest Party

Learning Outcome: To explore careers that fit the participant's personality in order to narrow down an academic area for postsecondary study.

1. Students play the Career Interest Party Game, using the Career Interests Party Game Sheet (available by accessing Springer Publishing Connect™ via the instructions on the opening page of this book and clicking on the drop down Show Supplementary, Student Materials) to determine their top three groups and then their Holland Code. Envelopes filled with careers to match each of the six groups are spread throughout the room, and students find their first group envelope and explore the careers inside. They pick their top three careers and write them down. The students repeat this until they have visited each of their top three groups and written down their top three

careers. All the students stay in their last group and talk about careers and potential secondary educational requirements.

2. The students take the Holland Code test and write down their scores.
3. Next, students explore possible postsecondary education interests and major profiles via internet resources.
4. Finally, students are asked to reflect on how their interests, personality, and future careers are linked, and then they research and think through their next academic and career choices.

A more detailed explanation of this activity is available by accessing Springer Publishing Connect™ via the instructions on the opening page of this book and clicking on the drop down Show Supplementary, Student Materials.

ETHICAL CORNER

In this section, the authors lead the reader through topical scenarios to surface common ethics questions and dilemmas faced by career professionals. They ask pertinent and personal questions to encourage reader reflection and insight into personal and professional ethics.

Azra Karajic Siwiec PhD, LPC, is a counselor educator employed by Capella University. She has been working in the counselor education field for over 14 years and has served as a committee member of the Ethics Committee of the NCDA since 2015 and served as the chair of the Ethics Committee since 2017.

Sharon K. Anderson, PhD, is professor of counseling and career development at Colorado State University. Sharon has taught the master's level ethics course for counseling students for over 20 years, teaching and mentoring a multitude of students. She has coauthored or coedited four professional ethics books used by practitioners in counseling and coaching.

As a student, the examination and assessment of your knowledge of counseling **theories** and trends is important to the gatekeeping process. You may view this examination and assessment as a stressful time in becoming a counselor and may even feel fear or anger that this is taking place. However, think of it this way: what if you were to see a medical doctor who could not pass exams and could not perform proficiently in surgery but is now scheduled to perform a surgical procedure on a member of your family. How would this impact your thinking about this doctor?

VIGNETTE

Sandi is stressed out about taking the National Councilor Exam (NCE); however, she has done everything in her power to prepare, including purchasing materials and taking self-tests that review all the information. When she takes the test for the first time, she learns that she has not passed. She is devastated, but she is guided by the virtues of humility and diligence and is committed to the ethical principle of beneficence—to do good. She wants to be an ethical counselor. She carries herself with integrity and speaks to her peers about her experiences. She states that while the test was difficult she learned what she needed to do a better job of preparing and will do better next time. Sandi thinks of the importance of gatekeeping and reflects this as she has conversations with her peers.

If someone close to you is thinking of seeking counseling but doubting the value of "laying on the couch and blaming their mother," how would you respond to their concerns and perceptions of counseling? Think about how you might share the standards of the profession and the importance of gatekeeping. How might you communicate to this person the process of who can enter the counseling profession and how the profession is kept ethical?

DIGGING INTO ETHICS

How will you reflect on your learning process in your counseling process regarding the actions you took from the beginning to now? How have you seen gatekeeping responsibilities implemented in your training? What do you see as going well for you in your training? What, if anything, do you wish was more rigorous and scrutinizing to prepare you and your colleagues? At times we hear of instances of plagiarism where learners in counseling programs pass off someone else's work as their own. What do you understand as the line between citing someone's work appropriately versus taking credit for it as if it is your own work? How have you encouraged yourself to demonstrate the highest ethical standards when it comes to writing and research?

Review the American Counseling Association (ACA) code of ethics and see if it addresses plagiarism. Please note that there are many levels involved in issues of plagiarism: program, university, profession, etc. You are examining a professional level of response. Can you find anything that your program or institution states explicitly about plagiarism? Do they have similar viewpoints, or do they diverge?

4.1 PRACTITIONER'S PERSPECTIVE

Megan Tajlili PhD, NCC, PMH-C, LCMHC is a private practice licensed clinical mental health counselor and supervisor. She has been a counselor since 2008 and has worked in the college career and counseling offices in a variety of universities. She is currently an adjunct professor of counseling with New York University and North Carolina State University and maintains a telehealth practice focusing on women's issues and work–life balance.

I would characterize my career path as a study of transitions, especially as they correlate to my life stages and roles. Five years out of college, I was working in marketing, and the part of my job that gave me the most joy and spark was recruiting and working with new college graduates. As I searched for a new career path to capitalize solely on those job tasks I enjoyed, career counseling enticed me because it combines helping people through life changes and teaching others how to promote themselves to be competitive. I enjoyed the energy and excitement that came with providing career counseling in a college setting.

After working in the career-counseling centers at three different universities, I longed for more ways I could serve a broader audience and decided to get a doctorate degree. I was particularly interested in understanding how career women conceptualize having a family and prioritize work–life balance, as I continued growing in my career and personal roles. For my dissertation, I surveyed millennial-generation college women, asking how they understand and enact work–life balance ideals in their future planning. I used grounded theory research methodology and the Kaleidoscope Career Model by Mainiero and Sullivan (2005) to survey 508 college women about their experiences and attitudes.

I now work in private practice with midcareer women who want to align their personal values and seminal care activities more closely to their career goals. I also teach career, internship, and college counseling at two universities, which feeds my desire to mentor and give back to the profession. I have found firsthand that crafting salient, cohesive personal and career identities across multiple life roles has allowed me to flourish and feel fulfilled.

I find that authenticity and purpose motivate me to continue my work. Many people share with me that they fell into a career that they don't love and do not feel that they can express their identity or values through this work. They work solely to pay the bills. This is a huge draw on creativity and flow, and it reduces productivity and health and costs the employer as well as the employee.

When working with these clients, I find that they do not feel that they have agency over their lives, and they lack intentional foresight in executing their next steps. I stay curious and ask a lot of questions, employing narrative therapy to help them craft the story of their life and identify where their gaps in satisfaction lie.

I believe having a social justice framework is ethically necessary to effectively engage in this type of work in our modern-day society. There are ways in which the world is not set up for any individual person's success; in fact, there are forces resisting equality and authenticity for the sake of oppressive professional standards and capitalism. A career counselor's job encompasses advocacy to assist and educate on systemic biases as well as tackle those biases head on. This may mean finding no-cost childcare so a client can participate in an interview or sourcing professional attire for a client who does not have appropriate career-fair clothing. This differs from the traditional notion of a career counselor reviewing cover letters, but I find that advocating in these ways is the true game changer for our clients. It takes a healthy dose of realism, combined with resolve, creativity, and bravery to craft the life and career one desires. I feel privileged to ignite the spark that allows people to grow into a more embodied sense of self.

CLASSICAL THEORIES/FRAMEWORKS

I find the following classical theories and frameworks particularly helpful in my practice:

- Work adjustment theory
- Life span, life space
- Personality theory of career choice
- Circumscription, compromise, and self-creation
- Vocational personality and work environment: John Holland's theory
- Social learning theory
- Social cognitive career theory
- Cognitive information-processing approach
- Career constructivist theory
- Integrative life planning

In my anecdotal experience, I do find that people with common interests tend to enjoy similar job opportunities, so my first step is a lengthy career intake. I ask about interests, hobbies, and key milestones in their life and career. From this information, the client and I collaborate on creating a narrative understanding of their career and what concerns they are facing now.

I start with the Holland Code when working with people that share that they've "fallen into" a career they don't love or find themselves completely lost as to what they'd like to do with their lives, I usually give the Self-Directed Search (Holland et al., 1994) to obtain a Holland Code. I never use just one assessment, however, and try to couple my results with the MBTI (Myers, 1962), values exercises, and the intake interview.

Additional powerful tools that I turn to regularly include O*NET OnLine, *Do What You Are* (Tieger & Barron-Tieger, 2001), and the online Life Values Inventory (Brown & Crace, 2002).

Once the client has taken the assessment, it is important that they discuss the results with a career counselor. Oftentimes, if left to their own devices, clients will only consider the list of job titles and their earning potential. Without the greater context and nuanced information, clients have strong reactions to their results, either completely embracing them or dismissing the assessment outright.

PERSONAL EXPERIENCE

When I worked with college students at a big agricultural and STEM school, many students had an interest in working with their hands and being outdoors, so the Realistic job family came up often. These students would react to receiving the job title farmer in their results, stating "I don't have to be in a 4-year school for that! Isn't this outdated? Why is that a job I want?" Through the nuanced information that I collected during the intake, I helped them step back from the traditional job tasks of a farmer and allowed them to see what similarities arose in their preferences— being outside, working with plants and animals, and possessing a strong scientific background. Many of these students eventually chose majors that were tangential to farming but required more sophisticated knowledge and rigor, for example, landscape architecture, agribusiness, and food science. Without receiving the interpretive skills of a career counselor who can zoom out on the big picture results, a client might jump at a job title without considering the full range of options available.

I like to share a personal example with my clients when discussing job title results. When I take these career assessments, I often get rabbi or pastor as a potential career path. I am not particularly religious in my everyday life and never had an interest in pursuing that field of study. So, should I drop everything and run to my nearest religious institution? No. Instead, I look at the ways that my counseling career might be similar to a ministry. I have a passion, zeal, and calling to help, lead, comfort, and work with people to enact an authentic and fully realized life.

4.2 PRACTITIONER'S PERSPECTIVE

Laura Inscoe, PhD, NBCT, is a school counselor and dean of students in a suburban public school in North Carolina. Dr. Inscoe has been a school counselor since 2000 and she oversees the school counseling department and program planning. She is an adjunct instructor

who enthusiastically and creatively supports, educates, and inspires future school counsel-
ors. She has earned the honors of district and state Secondary School Counselor of the Year
and was a national semifinalist for ASCA School Counselor of the Year.

I was fortunate to have had a wonderful school counselor in high school. I remember sitting in her office preparing for classes for my senior year. She had a natural calm nature and an innate ability to make everyone in her presence feel loved and appreciated. I remember thinking to myself that one day I would love to make others feel the same way she made me feel. In graduate school, I actually completed my internship at my old high school and had the pleasure of working with her during that time. I was sure to take mental notes that I have carried with me throughout my school counseling career.

I began my career as a school counselor at a middle school in a large urban district. It was the perfect place to begin my career! I was a part of a wonderful team of counselors and my principal was collaborative, involved, and supportive of counselors. I learned early on the importance of surrounding myself with awesome people, as well as the value of a strong relationship with my principal.

I then moved to another middle school in the largest school district in North Carolina and worked there for 9 years. My principal took a job "up the hill" at our feeder high school, and I transitioned into high school counseling where I have remained since. My role changed from school counselor to dean of students, and I moved to another local high school after 8 years.

As the dean, I have more managerial tasks and am fortunate to work with a team of terrific, hardworking counselors. We meet regularly as a team to share best practices, set goals, discuss ethical dilemmas, prepare for tasks, and reflect. Creating a cohesive department has always been my priority. Other goals include empowering my school counselors, learning what each counselor's strengths are, mentoring new counselors, and being a leader in the field. I had the honor of being my district and state Secondary School Counselor of the Year and a semifinalist for ASCA School Counselor of the Year. I attribute much of my success to the amazing people around me!

My job includes individual, group, and classroom counseling. I oversee the counseling department and ensure that we are data driven and student centered. I plan programming for students, parents, and staff on counseling-related topics such as mindful practice, registration, working with English learners, and equity. There was a time when our students did not feel they had a voice and wanted to have a place to talk about critical topics in a safe space, so I created a unity team for this, in which all student members are now trained as peer mediators by a local law school's restorative justice program.

TRAITS OF CAREER COUNSELORS

Students give me energy! Hearing their stories, guiding them in decision-making, and collaborating with others to help them have led to enjoyment and success in this field. I have found that people who thrive in this role have been able to find humor in everyday situations. This job is heavy! We cannot take students in need home, even if we know we could provide a more stable home for them. Being able to see a bright side and know that we have made a positive difference is the key to not burning out and feeling defeated. Also, finding other staff members to connect with who have common interests and provide a sense of belonging and friendship in (and out of) the building is helpful when we need to be recentered and grounded.

When I began my school counseling career, I thought I was the next Carl Rogers and would be client-centered forever. What I have realized, especially in a high school, is that many students need a counselor who is more direct, and I have found myself using Solution-Focused Brief Counseling as well as a reality approach. I find that I am able to change my theoretical approach depending on the student I am working with and their needs. For example, I worked with a senior who was having a difficult time figuring out his next steps after high school. After meeting with him two times, I realized that he was not growing nor figuring out what to do next. It was imperative that I change the way I was counseling him so that he became more empowered and able to come up with a solution. I always want to ensure that my students, staff, parents, and anyone else I am working with leave my office feeling supported and hopeful.

Student Voices

In Student Voices, students offer a unique viewpoint as they begin in the career-counseling field. Here, students share their thoughts and reflections about the career-counseling profession and offer personal takeaways.

SHEENA KELLY

Sheena Kelly graduated from Walden University with a master's degree in Marriage Couples and Family Counseling. Sheena is pursuing her LPC in Georgia and her LCMHC in North Carolina while working with individuals, couples, and families in a therapeutic setting.

My theoretical orientation is an existential-humanistic approach that is influenced by ecosystem structural family theory and trauma-focused cognitive behavioral theory (TF-CBT). The existential-humanistic approach views people as able to determine their impact on the world so that they can create their own destiny. This approach begins when a person makes the conscious decision to act in the world (Wolfe, 2016; Ivey et al., 2012). According to Lindblad-Goldberg and Northey (2013), ecosystem structural family therapy (ESFT) focuses on the way that members of a family respond and support one another within their system, combining attachment theory and structural family therapy in its interventions. According to Gurman (2008), attachment is important to individuals and how they develop relationships later in life (p. 107). If a client's family foundation is rocky due to negative attachment, the client will not fully form bonds with others outside their unit, especially not healthy bonds. Feeling secure is key in relationships to help us to regulate emotions and communicate clearly. TF-CBT may be used to reduce negative thoughts and feelings associated with trauma through exposure, inductive reasoning, and psychoeducation (Yasinski et al., 2016).

VIGNETTE

Jordan is a 17-year-old, single biracial male who was seeking therapy for concerns surrounding his sexuality and relationship with his parents. Jordan felt as

(continued)

though he was the reason for his parent's divorce resulting from him telling his mother about his father's affairs. After the divorce, Jordan lived with his father and visited his mother on holidays. Jordan's mother used religion to force Jordan into a heteronormative way of life. His mother would refer to him as the devil at times and would not allow him into her home. She believed that Jordan would change if he devoted himself to the church, and his father believed that his homosexuality was a phase. Jordan also had a history of substance misuse after completing high school early. He would smoke THC and drink alcohol that his father provided to him. Jordan has been dealing with isolation, low self-esteem, and anxiety for over 6 months.

According to Ivey et al. (2012), defense mechanisms such as repression, denial, projection, displacement, and fixation result from insecure attachment. With Jordan, he isolated and began misusing substances to reduce anxious thoughts and behaviors. Employing ESFT, the family benefited from increased support and resolved the unhealthy attachments. Religion was used to bring them together to support Jordan. The family also regained their structure, forming roles, rules, and boundaries with the father putting these mechanisms in place. Using TF-CBT, Jordan was able to tell his story to give Dad insight into how he felt about previous occurrences and about their relationship to reduce self-blame and negative beliefs while allowing reconnection (Hanson & Jobe-Shields, 2017). Over time, Jordan's symptoms subsided, and he was able to return to pleasurable activities as he went to college. Jordan and his father regained a better father–son relationship through healthy communication and support.

Tip: Counselors-in-Training

In the case Sheena shared, we see the impact of early relationships on both an individual and the larger family unit. In conjunction with a TF-CBT, Sheena might use a career construction approach to support Jordan. With a focus on empowering clients to take a proactive approach to their education and career goals, career construction integrates well with trauma-informed approaches.

Through the process of understanding attachments and family structures, Sheena may also aid Jordan in describing how his worldview and beliefs about his college or career opportunities have been shaped by his interactions with his family. Social construction may complement ESFT interventions and support clients' overall well-being.

COUNSELING SKILLS CONNECTION

Counselors-in-training are typically required to enroll in courses related to counseling theories and techniques. In these courses, the most foundational theories involve historical theories developed early on in the profession's infancy. Evidence-based theories provide a solid framework for practice. Throughout the counseling and related programs, there will be overlapping concepts that will be covered in various courses. The teaching and discussion related to the utility of theories and how theories can be applied to practice is one topic covered in multiple ways throughout a counseling students' plan of study.

One example of a theory that is highlighted in the counseling theories course involves Carl Roger's person-centered theory (Rogers, 1957). The theory posits "genuineness" and "unconditional positive regard" as the client and counselor develop rapport in the counseling relationship. The theory recognizes the importance of the counseling relationship as a foundation for the therapeutic alliance (Rogers, 1957). In comparison, Donald Super's theory of life span, life space spotlights the value of understanding the individual's career development and growth from a life-span approach. One link between Rogers' and Super's approach is the holistic way in which the theorists conceptualize the total person; they are both purposefully client-centered. Rogers leads with a complete acceptance of an individual's unique experience, and Super supports all of an individual's life roles within different life theaters. For more information about positive psychology and unconditional positive regard, the Positive Psychology website (positivepsychology.com) offers three free downloadable exercises to explore further.

MINDFUL MOMENT

Take a study break and practice bringing awareness using each of your five senses. Use this script to increase your mindfulness and to decrease any feelings of being overwhelmed or stress that you may be feeling. This exercise will take just a few minutes.

Take a deep, cleansing breath.

Looking around you, notice five things that you can SEE. Bring your attention to things that you might otherwise overlook, a leaf on the ground, pattern on a chair, etc. Take each thing in completely, naming it in your head or aloud.

Notice four things that you can currently FEEL with parts of your body. Focus your attention on the texture of a piece of clothing, the feel of a breeze across your face, the support of a chair on your back, and so on. Notice each sensation as you take a few deep breaths.

Rest your attention now on three things that you can HEAR. Notice sounds you hear in the background like the hum of a ventilation system, whir of a washing machine, or rustle of the leaves on a nearby tree.

Notice two things that you can SMELL. Focus on smells you may not regularly notice, like the faint scent of your shampoo or the smell of fresh-cut grass.

Rest your attention on one thing that you can TASTE right now. Take a bite or a drink of something nearby or simply take a moment to notice the taste in your mouth at this moment (Ackerman, 2017).

TECH TOOLS

If you are planning to pursue licensure as a counselor, you will likely need to take the NCE. As you might suspect, theory is a core element assessed on the NCE. The NCE Pocket Prep app (www.pocketprep.com/exams/nbcc-nce/) offers a free tool to support your exam preparation. The app offers both free and paid/premium subscriptions. Technology tools such as this can help you approach your exam preparation strategically, honing in on areas of strength and weakness. Gamification keeps you motivated and focused on consistency in your preparation. Keep your daily study streak alive!

REFLECTION ACTIVITY

Take a moment to reflect on the following questions related to the content of the chapter. What are some of the practical applications you can recall when applying the classical theories to career-counseling practice? Which classical theory or theories do you find yourself gravitating toward as a future counselor? Why? How might these various classical theories and approaches be used differently based on the counseling setting (i.e., school, industry, higher education) and the developmental stage of the client (i.e., child, adolescent, young adult, older adult)?

END-OF-CHAPTER RESOURCES

SUMMARY

Classical theories offer a context for practitioners to draw upon when counseling students and clients. Theories and approaches, such as work adjustment theory, Holland's SDS, Cognitive Information Processing, SCCT, and additional frameworks described in this chapter offer counselors-in-training and seasoned professionals tools to meet students and clients where they are in the moment. Many theories, such as Holland's theory, have been researched extensively with a multitude of populations across the world (Holland, 1959; Spokane et al., 2002). A rationale for reviewing and learning theories involves determining if and how the theories, frameworks, and approaches can be applied in practice. We encourage you to consider the key elements to each theory and determine how each theory resonates with who you are and how you want to show up in session and in the community with your clients, students, etc.

REFERENCES

Ackerman, C. (2017, January 18) *22 mindfulness exercises and activities for adults.* Positive Psychology.

Ackerman, C. E. (2018). *What is unconditional positive regard in psychology.* https:// positivepsychology.com/unconditional-positive-regard/#:~:text=Carl%20 Rogers%20described%20unconditional%20positive%20regard%20as%3A%20 %E2%80%9C%E2%80%A6caring,his%20own%20feelings%2C%20his%20own%20 experiences%E2%80%9D%20%28Rogers%2C%201957%29

Achieve, Inc. (n.d.). *College and career readiness.* Author. https://www.achieve.org

Achter, J. A., & Lubinski, D. (2003). Fostering exceptional development in intellectually talented populations. In W. B. Walsh (Ed.), *Counseling psychology and optimal human functioning* (pp. 25–54). Erlbaum.

Ali, S. R., & Menke, K. A. (2014). Rural Latino youth career development: An application of social cognitive career theory. *Career Development Quarterly, 62*(2), 175–186. https://doi.org/10.1002/j.2161-0045.2014.00078.x

American School Counselor Association. (2012). *The ASCA national model: A framework for school counseling programs* (3rd ed.). Author.

American School Counselor Association. (2019). *The ASCA national model: A framework for school counseling programs* (4th ed.). Author.

Ascencio, J. (2018). Offenders, work, and rehabilitation: Horticultural therapy as a social cognitive career theory intervention for offenders. *Journal of Therapeutic Horticulture, 28*(1), 21–28. https://www.jstor.org/stable/26598041

Bader, C. M. (2011). *An examination of contextual and process variables influencing the career development of African-American male athletes and non-athletes* (Publication No. 3506949). [Doctoral dissertation, University of North Texas]. ProQuest Central (1012121116).

Bak, S. (2012). Personality characteristics of South Korean students with visual impairments using the Myers-Briggs Type Indicator. *Journal of Visual Impairment & Blindness, 106*(5), 287–299. https://doi.org/10.1177/0145482X1210600504

Bandura, A. (1986). *Social foundations of thought and action: A social cognitive theory.* Prentice-Hall.

Betz, N.E., & Gwilliam, L.R. (2002). The utility of measures of self-efficacy for the Holland themes in African American and European American college students. *Journal of Career Assessment, 10*(3), 283–300. https://doi.org/10.1177/10672702010003001

Bigler, R. S., Averhart, C. J., & Liben, L. S. (2003). Race and the workforce: Occupational status, aspirations, and stereotyping among African American children. *Developmental Psychology, 39*, 572–580. https://doi.org/10.1037/0012-1649.39.3.572

Bishop-Clark, C., & Wheeler, D. D. (1994). The Myers-Briggs personality type and its relationship to computer programming. *Journal of Research on Computing in Education, 26*(3), 358. https://doi.org/10.1080/08886504.1994.10782096

Bozzato, P. (2020). The relationship between children's aspiration profiles and self-efficacy, life satisfaction, and academic achievement. *Social Sciences, 9*(5), 77. https://doi.org/10.3390/socsci9050077

Brown, D., & Crace, R. K. (2002). *Life values inventory: Facilitator's guide.* Applied Psychology Resources.

Cevik, B., Perkmen, S., Alkan, M., & Shelley, M. (2013). Who should study music education? A vocational personality approach. *Music Education Research, 15*(3), 341–356. https://doi.org/10.1080/14613808.2013.788140

Chauvin, I., Miller, M. J., Godfrey, E. L., & Thomas, D. (2010). Relationship between Holland's vocational typology and Myers-Briggs' types: Implications for career counselors. *Psychology Journal, 7*(2), 61–66.

Clemens, E. V., & Milsom, A. S. (2008). Enlisted service members' transition into the civilian world of work: A cognitive information processing approach. *Career Development Quarterly, 56*(3), 246–256. https://doi.org/10.1002/j.2161-0045.2008.tb00039.x

Cochran, L. (1997). *Career counseling: A narrative approach.* Sage.

Dames, L. S., Ghekiere, E., Zalaquett, C. P., Kromrey, J. D., Ellerbrock, C. R., Exum, H., & Paxton, R. J. (2019). Correlates of dysfunctional career thoughts in breast cancer survivors from the Bahamas. *Journal of Psychosocial Oncology, 37*(5), 665–675. https://doi.org/10.1080/07347332.2019.1580330

Degges-White, S., & Shoffner, M. F. (2002). Career counseling with lesbian clients: Using the theory of work adjustment as a framework. *Career Development Quarterly, 51*(1), 87–96. https://doi.org/10.1002/j.2161-0045.2002.tb00594.x

Datti, P. A. (2009). Applying social learning theory of career decision making to gay, lesbian, bisexual, transgender, and questioning young adults. *Career Development Quarterly, 58*(1), 54–64. https://doi.org/10.1002/j.2161-0045.2009.tb00173.x

Dutta, A., Kang, H.-J., Kaya, C., Benton, S. F., Sharp, S. E., Fong, C., da Silva Cardoso, E., & Kundu, M. (2015). Social-cognitive career theory predictors of STEM career interests and goal persistence in minority college students with disabilities: A path analysis. *Journal of Vocational Rehabilitation, 43*(2), 159–167. https://doi.org/10.3233/JVR-150765

Ettigi, S. (2017). *The role of family expectations and internalized model minority on career choices of South Asian American college students* [Doctoral dissertation Lehigh University] (Order No. 10619003). ProQuest Central (2188045595).

Fitzgerald, L., & Rounds, J. (1993). Women and work: Theory encounters reality. In W. Walsh & S. Osipow (Eds.), *Career counseling for women* (pp. 327–354). Erlbaum.

Forsman, J., & Barth, J. (2017). The effect of occupational gender stereotypes on men's interest in female-dominated occupations. *Sex Roles, 76*(7–8), 460–472. https://doi.org/10.1007/s11199-016-0673-3

Gurman, A. S. (2008). *Clinical handbook of couple therapy* (4th ed.). Guilford Press.

Gottfredson, L. S. (1981). Circumscription and compromise: A developmental theory of occupational aspirations. *Journal of Counseling Psychology, 28,* 545–579. https://doi.org/10.1037/0022-0167.28.6.545

Gottfredson, L. S. (2002). Gottfredson's theory of circumscription, compromise, and self-creation. In D. Brown & Associates (Eds.), *Career choice and development* (4th ed., pp. 85–148). Jossey-Bass.

Gottfredson, L. S. (2005). Applying Gottfredson's theory of circumscription and compromise in career guidance and counseling. In S. D. Brown & R. W. Lent (Eds.), *Career development and counseling: Putting theory and research to work* (pp. 71–100). Wiley.

Hackett, G., & Betz, N. (1981). A self-efficacy approach to the career development of women. *Journal of Vocational Behavior, 18,* 326–339. https://doi.org/10.1016/0001-8791(81)90019-1

Hanson, R. F., & Jobe-Shields, L. (2017). Trauma-focused cognitive–behavioral therapy for children and adolescents. In S. N. Gold (Ed.), *APA handbook of trauma psychology: Trauma practice* (pp. 389–410). American Psychological Association. Walden University databases.

Harper, M. C., & Shoffner, M. F. (2004). Counseling for continued career development after retirement: An application of the theory of work adjustment. *Career Development Quarterly, 52*(3), 272–284. https://doi.org/10.1002/j.2161-0045.2004.tb00648.x

Harris, L. N. (2014). Black, queer, and looking for a job: An exploratory study of career decision making among self-identified sexual minorities at an urban historically black college/university. *Journal of Homosexuality, 61*(10), 1393–1419. https://doi.org/10.1080/00918369.2014.928170

Hartung, P. J. (2020). Life-span, life-space career theory and counseling. In S. D. Brown & R.W. Lent (Eds.), *Career development and counseling: Putting theory and research to work* (pp. 95–128). John Wiley & Sons.

Herring, R. D. (2002). Multicultural counseling for career development. In J. Trusty, E. J. Looby, & D. S. Sandhu (Eds.). *Multicultural counseling: Context, theory and practice, and competence* (pp. 219–246). Nova Science.

Holland, J. L. (1959). A theory of vocational choice. *The Journal of Counseling Psychology, 6,* 35–45. https://doi.org/10.1037/h0040767

Holland, J. L. (1966). *The psychology of vocational choice.* Blaisdell.

Holland, J. L. (1973). *Making vocational choices: A theory of careers.* Prentice Hall.

Holland, J. L. (1985). *Making vocational choices: A theory of personalities and work environments* (2nd ed.). Prentice Hall.

Holland, J. L. (1992). *Making vocational choices: A theory of vocational personalities and work environments.* Psychological Assessment Resources.

Holland, J. L. (1997). *Making vocational choices: A theory of vocational personalities and work environments* (3rd ed.). Psychological Assessment Resources.

Holland, J. L., Powell, A. B., & Fritzsche, B. A. (1994). *The self-directed search (SDS): Professional user's guide* (1994 ed.). Psychological Assessment Resources.

Hornyak, D. A. (2007). *Utilizing cognitive information processing theory to assess the effectiveness of Discover on college students' career development.* The University of Pittsburgh website: http://www.pitt.edu/~hornyak/Dissertation.pdf

Hoskins, M. (1995). *Constructivist approaches for career counselors.* ERIC Digest. https://files.eric.ed.gov/fulltext/ED401505.pdf

Ivey, A. E., D'Andrea, M. J., & Ivey, M. B. (2012). *Theories of counseling and psychotherapy: A multicultural perspective* (7th ed.). Sage.

Jackson, M. A. (2006). Are success learning experiences and self-efficacy beliefs associated with occupational interests and aspirations of at-risk urban youth? *Journal of Career Assessment, 14*(3), 333–353. https://doi.org/10.1177/1069072706286489

Kennedy, R. B., & Kennedy, D. A. (2004). using the Myers-Briggs Type Indicator® in career counseling. *Journal of Employment Counseling, 41*(1), 38–44. https://doi.org/10.1002/j.2161-1920.2004.tb00876.x

Kirk, C. M., Lewis, R. K., Nilsen, C., & Colvin, D. Q. (2013). Foster care and college: The educational aspirations and expectations of youth in the foster care system. *Youth & Society, 45*(3), 307–323. https://doi.org/10.1177/0044118X11417734

Krumboltz, J. D. (1979). A social learning theory of career decision-making. In A. M. Mitchell, G. B. Jones, & J. D. Krumboltz (Eds.), *Social learning and career decision making* (pp. 19–49). Carroll Press.

Krumboltz, J. D. (1994). Improving career development theory from a social learning perspective. In *M. L.* Savickas & R. W. Lent (Eds.), *Convergence in career development theories* (pp. 9–32). Consulting Psychologists Press.

Krumboltz, J. D. (2009). The happenstance learning theory. *Journal of Career Assessment, 17*(2), 135–154. https://doi.org/10.1177/1069072708328861

Krumboltz, J. & Leven, A. (2010). *Luck is no accident: Making the most of happenstance in your life and career* (2nd ed.). Impact.

Lahner, J. M., Hayslip, B., McKelvy, T. N., & Caballero, D. M. (2014). Employee age and reactions to downsizing. *International Journal of Aging & Human Development, 79*(3), 225–255. https://doi.org/10.2190/AG.79.3.c

Lent, R. W., Brown, S. D., & Hackett, G. (1994). Toward a unifying social cognitive theory of career and academic interest, choice, and performance. *Journal of Vocational Behavior, 45*(1), 79–122. https://doi.org/10.1006/jvbe.1994.1027

Lindblad-Goldberg, M., & Northey, W. (2013). Ecosystemic structural family therapy: Theoretical and clinical foundations. *Contemporary Family Therapy: An International Journal, 35*(1), 147–160. https://doi.org/10.1007/s10591-012-9224-4. Walden University databases.

Lofquist, L. H., & Dawis, R. V. (1984). Research on work adjustment and satisfaction: Implications for career counseling. In S. Brown & R. Lent (Eds.), *Handbook of counseling psychology* (pp. 216–237). Wiley.

Lubinski, D., & Benbow, C. P. (2000). States of excellence. *American Psychologist, 55*(1), 137–150. https://doi.org/10.1037/0003-066X.55.1.137

Lyons, H. Z., Brenner, B. R., & Fassinger, R. E. (2005). A multicultural test of the theory of work adjustment: Investigating the role of heterosexism and fit perceptions in the job satisfaction of lesbian, gay, and bisexual employees. *Journal of Counseling Psychology, 52*(4), 537–548. https://doi.org/10.1037/0022-0167.52.4.537

MacLellan, C. R. (2011). Differences in Myers-Briggs personality types among high school band, orchestra, and choir members. *Journal of Research in Music Education, 59*(1), 85–100. https://doi.org/10.1177/0022429410395579

Mainiero, L. A., & Sullivan, S. E. (2005). Kaleidoscope careers: An alternate explanation for the "opt-out" revolution. *Academy of Management Executive, 19*, 106–123. https://doi.org/10.5465/ame.2005.15841962

Maxwell, M. (2007). Career counseling is personal counseling: A constructivist approach to nurturing the development of gifted female adolescents. *Career Development Quarterly, 55*(3), 206–224. https://doi.org/10.1002/j.2161-0045.2007.tb00078.x

McLennan, N. A., & Arthur, N. (1999), Applying the cognitive information processing approach to career problem solving and decision making to women's career development. *Journal of Employment Counseling, 36*, 82–96. https://doi.org/10.1002/j.2161-1920.1999.tb01011.x

Menon, P., & Anurekha, T. (2019). Personality type and birth order of women engineering students. *International Journal of Recent Technology and Engineering, 8*(4), 10932–10938. https://doi.org/10.35940/ijrte.D4881.118419

Mitchell, A., Levin, A., & Krumboltz, J. D. (1999). Planned happenstance: Constructing unexpected career opportunities. *Journal of Counseling and Development, 77,* 115–124. https://doi.org/10.1002/j.1556-6676.1999.tb02431.x

Mitchell, L. K., & Krumboltz, J. D. (1996). Krumboltz's learning theory of career choice and counseling. In D. Brown, L. Brooks, & Associates (Eds.), *Career choice and development* (3rd ed., pp. 233–280). Jossey-Bass.

Mohd Rasdi, R., & Ahrari, S. (2020). The applicability of social cognitive career theory in predicting life satisfaction of university students: A meta-analytic path analysis. *PLoS One, 15*(8), 1–22. https://doi.org/10.1371/journal.pone.0237838

Myers, I. (1962). *The Myers Briggs type indicator: Manual.* Consulting Psychologists Press.

National Center for O*NET Development. *O*NET online.* https://www.onetonline.org/

Neukrug, E., Sparkman, N., & Moe, J. (2017). The Holland code of members of the national organization for human services: A preliminary study of human services professionals. *Journal of Employment Counseling, 54*(4), 146–155. https://doi.org/10.1002/joec.12063

Osborne, L. K. (2014). Using a cognitive information processing approach to group career counseling with visually impaired veterans. *The Professional Counselor, 4*(2), 150–158. https://doi.org/10.15241/lko.4.2.150

Perrone, K. M., Zanardelli, G., Worthington, Jr., E. L., & Chartrand, J. M. (2002). Role model influence on the career decidedness of college students. *College Student Journal, 36*(1), 109.

Peterson, G. W., Sampson, J. P., Lenz, J. G., & Reardon, R. C. (2002). A cognitive information processing approach to career problem solving and decision making. In D. Brown and Associates (Eds.), *Career choice and development* (pp. 312–369). Jossey-Bass.

Peterson, G. W., Sampson, J. P., & Reardon, R. C. (1991). *Career development and services: A cognitive approach.* Brooks/Cole.

Pierce, L. M., & Gibbons, M. M. (2012). An ever-changing meaning: A career constructivist application to working with African refugees. *Journal of Humanistic Counseling, 51*(1), 114–127. https://doi.org/10.1002/j.2161-1939.2012.00009.x

Rocconi, L. M., Liu, X., & Pike, G. R. (2020). The impact of person-environment fit on grades, perceived gains, and satisfaction: An application of Holland's theory. *Higher Education, 80*(5), 857–874. https://doi.org/10.1007/s10734-020-00519-0

Rogers, C. R. (1957). The necessary and sufficient conditions of therapeutic personality change. *Journal of Consulting Psychology, 21,* 95–103. https://doi.org/10.1037/h0045357

Rounds, J. B., Henly, G. A., Dawis, R. V., Lofquist, L. H., & Weiss, D. J. (1981). *Manual for the Minnesota importance questionnaire.* University of Minnesota, Psychology Department, Work Adjustment Project.

Savickas, M. L. (1997). Career adaptability: An integrative construct for life-span, life-space theory. *Career Development Quarterly, 45*(3), 247–259. https://doi.org/10.1002/j.2161-0045.1997.tb00469.x

Savickas, M. L. (2002). Career construction: A developmental theory of vocational behavior. In D. Brown & Associates (Eds.), *Career choice and development* (4th ed., pp. 149–205). Jossey-Bass.

Scholl, M. B., & Cascone, J. (2010). The constructivist résumé: Promoting the career adaptability of graduate students in counseling programs. *Career Development Quarterly, 59*(2), 180–191. https://doi.org/10.1002/j.2161-0045.2010.tb00061.x

Sharf, R. (2013). *Applying career development theory to counseling* (6th ed.). Cengage Learning.

Shurts, W. M., & Shoffner, M. F. (2004). Providing career counseling for collegiate student-athletes: A learning theory approach. *Journal of Career Development, 31*(2), 95–109. https://doi.org/10.1007/s10871-004-0567-4

Spokane, A., Luchetta, E., & Richwine, M. (2002). Holland's theory of personalities. In D. Brown & Associates (Eds.), *Career choice and development* (4th ed., pp. 373–426). Jossey-Bass.

Super, D. E. (1953). A theory of vocational development. *American Psychologist, 8,* 185–190. https://doi.org/10.1037/h0056046

Super, D. E. (1990). A life-span, life-space approach to career development. In D. Brown, L. Brooks, & Associates (Eds.), *Career choice and development: Applying contemporary theories to practice* (2nd ed., pp. 197–261). Jossey-Bass.

Super, D. E. (1994). A life-span, life-space perspective on convergence. In M. L. Savickas & R. W. Lent (Eds.), *Convergence in career development theories* (pp. 63–74). Consulting Psychologists Press.

Super, D. E., Savickas, M. L., & Super, C. M. (1996). The life-span, life-space approach to careers. In D. Brown, L. Brooks, & Associates (Eds.), *Career choice and development* (3rd ed., pp. 121–178). Jossey-Bass.

Super, D. E., Thompson, A., & Lindeman, R. (1988). *Adult career concerns inventory: Manual for research and exploratory use in counseling.* Consulting Psychologists Press.

Tang, M. (2009). Examining the application of Holland's theory to vocational interests and choices of Chinese college students. *Journal of Career Assessment, 17*(1), 86–98. https://doi.org/10.1177/1069072708325743

Tieger, P. D., & Barron-Tieger, B. (2001). *Do what you are: Discover the perfect career for you through the secrets of personality type* (3rd ed.). Little, Brown.

Trujillo, M. (2010). Persons living with HIV/AIDS contemplating a return to work: A social cognitive career theory and constructivist theory perspective. *Journal of Rehabilitation, 76*(1), 51–56. https://www.researchgate.net/publication/289897665_Persons_living_with_HIVAIDS_contemplating_a_return_to_work_A_Social_Cognitive_Career_Theory_and_constructivist_theory_perspective

U.S. Department of Labor. (1982). *Manual for the USES general aptitude test battery: Section II. Occupational aptitude pattern structure.* U.S. Government Printing Office.

van Huizen, P., Mason, R., & Williams, B. (2021). Exploring paramedicine student preferences using Holland's vocational theory: A cross-sectional study. *Nursing & Health Sciences, 23*(4), 818–824. https://doi.org/10.1111/nhs.12870

Velez, B. L., Cox Jr., R., Polihronakis, C. J., & Moradi, B. (2018). Discrimination, work outcomes, and mental health among women of color: The protective role of womanist attitudes. *Journal of Counseling Psychology, 65*(2), 178–193. https://doi.org/10.1037/cou0000274

Williams, F. C. (2004). *An investigation of the relationships between racial identity development and career thoughts for black seniors at an urban high school* [Doctoral dissertation, University of Central Florida]. ProQuest Dissertations and Theses database (UMI No. 3163637).

Williams, R. G. (2015). *The effects of customized individual counseling interventions on the career and college readiness of adolescents in the foster care system* (Unpublished report). North Carolina State University, Raleigh.

Wolfe, B. E. (2016). Existential-humanistic therapy and psychotherapy integration: A commentary. *Journal of Psychotherapy Integration, 26*(1), 56–60. https://doi .org/10.1037/int0000023

Yarberry, S. & Sims, C. (2021). The impact of COVID-19-prompted virtual/remote work environments on employees' career development: Social learning theory, belongingness, and self-empowerment. *Advances in Developing Human Resources, 23*(3), 237–252. https://doi.org/10.1177/15234223211017850

Yasinski, C., Hayes, A. M., Ready, C. B., Cummings, J. A., Berman, I. S., McCauley, T., & Webb, C., & Deblinger, E. (2016). In-session caregiver behavior predicts symptom change in youth receiving trauma-focused cognitive behavioral therapy (TF-CBT). *Journal of Consulting and Clinical Psychology, 84*(12), 1066–1077. https:// doi.org/10.1037/ccp0000147

CHAPTER 5

THEORIES, FRAMEWORKS, AND APPROACHES IN CAREER COUNSELING PART TWO

Terri L. Tilford, Angie C. Smith, and Katie Peterssen

LEARNING OBJECTIVES

By the end of this chapter, you will be able to:

- Describe and compare key elements of postmodern career theories and approaches.

- Discuss limitations of postmodern career theories including applications for diverse populations.

- Evaluate and select theories to integrate into your counseling approach.

WARM-UP EXERCISE

As you reflect on today, how are you feeling? What are you noticing around you? Sights? Sounds? Movement? Are you alone or around people? How has your day been constructed? Have you had agency over aspects of your day? If so, what parts? What systems may be operating in the forefront and/or the background that you have control over or perhaps have no control over? As you consider your current state and any future orientation, how might you construct your narrative? Do you have any hopes, dreams, or wishes in the here and now and for the future?

INTRODUCTION

This chapter highlights references for several postmodern **theories**. In contrast to modern theories, postmodern theories include cultural contexts in which every person constructs their own reality. Theories offer a framework and "handles" for counselors to use as they seek to support clients and students throughout their life span. Although there are many theories that embrace many of the same principles that help facilitate change, guidance, and support, only six will be listed in this chapter. More specifically, highlighted in this chapter will be the following theories: cognitive information processing, integrative life planning, constructivist, narrative, chaos, and kaleidoscope model.

POSTMODERN THEORIES

Postmodern theories in career counseling, in contrast to modern theories, are important to today's career-counseling experience because they include cultural contexts that are significant for clients and students. In 2017, Bethany Bray quotes two authors, Busacca and Rehfuss describe postmodernism as "individuals construct meaning or perceive their own reality or truth. This contrasts with the modernist assumption that an external and objective mean can be discovered" (2016, p. 36). This change is noteworthy as the demographics of workers continue to change and be more diverse.

Another significant contribution of postmodern theories is that career counselors assist clients or students in discussing past experiences, interactions, and interpretations of their environment and then to revise their story and develop their identity in their cultural context (Bray, 2017). This approach is valuable to clients and students as it embraces a perspective that includes identity development, culture, a holistic perspective, gender identity, and approaches that support guidance for marginalized populations. There are also some postmodern theories that counselors can use to help engage youth by sharing personal experiences and influences, and other theories that allow marginalized clients to have alternative "back up" plans, which is often the way of life for economically disadvantaged individuals.

Also, postmodern theories are valuable approaches to career counseling as we consider the influences of COVID-19 pandemic challenges, remote working opportunities, and ongoing implications of relevant social injustices and quickly changing technology. These variables independently, and sometimes collectively, create a need for counselors to be inclusive of clients' environmental challenges that will impact career decision-making.

In clinical mental health counseling, when a treatment plan includes addressing stress, anxiety, or depression related to career issues, postmodern theories are valuable and relevant to provide support. Postmodern theories provide helpful approaches for clinical mental health counselors to provide career-related support. For example, narrative theory promotes clients sharing their story, as the clinical mental health counselor assists to reduce stress and anxiety within a cultural context. In most cases, clinical mental health counselors can use an eclectic approach while using these postmodern theories.

Six theories fall under the postmodern category, and each provides an opportunity for the "voice" of a client to come to the forefront and to be mindful of cultural considerations. Table 5.1 lists more details of each theory to help the reader compare and contrast the different theories.

COGNITIVE INFORMATION PROCESSING

Cognitive information-processing (CIP) theory evolved at the Curriculum-Career Information Services of the Florida State University Counseling Center, later called the Florida State Career Center (Sampson, 2017). It is a career-development theory that emphasizes effective career decision-making and problem-solving based on the content and process of career decisions. The major components of the theory are the pyramid of information processing domain and the communication-analysis-synthesis-valuing-execution (CASVE) cycle.

TABLE 5.1 THE SIX POSTMODERN THEORIES

THEORY	APPROPRI-ATE AGE	ALLOW-ANCES FOR CUL-TURAL CONTEXT	CONSID-ERATIONS FOR MARGIN-ALIZED POPULA-TIONS	ALLOW-ANCES FOR POSTPAN-DEMIC CHAL-LENGES
1. Cognitive information processing	Young adults & older	Yes	Some	Some
2. Integrative life planning	Young adults & older	Yes	Yes	Yes
3. Constructivist	Young adults & older	Yes	Some	Yes
4. Narrative	Young adults & older	Yes	Yes	Yes
5. Chaos	Young adults & older	Yes	Yes	Yes
6. Kaleidoscope	Middle school children and older	Yes	Yes	Yes

The five key definitions that set the foundation for the information-processing domain and the CASVE cycle are career problems, problem space, career problem-solving, career decision-making, and career development (Sampson et al., 2004). The career problem is the existence of a gap between being decided and undecided about a career. This dissonance can create stress and discomfort. These clients pursue career counseling to assist with problem-solving and decision-making. Problem space is the combination of affective concerns and career-related concerns. For example, it includes a person's concerns about marriage, work, family, finances, and children. Career problem-solving is the process of thinking through options and alternatives to select an option that will resolve the career problem. Career decision-making is the process of making a decision and completing the task of following through with the selection options. Career development is the implementation of career decisions that, combined, creates a career path over a lifetime (Sampson et al., 2020).

As clients and students meet with trained professionals who use the CIP theory, they will adequately process information by working with three domains. Figure 5.1 is a graphic of the domains.

The pyramid model shows three levels of information processing for career counseling. The knowledge level, which is the base of the pyramid, includes two domains, knowledge and occupational knowledge. Knowledge in this context is self-knowledge, which includes interests, abilities, skills, and values. The second part of the base of the pyramid is the occupational domain that focuses on the duties and responsibilities of educational and training for each career.

The second level of the pyramid is the CASVE cycle (Figure 5.2), which provides a system for clients and students to process information to select a career (Sampson et al., 2004). The CASVE cycle has six components.

FIGURE 5.1 Pyramid of information-processing domains.

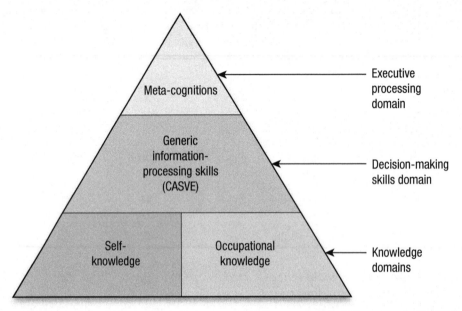

Source: Provided with permission from Peterson, G. W., Sampson, J. P., & Reardon, R. C. (1991). *Career development and services: A cognitive approach.* Brooks/Cole.

FIGURE 5.2 The five stages of the CASVE cycle of information-processing skills used in career decision-making.

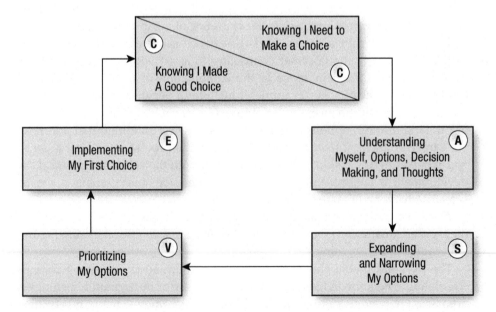

Source: Provided with permission from Peterson, G. W., Sampson, J. P., & Reardon, R. C. (1991). *Career development and services: A cognitive approach.* Brooks/Cole.

Communication: This represents the step in the process when information is received, and with the help of a counselor, the client can identify all of the career-related issues or gaps.

Analysis: The cause of the career-related problem or gap is identified, and the client is able to analyze and develop a mental model of the gap.

Synthesis: During synthesis, the counselor assists the client to identify possible options (synthesis elaboration) and then narrow down the career options with the best fit (synthesis crystallization).

Valuing: In this step, each option is reviewed, evaluated, and prioritized based on the best fit and likelihood of success to overcome the career-related problem or gap.

Execution: At this final stage, unless the client needs to begin the process again, an action plan is developed and implemented with the best fit. This becomes an executable goal for the client.

After the plan is executed, an evaluation is made again with the client at the communication step to ensure the decision has removed the gap or career-related problem (Sampson et al., 2020). In most cases, this model has proven to be successful for college students who can make multiple visits to a career center to meet with a college counselor. Most quality counseling takes place over time; thus, the model tends to be effective as students can take time to meet with a counselor, complete tasks, process thoughts, research options, document plans, and return to the career center for each step.

Although this theory is effective and creates a documented process for clients to follow, it may be cost prohibitive to socially or economically disadvantaged people who may not be able to return for multiple appointments due to cost or time restraints. However, the ability to serve clients in a way that embraces diversity and the cultural contexts of each client, and also presents the opportunity to gradually and deeply process information, has proven to be helpful. It may be possible to use this theory with economically challenged populations through grant -funded community organizations, religious organizations who may provide ongoing workshops with trained counselors, or K–12 schools where high school counselors may provide a series of appointments or workshops for students.

INTEGRATIVE LIFE PLANNING

Integrative life planning allows counselors to holistically approach career counseling beyond work (Hansen, 2002). This theory by Sunny Hanson, PhD, incorporates six themes, including finding work that needs doing, attending to our health, connecting family and work, valuing pluralism and diversity, exploring spirituality and life purpose, and managing transitions and organizational change (Hansen & Suddarth, 2008). The themes of integrative life planning are listed in Table 5.2 with the associated definitions for each.

Dr. Hansen created this theory in the 1990s to help her assist students in thinking beyond just "work" for a holistic approach to career counseling (Hansen & Suddarth, 2008). Dr. Hansen suggests that counselors help clients by developing a big picture, holistic view perspective. As described in her 1997 book, *Weaving Our*

TABLE 5.2 THEMES OF INTEGRATIVE LIFE PLANNING

CRITICAL THEMES	DEFINITION
Finding work that needs doing	Identifying passions, purpose, and concerns to support the community rather than searching for a career fit
Attending to our health	Helping students or clients identify tasks that will support their physical, mental, and emotional well-being
Valuing pluralism and diversity	The ability to understand and interact with individuals who are different from us
Connecting family and work	Identifying and embracing changes in gender roles and reducing stereotyping
Exploring spirituality and life purpose	The experience of interconnecting all of one's being and all of one's life to interrelate and experience wholeness
Managing transitions and organizational change	The ability to observe and embrace changes that have occurred in the workplace

Source: Adapted from Hansen, S., & Suddarth, B. (2008). *Using Integrative Life Planning (ILP) in your professional development.* NCDA. Retrieved August 1, 2022, from https://www.ncda.org/aws/NCDA/asset_manager/get_file/531352?ver=0

Lives Into a Meaningful Whole, she conceptualizes career counseling as the circle that supports the patches in the quilt (Hansen & Suddarth, 2008). The six pieces of the quilt are represented by six themes, and the circle is our life, which encompasses the six quilts or life themes.

Specifically, Dr. Hansen's theory includes an ILP model that guides clients in developing a perspective in which they can understand the cultural context of their lives and then use this information to address career-planning issues (Hansen & Suddarth, 2008). The goals of the ILP model are as follows:

1. Help clients to develop a perspective that is inclusive of multiple variables, including their culture.
2. Approach career counseling from a holistic instead of reductionist perspective that sees life in subparts.
3. Assist clients to prioritize major themes in their lives as they consider a career choice.
4. Encourage self-discovery with tools such as genograms, journaling, and other self-reflection activities.
5. Assist and support clients to embrace change in themselves and in their community from an integrative approach

This theory has great success assisting adults in transitions, college students, students in counselor education preparation programs, and international students across the globe. This theory allows counselors to guide students and clients to be authentic, share experiences in a cultural context, and allow them to develop a big picture perspective, beyond the limitations of former approaches in which clients fit into work without considering other important variables that influence and impact their career choice.

As counselor education programs continue to keep social justice in the forefront and are integrated in curriculums, counselors can keep this theory in mind as they assist a mosaic of people; especially women, marginalized populations, those who have experienced major transitions such as major life adjustments due to the pandemic, people who have experienced social injustice, and marginalized populations in the LBGTQIA+ community. Counselors can be assured as they implement this theory that they will be able to assist a client or student to envision their life in a holistic way and identify and discuss multiple themes of importance that can help navigate them to career success.

This theory allows a client to reflect, learn, share, and evolve during their career -counseling experience as they embrace multiple themes that impact their identity. This is important as one's experience can often be the motivation to change or support a community or could be a catalyst to select a career. An example would be a client who desires to become a social worker because of his childhood experience dealing with domestic violence, or another person may desire to be a police officer to make his community safer. Another example would be people who were incarcerated who would then have the opportunity to "unpack their story" of how a poor past choice led them to a difficult space and how this challenge and recovery can be integrated into the "quilt" of their identity. Similarly, in embracing the concept of the "quilt" with the ILP theory, people who are intentional about their faith and spirituality can be open with career counseling and discuss how their perspective may impede or drive their career choice. This holistic approach encourages building self-efficacy and resilience as people evolve in their career awareness.

In all of these examples, the clients have the opportunity to experience career counseling from a cultural context and integrate their journey, passions, and goals with a counselor. The ILP theory can provide an effective career-counseling experience for clients and students who experienced difficulties or marginalization.

CONSTRUCTIVIST THEORY

Mark Savickas created the **constructivist** theory to help clients create a **narrative** in which work fits into their lives, rather than their lives fitting into their jobs. This approach helps clients view their lives as a story being written and uses the recurring themes in the story to advance their life projects (Savickas, 2015). Counselors help clients listen to their inner voice and construct career decisions in spite of their life themes (Savickas, 2015). Overall, Savickas' theory has its roots in social constructionism and emphasizes that there are possibilities and no realities that predict the future.

When counselors use constructivist theory, they begin with career-style interview questions. With the assistance of the career counselor, clients' use their responses to the questions to develop life goals, and then these goals are connected to a career. Overall, the questions, responses, and the connection to a career are used to guide the client through self-exploration. Once the clients tell their story, the counselor retells the story in a manner that assists the client to consider career decisions. Together, the career counselor and the client discuss what the next chapter of their story might be. Specifically, counselors can help clients tell their story and then use their story to find work that fits into their life and is of value to them (Savickas, 2015).

This theory is most effectively implemented with people who have had a work history that can be discussed. Thus, people who have been dislocated due to changes in the economy, technology updates, and unemployment due to COVID-19 can work with a counselor to create a story for the next chapter in their lives. In sharing, reflecting, and listening, the client develops new perspectives and purpose on how work fits into their lives and adds value.

For marginalized populations, there may be limitations to using this theory due to lack of work opportunities or the ability to consider careers that one may not have been exposed to other than through media. Youth may also experience difficulty in sharing a narrative of work history. However, a career counselor may use volunteer experiences or work duties at home to help young people create a narrative. People who may have experienced work-related trauma may find that this theory is not ideal as they may experience cognitive and emotional distress. These challenges may impede their ability to write the next chapter with a positive perspective on how work fits into their life.

Mark Savickas offers a free workbook for practitioners on www.vocopher.com/CSI/CCI_workbook.pdf called My Career Story. This is a free downloadable form and resource that can be used with clients that take the client through developing their own personal narrative based on a specific process and questions. The workbook can be found at https://docobook.com/my-career-story-workbook-vocopher.html.

NARRATIVE THEORY

The narrative theory in career counseling allows the counselor to help clients engage in their personal story and then develop it so that they can make informed decisions about their career choices (Chope & Consoli, 2007). This approach is empowering for clients as they become the center focus of the counseling process. During the career-counseling process, clients tell their story, including key life events, favorite characters in stories, and role models. The career counselor collects the stories and then develops themes to help create goals and a draft of possibilities for a career (Chope & Consoli, 2007).

In career-counseling cases involving children, heroes and stories can evolve from mentors, role models, and television personalities (Chope & Consoli, 2007). Many children share a narrative for careers that are limited to their communities. In some cases, children may have heroes, mentors, and role models who have great character and integrity; yet many children see and experience another world. Many inner city youth may feel limited to careers that focus on illegal activities, professional sports, musical careers, or careers requiring little or no training or education beyond high school. When children watch their favorite shows, there are often many limitations regarding career. They are either cartoonish or unrealistic. It is important that counselor education curriculums integrate cultural competency experiences for future counselors to understand the context of these communities and work toward broadening opportunities to help students dream. Ideally, these children would be empowered by seeing the behind the scenes work that support their favorite show or video games, such as journalism, game design, or animation. Other opportunities that career counselors may offer are a career day within the school or unique field trips to visit college campuses or trade schools.

Adults who aspire to attend college may also feel limited in the career options available to them beyond the career roles portrayed on television. Unfortunately, many of these TV careers are limited and fail to represent occupations and pathways accurately. For example, when talking with students about the careers they see in crime shows, many students are unaware of the advanced degree in science that are requirements for those crime-solving jobs.

Narrative theory can help clients and students bring to the forefront their dreams and aspirations. Although this theoretical approach may be limited with marginalized groups, such as women, economically disadvantaged clients, and older adults. Yet, it can be effective with the assistance of a career counselor that provides additional resources, field trips, and career days. These new awareness experiences can help clients and students envision and develop a new narrative.

CHAOS THEORY

The **chaos theory** of career development by Bright and Pryor (2011) emphasizes that life is unpredictable, and thus career counselors must take this unpredictability into account with their clients as they plan a career. More specifically, the theory emphasizes that because life does not occur in isolation, but rather as a combination of events, such as family dynamics, world economic conditions, societal changes, and cultural influences, it is impossible to predict a career plan with assurance and necessary to understand that a career selection may be temporary. However, the theory embraces the constants such as personality and acquired skills.

The COVID-19 pandemic is a great example. During the pandemic, we often stated, "We are adapting to a new normal." We lived with being "on hold" with our careers, learned how to work remotely and differently, and, in some cases, learned how to be a schoolteacher as we simultaneously worked our jobs. Many careers were inconsistent, unstable, and unpredictable.

For people who needed to seek career counseling during the pandemic, and even now, with the frequent changes due to postpandemic challenges, the chaos theory can help clients by anticipating changes, creating backup plans, and learning how to maintain personal strength to be resilient. Often in marginalized communities, being resilient, having backup plans, and adapting to constant change is a way of life. As such, a client from a marginalized community may feel a career counselor using chaos theory offers a counseling session that may feel like a more realistic approach to career development. They have experienced "life does happen and will happen," thus the tenet of unpredictable being predictable, as stated in chaos theory, may be more comfortable.

KALEIDOSCOPE THEORY

Mainiero and Sullivan (2006) created the **kaleidoscope theory** in response to changing needs for authenticity, balance, and challenges within a changing internal and external life context. More specifically, the theory suggests that career counseling guides a client through a process of self-understanding, where clients recognize their needs of authenticity, balance, and challenge (Mainiero & Sullivan, 2006).

This model emphasizes that counselors help clients to understand three distinct needs in respect to various junctures in their life and then identify which need is most relevant to their career decision-making. Authenticity is being true to one's values, and in terms of career needs, it is expressed as the focal point in decision-making being the self rather than one's personal community. Balance reflects that people choose careers and find strategies to balance their work life with their personal lives. Challenge is the desire to learn and grow in one's career and find stimulating work (Mouratidou, 2019).

In using the kaleidoscope theory, counselors may use questions such as: "what motivates you in your career," "how do you understand work–life balance," "how do you understand challenges at work," and "what is your dream job" (Mouratidou, 2019, p. 7). Questions that include the phrases "work–life balance," "dream," and "challenges at work" may not be ideal for people who consider dreaming abstract, people for whom work–life balance may not be an option, and people for whom challenges at work may appear to be normal. In our world today, where many people strive to manage their work and maintain work–life balance, dreaming about a career change can pose some limitations. Ideally, the kaleidoscope theory allows clients to consider authenticity, balance, and to challenge the theory may be more difficult for people who have constant change and limitations.

Mouratidou (2019) found that in Greek culture the context creates conditions that influence people's perceptions of their career needs. She also found that there are no universal career needs and that career perceptions are socially constructed and context dependent. In another study, Elley-Brown et al. (2018) used the kaleidoscope theory to understand why women leave the workplace in midcareer. They found that authenticity was an important theme throughout the careers for professional women. Again, the kaleidoscope theory provides the opportunity for career counselors to help clients identify a good career path, but there are limitations, specifically for individuals who may not have developed a concept of work–life balance, embraced an understanding of pursuing stimulating work, or possessed the ability to live authentically by selecting a career that may meet their career needs.

There are additional postmodern theories that a counselor may consider when helping clients experience a holistic and cultural approach in searching for a career. One example is the happenstance learning theory by Mitchell et al. (1999). This theoretical approach emphasizes that chance in one's life can be both positive and negative. For example, during the pandemic, new careers evolved and became available, such as remote working, food delivery services, online retail company ownership, and careers in cryptocurrency. Another theory, nurturing aspirations and potential theory of excellence, is specifically applicable to promote career development for African American boys. This theory, developed by Dr. Marc Grimmett (2006), specifically defines excellence "as a state of awareness of one's potential and performance perseverance at the highest level of one's ability, in all areas necessary to achieve one's dreams, regardless of circumstances" (Grimmett, 2006, p. 95).

Postmodern theories are significant as they provide a **framework** for career counselors to engage clients and students in a cultural context. These theories also allow clients and students to share the stories of their experiences and dreams so that counselors can help them identify viable career options that fit their identity from a holistic perspective. As career counselors, we must be culturally competent as we consider helping clients that are diverse, marginalized, or have had difficult lived experiences, as these directly impact a client's perspectives about work and career choices.

As culture continues to evolve, postmodern theories are ideal approaches to help counselors help clients. Marginalized populations often need to believe that they are heard, and because of these needs, several of the postmodern theories allow the opportunity for clients to experience dynamic counseling sessions that encourage resilience, hope, and a vision for their future with an executable plan. With committed and competent counselors, clients and students can overcome limitations from childhoods that lacked opportunities and resources to envision sustainable career options that fit their needs. In consideration of all counseling professionals, our commitment to support, embrace diversity, and develop identities, as we facilitate change and hope, allows postmodern theories to be valuable in today's world and work environment.

The following activities, questions, and lesson plans using postmodern theories will serve as a great resource for practicing career counselors, graduate counseling students, and career consults.

QUESTIONS ON POSTMODERN THEORY

1. You are teaching a career decision-making workshop for freshmen students at your university as required in a first-year experience class. Your class is filled with decided, undecided, and indecisive students. How will you facilitate your workshop by using the CASVE cycle?

2. When using CASVE, role-play the counseling session after you have completed the first step in the pyramid (knowledge) with a client. What would you include?

3. You are providing counseling to youth in a rural county school in North Carolina. Your team of counselors have committed to using the ILP theory. What are the themes you should consider discussing with these clients?

4. A middle-age African American male has just been released from prison for selling marijuana in the 1990s. Provide context to themes that are important to discuss with this client.

5. When using the constructivist theory for career development, you are assisting nurses who worked diligently through the pandemic. Provide at least three strategies to help them create meaning in their work as you assist them to find a new career path.

6. You are working with a transgender man who lived a life as a Black female as a schoolteacher. Recently, he is considering pursuing a new career in diversity, equity, and inclusion consulting with a firm. By using the

constructivist theory, provide some practical examples of how he can use his knowledge of his past as a woman to find meaning for his future as he is learning to be a man.

7. When considering using a narrative theory for career counseling, what are safeguards to consider when providing an environment for people to share their story if they have experienced trauma?

8. Provide an example by using the narrative theory for career counseling to help a first-generation college student identify his/her/their strengths that have limited support from home due to lack of information.

9. As you use the chaos theory, what tools can you use to help clients anticipate change and help them to always have a mindset to reinvent themselves?

10. The current generation of youth values truth. As a school counselor, outline a discussion about the truth regarding the impact of social media postings and how they may impact career choices in their future.

LESSON PLANS

Insurance and Support for Transgender Youth

You are a part of a family that is seeking resources to support their transgender son. Call your Employee Assistance Program (EAP) resource with your employer or your insurance company to inquire about resources. How does what you have learned impact career choices and employment?

Genogram Activity

Create a work family genogram and discuss how this has impacted your journey to be a counselor and how this activity can be used to support your client.

Timeline Activity

Ex-offenders are often challenged with developing a fresh perspective and hope because of the lack of opportunities. Interview someone you may know that has a criminal record who is willing to disclose it, or interview someone who works with the court system to help understand this perspective. Ask them to respond to career-related perspectives in 5-year increments. What areas of growth did you experience from this activity?

Onetonline.Org Activity

Clients and students develop perspectives about a career by watching television. Watch two or three movies that bring to the forefront emphasis about careers. Create a grid that includes important contrast and comparison information based upon what you saw in the movie and truth/facts that are available in onetonline .org. Explain how you will use this tool with your clients/students.

ETHICAL CORNER

In this section, the authors lead the reader through topical scenarios to surface common ethics questions and dilemmas faced by career professionals. They ask pertinent and personal questions to encourage reader reflection and insight into personal and professional ethics.

Azra Karajic Siwiec, PhD, LPC, is a counselor educator employed by Capella University. She has been working in the counselor education field for over 14 years and has served as a committee member of the Ethics Committee of National Career Development Association (NCDA) since 2015 and served as the chair of the Ethics Committee since 2017.

Sharon K. Anderson, PhD, is professor of counseling and career development at Colorado State University. Sharon has taught the master's level ethics course for counseling students for over 20 years, teaching and mentoring a multitude of students. She has coauthored or coedited four professional ethics books used by practitioners in counseling and coaching.

VIGNETTE

Matt worked at a factory for 12 years and has earned seniority and sizable pay increases along the way. While remaining successful at his job, he transitioned to a female named Sandi. Now Sandi faces many obstacles at the place of employment that she loves. First, the women are uncomfortable with her using women's bathrooms, and the males are aggressive; they don't understand the process, and they refuse to call her Sandi or refer to her with female pronouns. Sandi is struggling and hates going to work and takes many days off. Between hormones, difficult work conditions, and so much change, she is now experiencing depression. Sandi is very close to quitting her job and is wondering what to do about the current situation. She likes what she does in her position and doesn't want to look at leaving her company.

DIGGING INTO ETHICS

Role-play that you are Sandi's counselor. What are the ethical issues of concern? What are the ethical issues of concern as it relates to you and your values set? How do your values align with or not align with Sandi's values set? What ethical virtues do you need to draw upon as you work with Sandi? Why those in particular? When you think about the ethical principles, how do you think about them specifically in this scenario?

How you would communicate with Sandi about your commitment to counseling and address how you see your role in working with her, especially in terms of your vision for improving her career.

Look at the American Counseling Association (ACA) and NCDA Codes of Ethics. How could you use the codes to advocate for greater understanding of Sandi and clients with similar concerns? Imagine you are talking to professionals in your field and use those codes to support your stance.

5.1 PRACTITIONER'S PERSPECTIVE

Amanda Friday, LPC, NCC, PhD is a licensed mental health therapist and career - counseling practitioner. Amanda has worked in higher education at the undergraduate and graduate levels, in elementary schools, and in hospitals. They are a fierce advocate for preparing individuals for their journey in life as well as to, through, and within the workplace.

My vocation and where I found purpose in my work unfolded over some time, and the key milestones that affected my career choices sit in many spaces, including health and wellness—not just the career space.

My career choices shifted dramatically in college. I was a NCAA Division I college volleyball athlete. I had initially desired to be an architect or engineer, but those majors did not match up well with my practice schedule. I took a psychology course my freshmen year on existentialism and was fascinated. I ended up majoring in psychology.

During my first year of college, I had to have heart surgery, which went awry. That experience propelled me toward a time of immense introspection and self-discovery around what I wanted to do in life. I also had a number of concussions during my collegiate volleyball career that affected my mental health and well-being. Coming out of college, I knew I wanted to help people, and I saw a number of my peers, and myself, struggle with mental health issues as well as the question, "What do I do after sport?" I wanted to help others solve that question and support them during times when their mental health was struggling.

I became a college volleyball coach for a short period before realizing that I wanted to help people and athletes more holistically. I stumbled on counseling and was accepted into a PhD program. It was not until I took my first career-counseling course that I really felt like I had found my calling.

During my internship year, luckily, my graduate program had a memorandum of understanding with Georgetown University's career-counseling center. I interned there and discovered that this work is extremely fulfilling and life-giving. It was then that I knew this was the profession for me.

At Georgetown, I work with college students, emerging adults, and minoritized students. The unifying characteristic of these populations is that they are all students trying to discover what comes next after college. My passion for social justice, inclusion, and equity revealed itself over the course of my time as a counselor-in-training and now a licensed professional counselor. As a queer Latiné, I have a passion for helping other minoritized and marginalized folks along their career journey. I work more generally with people trying to answer the questions "Who am I?" "What's out there?" "What's next?" and "How can I get there?"

Not every career center has career counseling, but Georgetown does. What I love about my work as a career counselor is that I get to work holistically with students and counsel them through their career and college journey. I also get the opportunity to teach career courses to undergraduate students where they learn empowering strategies, techniques, and resources to help them tell their career stories and navigate the world of work.

TRAITS OF CAREER COUNSELORS

The traits that make someone a good career counselor are the same traits that make someone a good counselor, such as someone who is an engaged listener and educator, creates a warm and growth-oriented environment, and is curious, thoughtful, and holistic. I also believe that to do this work well, counselors must be social justice advocates.

Whether it's in my work or what I do outside of work, it is the stories that drive me. I love helping others in crafting, discovering, knowing, telling, and restorying their story. I am also a learner by nature, and I learn something new with every client or student I meet with. It also doesn't hurt that I work in the best work environment I have known in my life. It's the people I work with and get to meet that keep me working here.

PROFESSIONAL ETHICS

In our career-counseling work at the center, we review our informed consent form with every student or client. We articulate the expectations and ethical standards we work by and are transparent about those standards. We also offer both individual and group supervision for our counselors to ensure any dilemmas or questions about ethics and boundaries are reviewed and discussed.

POSTMODERN THEORIES AND FRAMEWORKS

I draw on multiple postmodern theories in my work and would say I have an integrative approach. A core theory that we teach here at Georgetown's career center and to our counseling interns is CIP. Much of our training focuses on using this theory. Other postmodern theories I like to weave in and pull from include chaos theory, career construction theory, life design, intersectionality, critical theory, grief and loss, transition theory, and narrative theory. I also use these theories and frameworks regularly in my work as a career counselor:

- Work adjustment theory
- Life span, life space
- Personality theory of career choice
- Circumscription, compromise, and self-creation
- Vocational personality and work environment: John Holland's theory
- Social learning theory
- Social cognitive career theory
- CIP approach
- Career constructivist theory
- Integrative life planning

ASSESSMENTS, RESOURCES, AND INTERVENTIONS

As a career counselor, I draw on a few interventions regularly, including values card sorts, wandering maps, identity trees, decision space, peak experiences, and an intervention around superheroes and narratives that I designed. Assessments that I use include the Strong Interest Inventory and the Myers Briggs Type Indicator. We have a number of resources that we offer students that are available publicly on our website (https://careercenter.georgetown.edu/), including ResumeWorded, Interstride, Handshake, and Big Interview. We also offer a number of specific resources related to identity groups.

I use the wandering map quite a bit and have adapted that exercise to have a part two. Once a client has written down all the significant things, people, places, and events in their life, they then map those items onto a timeline. This added step helps clients see consistent and emerging themes between experiences while also providing them with temporal structure that is often a useful framework for telling their story.

VIGNETTE

A first-year college student came into our career-counseling center because she decided to take a leave of absence (LOA). (We offer services to students on LOA.) This student is an Asian American woman who was majoring in human sciences/pre-med but did not perform well her first semester. For this reason, she is considering transferring into an English major. She is the eldest of three and the first in her family to go to college. She feels immense pressure to succeed and "be perfect."

In our initial sessions, we used the CIP activity to help her explore and externalize the thoughts and influences affecting her decision, and this has been very helpful to her. She discovered that both the pre-med and English majors were suggestions made to her by other people, such as parents and mentors. She experiences grief and loss around transferring from pre-med and particularly loss around the person she "thought she was but didn't live up to." She is rediscovering answers to two key questions CIP notes: "who am I?" and "what's out there?" She feels she has wasted all of her prior experience and has no skills now.

A few potential next steps are to teach her about prototyping (life design) and how a career is about iterating instead of knowing at the get-go. She could then draw a wandering map to identify the transferable skills and experiences she has to build confidence and begin to restory her narrative. A values card sort may help her identify core foundational beliefs that can help her in making decisions as well as provide her with some direction in navigating her career journey.

5.2 PRACTITIONER'S PERSPECTIVE

Jonathan Adams has a master of arts in counseling from Wake Forest University and is pursuing a doctorate in counselor education and supervision at the College of William and Mary. He currently works at as a career counselor at Duke University in Durham, North Carolina.

From a young age I was very involved in athletics and enjoyed attending live sporting events, and this played a key role in identifying career possibilities for me. When it came time to choose my undergraduate major, broadcast journalism stood out due to my love of storytelling and following live sporting events. However, during a sports broadcasting internship at a local radio station, I distinctly remember taking stats for our broadcast and having an overwhelming feeling that I wanted to be anywhere else. It took me some time afterward to make sense of what happened and what it meant for my next steps.

As I continued to reflect on my past experiences, I realized that I had always gravitated to working with people, whether it was as a camp counselor, youth sports coach, or fitness instructor. As a result, I changed my major to psychology and eventually went on to a master's degree in mental health counseling.

A pivotal moment for me during the master's program was the opportunity to assist with an undergraduate career planning course. I noticed that I was highly energized, focused, and engaged when meeting with students to discuss meaning and purpose in their lives. Career counseling was not something I had considered or really been exposed to as a career possibility prior to that point. In my first position after graduate school as a community mental health counselor, I discovered early on that I need a career path that focused less on crisis management and more on coaching clients around wellness, meaning, and purpose.

During my 8 years as a career counselor, I have primarily worked with undergraduate students and large state institutions. As a generalist, I frequently worked with students across departments and majors as part of a brief and primarily short-term model. What stands out to me is the pressure that students face to make decisions about their majors and career paths. I've spoken to students who are overwhelmed by the prospect of making these decisions beginning as early as the summer before their first year of college. The impact of social comparison is also significant for college students and can contribute to a feeling of being behind their peers in regard to career milestones, even though students in different disciplines progress into recruitment for internships and other opportunities at different rates. Frequently I hear that students feel behind, overwhelmed, and often uncertain regarding next steps in their career decision-making journey.

As a college career counselor, I get to provide support to students in managing their stress and anxiety, and I enjoy incorporating breathing exercises and mindfulness activities into the work I do with students. I find that there is a great opportunity to teach these types of skills for enhanced self-reflection and stress management, along with the opportunity to normalize the process and the student experience.

VIGNETTE

I frequently draw on the CIP approach in my work with students. I began working with a student named Jeremiah during his second year of undergraduate studies. In going through the CASVE cycle of career problem-solving and decision-making, we talked together about what Jeremiah was thinking and feeling about his life and career. Jeremiah described a sense of commitment anxiety and feeling overwhelmed by the pressure to make the right choice, and as a result, he had been putting off taking next steps, like meeting with a career coach. Jeremiah completed the Decision Space Worksheet (DSW) to explore thoughts, feelings, people, and internal/external pressures associated with career decision-making process, and through this activity, he recognized the support and validation from family members when discussing changing his major from business to media production. It was almost as if the act of reflecting gave him permission to commit to and embrace his strengths and interests, specifically related to creating animated content.

A next step in our meetings was moving from the analysis component of the CASVE cycle toward execution, since there was not a need to focus further on narrowing or expanding options Jeremiah was able to prioritize what was most important in a career path through our conversations stemming from using the DSW: identifying options for continuing to build skills and experience in the media production and animation field. We worked together to build a list of tools Jeremiah could use to find out about internship opportunities and potential contacts to learn more about those options.

Another breakthrough for Jeremiah was in identifying a fellowship opportunity through the university that eventually led to an internship and full-time position in Hollywood. Jeremiah continued to build confidence through implementing choice and gaining experience in the field. Jeremiah's self-talk and affect continued to change at the same time, from commitment anxiety about making a decision to reflecting on the enjoyment he derived from the animation work and career.

Student Voices

In Student Voices, students offer a unique viewpoint as they begin in the career-counseling field. Here, students share their thoughts and reflections about the career-counseling profession and offer personal takeaways.

BRITTANY COLES

I attended Argosy University and The Chicago School of Professional Psychology as a MA student in the Clinical Mental Health Counseling Program. While, studying in the masters' program, I became very interested in children's and adolescent's psyche, which resulted in me completing an internship at Laurel Heights Residential Program.

While in my graduate program at Argosy University, I would live and die by humanistic counseling theory. Let me explain. In my younger years, I went through some very traumatic events that would shape my life and how I process and understand any decision I've made or will make. Growing up, I wholeheartedly believed that I pulled myself up from dark places and carried myself through everything.

Whenever friends would complain or vent to me about anything, I'd foolishly think they knew what needed to be done and how. From a humanistic perspective, individuals have all the resources, within themselves, to live healthy functioning lives; if they are not, they themselves are restricting themselves from the resources needed to solve their problems (McAdams, 2022). Now, I'm more of a systemic thinker. Don't get me wrong, I haven't abandoned my origins of humanistic thinking, I've just learned and evolved more within my thought process. My time working as a community therapist helped change my thought process because not everyone is given the same opportunity; not everyone thinks the same; nor does everyone have the same drive or focus.

At my current job, I think I started out with a systemic approach. I believed a lot of the emotions and behaviors my clients were/are displaying was a direct

(continued)

result of their environment and the lack of support and resources they were/are offered (McAdams, 2022). I apply theories to my work by first admitting there's some difficulty and accepting any challenges that may arise. Also, I check myself for any preconceived notions. Now, I am human, so I do fall short sometimes and have judgmental thoughts, but I hold myself accountable and reach out to my supervisor for additional education, support, and feedback on how to proceed. Most importantly, I'm always learning. I try not to limit myself because I don't want to limit my clients.

SHAMIKIA MCGHEE

I am a graduate of Alabama State University where I received a bachelor's in psychology and master's in clinical mental health counseling. I am also an Army veteran serving in the Alabama National Guard.

The theory that resonates with me, and one that I have used for most of my counseling career is cognitive behavioral theory. I believe that our thoughts become our actions (behaviors) that can influence rational or irrational decisions. One of the reasons that I enjoy using cognitive behavior theory is to get the client to recognize and identify faulty thinking that often impacts relationships, personal behaviors, and irrational decisions. Also, cognitive behavioral theory allows me as the therapist to collaboratively work with the client to understand the problem(s) in order to develop an effective treatment plan. Another theory that I use is person-centered, to help the clients focus on themselves rather than the problem. I like to use this theory as a clinician to help foster a positive environment for the client to grow and make rational independent decisions.

Currently working as a clinical mental health case manager with clients with severe mental illnesses such as schizophrenia, bipolar, and depression. I use cognitive behavior therapy to help my clients understand irrational decision-making when experiencing symptoms. In the past, I have also used cognitive behavior theory when working as a behavior health counselor working with female offenders. Cognitive behavior therapy was highly effective in this population because it allowed the offender to reflect on irrational decisions/behaviors that led up to their incarceration. In my experience, most female offenders who served long sentences were least likely to reoffend. Also, those offenders took advantage of individual and group counseling sessions to help develop healthy coping skills and strategies to reintegrate into society. There is not any one theory that will work for every client, as you will learn as you grow in your career as a clinician.

Counselors can integrate clinical skills and approaches with career development frameworks. While cognitive behavioral theory (CBT) provides a model to bring awareness to negative behavior patterns and distorted thinking, CIP provides a framework to improve decision-making and career problem-solving. A career counselor might employ CBT as they work with a client through the career decision-making process following the CIP model. For example, a career counselor supporting a client who has lacks a realistic self-appraisal would have difficulty within the self-knowledge domain in CIP. A CBT approach may be used to assist a client in creating knowledge of their skills, interests, values, and goals. Similarly, in the executive processing domain, a client may lack self-awareness or have negative self-talk, that may benefit from CBT interventions.

Tip: Your Theoretical Orientation

Finding your theoretical orientation can be a process and take time as well as patience. One strategy to consider as you explore various approaches, theories, and techniques is to reflect upon the client's or student's presenting issue(s) and identify related constructs that would support growth and healing, particularly during the practicum and internship when you have a strong supervisory relationship. One recommendation would be to discuss with your supervisor opportunities for shadowing and observing a variety of counselors within the setting. As you observe, be sure to take note of the diversity of approaches.

COUNSELING SKILLS CONNECTION

All counseling programs teach, review, and practice theories and techniques as a pivotal component for students in training. There is a multitude of counseling theories to explore and implement in practice (Corey, 2013). Counseling theories and models consist of tenets that counselors can use as they seek to support their clients and work through presenting issue(s) together with their individual client, community, and/or population of interest. Theories can be grouped into several types including, but not limited to psychoanalytic, existential, narrative, cognitive behavioral, and much more. (For a list of 12 popular counseling methods, visit https://positivepsychology.com/popular-counseling-approaches/)

Instructors teaching theories and techniques courses can draw parallels between the overall counseling theories compared to career-counseling theories. For example, when using the narrative approach, counselors encourage and invite clients and students to consider stories identifying them as the author. This provides students and clients with the agency to tell and craft their story as the expert of their personal experience. Similarly, using a career constructivist or career narrative approach, career counselors work through the process of telling their story and essentially constructing and or reconstructing their story in a way that promotes growth and wellness.

MINDFUL MOMENT

Many of us struggle to make time for our own wellness. As your roles and responsibilities in your life grow, whether in number or impact, it becomes even more important that we find simple, brief routines that can fit into those small windows of time we choose to devote to ourselves. Try these brief strategies for intentionally incorporating mindfulness into your daily routine:

■ Set aside time in your day to intentionally focus on yourself.

■ Choose an exercise to guide your mindfulness. Examples might include a body scan, mindful breathing, or mindful stretching.

■ Observe your environment. Indoors or out, focus on what is happening around you. Notice small details and bring your attention to each of your five senses.

- Practice gratitude by making list of things you are grateful for. Pause and reflect on each item you've added to your gratitude list. Notice how they made you feel.
- Eat mindfully. Focus on the present moment while you're eating. Notice textures, tastes, and smells. Bring your attention to how quickly or slowly you chew (Nortie, 2020).

TECH TOOLS

The NCDA's web magazine, Career Convergence, publishes a free monthly column focused on technology applications. The Tech Tips section provides brief reviews of technology platforms, apps, and other resources that may be useful for career counselors or coaches. Like counselors in other specialty areas, career counselors' roles often require maintaining websites, managing social media accounts, creating resources for client use, marketing, and more. This publication does a great job of highlighting tools useful across the broad scope of work. Dirk Matthews (2022, para. 1) recently highlighted the Creative Commons:

"When creating graphics, presentations, or logos for a professional brand, career practitioners often turn to the internet to find resources. Creative Commons provides information about fair use of media found online including how and when to attribute the owner and what can and cannot be modified. The site provides links for finding resources and ways to avoid copyright infringement."

REFLECTION ACTIVITY

Career theories are, in part, born out of reflection. If you were to create your own career theory, what tenets would you cover? How would your values show up in the way you create the theory? What would you name your theory? How would you empirically test, validate, and study your theory? What type of presenting issues would your theory address?

END-OF-CHAPTER RESOURCES

SUMMARY

Postmodern theories are identified and explored throughout the chapter. Theories offer a framework and "handles" for counselors to use as they seek to support clients and students throughout their life span. Theories and frameworks such as career construction, narrative, chaos, ILP, and kaleidoscope model are all options for counselors and coaches to use as they seek to assist clients in making meaning of their lives, current context, and future planning.

REFERENCES

Bray, B. (2017, October 14). *Behind the book: Postmodern career counseling: A handbook of culture, context and cases.* Counseling.Org. https://ct.counseling.org/2017/08/behind-book-postmodern-career-counseling-handbook-culture-context-cases/

Bright, J., & Pryor, R. (2011). *Chaos theory of careers.* https://marcr.net/marcr-for-career-professionals/career-theory/career-theories-and-theorists/chaos-theory-of-careers-pryor-and-bright/

Busacca, L. A., & Rehfuss, M. C. (Eds.). (2016). *Postmodern career counseling: A handbook of culture, context, and cases.* American Counseling Association.

Chope, R., & Consoli, A. (2007). A narrative approach to multicultural career counseling. American Counseling Association. https://www.counseling.org/resources/library/vistas/2007-V-online-MSWord-files/Chope.pdf

Corey, G. (2013). *Theory and practice of counseling and psychotherapy.* Cengage Learning.

Elley-Brown, M., Pringle, J., & Harris, C. (2018). Women opting in? New perspectives on the Kaleidoscope Career Model. *Australian Journal of Career Development, 27*(3), 172–180. https://doi.org/10.1177/1038416217705703

Grimmett, M. (2006). *Nurturing aspirations and potential theory of excellence: Career development of African American Boys.* American Counseling Association. https://www.counseling.org/knowledge-center/vistas/by-subject2/vistas-multicultural-issues/docs/default-source/vistas/nurturing-aspirations-and-potential-theory-of-excellence-career-development-of-african-american-boys

Hansen, L. S. (2002). Integrative life planning (ILP): A holistic theory for career counseling with adults. In S. G. Niles (Ed.), *Adult career development: Concepts, issues and practices* (pp. 57–75). National Career Development Association.

Hansen, S. S., & Suddarth, B. H. (2008). *Using Integrative life planning (ILP) in your professional development.* NCDA. https://www.ncda.org/aws/NCDA/asset_manager/get_file/531352?ver=0

Mainiero, L. A., & Sullivan, S. E. (2006). *The opt-out revolt: How people are creating kaleidoscope careers outside of companies.* Davies Black.

Matthews, D. (2022, June 1). Improving digital literacy with creative commons. NCDA. https://www.ncda.org/aws/NCDA/pt/sd/news_article/441898/_self/CC_layout_details/false

McAdams, C. (2022). *Counseling theories and approaches.* William and Mary School of Education. https://counseling.education.wm.edu/blog/counseling-theories-and-approaches

Mitchell, K., Levin, A., & Kromboltz, J. (1999). Planned happenstance: Constructing unexpected career opportunities. *Practice and Theory, 77*, 115–124. https://canvas .wisc.edu/files/42959/download?download_frd=1&verifier=caP62PzAqk5QStL Mj6KrA2onMByNOjgvvItndNeU

Mouratidou, M. (2019). Reconstructing the kaleidoscope career model to complex contexts. In *Eastern academy of management conference 2019*, 8–11th May 2019, Wilmington, Delaware (Unpublished).

Nortie, A. (2020, June 5) How to practice mindfulness: 11 practical steps and tips. Positive Psychology. https://positivepsychology.com/how-to-practice -mindfulness/

Sampson, J. (2017). A cognitive information processing theory for career choices: Challenges and opportunities for integrating theory, research, and practice. In J. Sampson, Jr., E. Bullock-Yowell, V. Dozier, D. Osburn, & J. Lenz (Eds.), *A cognitive information processing theory for career choices: Challenges and opportunities for integrating theory, research, and practice* (1st ed., Vol. 1, pp. 62–73). Florida State University.

Sampson J. P. Jr, Osborn D., Bullock-Yowell E., Lenz J. G., Peterson G., Reardon R. C., & Dozier V. C. (2020). *An introduction to CIP theory, research, and practice.* Florida State University, Center for the Study of Technology in Counseling and Career Development. http://purl.flvc.org/fsu/fd/FSU_libsubv1_scholarship _submission_1593091156_c171f50a

Sampson J. P. Jr, Reardon R. C., Peterson G. W., & Lenz J. G. (2004). *Career counseling and services: A cognitive information processing approach.* Brooks/Cole.

Savickas, M. L. (2015). Career counseling paradigms: Guiding, developing, and designing. In P. J. Hartung, M. L. Savickas, & W. B. Walsh (Eds.), *APA handbook of career intervention, Vol. 1. Foundations* (pp. 129–143). American Psychological Association. https://doi.org/10.1037/14438-008

CHAPTER 6

THINKING TO DOING: AN EXPLORATION OF YOUR OWN CAREER STORY

Katie Peterssen and Angie C. Smith

LEARNING OBJECTIVES

By the end of this chapter, you will be able to:

- Define your career interests, strengths, and values.
- Explore and identify job titles that align with your interests.
- Construct a plan to move forward toward your career goal.
- Practice articulating your values and describing experiences relevant to your career goal.

WARM-UP EXERCISE

When you were a child, who were your heroes? It might be a storybook character, a family member, a celebrity, and so on. Recall your pretend play as a child. Who did you emulate? If you played dress-up, what toys or attire did you choose? Did you use tools, tiaras, trucks? What adjectives would you use to describe these characters or heroes? Now, think about who you are today. Which of those adjectives would you use to describe your aspirations? What potential **careers** or occupations may have been budding in early stages of your development?

INTRODUCTION

In this chapter, you will curate your personal journey; we have designed it to be used as a workbook. In the following pages, you will reflect on who you are and what your values are, as well as your personality, skills, strengths, and aspirations. You will write a resume and cover letter and create a LinkedIn profile. Self-awareness is foundational for career development and counselor training, and it is very personal—it is also how you show up to your clients. Awareness of how our own life experience, background, family constellation, gender, racial identities, abilities, etc. is critical to counseling ethically and effectively.

WHO AM I? IDENTIFYING MY VALUES, INTERESTS, STRENGTHS, AND SKILLS

Self-awareness is a critical foundation for career development and decision-making. A hallmark within the counseling profession is to "know thyself." Starting with who we are and how we show up in spaces in the world seems like a natural progression as we begin to delve into career exploration. Key concepts to reflect on regarding self-awareness include **values, interests, strengths**, and **skills**.

Career Values

Beginning the career development process with identifying and prioritizing career and work values sets the standard by which we can make authentic, satisfying decisions. By honing in on our core values, we are defining what we need and want most in and from our work. There are a wide variety of values to consider, such as financial reward, work–life balance, recognition, independence, decision-making, creativity, stability, and more. Values themselves are neutral; no one value is better or worse than another. There are many cultural, social, and gender role messages that may affect how you feel about prioritizing a particular value. For example, American sociocultural norms may cause a woman to question or even feel some shame when prioritizing power and influence over family. Processing these choices with a client and discussing how these values integrate with their other life roles (i.e., friend, partner, parent, caretaker, etc.) enables a client to consider their values in the context of their multiple identities and roles. When working with clients through a career values activity, keep in mind that culture may have a significant impact on values for both you and your client. Reflect on your own bias and check-in with your clients to ensure that you are having conversations about similarities and differences in values within the therapeutic alliance.

ACTIVITY 1: VALUES CARD SORT

It's your turn. Review the following list of values. Sort the values in order of priority, from those you **always need** to those you **never need**. Re-review those you have identified as "always need" and select your top five values. Write these down. These values will be used to guide your exploration and decision-making (Exhibit 6.1).

ACTIVITY 2: APPLY YOUR VALUES

Once you've identified the career values that are most important to you, use them as a tool to inform your decisions. Use this as a resource to jumpstart your career investigation and evaluate opportunities.

List your top five career values in order of importance.

1.

2.

3.

4.

5.

EXHIBIT 6.1 VALUES CARD SORT

SELF-ESTEEM	GENUINENESS	COMMITMENT
To feel good about myself	To act in a manner that is true to who I am	To make enduring, meaningful commitments
ACHIEVEMENT	ACCURACY	COOPERATION
To have important accomplishments	To be accurate in my opinions and beliefs	To work collaboratively with others
HELPFULNESS	MASTERY	KNOWLEDGE
To be helpful to others	To be competent in my everyday activities	To learn and contribute valuable knowledge
SAFETY	POPULARITY	FAMILY
To be safe and secure	To be well-liked by many people	To have a happy, loving family
CONTRIBUTION	INDUSTRY	GENEROSITY
To make a lasting contribution in the world	To work hard and well at my life tasks	To give what I have to others
COMPASSION	CHALLENGE	FUN
To feel and act on concern for others	To take on difficult tasks and problems	To play and have fun
AUTONOMY	ORDER	PASSION
To be self-determined and independent	To have a life that is well-ordered and organized	To have deep feelings about ideas, activities, or people
RESPONSIBILITY	RATIONALITY	SELF-KNOWLEDGE
To make and carry out responsible decisions	To be guided by reason and logic	To have a deep and honest understanding of myself
SELF-CONTROL	SOLITUDE	REALISM
To be disciplined in my own actions	To have time and space where I can be apart from others	To see and act realistically and practically
FRIENDSHIP	ADVENTURE	POWER
To have close, supportive friends	To have new and exciting experiences	To have control over others

RESEARCH, ASK, OBSERVE ACTIVITY

Brainstorm and research values-based questions that will give you the information and insights needed to evaluate career options and make choices. Create questions for each of your values within three categories: those that will guide your digital information gathering (Research), those that will frame your conversations with professionals in the field (Ask), and those that will encourage critical thinking and insight gathering (Observe).

These prompts will engender deeper insights to guide your career planning (Exhibits 6.2–6.4).

EXHIBIT 6.2 RESEARCH ACTIVITY

RESEARCH	
	EXAMPLES
Research organizations via readily available digital sources. Review company websites, social media channels, LinkedIn, Glassdoor, job postings, databases, etc. and assess for values fit. Be mindful when evaluating company reviews; look for trends or themes but recognize that one poor review does not mean an opportunity or an employer is not a good fit. Include questions that: • Rely on information available across digital platforms • Challenge you to assess the job description, company website, or social channels • Encourage you to build inferences from trends in qualitative or quantitative data	*(Advancement)* Review the LinkedIn profiles of people at the company. How many people do you see who have had multiple roles or progressively more senior roles within the organization? Do you get a sense that employees had to leave to advance?
	(Challenging Problems) Review the job description carefully. Do you see mention of key skills such as analyze, devise solutions, evaluate results, solve problems?
	(Diversity) Visit Glassdoor and the company's social media pages. How inclusive is their communication? Is it consistent or does it just occur at certain times of the year?
	(Work-Life Balance) Review the benefits that the organization offers. Do they offer strong maternity and paternity leave benefits? Are flexible schedules and remote work written in as explicit benefits of employment? How does the PTO benefit fit with your needs? *(Even if you aren't planning to have children, this is an indicator of how the company values your other life roles.)*
	(Recognition) Visit the social media pages for the organization and its leaders. Are there regular "kudos," "thank yous," or other public recognition of employees?

EXHIBIT 6.3 ASK ACTIVITY

ASK	
Prepare questions to ask during discussions with professionals in your area(s) of interest. Build advocates for your search process while collecting the insights you need to make career choices. Ask questions during informational meetings, employer events, or **interviews.** Include questions that: • Are open-ended and positively framed. • Are NOT "spicy" or overly personal topics (Stay away from politics, religion, etc.) • Invite professionals to share their experience or expertise Before you ask a question, consider the following: • Is this the RIGHT PERSON to ask? • Is this the RIGHT METHOD to ask (e.g., email, phone, in-person)? • Is this the RIGHT TIME to ask?	*EXAMPLES* *(Advancement)* Who have been some of the most successful people you've managed and where have their paths led? *(Challenging Problems)* What is a project that you've worked on in the last two years that you're particularly proud of? *(Hint: the response should indicate the level of complexity of the project.)* *(Change & Variety)* What have been your favorite changes in your role over the past few years? *(Work-Life Balance)* What are some of your favorite things to do outside of work? *(Hint: you're looking to see if there is time for your other life roles and interests.)* *(Security)* What are some of your primary goals for the next five years? How do you see this role contributing to those strategic goals?

EXHIBIT 6.4 OBSERVE ACTIVITY

OBSERVE	
During informational meetings, interviews, employer events, etc., we can gather important insight to inform our career decision-making. Our observations can help us to infer priorities for a particular role or organization. Include questions that: • Rely on your senses, particularly what you are hearing or seeing • Invite you to pay attention to communication patterns and interpersonal skills or behaviors • Observe what is, and isn't, being said AND who is, and isn't, saying it • Assess the types and focus of the questions you're being asked by an employer	*EXAMPLES* *(Work-Life Balance)* Are you receiving communications from people within the organization outside of "normal business hours"? *(Stability)* Do the interviewers ask you multiple questions about your flexibility or adaptability? *(Honesty & Integrity)* Are employees/managers willing and able to acknowledge missteps, failures, or areas of weakness? *(Challenging Problems)* Are you being asked about your ability to be resourceful, trouble-shoot, or problem-solve? *(Fun & Humor)* How well do team members seem to know one another? *(Relationships are a foundation for humor.)*

CREATE EVALUATION CRITERIA

For each of your top career values, make a list of questions to research, observe, and ask during your search process. Your questions should help you to assess how a pathway, role, or company of interest aligns with your values (Exhibit 6.5).

EVALUATE YOUR FIT

Use these questions to guide your employer research, focus your discussions with people in your fields of interest, and drive your critical analysis of what you have learned or experienced. This activity can help you structure your thinking and provides a framework to test how your core work values align with a particular career path or organization.

Careers are rarely linear. More often, a career is an iterative process, and we design our path as we grow, learn, and experience life changes. There is no one "best" career path—each of us has many optimal outcomes. Test multiple career options as you attend employer presentations, **networking** events, informational meetings, and counseling or coaching sessions.

REFLECTION

How well does this opportunity align with your core work values? Do you have the resources you need to succeed in this path? If not, can you secure them? Based on what you have learned, how much do you like this path? How confident are you that you can succeed in this path? What more do you need to learn to feel confident in making your decision?

Interests

In infancy we start to form preferences, we recognize our parents' or caretakers' voices, and we gravitate toward certain toys or activities. Interests continue to

EXHIBIT 6.5 RESEARCH, ASK, OBSERVE QUESTIONS TO GUIDE YOUR JOB SEARCH

CAREER VALUES	RESEARCH Information that you can read	ASK Questions for discussion	OBSERVE Insights you can gather
1.			
2.			
3.			
4.			
5.			

develop through adolescence as we explore school subjects, extracurricular activities, and hobbies. John L. Holland defined interests across six different domains: realistic, investigative, artistic, social, enterprising, and conventional (Holland, 1973). Identifying our interests is another facet of discovering who we are in our personal and professional lives. For some, interests develop into monetary value, a sustainable income, or even an occupation. For others, interests remain hobbies or even a safe haven to escape the pressures of life. Let's investigate your interests and determine if and how your interests may align (or not) with your professional goals.

ACTIVITY: IDENTIFY YOUR INTERESTS

Step 1: Complete the O*Net Interest Profiler at www.mynextmove.org/explore/ip. After completing the profiler, reflect on the following prompts:

1. What two or three domains of interest rose to the top for you? Did any of the themes surprise you?
2. Are these interests you would like to view as part of your total wellness, or would you like to explore these interests further as part of your career aspirations (current or future)?

Step 2: Brainstorming
   Use the following question prompts to explore your interests. Write down notes or draw pictures or other representations of your reflections.

1. If you had a free day, and you could do whatever you want, what would you do?
2. Imagine you are in a bookstore, or perhaps you are searching through podcasts; what topics do you gravitate toward?
3. What types of things do your friends and family seek your input on?
4. What is a problem or challenge in the world that you'd love to fix?
5. What three things did you truly enjoy doing this week?
6. Which classes have been your favorites and why?
7. Who do you admire or look up to? What qualities motivate or inspire you?
8. What excites you? What could you talk about for hours?

Sometimes it's easier to determine what you don't enjoy than what you do. Reflect on these questions, and use the information to know what you may want to avoid in the future.

1. What subjects or topics do you like least or avoid most?
2. In what activities do you disengage in or dislike the most?
3. What hobbies would deflate you?

APPLY YOUR INTERESTS

Review careers that fit your interests and preparation level via the O*Net Interest Profiler that you completed. Click on occupations that interest you and learn more about the tasks, skills, knowledge, and activities of each career.

REFLECTION

How do you envision your interests being part of your life? Which interests do you want to prioritize for your career, if any? How do your interests align with your values?

Strengths and Skills

We often discount or undervalue our own strengths and skills. A skill is the "learned power of doing something competently: a developed aptitude or ability" (Merriam-Webster, n.d.). Unlike skills, strengths grow out of innate talent. Gallup defines a strength as "the ability to consistently provide near-perfect performance in a specific activity. The key to building a strength is to identify your dominant talents, then complement them by acquiring knowledge and skills pertinent to the activity" (Gallup, n.d., para. 1). Your unique value to an employer is the combination of skills and strengths that you bring. For an internship or job search, you will need to clearly articulate your skills and strengths in the context of the employer's needs and the value that you will add to the organization and its staff and clients.

ACTIVITY 1: DEFINE YOUR SKILLS

Create a list of your skills including soft skills, such as communication, leadership, collaboration, as well as hard or technical skills, such as software, languages, design, and analysis. Indeed.com provides a list of skills to help you brainstorm: 120 Skills to Include on Your Next Resume (Indeed Editorial Team, 2021; Exhibit 6.6).

EXHIBIT 6.6 SKILL IDENTIFICATION ACTIVITY

SKILL TYPE	MY SKILLS
Communication Skills (e.g., written communication, editing, teaching)	
Interpersonal Skills (e.g., patience, positivity, networking, coaching)	
Critical Thinking Skills (e.g., problem-solving, assessing, trouble-shooting)	
Leadership Skills (e.g., mentoring, managing, crisis management)	
Technical Skills (e.g., PowerPoint, Excel, coding, R, Tableau)	
Language Skills (e.g., translating, speaking, writing, proofreading)	
Design Skills (e.g., graphic design, user experience development, web design, video editing)	
Analytical Skills (e.g., researching, organizing, statistical analysis, surveying)	

Source: Adapted from Indeed Editorial Team. (2021, June 8). *120 essential skills to list on a resume.* Indeed.com. Updated September 1, 2022. https://www.indeed.com/career-advice/career-development/skills-list

REFLECTION

How do the skills in which you are most talented align with your career interests? Do you have skills in which you are also talented but have no interest in? How did you develop the skills that you have now? What skills do you feel motivated to develop? What gaps do you notice in your skill set, and how do you plan to address those gaps (e.g., through training, education, certifications)? Who or what can you use to support your skill development?

ACTIVITY 2: DEFINE YOUR STRENGTHS

We are often quite adept at quickly identifying strengths and talents in others, though we struggle to articulate our own gifts. As we identify our own strengths, it is important for us to model the value of amplifying our strengths in our work. Make a list of your top five strengths. You might use Gallup's CliftonStrengths, VIA Character Strengths, or other assessment tools to shine a light on your unique talents. The following reflection questions may also be used to identify your strengths:

- Think about an activity you did that, before you were finished, you thought, "when can I do that again?" What were you doing?
- For what do others often seek you out? Reflect on compliments or kudos that you've received.
- When do you frequently outpace others? What comes so naturally to you that you just know the steps to be taken?
- When are you most motivated, engaged, and energized? What are you doing?

PERSONAL BRAND ACTIVITY: SEEING YOUR STRENGTHS THROUGH OTHERS' EYES

If you are struggling to identify your strengths, we encourage you to gather feedback from others. Conduct a brief survey among your trusted friends, family, peers, colleagues, and others who know you well. Use a digital survey tool such as Google Forms, Survey Monkey, or Qualtrics to ask your connections to choose three words to describe you. Collect responses from at least 12 people. Your strengths are likely reflected in this crowd-sourced feedback. Take the feedback you gather and create a word cloud, displaying repeating responses larger and bolder than single responses. See Figure 6.1 for an example of a strengths word cloud.

- What themes do you see across the responses? What strengths are appearing?
- How do these words connect with how you view yourself?
- Is there something missing in the responses that you feel strongly about changing? How might you go about creating that change?

WHERE AM I GOING? DEVELOPING A VISION FOR MY FUTURE

Perhaps the most frequent type of question career counselors are asked is "what is the best career for me?" While some people early on in life have visions for their future, most discover opportunities and career paths organically, by happenstance.

FIGURE 6.1 Strengths word cloud.

Flexible
Initiator Bright
Inspiring Goal-setter
Leader Listener
Trustworthy Helpful
Resourceful
Passionate Responsible Empathetic
Determined Motivated
Writer Delegator Curious
Thinker Organized Compassionate
Thoughtful Skilled
Communicator Fast-learner
Open-minded Problem-solver
Creative

There are a multitude of ways to apply your skills and strengths to careers; for example, if you are skilled in science and enjoy solving problems, you might enjoy engineering, medicine, clinical research, or software development. What careers and pathways are you considering?

Activity: Identifying Job Titles of Interest

Explore possible career pathways by reviewing possible job titles. Make a list of job titles that you want to target. As you note job titles, also include potential employers and key words that appear in the job or occupation description. All of these key pieces will be helpful as you generate your professional documents and prepare for interviews (Exhibit 6.7).

1. Use O*Net (www.onetonline.org/) to search for occupations of interest to you. At the top of an occupational profile, after a brief definition of the career, review the list of sample reported job titles. Use the task and work activities list to generate key words for the occupation.
2. Visit job boards within relevant professional associations. Note job titles that interest you and briefly review job descriptions to assess how your skills and strengths align with that role.
3. You might use CareerOneStop's My Skills My Future (www.myskillsmyfuture .org) tool to identify potential careers and job titles based on your prioritized skills.

Note that organizations have creative freedom when it comes to job titles; what one organization calls a "mental health counselor" another might call a "behavioral health therapist." Visit organization or employer human resources or careers pages to clarify and learn the vernacular of that specific employer.

EXHIBIT 6.7 JOB SEARCH ORGANIZATION CHART

JOB TITLE	POTENTIAL EMPLOYERS	KEY WORDS
EXAMPLE *Career Counselor*	*ABC Career Consulting, LLC* *WestState University* *Ridgeway High School*	*Career coordinator, resume development, career exploration, career assessment, student services*

Write Your Resume

Before you write:

- Research and review job descriptions for roles that interest you.
- Identify required documents for applications (**resume** versus curriculum vitae [CV], transcript, diploma, license, etc.).
- Brainstorm your key experiences and accomplishments.
- Meet with professionals in the field to gain insight on expectations for content and formatting.
- View sample resumes from trusted sources to explore styles that you prefer.

Tip: For Resume and Cover Letters

Highlight relevant key terms within job descriptions to include on your resume and cover letter. These should guide your content.

STUDENTS

For students in high school, we recommend seeking support in the school counselor's office for assistance in creating a resume, candidate statement, and other documentation needed for applying to jobs and educational institutions. School counselors can offer specific strategies, tips, resources, and examples to review.

College students are encouraged to visit their university career centers early on in their academic career to begin the process of creating a resume, career portfolio, and cover letters, as well as explore career options within their field of interest. Career center websites offer concrete examples and resources for students majoring in a variety of subjects and can tailor resumes to the discipline of interest as well. Career counselors and coaches in higher education settings provide students at all levels (e.g., undergraduate, graduate, postdoctoral), with support in the creation of documents for employment, future training, and advanced educational pursuits. At some institutions, career services are offered to alumni through the career center or even an alumni office to help graduates navigate careers postgraduation. Career counselors in these settings often provide resume and cover letter support, connections for networking opportunities, career fairs to attend in person or virtually, and much more.

PRACTITIONERS

As practitioners begin in the counseling field and similar helping professions, questions often arise about how to conduct a job search and apply for relevant positions. As a graduate student, beginning to build a solid career network through connecting with peers, attending conferences, and joining related professional associations and organizations can be essential to making early career connections and remaining up-to-date with current trends in the field. Also, the relationships established during graduate programs can set the tone for future connections within the field. When applying for an agency, school, or higher education positions, practitioners are encouraged to create a resume tailored to their specialty area and positions that meet their values, interests, certifications, and skill set.

Activity: Write Your Resume

Begin to brainstorm content for your resume or CV using the following exhibit as a guide. This is not comprehensive, but it will help you generate ideas about the information you want to include on your professional documents (Exhibit 6.8).

EXHIBIT 6.8 RESUME CONTENT EXERCISE

Content Type	Your Information
Name	
Contact Information: Address (City, State), Email, LinkedIn	
Education (University Name, Location, Degree Name, Dates, Thesis, Dissertation)	
Other Education: Study Abroad, Relevant Courses, Honors, Awards	
Experiences (Work, Research, Leadership, Volunteer, etc.)	1. 2. 3. 4.
Skills (Languages, Certifications or Licenses, Technical)	

(continued)

EXHIBIT 6.8 RESUME CONTENT EXERCISE (*CONTINUED*)

Content Type	Your Information
Professional Affiliations and Organizational Membership	
Presentations and Publications	
Other Accomplishments or Relevant Experiences	

DIFFERENTIATING BETWEEN RESUME AND CURRICULUM VITAE

Different occupations and roles will require varying formats and content. Pay close attention to the required documentation when applying to a job to determine the appropriate materials. Roles in research, academia, and sometimes government will require a CV in lieu of a resume. You would not use a CV for a corporate, school (K–12), or higher education staff role. Most graduate students entering the counseling field will use a resume.

Doctoral level graduate students and postdoctoral seeking faculty or research-oriented roles would create and submit a CV. The core information in a CV resembles a resume but includes additional sections to highlight accomplishments in research, publications, teaching, presentations, service and leadership, extension outside the college or university, and other scholarly work. A key difference between resumes and CVs is the expected length of the document. While resumes are expected to be brief, one or two pages, CVs are quite a bit longer, often in excess of three pages, depending upon career stage and discipline.

DRAFT YOUR RESUME AND GATHER FEEDBACK

Choose a format appropriate for your career path and representative of your professional brand. Include the content you began to curate in the previous activity. Continue to add experiences and describe your skills and accomplishments.

Once you have a draft of your document, and before applying for a job, meet with a career counselor, coach, mentor, or experienced professional in the field to gather feedback and insight on your document. Make revisions and have your document reviewed by a few other trusted people to identify any content, grammar, or other concerns you may have missed. As you gather feedback, think about your vision and purpose and keep in mind what you know about the company and role to which you are applying.

As you apply, be sure to tailor your resume to the job and organization. Review the application directions and requirements carefully to ensure that you include all required information. Follow directions.

Tip: Short Resumes

Brevity is key for resumes. Studies suggest resumes are reviewed in 8 seconds or less (Bortz, 2021). Aim for one page that packs a punch!

Learn From Experienced Professionals: Informational Interviews

One of the best ways to learn more about a career of interest, organizations, employers, and opportunities is to talk with experienced professionals in the field. They can share insights and first-hand accounts of the profession and workplace that you won't find online. In fact, research suggests that up to 85% of jobs are filled through networking, and at least 70% of jobs are not even listed (Adler, 2016; Belli, 2017). Having these informational conversations provides you the opportunity to build advocates for your job search, prepares you to shine in the interview process, and may well uncover job opportunities (The HT Group, 2018).

Identify professionals in functional roles one to two levels above where you plan to enter the field. Focusing on this level helps you connect with people who have relevant experience, are likely to have some influence in hiring decisions, and are connected to the daily activities of the role to which you aspire. Someone in a higher level position may have less availability and have less information about the regular functions and responsibilities of the role and career path that interest you. If you are currently in a leadership role, you may well be seeking out senior managers within the organization. LinkedIn can provide a broad source for finding professionals connected with your field of interest; use advanced search features to filter for professionals affiliated with your university. Students may leverage the career center and faculty recommendations to tap into alumni networks and departmental connections.

ACTIVITY: CONDUCTING AN INFORMATIONAL INTERVIEW

Informational interviews are an opportunity to build a relationship that should be mutually beneficial. You are reaching out with the goal of gathering information; do not ask for a job or internship. Focusing on developing rapport and learning from the expertise and experience of your contact provides the foundation for a longer term interaction.

Tip: Informational Interviews

1. Be prepared with positive, informed questions that can't be Googled and are relevant to your career path.
2. Share relevant information about your interests and experiences.
3. Seek to develop rapport.
4. Choose an environment conducive to open conversation and convenient for the professional.
5. Send a thank you note within 48 hours of your conversation.

ASKING GREAT QUESTIONS

Revisit the values-based questions that you developed in the Research, Ask, Observe activity. Select questions that are appropriate for the person with whom you are speaking. Consider beginning with lighter questions that invite the professional to share their career path and successes. These provide a positive foundation for the conversation and establishing rapport.

Sample questions and prompts for informational interviews include:

- What is your favorite part of your work?
- I noticed from your profile that you have done X and Y. How did you navigate the transition into X?
- What are some of the unique characteristics or needs of the population that you work with?
- Which theoretical frameworks or techniques do you gravitate toward and find most effective for your work?
- Describe a client or student who has been particularly impactful in how you approach your work.

HOW DO I GET THERE? CREATING MY PATH AND CONNECTING WITH PROFESSIONALS IN MY FIELD

Creating your path takes time and many relationships will be formed in the process. Informational interviews provide you with an avenue to establish connections with professionals who may be influential in your decision-making process and open doors to opportunities. You have agency in creating your own career pathway. As you curate this path, it is essential to be intentional and purposeful about who you want to invite to join your professional network. Challenge yourself to expand your network by connecting with professionals and colleagues with diverse experiences and ideas. This may be a time to consider stepping outside your comfort zone.

Activity: Set Up a LinkedIn Profile

Continue to build your connections by creating an online professional profile on LinkedIn. As the world's largest professional networking platform at more than 830 million members globally, LinkedIn is a great place to share your experience, your goals, and connect with a wide variety of professionals (LinkedIn, 2022a). Review profiles for professionals in your field, related fields, and mentors to generate ideas for content and style for your own profile. After you've created a profile, share your experiences, goals, and accomplishments. Use the LinkedIn guide for creating your profile and presenting a strong professional brand. The link offers helpful tips and strategies for creating your online professional presence through the LinkedIn platform. How do I create a good LinkedIn profile (LinkedIn, 2022b)?

Tip: LinkedIn

1. When creating your profile, use the name that you use to introduce yourself.
2. Include a professional headshot that focuses on your face and not a backdrop.

3. Engage with content on the platform and always customize your connection requests.
4. Consider seeking recommendations from your supervisors and colleagues to demonstrate your impact.
5. Don't accept every connection request. Consider your relationship with that person and how they may be connected, or not, with your areas of interest.
6. Keep your profile up-to-date with your experiences and accomplishments.

Create a List of Possible Internship Sites

Begin creating a list of sites where you would like to explore potential practicum or **internships** (Exhibit 6.9). To generate ideas, ask your faculty coordinator for a list of sites where prior students have interned. Review LinkedIn profiles for program alumni—their experience will likely indicate their internship site. Use search engines such as Indeed or LinkedIn to search for open jobs in your field. Note the organizations that populate in the search results; these organizations may also host interns in your field. Include the organizations with whom your informational interviews are connected.

CONSIDERATIONS FOR SELECTING AN INTERNSHIP SITE

- Schedule: Days per week, number of hours available, time of day on-site/virtual.
- Paid or unpaid.
- Location: Proximity to your residency or school.
- Requirements: Will work be performed on-site and/or virtually?
- Supervision: Background of supervisor (i.e., meet educational requirements), skill set, and availability.
- Mentorship: Peer, colleague, and supervisor opportunities for mentorship.
- Opportunities for employment postgraduation.
- Quality of training program.
- Client volume and potential to gain required hours toward graduation.
- Opportunity for both individual and group sessions.
- Interest in the population served.
- Development of specialty area or specific skill set.

HOW CAN I STAND OUT? SHOWCASING MY EXPERIENCE AND ARTICULATING MY VALUE

Applicants inevitably ask career counselors for strategies to stand out in the application process. Standing out requires intentional planning. A key to standing out is building advocates in organizations and roles that excite you and having an informational interview that will set the foundation for these influential relationships.

EXHIBIT 6.9 YOUR TARGET INTERNSHIP SITES

Name: Internship Sites	Location	Contact Person and Information (e.g., Name, email address, etc.)	(+) Positive Attributes	(−) Drawbacks or Potential Concerns

These conversations also should provide critical information with which you can prepare for your application process and interview. For example, if you learn during the informational interview that the site serves a Spanish-speaking population and you are bilingual, you can intentionally highlight that skill set on your documents and in your interview process.

Activity: Write a Cover Letter

Cover letters offer you the opportunity to provide a narrative alongside your resume. Here, you can make a case for your candidacy. It can be a key place for you to stand out. Unfortunately, there are many mixed feelings about cover letters among hiring managers. You will see some organizations that require cover letters, others that accept them but don't require them, and still others that don't accept them at all. Best practice is to create a tailored cover letter and include it where possible.

Begin with reviewing the job description for the role and highlight key words and phrases that appear in the posting. What are two or three of your skills or experiences that prepare you to quickly add value or make an impact in the role? Keep these in mind as you write. As with a resume, brevity is important. Your final document should be less than one page long. Share your cover letter with trusted professionals to gather feedback and hone your document.

Interviewing

Interviewing is a skill and requires practice. Practicing can highlight areas of strength and weakness and help you polish your responses. Even experienced professionals can feel anxious in an interview setting. Mock interviews provide insight to help you know how you might feel and present yourself during the interview. This feedback is invaluable to give you additional control and help you stand out in the process. Ask professionals in the field, perhaps some of the same people who you have interviewed, to help you practice with a mock interview. Students can often request mock interviews with career counselors or coaches at the university career center, too. Similar services may also be available to alumni. Ensure that your mock interview is tailored for the position you are targeting by sharing the job description and your resume with your interviewer before your meeting.

ACTIVITY: INTERVIEWING PRACTICE

Schedule a mock interview with a professional in the field, a career counselor, or coach. Share your updated resume and a sample job description for a role that interests you before you meet. Prepare for your interview by practicing introducing yourself, describing your key experiences and accomplishments, and communicating why you are interested in the job and field. Plan to have your mock interview in a setting (e.g., virtual, in person, on the phone), similar to what you expect for the real thing, and dress for the interview. This will help you to more closely mirror the interview experience. Afterward, gather feedback about your performance, both the positives and the areas needing growth.

After completing your mock interview, reflect on your experience and make a plan to address any gaps or areas of weakness.

REFLECTION

How did you feel while you were interviewing? Did your introduction confidently lay out your fit and qualifications for the role?

What questions were easiest for you to answer? Which questions did you struggle with or stumble through? Which experiences or accomplishments did you share in the interview? Were these the ones that you wanted to highlight? With what do you need additional practice? What steps can you take to be more prepared to stand out in an interview?

Standing Out in Different Spaces

CAREER FAIR

Career fairs can be a useful avenue for connecting to employers and learning about opportunities within your field. Career fairs may be offered virtually or in person. Preparation is key to attending any of the career fair events. Career counselors are a terrific resource for developing a concrete plan for attending and engaging in career fair events. See the following box for tips for both in person and virtual career fairs (Exhibit 6.10).

ONLINE

In a time where social media is a part of our everyday lives, it is essential to consider how we are showing up in online spaces, including social media outlets. Developing your own professional brand will be essential for your career throughout your lifespan. As mentioned in the chapter, LinkedIn can be a useful tool to showcase your brand. Keep in mind that you can always consult with a career counselor or helping professional to discuss ways to capture your professional image to showcase your strengths, interests, accomplishments, and career goals.

EXHIBIT 6.10 CHECKLIST FOR IN-PERSON AND VIRTUAL CAREER FAIRS

In Person	Virtual
• Visit the career center for career fair tips and strategies • Arrive early to the event • Be mindful that as you enter the career fair you are "on" and recruiters, hiring managers, etc. are watching • Dress for the event in professional attire • Prepare a resume and be ready to share with employers • Review and research the employers in attendance • Create a list of employers to connect with at the event • Prepare a few targeted questions for employers • Develop a 1 minute introduction and practice beforehand • Be positive, approachable, and smile • Follow up via email with connections you meet at the event	• Determine where you will be joining the event • Consider logistics: background noise, computer background, internet connectivity, sound (i.e., use of a headset) • Research employers before the event • Test technology and platform before the event • Locate instructions for engaging in the online platform • When possible, use your camera to engage with employers • Prepare a list of employers to "visit" • Have your resume, cover letter, ready to share • Prepare a 1 minute introduction and practice beforehand • Smile • Send thank you notes after all conversations

In Class

As a graduate student, consider your level of engagement and participation in your graduate program. What professional organizations, committees, associations, and other university opportunities may be available to develop your professional career, enhance your leadership skills, and create strong networks that could lead to future career possibilities. Consider the relationships you may cultivate while you are in your program with fellow colleagues and peers, faculty, administrators, and staff. Often these relationships can lead to unexpected outcomes and professional experiences that can be included on your resume, cover letter, and related employment documentation. As a student, it is important to remain connected with faculty as they may serve as a reference for you and offer recommendation letters and complete documentation for licensure, certification, and additional educational pursuits.

Professional Etiquette

As the saying goes, a picture can be worth a thousand words. Take care of your personal image and branding to ensure you are placing yourself in the most positive light in all social media outlets, both personally and professionally. People talk and often are connected. Be careful in posting any content, images, and related materials to any online platform, as it lasts forever. A negative post can tarnish your image for years to come.

In this section, the authors lead the reader through topical scenarios to surface common ethics questions and dilemmas faced by career professionals. They ask pertinent and personal questions to encourage reader reflection and insight into personal and professional ethics.

Azra Karajic Siwiec, PhD, LPC, is a counselor educator employed by Capella University. She has been working in the counselor education field for over 14 years and has served as a committee member of the Ethics Committee of the National Career Development Association (NCDA) since 2015 and served as the chair of the Ethics Committee since 2017.

Sharon K. Anderson, PhD, is a professor of counseling and career development at Colorado State University. Sharon has taught the master's level ethics course for counseling students for over 20 years, teaching and mentoring a multitude of students. She has coauthored or coedited four professional ethics books used by practitioners in counseling and coaching.

VIGNETTE

Sandi is developing her own lifeline by plotting her career on a line. She lists all of her desires from as early as she can recall, and then moves through the line to her middle school and high school aspirations. She continues to plot what she would like to do with her life. Sandi begins to ask herself some really big questions: What ethical challenges have I struggled with? Why? How do I need to address those challenges in the future? How are these challenges related to my purpose in life? How do I know my purpose in life? How can that purpose be fulfilled in my career? Who will be impacted by my purpose? How will I know that impact is for good and not for harm?

DIGGING INTO ETHICS

Now, it's your turn. Have you ever plotted your lifeline? If not, consider doing so right now. Consider asking yourself the same questions that Sandi is asking of herself. What ethical challenges have I struggled with? Why? How do I need to address those challenges in the future? How are these challenges related to my purpose in life? How do I know my purpose in life? How can that purpose be fulfilled in my career? Who will be impacted by my purpose? How will I know that impact is for good and not for harm?

6.1 PRACTITIONER'S PERSPECTIVE

Sara Concini holds a bachelor of arts in psychology and a master of science in counseling both from West Chester University of Pennsylvania. She is a licensed clinical mental health counselor in the state of North Carolina and has served in a variety of higher education and human resources roles, spending the last 16 years in career services. She is currently the director of graduate career services and corporate relations for the Electrical and Computer Engineering Department at North Carolina State University.

This work in career service chose me. I began my career in higher education with a focus on student activities and leadership. Career development was not on my radar as a graduate student or early in my professional life. Yet, as my personal life changed, my own career needs changed, and I added a recruiting role to my skill set. Career counseling became an obvious next step in my journey. I have now proudly served a wide breadth of students for almost two decades.

I currently serve master and doctoral students in electrical and computer engineering. These students have a high degree of technical training but are keenly aware of the need for career exploration and professional development. I enjoy serving MS and PhD students with a technical/STEM focus because they take a great amount of interest and care in their career and professional development. Over 50% have prior professional experience, and more than 60% are international students. Working on getting a degree is often their first experience in the United States.

My role serves a variety of constituents: students, employers, alumni, faculty, and strategic department partners. I spend a significant amount of time counseling students and providing supervision to a professional staff member who also counsels students. I also interact with the companies that hire our students; whether it be a CEO or a talent acquisition team member from a company, I get to market NC State Electrical College of Engineering talent to them and provide services via a partnership program that helps their company reach their goals. It's a true pleasure to serve students by teaching, counseling, advising, and guiding them while also serving employers by creating unique ways for them to connect with our students.

I find this vocation and experience very satisfying. I love the "light bulb" moment for students when they see themselves through my eyes. I like to hear employers say "your students are a joy to have on our team" and the student who says "I am more confident in my abilities after working with you." Those are the moments that make me proud to be in my profession.

TRAITS OF CAREER COUNSELORS AND CAREER-COUNSELING INTERNS

There are several traits of good career counselors. They are curious to learn about their students and about different industries, hiring trends, new techniques, and tools. Career counselors are also compassionate, understanding that students are learning and developing at a rapid rate in their college years and that they need a listening ear and guidance from a trusted source. Career counselors are creative—and this is a must-have characteristic because there is a lot of problem-solving and knowing how to do more with less as budgets are always tight. Finally, a career counselor needs to take initiative, before or without being asked, to create workshops, classes, events, and online training that will support the students' needs.

Informational interviews are a great way for those entering the profession to gather critical insight. What questions should a prospective professional in your field ask you?

- What do you love about your job?
- What do you wish you could change?
- What do you wish you would have known before you started in this profession?
- Who else should I be speaking with to learn more?

PROFESSIONAL ETHICS

Ethical standards are multilayered in this profession. I am always mindful of Family Educational Rights and Privacy Act regulations for paperwork, documentation, and other items to protect the student. I also adhere to the ACA code of ethics in particular, as it applies to making sure that I am only acting in a career-counseling manner with my students and *not* as a licensed professional counselor. I refer students to ensure that they are receiving mental health counseling from a professional. I also teach the students about the ethical job search, and I keep their salary data in the strictest of confidence.

When teaching and coaching students regarding the ethics of a job search, I guide them to interview in good faith: keep an open mind to learn about the role, provide honest answers to questions, and communicate with the prospective employer in a timely manner. Upon receiving a desired offer, I delicately counsel students to accept and negotiate in a reasonable, fact-based way. I also help the student understand that verbally accepting an offer does obligate the relationship with the company. Ethical dilemmas arise when students decline an offer after they have accepted it, and then the employer is left with an unfilled position and a tainted professional view of that student. Finally, I educate employers about ethical hiring practices if their behaviors are in violation.

CREDENTIALS, CERTIFICATIONS, AND DEGREES

My particular role requires at least a bachelor's degree, yet a master's degree is preferred. A bachelor of arts or bachelor of science degree can be in psychology, human development, human resources, business, or related fields. An MS in counseling, higher education, or business administration is a huge plus. Advanced degrees carry some weight, particularly when working in an academic setting. A counseling license or human resources certification is a plus but not required or necessary.

Student Voices

In Student Voices, students offer a unique viewpoint as they begin in the career-counseling field. Here, students share their thoughts and reflections about the career-counseling profession and offer personal takeaways.

ERICA M. JIMENEZ

I have a bachelor of science in social psychology, and I am a masters' in education student at North Carolina State University, studying college counseling and student development. I currently serve in the United States Air Force Reserves in a Special Duty Assignment for Airman and Family Readiness. I am completing my internship at the University of North Carolina-Chapel Hill as a student care specialist, focusing on empowering students to succeed in navigating academic and personal life.

(continued)

Student Voices (*continued*)

I am married with three children, and I work full time and serve in the military as a reservist. Before fully committing to the College Counseling and Student Development program at North Carolina State University, I had to ensure that all other obligations and areas in my life were in order.

When I first learned of the counselor education master's program in 2017, everything about it aligned perfectly with what I wanted to do for my career. However, the timing was not right for the other facets of my life. My husband was in a master's program, and I had other military career development requirements that needed my undivided time and dedication. I had to sit down and really map out timelines that included realistic due dates on the three military courses I had to complete and when my husband would graduate. It was important to me that only one parent was enrolled in a master's program after seeing how much time was taken away from our children as we both worked on our undergraduate degrees.

I made applying to the counselor education master's program 2019 cohort my goal. I completed all three military courses, for which I was given 1 year each to complete, in less than 2 years. I cannot take full credit for this, as I had many people, from colleagues, mentors, family members, and most importantly, my husband, who checked in with me consistently. Their kind words of encouragement held me accountable and kept me motivated. When it came time to focus on the program application process, that very same support system proofread my personal statement, provided amazing letters of recommendation, and even practiced graduate interviews with me.

The military and education both hold a special place in my heart. At the time of application, I was a military academic advisor for our local community college on a military base. As an advisor working with nontraditional students, I learned early on that these students trusted me with so much more than just their academics. Completing a master's in education in college counseling and student development would provide me with the skills, techniques, and experience needed to better support my students and their futures.

This journey has been anything but easy, but the quality of education I have received and the relationships I have made are indescribable. This past fall, I was particularly proud of myself because I was also going to graduate a semester early. Yet, 2 weeks into the semester my family experienced a life-changing emergency and at the same time, major events and changes occurred at my place of employment. I had to make the hard decision of taking the semester off. However, during one of the hardest times in my life, I have never felt more supported. I will forever be grateful for the support my classmates and instructors provided, not only to me, but to my family, without hesitation.

I will graduate in fall 2022, and I plan to obtain licensure. While I see myself continuing a career in higher education, I would like to dedicate a few years to being a military family life counselor (MFLC). I am fortunate to be in a program that allows so much versatility and limitless options.

I do not take any of this journey for granted, and I know I would not be where I am without the support, dedication, and sometimes sacrifices, of my support system.

COUNSELING SKILLS CONNECTION

Feedback is a gift. It can also be just as challenging to receive as it is to give. As a counselor, you will be charged with providing thoughtful feedback to your peers, colleagues, and clients. You will also receive feedback from many of these same people. Career counselors play a special role in educating clients about resume standards, job search strategies, and more. Counselors must be intentional about developing the necessary counseling relationship before confronting or challenging clients about poor job search behaviors in the same way that they would take caution before challenging a client on an unhealthy relationship or other area of clinical concern. One tip in building rapport is to learn more about your student or client before delving into sensitive topics. An approach counselors can use to share challenging feedback is the "sandwich" approach or "hamburger model," which is sharing something positive and affirming first, then highlighting any constructive feedback next, then following up with another affirmative comment (Rubin, n.d.).

MINDFUL MOMENT

Take a moment of reflection and answer the following questions in your journal. Make an inventory of your strengths. When are you at your best? Think about a time when you felt proud of yourself. What made you feel proud and how did you accomplish it? For what do others frequently seek your advice, skill, or expertise? When times get tough, how do you rest and take care of yourself in these moments?

TECH TOOLS

A great place to start your internship search is with a conversation with your faculty advisor or internship coordinator. They will point you to a number of sites where recent students have completed their practicum and internship. Here are a few tech tools you might also use to identify internship sites:

- Idealist.org: Navigate to the organization search on this tool. Refine your search by location and "issue areas," that is, mental health, LGBTQ, job and workplace, and so on.
- NCDA.com: If you are a member, use the member directory to identify career-development professionals in your area. Review their profiles and note their organizational affiliation. (You can apply this same method with other professional associations, too.)
- LinkedIn.com: Search for your educational institution, then use the alumni tool to find graduates of your program. Review profiles of professionals who have titles of interest and note in their experience section where they completed their internship.

REFLECTION ACTIVITY

What part of this career-exploration process did you find most challenging and why? Flash forward 15 years. What kind of work are you doing? Describe your work environment. What are you known for? Write a letter to yourself to open in 1 year. What are your career aspirations? What are your worries, concerns, or frustrations? What are you excited about? Add details to describe your honest thoughts and goals. Pro-Tip: Try using FutureMe, a free tool that holds and delivers email at a set date in the future (www.futureme.org/).

END-OF-CHAPTER RESOURCES

SUMMARY

This chapter focuses on *you* and an abundance of practical tips and strategies for "thinking and doing" throughout the career exploration and development process. We have explored a roadmap and framework along with prompts and reflection questions to help you identify key aspects of who you are, where you are going, and how you can get there. Tips for resume and cover letter "dos and don'ts" will elevate your resume and support your document creation. Personal branding tips and reviewing "how you can stand out" in a job search were considered.

Several concrete activities and exercises are presented to dig deeper into your values, interests, skills, and strengths. These activities are offered as a tactile way to begin asking yourself intentional questions related to your career. As always, we encourage you to share with trusted colleagues and/or career professional to review the ideas you have generated thus far and as you plan for the future.

As we conclude the chapter, we would like to offer you an opportunity to consider five pivotal questions as a way of a self-check.

Self-Check: Top Five Things to Do for Yourself

1. Identify and select a counselor for yourself.
2. Maintain professional mentorships and relationships for consultation and support.
3. Embrace continuing education, both formal (CE credits toward licensure) and informal (attend a lunch and learn about a topic of interest to you).
4. Develop self-care practices and regular routines, formal and informal. (Do things that bring you joy.)
5. Advocate for yourself. Revisit your goals and values as you move through phases of life and your journey, and use your voice to promote the aspects of your life that are of most importance to you. Try talking to yourself the way you would talk to your best friend. No one else will do it for you.

REFERENCES

Adler, L. (2016, February 29). *New survey reveals 85% of all jobs are filled via networking.* LinkedIn Pulse. https://www.linkedin.com/pulse/new-survey-reveals-85-all-jobs-filled-via-networking-lou-adler/

Belli, G. (2017, April 10). At least 70% of jobs are not even listed—here's how to up your chances of getting a great new gig. *Business Insider.* https://www.businessinsider.com/at-least-70-of-jobs-are-not-even-listed-heres-how-to-up-your-chances-of-getting-a-great-new-gig-2017-4

Bortz, D. (2021, May 25). What your HR resume should look like after the pandemic. *SHRM.* https://www.shrm.org/hr-today/news/hr-magazine/summer2021/pages/what-your-hr-resume-should-look-like-after-the-pandemic.aspx

Gallup. (n.d.). *About CliftonStrengths. CliftonStrengths for students.* https://www
.strengthsquest.com/help/general/142466/strength.aspx#:~:text=A%20
strength%20is%20the%20ability,Copyright%20%C2%A9%202022%20
Gallup%2C%20Inc

Holland, J. L. (1973). *Making vocational choices: A theory of careers.* American Psychological Association.

Indeed Editorial Team. (2021, June 8). *120 skills to include on your next resume.*
Indeed.com. https://www.indeed.com/career-advice/career-development/
skills-list

LinkedIn. (2022a). *About LinkedIn.* https://about.linkedin.com/

LinkedIn. (2022b). *How do I create a good LinkedIn profile.* https://www.linkedin.com/
help/linkedin/answer/a554351/how-do-i-create-a-good-linkedin-profile-?
lang=en.

Merriam-Webster. (n.d.). Skill. In Merriam-Webster.com dictionary. https://www
.merriam-webster.com/dictionary/skill

O*Net Online. (n.d.). Home page. https://www.onetonline.org/

Rubin. (n.d.). Sandwich feedback model/Hamburger model [steps & examples].
Happy Rubin. https://happyrubin.com/nlp/sandwich-feedback-model/

The HT Group. (2018, June 12). *Are 1/3 of your jobs filled by employee referrals?* https://
www.thehtgroup.com/one-third-jobs-filled-employee-referrals/

CHAPTER 7

ASSESSMENTS IN CAREER COUNSELING

Christopher T. Belser, Angie C. Smith, and Katie Peterssen

LEARNING OBJECTIVES

By the end of this chapter, you will be able to:

- Identify specific assessment tools used within the career-counseling settings.
- List the rationale and considerations for selection and use of assessment instruments.
- Compare and contrast formal versus informal assessment instruments.
- Review assessment instruments and highlight the different types of assessments used with individuals in various settings.

WARM-UP EXERCISE

What has your experience been with career assessments? If you've taken a career assessment previously, who administered it, or how did you choose the assessment? What were your impressions of the results, and how did they influence your thoughts about your career or education opportunities? If you've not taken a career assessment, what would you want to see in an assessment? Are there particular results or insights you would hope to gain from a career assessment?

INTRODUCTION

This chapter focuses on the assessments commonly used in career-counseling practice, including assessment tools to be used with clients in various settings. Assessment tools are instruments to help practitioners assist people as they explore and navigate their career choices. These tools assess interests, abilities, skills, values, and personality. We will explore formal and informal career assessments, including career readiness, career decision-making, and career exploration, and how to use them effectively and ethically. We will also consider the interrelatedness of the career and mental health assessment processes and applications with historically marginalized populations. We will also connect these tools to aspects of mental health and the Council for the Accreditation of Counseling and Related Educational Programs (CACREP) standards.

SELECTING AND ADMINISTERING ASSESSMENTS

In 2010, the National Career Development Association (NCDA) and the Association for Assessment and Research in Counseling (AARC; formerly the Association for Assessment in Counseling and Education) identified the effective use of career assessments as vital to the practice of career counseling. Counselors can use assessments with clients and students for various purposes, including increasing client self-knowledge, identifying potential careers, and gaining insight into how clients or students approach the career decision-making process. Because of the multifaceted scope of career assessments, it is critically important for counselors to know that career assessment is not just for professionals with Career Counselor in their title.

The roots of career-assessment tools date back more than 100 years to Jessie B. Davis's development of an interest inventory for use with high school students (Harrington & Long, 2013). In the years since that first inventory, career assessments were the subject of work by educators, psychologists, and counselors and have expanded in use to all age groups. Today, these tools have applications for school counseling, academic advising, career services, private practice, human resources, and beyond.

The career-assessment process begins with selecting and understanding assessments that fit with your setting, client population, and intended purpose and continues through the interpretation and use of those results with a client or student. The roots of this process are with interest inventories (Harrington & Long, 2013), where the majority of career assessments continue to be. As career theories evolved and added other constructs to the career-development process, new categories of assessments emerged, including abilities, skills, personality, values, career readiness, and **informal assessments.** The sections that follow will highlight key considerations for each type of assessment along with implications for use with different populations.

Assessing Interests

Research tells us that most people do not randomly end up in a career field, but rather they enter one that aligns to some degree with their interests (Nauta, 2010). The most frequently used category of career assessments, interest inventories, are designed to help people understand their career interests by weighing their likes and dislikes across a wide set of activities. Basic interest scales match a person's interests with career environments (e.g., artistic, social, realistic), career clusters (e.g., hospitality and tourism, human services), or specific career fields (e.g., engineering, education), by highlighting patterns observed within a person's interests.

Examples of this type of assessment are the Self-Directed Search (Holland & Messer, 2017; Reardon & Lenz, 2015), O*Net Interest Profiler (National Center for O*Net Development, 2021; Rounds et al., 2021), the Strong Interest Inventory (Donnay et al., 2004; Harmon et al., 1994; Herk & Thompson, 2012), the Kuder General Interest Survey (Kuder, 1964), and the Campbell Interest and Skill Survey (Campbell, 1992, 2002), all of which have electronic or web-based administration and scoring. There are also a variety of nonstandardized paper-based interest inventories, such as the Career Clusters Interest Survey (Primé & Tracey, 2009), as well as variations for children and adolescents.

Another feature of interest inventories are occupational scales, which compare a person's interest inventory results to the interests of people in specific career fields; for example, they compare the test taker to other respondents who identify as accountants. This scale allows people to see how congruent their interests are with others who are in a field of interest. Both the Strong Interest Inventory and the Campbell Interest Inventory have occupational scales that have been researched and validated; a key difference between these two is that the Strong Interest Inventory divides occupational scales on a gender binary, whereas the Campbell Interest Inventory uses combined occupational scales (Hays, 2017).

SELF-DIRECTED SEARCH

The Standard Self-Directed Search (SDS; Holland & Messer, 2017) is one of the most widely used career assessments. The SDS has been normed on ages 11 to 70 and employs John Holland's RIASEC (Realistic, Investigative, Artistic, Social, Enterprising, and Conventional) codes to match a person's personality type to their work environment type (Holland & Messer, 2017). The assessment is designed so that it can be used by a client or student on their own or with a counselor. The scoring report provides the test taker with a summary code, the three-letter RIASEC code, a list of occupations that match the test taker's summary code, and a comparison of the test taker's summary code with occupations identified as "daydream occupations" and prior jobs. The SDS is a paid assessment that can be accessed through www.Self-Directed-Search.com.

O*NET INTEREST PROFILER

The O*Net Interest Profiler (National Center for O*Net Development, 2021; Rounds et al., 2021) is a free online assessment housed within the Occupational Information Network (O*Net) website sponsored by the U.S. Department of Labor/ Employment and Training Administration. Like the SDS, the Interest Profiler is built on Holland's RIASEC codes and asks test takers to rate 60 work activities on a five-point scale ranging from Strongly Dislike to Strongly Like. According to Rounds et al. (2021), the Interest Profiler was developed with an eighth-grade reading level in mind (for populations age 14 and up); however, they note that the tool can be used with younger grades for purposes of career exploration and exposure. The readability, ease of use, and no cost of this assessment make it an excellent tool for classroom-level career-development programming by middle and high school counselors.

STRONG INTEREST INVENTORY

The Strong Interest Inventory is another widely used interest assessment based on Holland's RIASEC theory. The Strong Interest was initially developed in 1927 but has undergone numerous revisions in its nearly 100 years of use to make a more succinct instrument that is reflective of both the contemporary workforce and present diversity in the United States (Donnay et al., 2004; Harmon et al., 1994; Herk & Thompson, 2012). Designed with a ninth-grade reading level, the Strong has approximately 300 items, and the results report provides the test taker with their three-letter Holland code, a list of interest areas that most highly associate with their code, a comparison of one's results with those of occupations that highly correlate, a summary of work style preferences, and summaries. The Strong can also be taken in conjunction with the Myers-Briggs Type Indicator to get a combined and synthesized results report. The Strong Interest Inventory is a paid assessment available through www.themyersbriggs.com.

Interest Assessments in Marginalized Populations

Prior research has illustrated observed differences in career interest based on demographic factors (i.e., race, ethnicity, gender; Ertl & Hartmann, 2019; Fouad & Mohler, 2004; Morris, 2016); however, Fouad and Kantamneni (2013) posited that these differences are more likely due to socialization, differences in exposure to career options, and intersecting differences in opportunities based on sociocultural factors. Ludwikowski et al. (2020) noted that people may respond to occupational scales using prior knowledge based on occupational stereotypes, such those of gender or ethnicity.

Professionals should also take caution to ensure that they are using assessments with populations represented in instrument development processes that can be determined by reviewing instrument manuals and validation studies. For example, Schaubhut and Thompson (2016) issued a brief on the use of the Strong Interest Inventory with LGBT+ clients, including revised directions related to gender identification, and initial validation data with LGBT+ individuals. Regardless of the inventory's psychometric properties, professionals should consider interest assessment results in conjunction with career values and cannot assume that a client approaches interest assessment from an individualistic perspective (as opposed to a collectivist view; Leong, 2010).

ABILITIES AND SKILLS

Although abilities and skills both reflect an individual's unique strengths, the two terms are not completely synonymous. O*NET (2022, para. 1) defines abilities as "enduring attributes of the individual that influence performance" and defines skills as "developed capacities that facilitate learning or the more rapid acquisition of knowledge." In essence, abilities are things that a person has the aptitude or capacity to do, whereas skills are things that a person has learned to do through training or experience (Lowman, 2022). It is imperative for clinicians to consider this distinction when selecting what constructs to assess, as the two categories would have different implications for developing a plan to help the client or student. O*NET (2022) lists four categories of abilities—cognitive, physical, psychomotor, and sensory—and six categories of skills—basic, complex problem-solving, resource management, social, systems, and technical.

Assessing clients' abilities can help them gain understanding of traits and strengths they can bring to a job or career, and this can be very useful for individuals with limited work experience or high school students who are early in the career decision-making process. Assessments commonly used in high schools include academic assessments such as the ACT and SAT and comprehensive assessments such as the Armed Services Vocational Aptitude Battery (ASVAB; 2022). It must be noted, though, that despite the wide use of academic aptitude tests, these tests have come under scrutiny for potential racial bias, and contemporary research has indicated that current grades are a better predictor of future academic success (Hays, 2017).

Skills assessments look more at constructs that clients have gained through personal and professional experiences, including education and hobbies. Examining skills can be helpful for identifying entry-level skills of first-time job seekers such as high school students and the transferrable skills of clients making a job or career change. Assessing one's skills helps shed light on the unique qualifications and assets that a person could bring to a job or career and also highlights skill areas in which the person may want to get additional training. Counselors should consider using interest assessments in tandem with skills assessments to help clients and students identify interest areas that overlap with skills, as well as interest areas that require additional training or experience.

CliftonStrengths

The CliftonStrengths assessment (formerly StrengthsQuest; 2022) is a standardized assessment that creates a profile of one's strengths based on Don Clifton's identified themes that fall into four domains: strategic thinking, relationship building, influencing, and executing. Though this assessment is more geared toward managerial, business, and organizational career pathways, there are versions for middle and high school students, and it has been tested on hundreds of thousands of people over decades (Asplund et al., 2014). Because the concept of abilities covers such a wide range of areas, clinicians may also want to consider assessing specific areas or referring for assessment of specific areas that fit with the client's identified interests (e.g., emotional intelligence, musical rhythm, managerial abilities).

ACT WorkKeys

The ACT WorkKeys exams evaluate various workplace skill areas, including applied math, graphic literacy, workplace documents, applied technology, business writing, workplace observation, fit, and talent. These identified areas represent essential hard and soft skills that are relevant to a wide range of occupations. Results from WorkKeys assessments help match test takers to National Career Readiness System credentials and related jobs based on scores in each area (ACT, 2022). Potential test takers can access study materials to help improve scores on the tests, and ACT also has developed curricula that can be used in schools to help students prepare for the tests. Research on WorkKeys indicates that these assessments performed comparably to other similar assessments regarding race, ethnicity, and gender (LeFebvre, 2016). ACT WorkKeys is a paid assessment program that must be offered through an ACT-approved testing center, often a school, school district, or technical/vocational training center.

Career One Stop Skills Matcher

The Career One Stop Skills Matcher (2022) allows test takers to self-assess their skill level in 40 areas, such as clerical, instructing, programming, and repairing. Results are presented using a scale of Beginner to Expert, and the results link the test taker to information about jobs that match their score profile using data from O*Net and other resources from federal agencies. The Career One Stop website does not currently report information about the test's development or psychometric properties. However, it is a free, easy-to-use web-based tool.

YouScience Discovery

YouScience Discovery (2022) is a web-based system that allows middle and high school students to assess their aptitudes, explore careers that fit, and develop career and educational plans. The platform uses a series of short brain games to help students better understand their aptitudes and interests. It has an abbreviated version for seventh- and eighth-grade students and a full version for students in ninth grade and beyond. YouScience Discovery also provides a wealth of resources and reports for educators that aid students in their exploration process. Though the platform is designed for schools and districts to pay for licenses for a large number of students, the YouScience website also allows individuals to purchase access. Users retain access to their Discovery results for 10 years.

Motivated Skills Card Sort

Richard Knowdell (2018) has a Motivated Skills Card Sort that allows clients to sort work skills into various categories. This card sort asks individuals to sort various skills based on two dimensions: how much the individual desires to use the skill and how proficient the person is with that skill. Motivated skills are the skills that a person enjoys and has proficiency with, whereas unimportant skills are the opposite. These are skills that a person does not enjoy and does not feel proficient with. Developmental skills are those that a person has an interest in using but does not yet feel proficient using, indicating a desire for training, education, and experience. Burnout skills, on the other hand, are those that a person may have some proficiency with but does not enjoy using (i.e., the person can exercise the skill but will likely burnout if it is their primary task). These four categories help people connect their thoughts about various skills to goal-oriented planning. Because the Skills Matcher and the Motivated Skills card sort both rely on self-reported skill information, the clinician should be mindful that clients' reported skill levels may be incongruent with their actual skill level due to either exaggerating or underrating skill level.

VALUES

Work values, or career values, represent the characteristics of a job or work environment that help a person derive meaning or fulfillment from their work (Choi, 2017). They are a subset of one's personal values and are a predictor of one's fit with a particular job. Examples of career values include working in a prestigious field, working collaboratively with a team versus working alone, the ability to earn a high salary, and the ability to maintain a desired work–life balance, among many others. Leuty and Rounds (2021) note that work values are rooted in individual needs and help explain why all members of a particular field who may share similar interests are not "equally successful in and satisfied with their work" (p. 132). Assessing interests can help a person understand *what* they like about a particular career field; assessing work values can help a person understand *why*.

Professionals can assess a client's work values through formal inventories, including both paper-based and computer-based. The O*NET Work Importance Locator (2000) is a free paper-based tool that measures the importance of six work values: achievement, independence, recognition, relationships, support, and working conditions. Super's Work Values Inventory-Revised (Zytowski, 2006) is part of the Kuder Career Planning System and helps clients evaluate the importance of 12 work values: achievement, coworkers, creativity, income, independence, lifestyle, mental challenge, prestige, security, supervision, work environment, and variety. Both of these inventories are standardized and have been validated on a variety of populations. Career-development sites aimed at K–12 students, such as California Career Zone and Pennsylvania Career Zone, have online variations of these work values assessments.

Values Clarification Exercises

Values clarification exercises offer another method of aiding clients in understanding their work values. One example is a career values card sort, which has a client literally sort through a deck of cards, each card with different career values based on their importance to the client. The Knowdell Career Values Card Sort (Knowdell, 2018) has a physical deck of values cards, as well as an online version, that can be used with clients. Curry and Milsom (2021) describe a group activity that school counselors can use with middle and high school students similar to Go Fish. Similarly, the career-values auction is another group activity that adds a game-like element to values clarification. In a values auction, people are given a budget of fake money they can use to "bid" on different career values, that is, the monetary value they are willing to place on a specific career value communicates the importance of that value to them. Numerous templates and lesson plans for values auctions exist online.

Assessing Values in Marginalized Populations

Because values can be reflective of both individual and cultural characteristics, counselors must ensure that any assessment practices they are using are culturally valid and appropriate. Various values instruments have been researched across racial and ethnic minority groups, international populations, generations, and ability/disability levels with a general consensus that cultural and demographic variables are a factor in how clients develop and make sense of their values (Leuty & Rounds, 2021). It is imperative for counselors to consider how individual and cultural values may be congruent or in conflict with each other for the client. Thus, the counselor has an added responsibility to create a safe space for the client to process any results derived from values assessment.

Career Genograms

Career genograms (Curry & Milsom, 2021; Gibson, 2008) offer a strategy for clinicians to explore occupational and educational patterns that exist within a person's family tree that may have influenced one's beliefs, choices, and values. As with the card sorts, these genogram activities can be modified to fit clients and students across the life span. Curry (2017) and Curry and Milsom (2021) highlight the benefit of using career games and career play to help elementary and middle school students learn about careers and explore their interests.

PERSONALITY

Measuring elements of one's personality provides another piece of the puzzle in helping clients identify jobs and careers that fit with their unique profile. Similar to career values, gaining understanding of personality elements can aid the client in narrowing decisions about various specialty areas or career environments within a particular field that fits with one's interests. For example, someone interested in medical careers may find that working behind the scenes in a laboratory research job fits better with their personality based on introversion than would a direct patient-care job. The most common personality assessments fall into two categories—those based on Carl Jung's typology (e.g., the Myers-Briggs Type Indicator [MBTI]; Myers et al., 2018) and those based on the Five Factors of Personality personality traits (e.g., the NEO-PI-3; Costa & McCrae, 2008), although there is some overlap between the two (Lowman, 2022). Further measures of personality are either based on other specific theories of personality (e.g., the DiSC; Marston, 1928; Scullard & Baum, 2015) or have a basis in measuring psychopathology (e.g., Minnesota Multiphasic Personality Inventory 3 [MMPI-3]; Ben-Porath & Tellegen, 2020).

Jung typology assessments like the MBTI, the 16PF (Cattell & Mead, 2008), and the MyPlan Personality Test (MyPlan, 2019) are commonly used in career-counseling work and help clients understand typology on four subscales: Introversion/Extraversion, Sensing/Intuition, Thinking/Feeling, and Judging/Perceiving. Score reports for this type may include a continuum score for each of the subscales, a four-letter profile code (e.g., ISTJ, ENFP), or both, although contemporary research is less supportive of the 16 unique personality types indicated by the four-letter code (Hays, 2017; Lowman, 2022). Research on the MBTI indicates strong reliability with the four subscales across racial and ethnic groups (Schaubhut et al., 2009). The MBTI can be taken in tandem with the Strong Interest Inventory to get a combined score report.

In contrast, the Big Five personality assessments (e.g., NEO-PI-R) provide scoring based on five subscales: openness to experience, conscientiousness, extraversion, agreeableness, and neuroticism (Lowman, 2022). Assessments of the Big Five typically provide more in-depth information, have stronger empirical support, and are more highly regarded as true personality measures than those based on Jung's typology (Lowman, 2022). Although Big Five assessments, such as the NEO-PI-R, are more often used for purposes of psychological testing and evaluation, Costa and McCrae (2011) highlight dozens of applications of these constructs within career development and organizational psychology contexts, such as psychological fit for specific career fields, connections between personality and leadership/entrepreneurship, and predictors of burnout. However, this category of assessments typically requires additional training or professional licensure as set by the test publisher, and license-granting regulatory agencies (i.e., state-level counselor licensure boards) may have different requirements or limitations regarding using personality assessments.

Though not as well represented in a wide range of assessments, William Moulton Marston's (1928) primary emotions uses a similar structure of assessing in which people score on a continuum of identified constructs. Marston, who also developed the blood pressure–based polygraph test and created the comic book character Wonder Woman, held that people can be described based on four primary emotions: dominance, influence, steadiness, and conscientiousness (Everything DiSC, n.d.; Scullard & Baum, 2015). The DiSC assessment is the primary method of assessing these primary emotions.

Myers-Briggs Type Indicator

The MBTI (Myers et al., 2018) is a measure of personality widely used in business, employment, and human resource settings. As noted earlier, the MBTI uses Carl Jung's personality typologies to provide test takers with an understanding of their preferences on four dimensions: Introversion/Extraversion, Sensing/Intuition, Thinking/Feeling, and Judging/Perceiving. Test takers receive a four-letter profile (e.g., INFJ, ESTP) based on their results with the four scales. Career and human resources professionals have helped people link these results to careers and occupations. For example, a person with the ESTP type may fit well in leadership positions that require attention to changing circumstances and adaptability. It's worth noting that the four subscales have a stronger evidence base than the 16 unique personality types (Hays, 2017; Lowman, 2022). The MBTI features 93 items and is written at a seventh grade reading level. It is intended for use with ages 14 and above and can be accessed for a fee at www.themyersbriggs.com. Similar assessments using Jung's personality typology include the 16PF (Cattell & Mead, 2008) and the MyPlan Personality Test (MyPlan, 2019).

NEO Assessments

The NEO assessments (Costa & McCrae, 2008, 2011) are measures of personality based on the Five Factor Model of personality (Big Five). These five scales include openness to experience, conscientiousness, extraversion, agreeableness, and neuroticism (Lowman, 2022). The NEO Personality Inventory-3 (NEO-PI-3), a revised version of the NEO-PI-R, is normed for ages 12 and up and includes 240 items written at a sixth-grade reading level. A related assessment, the NEO Five Factor Inventory-3 (NEO-FFI-3), is also normed for ages 12 and up and includes an abbreviated 60 items written at a sixth-grade reading level. Administration of the NEO assessments is limited to certain degree fields and licensure requirements based on publisher requirements and state licensing boards; they may not be accessible to all career counselors. However, previous research has demonstrated the usefulness of considering the Big Five when aiding clients with career decision-making and career concerns (Di Fabio et al., 2015; Martincin & Stead, 2015; Xu, 2020).

DiSC

Based on Marston's (1928) primary emotions, the DiSC (Everything DiSC, n.d.; Scullard & Baum, 2015) is a web-based assessment with a Classic version with 28 items, a 79-item Everything DiSC version, and an adaptive testing version. In general, the DiSC measures eight subscales, including the four primary emotions (dominance, influence, steadiness, and conscientiousness), and four subscales that measure interactions between the four primary emotions: Di, iS, SC, and CD. Scullard and Baum (2015) describe each subscale in further detail and outline the evidence of reliability and validity for the DiSC. Career counselors can help clients relate their results to work settings that may allow them to thrive. For example, people with high scores on the Di and i subscales may work well in coaching and supervisory positions that use their disposition as an active, dynamic leader, whereas people scoring high on the SC and C subscales may work better in environments that use their quiet discernment and decision-making skills. Though the DiSC has a fifth-grade reading level, it is recommended for use with adults only and can be accessed for a fee at www.discprofile.com.

Minnesota Multiphasic Personality Inventory

The Minnesota Multiphasic Personality Inventory 3 (MMPI-3; Ben-Porath & Tellegen, 2020) is an adult personality assessment often used in mental health, forensic, and public safety settings. Test takers are asked to respond to 335 items and is estimated to take 25 to 50 minutes to complete. The MMPI-3 generates scores for 52 scales, including 10 validity scales, three higher order scales (e.g., emotional, thought, and behavioral dysfunction), eight restructured clinical scales (e.g., demoralization, antisocial behavior), four somatic/cognitive dysfunction scales (e.g., malaise, eating concerns), 10 internalizing scales (e.g., self-doubt, stress, anger proneness), seven externalizing scales (e.g., family problems, substance abuse), five interpersonal scales (e.g., self-importance, social avoidance), and five Psy-5 scales (e.g., psychoticism, aggressiveness). The third edition of the test has been updated to reflect greater diversity in the validation process and adjusts scales based on years of research. Various versions of the assessment have been used to determine whether job candidates were fit for careers that are psychologically demanding (e.g., police officers, astronauts). Administration of the MMPI-3 is reserved for highly trained professionals, most often licensed psychologists.

CAREER DEVELOPMENT

Career Readiness and Decision-Making

Unlike previously discussed measures meant to help people match with careers, career development and career readiness assessments are meant to bring insight to how people approach the career decision-making process (Hays, 2017). These assessments relate primarily to cognitive constructs and processes that promote or hinder the process of making career decisions or enacting career plans.

Examples of these constructs include adaptability skills, negative career thoughts, decision-making self-efficacy, and career beliefs. The primary reasons for professionals to assess these constructs include evaluating a person's readiness to make career decisions (e.g., career maturity), identifying potential areas of concern (e.g., negative career thoughts) that would need to be addressed prior to engaging in decision-making, or identifying cognitive or internal resources that a person has to enhance their career decision-making process (e.g., self-efficacy). Tapping into this information can bring insight for clients who have struggled with the decision-making process despite completing a variety of interest, values, and skills assessments.

There are numerous assessments that would fit this category, and several have been around for some time, with extensive research on their use across a wide range of racial and ethnic groups, languages, and disciplines. Although this chapter does not provide a comprehensive review of readiness assessments, there are a number that are available for free use, covering a range of constructs.

VOCOPHER INSTRUMENTS

The Vocopher website includes access to a variety of free instruments under the umbrella of career readiness and decision-making. The Career Maturity Inventory (Savickas & Porfeli, 2011) is a free 24-item survey that assesses overall readiness to make career decisions, as well as career concern, career curiosity, career confidence, and preferred relational style when making career decisions. The Career Adapt-Abilities Scale (Savickas & Porfeli, 2012) is a free 24-item assessment that helps clients identify strengths in the areas of control, concern, curiosity, and confidence in relation to career changes and work traumas. Additional constructs are available for assessment through Vocopher, including career concerns, work adjustment, and career mastery.

CAREER THOUGHTS INVENTORY

The Career Thoughts Inventory (CTI; Sampson et al., 1996) is a heavily researched instrument with 48 items that help clients understand the influence of negative career thinking on career choice. The CTI is normed for use with ages 17 and up and has norming standards for high school and college students and general adult populations. The scoring report provides raw and standard scores for an overall total scale, as well as three subscales: decision-making confusion, commitment anxiety, and external conflict. It is important to note that items on this assessment measure negative thoughts and, as such, use negative or pessimistic wording. In my experience using this assessment, this can lead test takers to feel overwhelmed or deflated after completing the assessment and make it necessary for the career counselor to debrief with the client. The CTI and its accompanying workbook are available for a fee through www.parinc.com.

CAREER BELIEFS INVENTORY

The Career Beliefs Inventory (CBI; Krumboltz, 1994) is a 96-item assessment that evaluates peoples' "assumptions, generalizations, and beliefs about themselves and the world of work" (MindGarden, 2022, para. 2). Understanding these underlying beliefs can provide more context regarding where a person's career interests and values may originate and can help the counselor understand why a client may be stuck in the decision-making process. Krumboltz recommends using the CBI early in the career-counseling process so that there is adequate time to explore the origin and impact of these beliefs. The CBI is available for a fee through www.mindgarden.com.

Career Decision Self-Efficacy Scale

The Career Decision Self-Efficacy Scale (CDSE; Betz & Taylor, 2012) measures the degree to which people feel capable of making career decisions and completing steps toward making career decisions. The CDSE includes a 50-item form and also has a 25-item short form that is recommended for use with ages 16 and up. The score report for the CDSE provides scores for five scales: self-appraisal, occupational information, goal selection, planning, and problem-solving. Career counselors can use this information to assess a client's self-efficacy in these areas and then develop a plan to help support the client in improving any problematic areas. The CDSE is available for a fee through www.mindgarden.com.

Career Decision-Making System–Revised

The Career Decision-Making System–Revised (CDM-R; O'Shea & Feller, 2012) is a series of assessments that helps test takers explore career interests, values, abilities, and related school subject preferences. The Level 1 assessment is designed for middle school students and features a 96-item inventory, whereas the Level 2 assessment is designed for high school students and adults and uses a 120-item inventory. The CDM-R results allow test takers to connect the test's interest areas to Holland's RIASEC areas, as well as career clusters. Because of its usefulness with middle and high school students, this assessment could be useful for school counselors. The CDM-R is available for a fee through www .pearsonassessments.com.

Comprehensive Career Exploration Programs

No single assessment provides all pieces to the career development puzzle, and thus comprehensive career exploration programs offer an avenue to pool the benefits of various assessments into a combined battery. Some of the assessments mentioned in the previous section are part of comprehensive career exploration programs. Most commonly, comprehensive programs include assessments of interests, values, and skills, with personality as a possible fourth construct. The purpose of these programs is to help clients or students obtain a more comprehensive picture of their career development profile and then link their results to a database of information about career options that align with the achieved results. Table 7.1 compares five common career exploration programs with some key characteristics of each. Although this table includes some of the most popular programs, there are likely others available that include similar assessment options.

TABLE 7.1 COMPREHENSIVE CAREER EXPLORATION PROGRAMS WITH AVAILABLE ASSESSMENTS

	ASVAB	CAREER ONE STOP	KUDER	MYPLAN	O*NET
Target Population	High school and young adults	High school and adults	Middle and high school	College students	High school and adults
Linked to Career Information	Yes	Yes	Yes	Yes	Yes
Interest Assessment	Yes	Yes	Yes	Yes	Yes
Values Assessment	Yes	Yes	Yes	Yes	Yes
Abilities/ Skills Assessment	Yes	Yes	Yes	Yes	No
Personality Assessment	No	No	No	Yes	No

ASVAB, Armed Services Vocational Aptitude Battery

INFORMAL AND QUALITATIVE ASSESSMENTS

Clinicians do not need to rely solely on formal instruments to gather information. Informal and qualitative assessments can add depth to the information gathered and also can be better adapted for younger children and adolescents. Card sorts qualify as informal assessments that can be used as directed or modified in various game formats. The Knowdell Card Sorts (Knowdell, 2018), mentioned earlier, include card packs for interests, career values, motivated skills, and leisure/retirement activities.

Odyssey Plan

The Odyssey Plan is an activity from the book *Designing Your Life* by William Burnett and David J. Evans (2016). The purpose of the activity is to help people map out their current plan, as well as some alternative plans. The Odyssey Plan can be drawn out on paper or a whiteboard to aid in visualizing the different plans together. First, the person draws their current life plan for the next 5 years. Next, the person draws the backup 5-year plan in case the primary plan cannot happen. The final 5-year plan maps out the "pie-in-the-sky" plan that could happen if time, money, and resources were no object. For each plan, people should also write down relevant resources, confidence, and questions they have, and career counselors can use this to help the client explore the various plans.

Career Construction Interview

The Career Construction Interview (Savickas, 1998, 2013; Savickas & Hartung, 2012) involves a lengthy interview protocol to identify themes. The questions range from childhood heroes to mantras to earliest recollections. The interview process integrates concepts from Adlerian Theory and narrative counseling and provides a strategy for collaboratively explore themes from the person's life. The full interview protocol is available for free on www.vocopher.com.

Life Career Rainbow

The Life Career Rainbow (Super, 1980; Super et al., 1992) is a tool that helps clients evaluate the salience of various life roles across the life span. The rainbow is a visual tool with Super's life stages and approximate age ranges on the outermost arc of the rainbow. Various life roles (e.g., child, parent, spouse, worker) are listed in the different colored bands of the rainbow. The client can use shading to indicate the salience of each role at different stages of the life span. Counselors can help clients make sense of this information, such as exploring how some roles may have competing importance that can lead to role conflict.

Narrative Career Activities

In an exercise that combines narrative and developmental concepts, counselors can lead activities with middle school students to write their career autobiographies (see the Career Autobiography Activity later in the chapter), including chapters related to events that have not yet occurred (e.g., high school activities, time at college, my first job). In this activity, drafting the chapters involves visualizing and describing one's future in depth. These assessments can also be enhanced by using some of the formal assessments mentioned earlier in the chapter.

CAREER COUNSELORS' USE OF MENTAL HEALTH ASSESSMENTS

Career readiness assessments demonstrate the impact that cognitive factors can have on the career decision-making process. Similarly, a person's mental health can impact the process of making career decisions, as well as one's satisfaction in their current job or career (Hayden & Osborn, 2020; Kronholz & Osborn, 2022; Saunders et al., 2000). Notably, researchers have found connections between negative career thoughts (as measured by the CTI) and symptoms of depression and anxiety (Hayden & Osborn, 2020; Kronholz & Osborn, 2022; Saunders et al., 2000), indicating that higher levels of mental health distress correlate with higher levels of dysfunctional career thinking. The loss of interest in hobbies and previously enjoyed activities can be a sign of depression, and this may show up on interest inventory results in the form of a flat profile (i.e., no indicated interests). A client's circumstance may determine if career distress is leading to mental health distress *or* mental health distress is exacerbating career distress. Nevertheless, clinicians should be prepared to recognize these connections and use assessments to facilitate insight and change.

Career professionals may be able to integrate mental health assessment into their practice. However, they should be very clear regarding their role and purpose, the ethical implications for assessment usage, and any certification or licensure requirements or limitations that may apply to professionals in their area (Lenz et al., 2010). Connections between career indecision and symptoms of anxiety and depression have the most documentation in professional literature (Hayden & Osborn, 2020; Kronholz & Osborn, 2022; Saunders et al., 2000; Walker & Peterson, 2012), so career professionals should be prepared, at a minimum, to conduct screenings for these symptoms. Training programs such as Mental Health First Aid (National Council for Mental Wellbeing, 2022) can be a great resource for career professionals who do not have strong training in mental health intervention; these trainings cover topics that may help you recognize, understand, and respond to various mental health concerns.

Procedurally, professionals may want to use a career readiness instrument like the CTI first to gauge whether any mental health screenings may be warranted. Or, mental health screening could be built into the intake process if permitted by the professional's workplace and credentialing body. Examples of mental health screening tools include the Patient Health Questionnaire-9 (PHQ-9; Kroenke et al., 2001) or the Generalized Anxiety Disorder 7-Item (GAD-7; Spitzer et al., 2006), which are freely available screening instruments for depression and anxiety. The *DSM-5* website (American Psychiatric Association, 2022) includes a few additional online assessment measures. Again, professionals should ensure that they have the proper training and necessary credentialing before using any mental health assessments and should make sure that their clients adequately understand the purpose of any assessments used and the nature of the professional relationship (i.e., career counseling, mental health counseling, or both). Moreover, if you intend to assess for mental health concerns but are not working in the capacity to address them (i.e., working in a university career center or advising), it is imperative to have referral options for the client or student.

CONNECTIONS TO COUNCIL FOR THE ACCREDITATION OF COUNSELING AND RELATED EDUCATIONAL PROGRAMS STANDARDS

Career assessment is an integral part of the CACREP (2016) standards, most notably in Section 2.F.4: *Career Development* and Section 2.F.7: *Assessment and Testing*. The standard focused on theories and models of career development (2.F.4.a) is of particular importance because many of the most popular career assessments are grounded in career theories in their interpretation and operation. Similarly, learning about connections between career, mental health, and life roles is important for understanding the importance of readiness assessment and mental health assessment in the career development process. Standards in the *Assessment and Testing* section matter for any type of assessment activities, including the importance of ethical practice, multicultural competence, and understanding statistical and psychometric properties of the instruments being used.

With career development and assessment composing two of the eight CACREP core areas, it's not surprising to see career, vocational, or work concepts mentioned in nearly every entry-level specialty area in Section 5. Career assessment is specifically mentioned in a few specialty areas (e.g., school counseling, career counseling, rehabilitation counseling), where vocational work is more obviously expected. However, due to the influence of career development on various life roles, professionals in other specialty areas should not shy away from using career assessments when presenting concerns related to some elements of work. Surprisingly, the Clinical Mental Health Counseling standards (5.C) is the only area that does not specifically address some element of career or vocational work, but it is hoped that this is corrected in the next set of standards due to the growing body of research connecting career and mental health concerns.

CASE STUDY

COLLEGE STUDENT WITH PANDEMIC-INDUCED CAREER ANXIETY

Agnes is a second-year college student who is majoring in business management with the hope of opening her own small business to sell merchandise made by local artists, including her own art. Amid the COVID-19 pandemic, she began to reevaluate that plan after seeing many small businesses struggle to stay open. She made an appointment with her university's career center to help her sort out her future plans. She arrives at her first appointment with Javon, a career counselor, feeling very anxious about the possibility of shifting away from a plan she's had for years.

After learning a bit about Agnes and why she's came in for career counseling, Javon asks her to talk about her experience during the pandemic and how it has influenced her decision to change her career plans. Agnes explains that she had been working part time at two small businesses, one focused on art and another a general retail store, and the owners of both decided to close up shop due to COVID-related closures and supply chain issues. To make ends meet for a while, Agnes started teaching basic art classes through Zoom to whoever was interested and willing to pay.

Agnes agrees to participate in several career assessments with Javon, including the CTI, the O*Net Interest Profiler, and card sorts for career values and motivated skills. Table 7.2 displays key results from the assessments.

Her overall score on the CTI is slightly in the area of mild concern, and commitment anxiety seems to be the most problematic area, which matches with her description of her situation. Her Interest Profiler results are not surprising and seem to fit well with her pandemic gig of teaching online art classes. Similarly, her experience with the values card sort indicates a strong inclination for creative expression and social contact. The skills card sort revealed motivated skills in the areas of planning and making arrangements, which is something Agnes says she hadn't previously considered.

In the next meeting with Agnes, Javon helps her make sense of the results. She said that after reflecting on the results, she realizes that the idea of owning a business is still very important to her, but the riskiness of opening a brick-and-mortar establishment still concerns her. Javon asks if she's ever considered operating an online business similar to her pandemic teaching gig. Agnes acknowledged that she really enjoyed the online teaching and could see herself expanding that to include other artists, as well. She recognizes that she has some skill and knowledge areas to work out and would like to explore some elective classes or a potential undergraduate minor that could help bolster these areas. Their meeting ended with Agnes feeling less anxious about her business management major and more excited about potentially starting a business offering art classes online.

(continued)

CASE STUDIES (*CONTINUED*)

TABLE 7.2 THE CASE OF AGNES: KEY FINDINGS FROM CAREER ASSESSMENTS

ASSESSMENT	KEY RESULTS
Career Thoughts Inventory	CTI Total Score: 50 (*T* score = 51) Decision-Making Confusion subscale: 8 (*T* score = 46) Commitment Anxiety subscale: 21 (*T* score = 65) External Conflict subscale: 4 (*T* score = 53)
Interest Profiler	Identified Holland Code: AES 1. Artistic 2. Enterprising 3. Social
Values Card Sort	Always Valued: Artistic creativity; Public contact; Community; Helping others; Work with others Never Valued: Physical challenge; Competition; Fast pace; Work under pressure
Skills Card Sort	Motivated Skills: Plan/Organize; Teach/Train; Make Arrangements Developmental Skills: Maintain Records; Mentor; Delegate; Computer literate Burnout Skills: Mediate; Classify; Use mechanical abilities

Discussion Questions
1. Reflect on the assessments administered to the client. Are there any areas that you would want to explore further given the data shared in Table 7.2?
2. After reading this chapter and are there any additional assessments that you would want to include, formal or informal, based on Agnes's presenting issue?
3. Discuss or role-play the conversation that might ensue between Javon and Agnes as the client and counselor process the presenting issue and discuss assessment results.

PROFESSIONAL INSIGHTS FROM CHRISTOPHER T. BELSER

My professional experiences include middle school counseling, teaching undergraduate career planning, conducting career research, and now, training school and mental health counselors. Interest assessments and values card sorts were the most commonly used career assessments during my time as a middle school counselor. In my experience, the students appreciated these, and they were a great place to start if students hadn't previously been exposed to career assessments. Using assessments that were computer-based, such as California Career Zone's Interest Profiler, added an extra element of fun to them.

Career assessment was a huge part of my work when I taught a STEM-focused undergraduate career-planning course. The course was part of a larger STEM program for students who were interested in STEM but who had not yet committed to a major (Dagley et al., 2016). Within the course, students completed the CTI, the Career Development Inventory (CDI), an interest inventory, a values inventory, a skills inventory, the Jung Typology Test, and card sorts for Career Values and Motivated Skills. They were able to build a more complete profile of themselves and use that data during the career exploration activities within the course. From a research lens, we used the CTI and CDI as pre- and posttests to evaluate change for students after completing the course, and overall, the course was effective in improving students' career readiness, particularly reducing negative career thinking (Belser, Prescod, et al., 2018; Belser, Shillingford, et al., 2018). Anecdotally, the subscales of the CTI helped give students language to discuss their career indecision and helped differentiate their sources of career indecision. My students generally liked the values and skills card sorts more than the formal assessments because the card sorts listed more examples and involved more opportunity for discussion. For those working with STEM-interested students or professionals, I've found that assessments that tap into the cognitive and meaning-making spaces were particularly useful because these students were less likely to have engaged previously in that work in career assessments.

Now, as a counselor educator, I've managed to work career assessment into graduate courses, such as Introduction to School Counseling, Analysis of the Individual (our assessment and evaluation course), Lifespan Development, and Counseling Theories. Based on the growing body of research that connects career concerns to mental health concerns, it is imperative that counselors-in-training are equipped to use career assessments, even if it isn't their primary work. When I taught the assessment and evaluation course, we evaluated existing career assessments based on their psychometric properties, their researched performance with diverse populations, and the properties that relate to diversity and inclusion. For example, we examined existing assessments to see how they handle or solicit information related to gender identity and how inclusive their validation samples are. Students generally concluded that many of our popular career assessments still have work to do when it comes to research with diverse populations, and that calls for professionals in the field making better, informed decisions about test selection.

CAREER AUTOBIOGRAPHY ACTIVITY

The Career Autobiography activity discussed previously in this chapter was designed for middle school students in a group or whole-class format, but it can be adapted for work with younger or older populations and with individuals. Within the activity, students tap into their future goals using story and solution-focused concepts and develop their autobiography for stages of life that have not yet occurred. To begin, introduce students to the overall project and the different "chapters" that they'll develop. Examples include the following:

- Who am I? (Current self-description, including interests, hobbies, personality, etc.)
- My family (Explore the family of origin and careers/hobbies in the family)
- My heroes (Heroes and role models)

- My first "when I grow up . . ." career (Can include realistic or "fantastical" careers)
- Middle school goals (Short-term goals for the remaining middle school years)
- High school goals (Short and long-term goals for high school, including the school, classes, extracurricular activities, leadership opportunities, etc.)
- My first job (Exploring the first paid job)
- Postsecondary goals (What is my plan for after high school?)
- Subsequent chapters can be developed based on individual interests and goals (e.g., Starting a family, owning a business, getting a specific graduate degree)

Once students have discussed the chapters they intend to include, work with them to identify how they would like to complete the autobiography. Some students may prefer to write it in a story format, some may prefer to create a mixed-media collage (magazine cutouts, printed pictures, drawings, etc.), and some may prefer a blended format. Blank books (preassembled blank cardstock books), can be useful for students who wish to put their autobiography together in a more artistic format. In subsequent sessions or lessons, students can complete a chapter or set of chapters and share their project with peers. Along the way, the counselor can aid the student in their self-assessment and research by using various formal and informal career assessments. In the end, they will have explored their goals and developed a short- and long-term plan.

It is good to remember that a single assessment is typically insufficient to help a client make a well-informed career decision. Using a combination of assessments or a comprehensive assessment program can help clients examine a variety of career-development constructs and form a more holistic picture of themselves. Despite the fact that assessments of the career development process and career readiness have grown more popular, there is still room to expand their use in tandem with other career assessments, particularly due to the increasing body of research establishing strong correlations between career concerns and mental health concerns.

Counselors should be versed in the ethical and appropriate use of any career assessment they select and should understand each instrument's psychometric properties, purposes, and limitations. Treat each career assessment with the same levels of importance and rigor as assessments of mental health constructs such as anxiety and depression. But most importantly, don't overlook the value of what career assessments can bring to the working alliance with a client or student. When used effectively, clients should feel supported and understood and should gain insight that can aid in career decision-making.

ETHICAL CORNER

In this section, the authors lead the reader through topical scenarios to surface common ethics questions and dilemmas faced by career professionals. They ask pertinent and personal questions to encourage reader reflection and insight into personal and professional ethics.

Azra Karajic Siwiec PhD, LPC is a counselor educator employed by Capella University. She has been working in the counselor education field for over 14 years and has served as a committee member of the Ethics Committee of NCDA since 2015 and served as the chair of the Ethics Committee since 2017.

Sharon K. Anderson, PhD, is professor of counseling and career development at Colorado State University. Sharon has taught the master's level ethics course for counseling students for over 20 years, teaching and mentoring a multitude of students. She has coauthored or coedited four professional ethics books used by practitioners in counseling and coaching.

VIGNETTE

Sandi, a supervisee, hears another supervisee discuss a client's career assessments in a relaxed manner. Sandi believes the supervisee is misrepresenting to a client the information about the Strong Interest Inventory. Sandi wonders what her professional responsibility might be.

If you were Sandi's supervisor and she came to you for guidance, what would you suggest she do? What parts of the NCDA ethics code might you reference? What ethical principles do you think would be important to bring into the conversation with Sandi? What virtue ethics might you ask Sandi about as she considers her next steps? Lastly, are you aware of any steps you might need to take with the supervisee who is misunderstanding the inventory?

DIGGING INTO ETHICS

Examine your perceptions on assessments. How would you gauge your perceptions? How did you come to have these perceptions? How will your views on assessment, your perceptions, impact your work with clients?

7.1 PRACTITIONER'S PERSPECTIVE

Trinka Polite, LPC, NCC is a Georgia native serving over 18 years as a career counselor providing education planning and career- guidance support. In her roles as counselor and poet, her mission is to empower and equip others to live to their full potential.

When I was in high school, my friends and other classmates would always come to me for advice. They would give me a folded letter in the morning or ask during our lunch break if I could respond by the end of the day. Little did I know that Trinka Polite, "the counselor," was being formed from ninth grade until my senior year. I enjoyed reading the letters and remember being in awe of the amount of trust others had in me. The impromptu advice seeking continued outside of school with my family and people in laundromats and doctors' waiting rooms. Obviously, helping others was going to be my contribution to the world, and I discovered the title of my contribution was counseling.

My career path started in a clinical psychology program, which I did not continue due to the incongruence with my natural way of being with people. Soon after making this decision, serendipity stepped in to deliver a postcard from a master's level humanistic psychology program. Discovering humanistic psychology, defined as "a perspective that emphasizes looking at the whole person and the uniqueness of each individual," reignited my passion and motivation to continue the career path to become a licensed counselor (McLeod, 1970, para. 2).

Why career counseling? A mentor in graduate school suggested a second major to have career options in the future, and after dealing with burnout as a mental health counselor, I made the decision to explore careers related to career counseling. Over 6 years, I worked as an education specialist for active-duty military members in which I provided counseling on education and career options in the civilian world. After experiencing a layoff, the opportunity presented itself to continue serving our military and their families through a program dedicated to education and career support for military spouses.

Currently I provide career counseling for military spouses. I also have a private practice where I provide career-planning support for families seeking career and education guidance for their children. Significant aspects of my job working with military spouses include individualized career counseling, staff development through new employee training/mentorship, and ongoing contact with spouses for support. Typically, characteristics of spouses include married less than 2 years, first-time college students, recent high school graduates, and reentering the workforce. Our work setting is a completely virtual career center providing all services, including career counseling, mock interviews, and career-related training through online and telephonic mediums.

When assessing clients, I draw regularly on Career OneStop Skills Matcher, Career OneStop Work Values Matcher, Myers-Briggs, Strong Interest Inventory, Department of Labor websites (i.e., Occupational Outlook Handbook, O*Net Online, and MyNextMove), and the Small Business Administration. Assessments are integrated into my work, especially with clients who are reentering the workforce after being unemployed for a number of years. One client was out of the workforce for over 8 years, and she completed a skills, interest, and personality assessment. The results from this combination revealed which careers overlapped her skills and interest areas with her personality type, and it provided more clarity for the specific path she should take.

My clients are my motivation to stay in the career field. Witnessing them set goals, develop objectives, and experience the reality of completing their goals is a huge source of inspiration. When clients go from failing at others' definition of success to winning based on how they define success, I am reminded of the rewards of serving as a career counselor.

TRAITS OF CAREER COUNSELORS

The people who are best suited for this work are people who have empathy, a desire to see others succeed, an understanding of process, creative approaches to helping others, and an ability to honor the individuality of each client.

PROFESSIONAL ETHICS

To maintain legal and ethical standards as well as boundaries within my work, I commit to having a working knowledge of my profession's code of ethics, and completing annual training keeps the code of conduct at the forefront when counseling clients. Respecting a client's privacy is an example of an important guideline to consider when working in a virtual setting. Clients may feel that they can connect with you on social media sites, and this could present a conflict and an invasion of the client's privacy.

7.2 PRACTITIONER'S PERSPECTIVE

Devan Lane, EdS, is the director of Career Development for the College of Communication and Information at The University of Tennessee, Knoxville. She has worked in a variety of career-development roles, including career coaching, experiential learning, and employer relations.

I chose to work in career counseling through self- and options-analysis and a little bit of happenstance. After working in the field of my undergraduate major—marketing—for about 5 years, I realized I wanted to help people more directly and less so in the business-to-business context. I started exploring my options using *What Color Is Your Parachute* and landed on pursuing an alternative teaching certification until I met a career coach on the rooftop of my gym. After learning about the career coaching profession, I was hooked and just had to go to one of the (eight at the time) CACREP-accredited career counseling programs. Florida State University was an easy choice after doing an informational interview with Dr. Robert Reardon.

I have worked with a wide variety of populations over my career, including adults transitioning out of government work, military spouses, government employees, and traditional and nontraditional college students. Currently, I work with undergraduate students studying communication and information.

Here is an example of one of my career assessment students: A student came to see me for help exploring their postgraduate options. The student had previous experience in healthcare before deciding to return to school for a bachelor's degree in biology to pursue a career in advanced medicine. Prior to our meeting, the student had failed several classes in the major and was encouraged by their academic advisor to pursue something different. But the student did not want to change majors.

Before administering any formal assessment, we spent our sessions talking about the student's general interest in healthcare. I decided to use the Strong Interest Inventory because it offered the opportunity to compare the student's interest with people actually working in the healthcare field, and it offered some insight into learning styles. I wanted to help this student understand that there were other ways to pursue a healthcare interest without directly helping in a physician's role.

We spent several sessions exploring occupations together and discussing how the student's strengths aligned or did not align with each of them. The student excelled at conventional work but did not feel comfortable with investigative work and decided to pursue office work in healthcare instead. We also used our institution's career management platform to simultaneously review position qualifications in the healthcare field. This allowed the student to see "real" positions and expedited the job search when our session goals naturally shifted to be job-search focused.

I love this work! Having the opportunity to pursue higher education changed my life. I love having the opportunity to do that for others at scale through the programs I develop. I spend a significant amount of time building out programs that will scale, measuring impact through data, creating pipelines to talent for employer partners, and helping faculty incorporate career readiness into the classroom.

In my current role, I mainly use assessment to measure the success of programs. The assessments and tools that I use most often include Handshake model, Holland theory, human performance, and instructional design methodologies, such as ADDIE (analyze, design, develop, implement, and evaluate) and the Kirkpatrick model. It is important to build in success measurements during the program-planning phase. Any time I work with a team on implementing a new program, I challenge them to think about what outcomes they would need to see to continue running the program. Sometimes this task is made easier by pointing to a clear learning objective or strategic initiative.

Often, though, practitioners may find themselves considering additional factors, especially as career development professionals are increasingly asked to deliver a wider variety of programs and services. For example, my team was asked to host an internship-only fair when we had already hosted a combined career and internship fair that semester. My team was not thrilled about duplicating work, so we worked with leadership to determine what would make this separate fair a success and built those factors into the postevent evaluation. The team wanted to attract a more diverse set of employers and designed a more focused event to increase the satisfaction of the employers served.

Postevent, we found the opposite was more successful; more students searched for internships at the combined career and internship fair than at the internship-only fair. Deciding not to host the event again was an easy decision because we mutually agreed on the success factors during the planning phase, and we were able to review the data without bias.

TRAITS OF CAREER COUNSELORS

Career development work often overlaps with other disciplines. It can be part workforce development, part academic advising, part talent development . . . and the list goes on. Folks who can articulate the expanded career development vision to varied audiences while educating constituents on the importance of ethical best practices and professional standards will do well in leadership roles in the field.

PROFESSIONAL ETHICS

Ensuring that equitable hiring processes are in place for referring students to open positions is something that our professional association, NACE, has embedded in its Principles for Ethical Professional Practice. Specifically, there is a Faculty Guide to Ethical and Legal Standards in Student Hiring that I share often with faculty and academic administrators.

Student Voices

In Student Voices, students offer a unique viewpoint as they begin in the career-counseling field. Here, students share their thoughts and reflections about the career-counseling profession and offer personal takeaways.

BYRON J. DICKEY

Byron J. Dickey is a MA graduate of the Counselor Education: Career Development & Placement Program at North Carolina Central University (NCCU). Byron serves as the career development coordinator for the Career and Professional Development Center at NCCU.

In graduate school, when it was time for me to pick a clinical placement site, I had the honor of completing my practicum, internship, and now my first job in my career with the Career and Professional Development Center at NCCU. As I continue to grow in the career-counseling world, I often look back to my graduate program experiences.

As a graduate student, I often wondered what assessment tools I would use and which ones I agreed with the most. After walking through multiple assessments, I must say that my top two assessments must be MBTI and Holland Code. MBTI resonates with me because it is one of the most used personality assessments, and the possibilities are endless. This assessment does not measure or categorize individuals by their abilities, likelihood to succeed, skills, intelligence, or even mental health, but instead reflects on preferences. This is one of the few assessments that make some of the theories that we learn practical.

MBTI can be used in organizations, education settings, counseling, team building, improving relationships, leadership development, and college and career development. For me, MBTI is an assessment that helps people understand their preferences and how they can use these preferences to work as an advantage in their prospective careers.

Holland Code assessment measures personality and helps people understand how their personality relates to their occupation. This assessment works well in sessions and allows me, as a counselor, to break down results from an assessment to a student who does not have a background in career counseling or self-awareness as it pertains to career development.

Here at NCCU, we refer to this assessment as RIASEC, which stands for realistic, investigative, artistic, social, enterprising, and conventional. In sessions with clients, I enjoy taking the terms of the assessment and explaining to them the areas that they can go into occupationally and not feel like they are stuck. The exciting part about this assessment is that it gives each personality type a nickname and different careers to explore. For instance, realistic people are "do-ers," artistic individuals are "creators," and those that are conventional are "organizers." So, when my students see this, they tend to say things like, "I think I am more like this category rather than that one." As a counselor, I have discovered that when the lightbulb moments happen for students, they have this indescribable feeling. That is exciting for me because I get a chance to help ignite a fire in them and show them that their options are endless.

Every counseling appointment varies, but assessments are applied in some way. In our career services center, we have an assessment tool that allows us to mix multiple assessments in one to help students understand better. Although I might not get a chance to do assessments in every session, I refer to assessments often to help fulfill the needs of the learners.

COUNSELING SKILLS CONNECTION

Mental health disorders can significantly impact a client's responses on a career assessment or influence their experience while taking the assessment, and recognizing signs of mental illness is critical when selecting, administering, and interpreting career assessments. For example, a client experiencing anxiety may have a difficult time making choices on an interest inventory such as the Strong Interest Inventory. When reviewing the assessment report, the profile may be elevated as a result of not wanting to close off any career options. As a counselor, you would want to be prepared to process the results along with the anxiety that may be affecting those results. Similarly, depressive symptoms may create a flat profile on an instrument like the Strong Interest Inventory. A client experiencing depression may lack significant interest in any one thing and have little motivation or energy to devote to their career exploration process, thus creating a flat profile. Career counselors should be prepared to refer clients to local clinicians or therapists licensed to diagnose and treat mental health disorders.

MINDFUL MOMENT

Both for our clients and for ourselves, mindfulness is a great daily practice to manage stress. The American Institute of Stress provides a breadth of wonderful mindfulness exercises. A few examples include: Rise and Shine—Morning Intention, Rub-a-dub-dub Mindfulness Exercises, and Mindful Food Practices.

A thoughtful mindfulness prompt from the Rise and Shine—Morning Intention activity offers several options people to engage with, such as intentional journaling and writing upon rising in the morning, a calming guided meditation, exploration of reading materials related to one's interests, and encouragement to move our bodies to create the mind, body, and spirit connection (Ikonomov, 2021). The intent is not necessarily to engage in all the activities at once or even in the same session but rather to identify the activities that bring you peace, calm, and joy.

There are a plethora of examples of mindfulness practices, including descriptive, automated, and visual videos to walk you and your clients or students through mindfulness exercises. We encourage you to try one of these activities or similar practices offered online and incorporate it into your daily routine.

TECH TOOLS

Counselors often rely on thin budgets, it's often necessary to seek out free tools to support our work. If you've spent any time on social media, you've likely seen quizzes purporting to predict any number of characteristics, personality traits, or even the future. With the click of a few pictures, a quiz could tell me if I would get expelled from Hogwarts or categorize my personality in a pseudo-Enneagram style quiz. It can be so tempting to click on these quizzes and seek answers; I admit to being curious if I would make it through Hogwarts. Counselors must be intentional about vetting any assessment, particularly the free ones. A few questions to research:

1. What is the theoretical foundation of this assessment? How does that theory align with my perspective as a counselor?
2. How was this assessment normed? To what extent does the norm group represent my client and their unique identity?
3. What is the reliability and validity of this assessment? Are there limitations that I need to be aware of?
4. How are results communicated to the client or counselor? What identifiable data is collected and saved by the assessment administrator?

Example: NERIS Type Explorer on 16 Personalities

From the 16Personalities.com site you can quickly dive in and learn that the assessment, the NERIS Type Explorer, builds from foundations of Myers-Briggs theory and Big Five personality traits. The website provides articles outlining reliability and validity testing, including internal consistency and test–retest validity. This particular assessment is available free in over 30 languages worldwide. The theory page notes that the assessment was tested in English and that translated versions have gone through "multiple iterations" (16 Personalities, n.d.-a, n.d.-b). As a counselor, you would want to be intentional about using a foreign language version of the assessment or administering the English language version with a non-native English speaker. Be mindful that nuances in language and cultural context may influence how a client may respond to a particular prompt. Queue your multicultural counseling skills!

You may find that it's difficult to find information about how a free assessment was developed. If it is difficult or impossible to find, you may conclude that the assessment has limited value and may even be harmful for your client. While the ease of use is tempting, it is critical to review digital assessments before recommending them to a client.

REFLECTION ACTIVITY

Reflecting on your past experience taking career assessments, what specific assessments or categories of assessments would have been helpful in your decision-making process? What populations can you see yourself working with and what categories of career assessments do you see being useful? How can you meaningfully integrate formal and informal assessments in your assessment practices? What career development or career readiness constructs will be useful to measure in your work setting? How can you see yourself integrating career assessment and mental health assessment in a meaningful way in your future work?

END-OF-CHAPTER RESOURCES

SUMMARY

Assessments are useful tools for career counselors to assist clients across the career development process. This chapter explored a variety of assessment tools used by career counselors within disparate settings. Intentional selection of assessment tools requires counselors to be mindful of their unique client and ethical application of a particular tool. While some assessment tools are formal, require certification, and can be costly, counselors can also draw from a host of informal tools to assist clients in evaluating their values, interests, personality, and career options. Assessments are not a substitute for the counseling process; rather, the value of these tools is best leveraged through the counseling relationship as you assist a client in understanding, connecting, and applying results. As a counselor-in-training, consult with peers and supervisors who have worked with populations of interest about which assessments have been most useful, relevant, affordable, and accessible.

REFERENCES

16 Personalities. (n.d.-a). *Core theory, our framework.* https://www.16personalities .com/articles/our-theory

16 Personalities. (n.d.-b). *Core theory, reliability and validity.* https://www .16personalities.com/articles/reliability-and-validity

ACT. (2022). *WorkKeys assessments.* https://www.act.org/content/act/en/products -and-services/workkeys-for-job-seekers/assessments.html

American Psychiatric Association. (2022). *Online assessment measures.* https://www .psychiatry.org/psychiatrists/practice/dsm/educational-resources/assessment -measures

Asplund, J., Agrawal, S., Hodges, T., Harter, J., & Lopez, S. J. (2014). *The Clifton StrengthsFinder 2.0 technical report.* https://www.gallup.com/cliftonstrengths/en/ 253790/science-of-cliftonstrengths.aspx

Armed Services Vocational Aptitude Battery (ASVAB) Program. (2022). *Understanding your ASVAB results.* https://www.asvabprogram.com/media-center-article/46

Belser, C. T., Prescod, D. J., Daire, A. P., Dagley, M. A., & Young, C. Y. (2018). The influence of career planning on negative career thoughts with STEM-interested undergraduates. *The Career Development Quarterly, 66*(2), 176–181. https://doi.org/ 10.1002/cdq.12131

Belser, C. T., Shillingford, M. A., Daire, A. P., Prescod, D. J., & Dagley, M. A. (2018). Factors influencing undergraduate retention in STEM majors: Career development, math ability, and demographics. *The Professional Counselor, 8*(3), 262–276. https://doi.org/10.15241/ctb.8.3.262

Ben-Porath, Y. S., & Tellegen, A. (2020). *Minnesota Multiphasic Personality Inventory 3.* Pearson.

Betz, N. E., & Taylor, K. M. (2012). *Career decision self-efficacy scale manual.* Mindgarden.

Burnett, W., & Evans, D. J. (2016). *Designing your life: How to build a well-lived, joyful life*. Alfred A. Knopf.

CACREP. (2016). 2016 CACREP standards (2.F.4-2.F.7). https://www.cacrep.org/for-programs/2016-cacrep-standards/

Campbell, D. P. (1992). *Campbell interest and skill survey*. National Computer Systems.

Campbell, D. P. (2002). The history and development of the Campbell Interest and Skill Survey. *Journal of Career Assessment, 10*(2), 150–168. https://doi.org/10.1177/1069072702010002002

Career One Stop Skills Matcher. (2022). *Skills matcher*. https://www.careeronestop.org/Toolkit/Skills/skills-matcher.aspx

Cattell, H. E. P., & Mead, A. D. (2008). The Sixteen Personality Factor Questionnaire (16PF). In G. J. Boyle, G. Matthews, & D. H. Saklofske (Eds.), *The SAGE handbook of personality theory and assessment, vol. 2. Personality measurement and testing* (pp. 135–159). Sage. https://doi.org/10.4135/9781849200479.n7

Choi, Y. (2017). Work values, job characteristics, and career choice decisions: evidence from longitudinal data. *The American Review of Public Administration, 47*(7), 779–796. https://journals.sagepub.com/doi/10.1177/0275074016653469

Costa, P. T., & McCrae, R. R. (2011). *NEO inventories: Bibliography for the NEO Personality Inventory-3 (NEO-PI-3), Revised NEO Personality Inventory (NEO-PI-R), and NEO Five-Factor Inventory-3 (NEO-FFI-3)*. https://www.parinc.com/Portals/0/webuploads/samplerpts/NEO_Biblio_2011.pdf

Costa, P. T., Jr., & McCrae, R. R. (2008). The Revised NEO Personality Inventory (NEO-PI-R). In G. J. Boyle, G. Matthews, & D. H. Saklofske (Eds.), *The SAGE handbook of personality theory and assessment, Vol. 2. Personality measurement and testing* (pp. 179–198). Sage. https://doi.org/10.4135/9781849200479.n9

Curry, J. R. (2017, December). *Careers from day one*. ASCA School Counselor. https://www.ascaschoolcounselor-digital.org/ascaschoolcounselor/november_december_2017/MobilePagedArticle.action?articleId=1251633#articleId1251633

Curry, J. R., & Milsom, A. (2021). *Career and college readiness counseling in P-12 schools* (3rd ed.). Springer.

Dagley, M. A., Young, C. Y., Georgiopoulos, M., Daire, A. P., Parkinson, C., Prescod, D. J., & Belser, C. T. (2016). Recruiting undecided admits to pursue a STEM degree. *Proceedings from the American Society for engineering education 123rd annual conference & exposition*. https://peer.asee.org/recruiting-undecided-admits-to-pursue-a-stem-degree

Di Fabio, A., Palazzeschi, L., Levin, N., & Gati, I. (2015). The role of personality in the career decision-making difficulties of Italian young adults. *Journal of Career Assessment, 23*, 281–293. https://doi.org/10.1177/1069072714535031

Donnay, D. A. C., Thompson, R. C., Morris, M. L., & Schaubhut, N. A. (2004). *Technical brief for the Strong Interest Inventory Assessment: Content, reliability, and validity*. The Myers-Briggs Company.

Ertl, B., & Hartmann, F. G. (2019). The interest profiles and interest congruence of male and female students in STEM and non-STEM fields. *Frontiers in Psychology, 10*, 1–18. https://doi.org/10.3389/fpsyg.2019.00897

Everything DiSC. (n.d.). *About everything DiSC: Theory and research*. http://www.discprofile.com

Fouad, N. A., & Kantamneni, N. (2013). The role of race and ethnicity in career choice, development, and adjustment. In S. D. Brown & R. W. Lent (Eds.), *Career development and counseling: Putting theory and research to work* (pp. 215–243). Wiley.

Fouad, N. A., & Mohler, C. J. (2004). Cultural validity of Holland's theory and the Strong Interest Inventory for five racial/ethnic groups. *Journal of Career Assessment, 12*(4), 423–439. https://doi.org/10.1177/1069072704267736

Gibson, D. M. (2008, May). *Using career genograms in K-12 settings.* Career Convergence. https://www.ncda.org/aws/NCDA/pt/sd/news_article/5473/_PARENT/CC_layout_details/false

Harmon, L. W., Hansen, J. C., Borgen, F. H., & Hammer, A. C. (1994). *Strong interest inventory: Applications and technical guide.* Consulting Psychologists Press.

Harrington, T., & Long, J. (2013). The history of interest inventories and career assessments in career counseling. *Career Development Quarterly, 61*(1), 83–92. https://doi.org/10.1002/j.2161-0045.2013.00039.x

Hayden, S. C. W., & Osborn, D. S. (2020). Impact of worry on career thoughts, career decision state, and cognitive information processing skills. *Journal of Employment Counseling, 57*(4), 163–177. https://doi.org/10.1002/joec.12152

Hays, D. (2017). *Assessment in counseling* (6th ed.). Wiley.

Herk, N. A., & Thompson, R. C. (2012). *Strong interest inventory manual update: Occupational Scales update 2012.* Consulting Psychologists Press.

Holland, J. L., & Messer, M. A. (2017). *Standard self-directed search* (5th ed.). Psychological Assessment Resources.

Ikonomov, J. (2021, February 10). *12 fun mindfulness exercises.* The American Institute of Stress. https://www.stress.org/12-fun-mindfulness-exercises

Knowdell, R. L. (2018). *Knowdell card sorts.* https://www.knowdellcardsorts.com/

Kroenke, K., Spitzer, R., L., & Williams, J. B. (2001). The PHQ-9: Validity of a brief depression severity measure. *Journal of General Internal Medicine, 16*, 606–613. https://doi.org/10.1046/j.1525-1497.2001.016009606.x

Kronholz, J., & Osborn, D. S. (2022). Dysfunctional career thoughts, profile elevation, and RIASEC skills of career counseling clients. *Journal of Employment Counseling.* https://doi.org/10.1002/joec.12178

Krumboltz, J. D. (1994). The career beliefs inventory. *Journal of Counseling & Development, 72*(4), 424–428. https://doi.org/10.1002/j.1556-6676.1994.tb00962.x

Kuder, G. F. (1964). *Kuder general interest survey: Manual.* Science Research Associates.

LeFebvre, M. (2016). *A summary of ACT WorkKeys validation research.* https://www.act.org/content/dam/act/unsecured/documents/5350-Research-Report-2016-4-A-Summary-of-ACT-WorkKeys-Validation-Research.pdf

Lenz, J. G., Peterson, G. W., Reardon, R. C., & Saunders, D. E. (2010). *Connecting career and mental health counseling: Integrating theory and practice.* http://counselingoutfitters.com/vistas/vistas10/Article_01.pdf

Leong, F. T. L. (2010). A cultural formulation approach to career assessment and career counseling: Guest editor's introduction. *Journal of Career Development, 37*(1), 375–390. https://doi.org/10.1177/0894845310363708

Leuty, M. E., & Rounds, J. (2021). Work values: Understanding and assessing motivation to work. In D. R. Strauser (Ed.), *Career development, employment, and disability in rehabilitation: From theory to practice* (2nd ed., pp. 131–141). Springer.

Lowman, R. L. (2022). *Career assessment: Integrating interests, abilities, and personality.* American Psychological Association.

Ludwikowski, W. M. A., Schechinger, H. A., & Armstrong, P. I. (2020). Are interest assessments propagating gender differences in occupations? *Journal of Career Assessment, 28*(1), 14–27. https://doi.org/10.1177/1069072718821600

Marston, W. M. (1928). *Emotions of normal people.* Harcourt Brace.

Martincin, K. M., & Stead, G. B. (2015). Five-factor model and difficulties in career decision making. *Journal of Career Assessment, 23*, 3–19. https://doi.org/10.1177/1069072714523081

Mcleod, S. (1970, January 1). *Humanistic approach.* Humanistic Approach | Simply Psychology. https://www.simplypsychology.org/humanistic.html

MindGarden. (2022). *Career beliefs inventory.* https://www.mindgarden.com/78-career-beliefs-inventory#horizontalTab3

Morris, M. L. (2016). Vocational interests in the United States: Sex, age, ethnicity, and year effects. *Journal of Counseling Psychology, 63*(5), 604–615. https://doi.org/10.1037/cou0000164

Myers, I. B., McCaulley, M. H., Quenk, N. L., & Hammer, A. L. (2018). *MBTI® manual for the Global Step I™ and Step II™ assessments* (4th ed.). The Myers-Briggs Company.

MyPlan. (2019). *MyPlan personality test.* https://www.myplan.com/assess/personality.php

National Center for O*NET Development. (2000). *O*NET work importance locator.* https://www.onetcenter.org/WIL.html#paper-pencil

National Center for O*NET Development. (2021). *O*NET interest profiler.* https://www.mynextmove.org/explore/ip

National Center for O*NET Development. (2022). *Browse by O*NET data.* https://www.onetonline.org/find/descriptor/browse/1.A

National Council for Mental Wellbeing. (2022). *Mental health first aid.* http://www.mentalhealthfirstaid.org

Nauta, M. M. (2010). The development, evolution, and status of Holland's theory of vocational personalities: Reflections and future directions for counseling psychology. *Journal of Counseling Psychology, 57*(1), 11–22. https://doi.org/10.1037/a0018213

O'Shea, A. J., & Feller, R. (2012). *The career decision-making system-revised.* Pearson.

Primé, D. R., & Tracey, T. J. G. (2009). Psychometric properties of the Career Clusters Interest Survey. *Journal of Career Assessment, 18*(2), 177–188. https://doi.org/10.1177/1069072709354202

Reardon, R. C., & Lenz, J. G. (2015). *Handbook for using the Self-Directed Search: Integrating RIASEC and CIP theories in practice.* Psychological Assessment Resources.

Rounds, J., Hoff, K., & Lewis, P. (2021). *O*Net interest profiler manual.* www.onetcenter.org

Sampson, J. P., Peterson, G. W., Lenz, J. G., Reardon, R. C., & Saunders, D. E. (1996). *Career thoughts inventory: Professional manual.* Psychological Assessment Resources.

Saunders, D. E., Peterson, G. W., Sampson, J. P., & Reardon, R. C. (2000). Relation of depression and dysfunctional career thinking to career indecision. *Journal of Vocational Behavior, 56*, 288–298. https://doi.org/10.1006/jvbe.1999.1715

Savickas, M. L. (1998). Career style assessment and counseling. In T. Sweeney (Ed.), *Adlerian counseling: A practitioner's approach* (4th ed., pp. 329–359). Accelerated Development.

Savickas, M. L. (2013). Career construction theory and practice. In S. D. Brown & R. W. Lent (Eds.), *Career development and counseling: Putting theory and research to work* (2nd ed., pp. 147–183). John Wiley.

Savickas, M. L., & Hartung, P. J. (2012). *My career story: An autobiographical workbook for life-career success.* http://www.vocopher.com

Savickas, M. L., & Porfeli, E. J. (2011). Revision of the career maturity inventory: The adaptability form. *Journal of Career Assessment, 19*(4), 355–374. https://doi.org/10.1177/1069072711409342

Savickas, M. L., & Porfeli, E. J. (2012). Career adapt-abilities scale: Construction, reliability, and measurement equivalence across 13 countries. *Journal of Vocational Behavior, 80,* 661–673. https://doi.org/10.1016/j.jvb.2012.01.011

Schaubhut, N. A., & Thompson, R. C. (2016). *Technical brief for the strong interest inventory assessment: Using the Strong with LGBT populations.* https://www.cpp.com/download/item/9a0a56f23e5b4fd99a40bda64eef6f54

Schaubhut, N. A., Herk, N. A., & Thompson, R. C. (2009). *MBTI Form M manual supplement.* https://www.mbtionline.com/-/media/Myers-Briggs/Files/Resources-Hub-Files/Practitioner-Resources/MBTI_FormM_Supplement.pdf?la=en-US

Scullard, M., & Baum, D. (2015). *Everything DiSC manual.* Wiley.

Spitzer, R. L., Kroenke, K., Williams, J. B., & Löwe, B. (2006). A brief measure for assessing generalized anxiety disorder: The GAD-7. *Archives of Internal Medicine, 166*(10), 1092–1097. https://doi.org/10.1001/archinte.166.10.1092

Super, D. E. (1980). A life-span, life-space approach to career development. *Journal of Vocational Behavior, 16*(3), 282–298. https://doi.org/10.1016/0001-8791(80)90056-1

Super, D. E., Osborne, W. L., Walsh, D., Brown, S. D., & Niles, S. G. (1992). Developmental career assessment and counseling: The C-DAC model. *Journal of Counseling & Development, 71*(1), 74–80. https://doi.org/10.1002/j.1556-6676.1992.tb02175.x

Walker, J. V., & Peterson, G. (2012). Career thoughts, indecision, and depression implications for mental health assessment in career counseling. *Journal of Career Assessment, 20*(4), 497–506. https://doi.org/10.1177/1069072712450010

Xu, H. (2020). Big five personality traits and ambiguity management in career decision-making. *The Career Development Quarterly, 68*(2), 158–172. https://doi.org/10.1002/cdq.12220

YouScience. (2022). *YouScience discovery.* http://www.youscience.com

Zytowski, D. (2006). *Super's work values inventory-revised: Technical Manual.* http://www.kuder.com

CHAPTER 8

CAREER AND TECHNOLOGY

Melissa A. Venable, Katie Peterssen,
and Angie C. Smith

LEARNING OBJECTIVES

By the end of this chapter, you will be able to:

- Evaluate online resources or tools and their ethical use.
- Review key technology resources for networking, organizational research, career information, professional practice, and so on.
- Compare delivering career counseling via distance modalities.
- Examine social media and LinkedIn applied to professional branding, networking, and job searching.
- Explore concepts related to ethics and technology.

WARM-UP EXERCISE

Right now, how close to you is your phone, computer, or electronic device(s)? What applications are currently on your phone or computer that you could use for a job search process or career exploration? Review your electronic devices to search the applications you would use for your own career journey. Reflect on the technology that could aid you and your clients as they seek specific career information, regardless of where they may be on their career path. Create a list of viable sites, applications, and technology.

INTRODUCTION

Technology is a part of our work and lives over the past several decades, and it's probably no surprise that it has gained popularity in career counseling and coaching as well and is referenced in some form throughout the chapters of this book. To have a separate chapter focused exclusively on technology seems somewhat deceptive since it's no longer easy to compartmentalize technology as a separate type of resource or work, but it is a necessary pleasure to address.

Whether you are or will be delivering career-development services online or in person, promoting programs and events, conducting outreach for new clients and partnerships, or facilitating career courses and workshops with learners and job seekers, technology will likely play a role in how you accomplish these tasks. A variety of websites, applications, social platforms, devices, and other tools can be leveraged to enhance your career- development work when implemented purposefully.

EVALUATING ONLINE TOOLS AND RESOURCES

Evaluating the **technology tools** you are using or are thinking about adopting is an ongoing process. It's also part of staying up to date with available tools and also your specific needs in working with students and clients. In your priorities, the latter should come first. Once you have identified a need, which may come in the form of a gap to fill or a problem to solve, then you can effectively search for tools that address these needs and add to your practice. You will likely discover many new, exciting, and popular tools, but that doesn't mean they are necessary or that they will improve your interactions with students and clients.

Evaluating tools and resources can involve many steps; start by creating a list of questions and requirements specific to your gap or problem. The following is a list of the basic considerations when adopting a new tech tool.

Associated Costs

How much will it cost? This is often the primary question asked when evaluating and comparing prospective technology tools because you'll likely be required to work within a budget. But this question can be challenging to answer. Is a free or trial version of the tool you are considering available? If so, use this as a place to start your exploration and evaluation.

When pricing technology, particularly software and online or cloud-based applications, note that costs may come in different categories, such as one-time fees, monthly or annual subscriptions, and rates that vary by number of users, amount of storage, number of projects, and other variables. Careful consideration is a must since comparing options, even options in the same category, may not be comparing apples to apples due to varying price structures.

Financial costs can be incurred directly and indirectly. The purchase of a software package will have a fee associated with it, but implementing new tools also incur costs related to time and effort. This area of expense includes providing training to current staff members and creating training for students and clients.

Accessibility

Using technology tools can improve or inhibit access to your programs, services, and resources. With a goal of increasing **accessibility** in mind, look for features and functions that address a wide scope of abilities, and include options such as closed captioning of live video, audio recordings of text-based materials, and text transcripts of audio-/video-based materials.

It's also important to consider access to the hardware (e.g., computer or smartphone), software applications (e.g., web conferencing and word processing), and broadband internet connectivity. Identify what each tool requires of your clients or students and also what they have access to before making the decision to adopt a specific technology. The Web Accessibility Initiative (www.w3.org/) provides detailed guidance to help tech users avoid barriers that make it challenging for some students and clients to use online resources.

Customer Support

Technology tools vary regarding how much training and support you, your clients, and students will need to use the tools effectively. Some technology tools are more intuitive to use, while others present a substantial learning curve. If you need a new tool to use with a team or with students and clients, it's important to think about whether they may already be familiar with it or something similar to it. If they are not, some sort of training or orientation will be helpful as well as quick reference guides and job aids to support teams, students, and clients use of the technology. When selecting a new tool, think about whether references and aids are available through the tool itself or if these are resources you will need to create.

Consider giving the new tool a trial run with a small group, or internally with your team, as a pilot test before making any big purchasing decisions and contract commitments.

KEY TECHNOLOGY RESOURCES

Technology is a great research tool. It can help you conduct a research project, connect with others interested in similar work, and share your research with the larger community of career practitioners. Google has become a first stop for online research, with more than 270 million unique visitors in January of 2022 in the United States alone (Johnson, 2022). But, advanced search engine techniques, such as Boolean searching (Burns, 2011) and the use of additional search engines (e.g., Bing, Yandex, CC Search, and Duck Duck Go), allow you to make the most of your time spent looking for relevant information and resources (Price, 2021). Extending your search to different search engines may help you avoid getting caught in a filter bubble, which actually narrows the results of your search rather than widen the scope (GCFGlobal, 2022a).

Online Databases

Those working for an education employer (i.e., school, college, or university) likely have access to a wide variety of digital publications and databases through the institution's library subscriptions. Connect with the research librarians at your institution for assistance and suggestions for the best options for your area of interest. If you don't have access to these kinds of resources through your employer, they can be expensive to subscribe to on your own. Start with open access options, such as Google Scholar, MERLOT, and CORE. Local and regional public libraries also offer free research support and may have relevant tools for employer and career-development research.

Organizational Research

Significant organizational research can be conducted via **online databases**. For example, you might compile a list of companies or organizations within a particular industry, geographic area, size, or other variable of interest to your students and clients. For example, Mergent Online or Hoover's Company Records can be applied to interview preparation. These resources provide snapshots of individual company financials, competitors, products, leadership, and more. Websites such as Glassdoor.com coordinate company reviews from the employee perspective. The U.S. Chamber of Commerce is touted as the largest business organization in the world that advocates and supports business of any and all sizes. Consider adding your local chamber of commerce to your professional network.

Career and Labor Market Information

Online databases provide easy access to information related to employment and careers that are commonly used to research both specific occupations and trends anticipated in the future. The U.S. Bureau of Labor Statistics (BLS) website (bls.gov) is home to a wide variety of resources, such as national compensation data, unemployment rates and research, an inflation calculator, geographic comparisons, and the Occupational Outlook Handbook (OOH). The OOH is updated regularly and provides a searchable database featuring pay scales, training and education, and projected growth by job title within 20 fie occupation groups (e.g., architecture and engineering, healthcare, media and communication).

There are several additional online resources that work with BLS and other government data sources to provide easy access to career information. O*NET OnLine (onetonline.org) is one such resource. It offers unique ways to search, such as by job duties, technology skills, work values, and abilities. O*NET also offers a suite of assessment tools, such as the Interest Profiler, to provide a personalized experience. The Crosswalk tools allow users to search for military occupational classifications to identify similar employment roles in the civilian sector. A related site, CareerOneStop (careeronestop.org), focuses on career planning, as well as the job search process, providing tools to explore careers and find training. This site also categorizes resources by specific need or motivation, such as entry-level workers, workers with disabilities, and workers aged 55 and over.

Technology Adoption and Use

It can be helpful to understand how other people are using technology as you make decisions about your own personal and professional use. The Pew Research Center, a nonpartisan fact tank, conducts public opinion surveys about topics including social media, internet use, and emerging technologies. Pew reports share how Americans, specifically, use technology for a variety of reasons including for work, career development, and education and training. Reviewing their reports may help you narrow down your own tech tool search or introduce you to new tools that Americans find helpful.

Technology for Everyday Use

Technology can help you do your work from communication and office administration tasks to more complex projects and collaboration. Here are a few more categories that you may want to explore.

- Collaboration applications: Discord, Google Chat, Microsoft Teams, Slack
- Event registration platforms: Eventbrite, Google Forms, Splash
- Project management systems: Asana, Basecamp, Monday.com, Trello
- Scheduling tools: Calendly, Doodle
- Web conferencing platforms: GoToMeeting, WebEx, Zoom
- Assessment or survey tools: Qualtrics, Survey Monkey, Google Forms

The Centre for Learning and Performance Technologies has been tracking the top tools for personal learning, workplace learning, and education since 2007. Its annual lists of these top tools are derived from submissions from professionals across the globe and can be searched by category, which includes many of the items listed earlier. This site can be a good place to start once you've identified a need.

Do you want to explore something new, but aren't sure whether to invest the time, energy, and expense to try it for yourself? Connect with your network, whether that means a LinkedIn post or a call with a few colleagues, to ask for feedback. You can also try the buddy system. Find a friend and colleague who will challenge you, and you in turn challenge them, to try new things and share notes about what you find along the way. There's a benefit to tapping this collective knowledge and experience base—you don't have to start from scratch. Also, there's safety in working with a friend to explore the possibilities and freely ask questions.

Networking Tools

As of May 2022, LinkedIn remains one of the top sites for professional networking; however, it's not the only networking option. Many niche career sites, such as Dice.com for tech-oriented jobs (e.g., software development, artificial intelligence), and Idealist.org for nonprofit opportunities (e.g., community organization, fundraising), offer job listings and also have devoted communities of coordinators and followers who actively share advice and current trends related to the work. These sites and other online communities can be particularly helpful for students and clients who are interested in switching to a new field or entering a new industry to familiarize themselves with the new field and begin to meet new people outside their existing circles.

Online communities are not the only way technology can help us connect with each other for career-development purposes. Many conferences now use mobile apps to enhance networking at professional development events. These apps, Cvent for example, allow participants to create a profile, message other participants, link to social feeds (e.g., Twitter, Facebook, and LinkedIn), and search for sessions and participants by keyword. These tools can be useful ways to connect with others at these events, whether they are held in person or online, and can be used to conduct virtual job fairs.

CAREER DEVELOPMENT AT A DISTANCE

There's a certain level of convenience in connecting at a distance or online to deliver or receive career-development programs and services. Many people realized the benefits and challenges, some for the first time, when schools and offices closed their physical locations during the coronavirus pandemic, while maintaining to some degree services and programs through technology tools. As we reach a postpandemic place, it's anticipated that teaching, learning, and working at a distance will continue (Maurer, 2022), including career-development work. The following is a list of basic technology considerations to keep in mind when providing career-development activities at a distance.

Learning Management Systems

Platforms such as Canvas, Moodle, TalentLMS, and Teachable allow learners to log in and access all course materials and requirements in one place; these are called **learning management systems (LMS)**. These systems can also be used to augment in-person courses with online communication and access to materials between class meetings. There are many LMS options already, and new systems are being developed every year. Finding an option that has the combination of features and functions that you need to administer and deliver an online career course will take some time and research.

These systems also often include the integration of tools that you and your students may already be using, such as Gmail, Zoom, and textbook publishers. You may not need something as robust as an LMS to offer your courses. But for those focused on education and training aspects of career development, they may be beneficial investments.

Engagement

Engagement tools allow you to build your own community of like-minded people, including students and clients. Meetup is a platform designed to attract members to groups organized around a specific topic or goal, including professional networking and career development. This app also includes discussion and messaging functions, event (virtual and in-person) communication, and registration. Slack is a virtual workspace that includes individual user profiles, topical channels for conversation and group project work, and integration of other tools, such as calendars (e.g., Outlook) and file sharing (e.g., Google Drive, attachments).

Setting Expectations

Communication is at the center of all successful engagement at a distance. Identifying your expectations for engagement in an online career course, one-on-one virtual counseling session, a webinar, or use of email and text messaging, is an important first step. Clearly conveying these expectations to your clients and students is also key. In some cases, it might also be advantageous to open a discussion, with group counseling clients, for example, to identify and agree on ground rules before beginning a program or starting a service.

IMPACT OF TECHNOLOGY ON THE WORLD OF WORK

Conversations about the **future of work** typically focus on technology. The tools used to perform work are rapidly changing and becoming more capable every year. This is certainly the case in our work as career-development professionals and for others in almost every field and industry from the arts and education to medicine and manufacturing. While advances in technology eliminate some jobs, they are also creating others. As a career counselor, you may want to reflect on and identify new job trends related to new technology so that you can give your clients a head start.

Trends and the Future of Work

Technical skills are essential for career coaches and counselors, from using the latest data analytics and virtual workplace software to operating and evaluating technical solutions. But it's not just about technology trends in terms of the tools implemented to do the work. We must also understand how the tools impact the worker (Career Practitioner Conversations with NCDA, 2022).

AUTOMATION

Automation is the result of implementing a technology or tool to perform tasks that remove or reduce the need for human labor to perform those tasks. The goals and outcomes of automation can include things like cost savings, increased production, human safety, and a reduction in errors. Examples of automation include modern manufacturing facilities in which machines, in lieu of humans, are programmed to assemble components (Fatehpour, 2022).

ARTIFICIAL INTELLIGENCE

Artificial intelligence (AI) is the development of complex computer programs that are able to solve problems and make decisions rationally, often in ways that mirror human problem-solving and decision-making. This AI trend includes machine learning and deep learning. Examples include virtual customer service agents, speech recognition, and search capabilities, such as Apple's Siri (IBM Cloud Education, 2020).

AUGMENTED REALITY AND VIRTUAL REALITY

Augmented reality (AR) involves a combination of real-life and digital elements in which digital elements are layered or projected on the physical world. AR can be achieved through a smartphone camera—you may remember the mobile Pokemon Game in 2016 where virtual creatures appeared around you. That's AR. Virtual reality (VR) involves total immersion in a digital environment and typically requires a device such as a headset with a built-in viewing screen, for example, Oculus Rift, and PlayStation VR (GCFGlobal, 2022b).

Upskilling and Reskilling

You can likely identify some sort of technology that's involved in how most work is done across jobs and industries. This is the case even for jobs we don't think of as "tech jobs" and work that takes place at non-tech companies. We don't all need to become programmers, but we do need to adopt a continuous learning approach that includes staying current with the technologies integrated within our jobs. Think of **upskilling** in this context as learning how to use a new technology, such as a software application, that helps you perform your job better and may even help you advance in your role. Think of **reskilling** as learning how to use new tech tools so that you can change jobs or move into a new role that might require that skill. Staying skilled as technology evolves so that we can grow in our roles or move to new roles as the work changes is critical to maintaining relevance in the workforce.

Remote Work

In the wake of the coronavirus pandemic, technology has allowed many businesses to continue operating remotely. If a worker had a computer, and in some cases just a smartphone with an internet connection, their work could continue. There were many challenges at first, but now, after months and years of remote operations, many employees want to remain "**remote workers**" at least some of the time (Parker et al., 2022). This emergence of employee agency, fueled by the possibilities that technology allowed, meant that employees came out of the pandemic with expectations for more flexibility in how and when they do their work, as well as a voice in making those decisions (La Duke, 2021).

ETHICAL USE OF TECHNOLOGY IN CAREER DEVELOPMENT

"If you are concerned about whether or not a particular practice is ethical, then you should not engage in that behavior without getting confident advice" (National Career Development Association [NCDA], 2015b, p. 1). Making decisions about the ethical implementation of technology in the workplace is a required skill for career counselors and coaches.

The NCDA Code of Ethics (2015b) provides specific guidance for the use of technology. The NCDA Code states that "career professionals understand the additional concerns related to providing career services online and using technology and/or social media, and make every attempt to protect confidentiality and data security, ensure transparency and equitable treatment of clients, and meet any legal and ethical requirements for the use of such resources" (NCDA, 2015b, p. 15). Considerations addressed in the code are outlined here. Add the full resource to your reading list and use it as a reference in your work.

National Career Development Association Code of Ethics Overview

Knowledge and Legal Considerations

Your work should include developing an awareness of laws and statutes in your location as well as that of your students and clients.

INFORMED CONSENT AND SECURITY

Disclose your use of technology, related policies, and expectations to your clients. Address confidentiality in the exchange of information through technology and how any collected data will be secured.

CLIENT VERIFICATION

Establish ways to confirm the identity of students and clients you may be working with at a distance or through various technology tools and social media.

PROVIDING ONLINE CAREER SERVICES

Address the benefits and challenges of providing services at a distance, including areas such as professional boundaries, availability of technical assistance and internet access, communication strategies, and the use and interpretation of online career-development assessments.

WEB MAINTENANCE AND TECHNOLOGY DEVELOPMENT

It's important to ensure that the information you provide via technology (e.g., websites, databases), is up to date. It's also critical for security to make sure that the technology tools you use are updated regularly. Check and recheck privacy settings and terms of agreement as they change often. And ensure that the resources you provide are accessible, which may require additional steps, such as audio or text transcripts.

SOCIAL MEDIA

Social media use is widespread as a way to create a virtual or digital presence in the workplace. Be aware of social media policies in your workplace, particularly as they relate to privacy and confidentiality. NCDA also provides a separate set of more detailed guidelines in its *Ethical Use of Social Networking Technologies in Career Services* (2015a) resource.

   While this particular code will evolve through updates and revisions, this overview provides a place to start your exploration. There's a lot to learn, but there are also many resources available to help you. Don't wait to begin building your professional network and don't hesitate to seek professional consultation and ask for help when you need it.

EXAMPLE OF TECHNOLOGY SELECTION IN PROFESSIONAL PRACTICE

During a recent LMS selection project for a small nonprofit organization, I created a matrix similar to the one following, listing specific items to be considered along with the structure to compare multiple options. The categories and capabilities were based on the organization's needs. This matrix is not inclusive of all considerations but provides a place to start and can be modified (Exhibit 8.1).

EXHIBIT 8.1 LEARNING MANAGEMENT SELECTION COMPARISON MATRIX

CATEGORY	CAPABILITY	LMS 1	LMS 2	LMS 3
Administration/ Management	Hosting service versus self-hosting			
	Integration of third-party tools (e.g., video tools, Google apps), CRM (e.g., Salesforce), others			
	How do new users access and/or get registered? (enrollment versus self-registration)			
	User limits (number or time)			
	Branding options (i.e., logos, color schemes)			
	Tech support (for all admin and user roles)			
	Security—collection, storage, and use of user data			
Access	Accessibility			
	Mobile capabilities (apps and reactive design)			
	Languages/translation			
Courses	Creation options (course builder tools, uploading exported courses from other platforms)			
	SCORM, xAPI, AICC specifications/ compatibility			
	Collect learner feedback/surveys			
	Reporting/tracking learner progress/ notifications			
	Student view versus admin/instructor view			
	Gamification, badges			
	Content ownership			
Assessment	Learner assessment types (e.g., multiple-choice, essay)			
	Automated/self-grading			
	Test creation services			
Price Structure	Per learner Per login Subscription—monthly, annual			
Sample course	Can we access a sample course from the admin side?			

This is just a starting point from which to develop your knowledge and skills related to the application of technology in a career-development context. Remember that you don't need to be a technology expert—that is an unrealistic and potentially overwhelming goal and an unnecessary one. But you can identify "go-to" people in your network, publications that answer your questions and guide your effective and efficient use of technology, and resources that support your decisions about and use of technology in your practice.

The dynamic nature of technology means adopting a continuous learning approach. As you implement one tool to solve a particular problem, it will require periodic version updates and eventually even replacement as you either identify additional problems that the tool you are using cannot adequately address or find that the tool will be discontinued or otherwise no longer supported, requiring you to find a new solution altogether. Embrace the inherent nature of technology—it is always changing. And always question the appropriate use of the tools and the data they store.

ETHICAL CORNER

In this section, the authors lead the reader through topical scenarios to surface common ethics questions and dilemmas faced by career professionals. They ask pertinent and personal questions to encourage reader reflection and insight into personal and professional ethics.

Azra Karajic Siwiec, PhD, LPC, is a counselor educator employed by Capella University. She has been working in the counselor education field for over 14 years and has served as a committee member of the Ethics Committee of NCDA since 2015 and served as the chair of the Ethics Committee since 2017.

Sharon K. Anderson, PhD, is professor of counseling and career development at Colorado State University. Sharon has taught the master's level ethics course for counseling students for over 20 years, teaching and mentoring a multitude of students. She has coauthored or coedited four professional ethics books used by practitioners in counseling and coaching.

Technology plays a significant role in career-counseling practice. How do technology and ethics intersect in counseling professions?

VIGNETTE

Sandi recognizes that technology is ever changing. In her ethics class, they discussed if counselors should have a visible presence on social media because it may hinder the professional relationship if clients see the postings. Sandi was willing to adjust her social media settings to be less visible, but at the same time, she wonders if it is as big an issue as the instructor seems to suggest.

Later that semester, Sandi recognizes one of the career-counseling center's clients on social media. She is intrigued and clicks on the person's page. The client identifies you, Sandi's supervisor, on social media as the key changer in his life and he lists you by name as his counselor. He even comments about your social media presence. Sandi asks you about this situation and is curious about your perspective.

DIGGING INTO ETHICS

What do you recognize as concerns? What ethical principles do you draw upon in the discussion and why? What ethical virtues seem important to you? What parts of the ethics code do you consider to be relevant to the discussion and why?

Review American Counseling Association (ACA) and NCDA Codes of Ethics. What sections connect to this section? How do you use the codes to inform your next steps? Be sure to cite the codes that are relevant.

8.1 PRACTITIONER'S PERSPECTIVE

Marcy L. Bullock, MS, has over 30 years of career-counseling experience at four universities, and she hosts a weekly podcast, Wolfpack Career Chats. She teaches classes on career exploration and women in the workforce, where she empowers others to reach their potential while offering creative solutions to career fulfillment.

I chose my career path after volunteering in my college career center at University of California at San Diego while studying sociology and communication as an undergraduate. I quickly realized that I never wanted to leave college and that I could devote my life to helping others figure out what to devote theirs to. This led me into completing a master's of science in counseling. We spend one-third of our waking hours at work, and I wanted to impact the choices others make to ensure those hours are meaningful to them.

I moved to North Carolina, where I have spent the majority of my career inspiring students to reach their potential. I enjoyed a sabbatical for 6 months visiting career centers in Australia, and I realized that no matter where you are on the globe, "Who am I now and who will I be when I grow up" is a dominant question throughout one's life.

In my job, I strive to provide transformative experiences to students. I facilitate a process by which my career explorers identify a previous, current, and future version of themselves. I believe that every human life is a canvas seeking inspiration to find their worth as they carve out their unique masterpiece. I lead teams and teach classes on career exploration, career readiness, practicing happiness, women in the workforce, and professional development at North Carolina State University. Milestones in my career have been the Governor's Award for Excellence, the Outstanding Faculty Award from the alumni society, and being invited to speak nationally and internationally.

I have expertise in building trust in teams, careers, Gallup's CliftonStrengths, job search, building relationships, finding your purpose, achieving goals, professionalism, leadership, and values alignment. I encourage others to reach their full professional potential by enthusiastically sharing what I have learned. I have done it for thousands over my career at four universities from Australia to California to North Carolina.

P5 MANTRA

I created a mantra that embodies my personal philosophy for career exploration, and I share it with my students: "Be fully present and trust the process as you explore your path, releasing the pressure valve to unleash your potential." I coined this phrase because it ties together successful strategies to deal with challenges that I see career explorers facing. Students agree to embrace my P5 mantra, and course evaluations prove the positive impact as graduates report higher confidence about their career direction (Bullock, 2018).

Here is the full mantra that my students agree to embrace:

1. **Be fully present.**
   Students struggle to stay present in the moment. They are pulled by worry over what has already happened and fear of what may happen next. "What if I make the wrong choice?" is echoed frequently. We intentionally turn off our devices to let go of the weight of the past while practicing mindfulness. We acknowledge our fears of the future and return to the present.

2. **Trust the process.**
   College students report high levels of anxiety during and after the pandemic (Larson, 2022). The process of choosing a future goal can be paralyzing. Leaning in with trust can free up the permission to be vulnerable and explore without boundaries. Students learn to align their actions with top values they have identified. Alumni stories of overcoming obstacles prove to be reassuring.

3. **Explore your path.**
   The path ahead looks foggy early on, but career-counseling activities lead to expanded self-knowledge and thoughtful decisions. While the FOCUS 2 (www.focus2career.com) assessment provides concrete examples of career paths that match a student's interests, values, personality, and skills, it is not a panacea, and I refer to the decade of your twenties as being "The trying 20s" as it feels trying while you try lots of things. We learn to embrace the uncertainty. Students report the relief that they are not alone as they work together to leave their comfort zone.

4. **Release the pressure valve.**
   The pressure to make "the right" decision causes stress and leads to mental health struggles, which is why we practice breath work, which is proven to activate the parasympathetic nervous system and lower the heart rate of a frequent flight/flight/freeze response (www.mrjamesnestor.com/breath-book). Students also compare themselves to others, which causes insecurities. We release this tendency and learn that we can admire others without questioning ourselves. We embrace our journey; just as there are many beautiful flowers in a field that are all unique, one is not better than another.

5. **Unleash your potential.**
   I believe every human has enormous potential, and I have seen that we often hold ourselves back with doubt. We are our worst enemy. Yet, there is a 1 in 300 trillion chance that each of us would be here, and taking a career exploration class reminds us that we have a reason for being here. It also provides the power to unleash what is inside of us.

The magic of a group of like-minded people striving together to unlock their potential while embracing the P5 philosophy is inspiring.

Activities that are useful include the values auction, where students use pretend money to purchase important values in a gamified format.

TRAITS OF CAREER COUNSELORS

The people best suited for work in career services share a connection to the P5 mantra, have a caring mindset, and have a desire to continually learn. After receiving recent offers to leave, I revisited my values, which include having a creative license to design new ways to support both struggling and thriving students. The pandemic forced me to take my pulse and connect to fulfilling experiences because nothing is guaranteed. When a student I impacted later shares how they grew from my counsel and how it helped them to succeed, it reminds me that this is where I am supposed to be.

PROFESSIONAL ETHICS

An ethics issue that I see more of recently is reneging on a job offer after accepting it earlier. The ethical code of conduct from the National Association of Colleges and Employers advises that job applicants accept one job offer and then cease interviewing. I have observed Generation Z morally challenged by this dilemma. They sometimes want to continue interviewing after accepting an offer just in case something better arises, but they don't want the hiring manager to continue seeking applicants for the job they accepted. Enter me and my ethics lesson.

TECHNOLOGY IN CAREER SERVICE

Technology has revolutionized my work, and there is simply nothing I do now in my career that I did a pandemic ago. I host virtual career fairs and online learning systems. I use Symplicity, Moodle, Zoom, and SoundCloud for my podcast, which has over 130 episodes and over 30,000 downloads. The pandemic forced me to offer services asynchronously and create new digital content.

I have added yoga breaks in my online class, and I begin with a mindful meditation. I give students active learning challenges instead of lectures. In career-counseling sessions, I walk and talk outside, allowing students the freedom to be vulnerable and talk about the issues underneath the resume critique, such as imposter syndrome and a paralyzing fear of the future.

Zoom counseling sessions are convenient and have a place in my work but do not offer the same success outcomes. During the pandemic, I began hosting events like "Puppies and Pizza" where the only outcome sought is stress relief. Technology offers new frontiers, but it does not replace face-to-face college community building and the need for human connection.

Student Voices

In Student Voices, students offer a unique viewpoint as they begin their career in the career-counseling field. Here, students share their thoughts and reflections about the career-counseling profession and offer personal takeaways.

AMBER LOVELL

> Amber Lovell is a student conduct officer at University of California Irvine. She attended North Carolina State University where she completed her masters of education degree.

I am a student conduct officer at UC Irvine, and technology is very important in my job. My department currently works 100% remotely, and technology has afforded me and my team the opportunity to travel and work from anywhere in the world and to be able to spend more time with friends and family members. It has also given our students better access to me and my team as they do not have to physically come to campus to meet with us.

I meet with my team virtually via Zoom several times a week and we attend professional development trainings via Zoom. We also use technology to connect socially and practice team building by participating in virtual social activities, such as virtual escape rooms. Our department uses Symplicity Software (Advocate) to store student data, notes, and documents, and to populate sanction letters.

I use technology to meet virtually one on one with students on Zoom to adjudicate student conduct and academic integrity cases. Working in student conduct, we've seen online learning lead to more academic cheating cases, yet it also offers solutions. For example, there is software available for professors (i.e., MOSS Matching software, TurnItIn, etc.), to use to check if students are submitting work that is entirely their own.

I have spoken with many students who express feeling "disconnected" from their professors and don't feel like they have the opportunity to establish a relationship with the professor when they are taking an online course. Students often also express feeling "confused" about what is and isn't considered cheating in online courses because they rely so heavily on technology. As an example, we see a lot of students who collaborate via a messenger app while taking an exam in an online course, even though collaboration was not permitted by the instructor. I think that being disconnected from the professor makes students feel like they can cheat, in the same way that people often will say negative things online where it's anonymous but may be inhibited from expressing those things to someone in person.

COUNSELING SKILLS CONNECTION

American Counseling Association and National Career Development Association (NCDA) set guidelines for client–counselor relationships and confidentiality. Counselors providing distance counseling, telehealth services, or using social media must be mindful of ethical standards that direct the protection of professional boundaries. Section H of the ACA Code of Ethics sets these core ethical standards. For example, when using social media, counselors should separate personal and professional profiles to maintain boundaries.

As you begin your counseling relationship, discuss these boundaries to set expectations for clients. Particularly in career counseling with emerging adult and adult populations, the prevalence and centrality of LinkedIn can create ethical challenges. Will you connect with your clients on LinkedIn or other platforms? Will you respond to direct messages via the platform? Here are a few things to consider if you are responding via the platform: Are these billable hours? Who has access to this information? What information about your client might you see that has an impact on your perception of your client? Having conversations about your practices and the limitations of confidentiality within each tool is essential to protect yourself and your client. What ethical challenges might you envision relative to technology usage for the setting in which you practice?

MINDFUL MOMENT

Take a screen break. Technology is great, but we need limits. Improve your mindfulness and disconnect from technology by taking a brief walk, looking out a window, or simply closing your eyes for a few minutes. If you have difficulty making time to disconnect, add brief breaks to your calendar the same way you would add a class or a meeting.

TECH TOOLS

Discover new technology tools and watch for emerging trends by reading professional publications and following thought leaders in your specialty area on social channels such as Twitter or LinkedIn. NCDA's Career Convergence Web Magazine includes a Tech Tips section (https://ncda.org/aws/NCDA/pt/sp/CC_home_page) that highlights technology applications for career counselors each month. Career Thought Leaders (www.careerthoughtleaders.com/) often highlights technology trends and emerging digital tools for career counselors in a variety of settings. You can follow them on social media!

REFLECTION ACTIVITY

What technologies do you use in your current education and work settings? How did you decide to use them? If they were chosen for you, think about the process that might have taken place for their selection. If you could find a tool to solve a current problem or meet a specific challenge you are working with, what would it be able to do? What keeps you engaged in learning and working activities at a distance? What are your predictions for how technology might impact the future of work? Have you experienced concerns about your own privacy or challenges impeding your ability to access needed information online? How do you or could you share your technology-related success stories and lessons learned with others working in the career-development field?

END-OF-CHAPTER RESOURCES

SUMMARY

Technology continues to play a significant role within the counseling profession. Remaining current with trends and upcoming technical developments is paramount to staying relevant, regardless of the setting you may be employed in now and in the future. The chapter offers suggestions for evaluating tools and resources pertaining to career-counseling practices. A matrix for comparing learning management systems is provided as a sample for technological selection.

We encourage you to review and explore the reflective questions related to technology, career counseling, and the overall helping professions. These questions provide strong guidance for ethical selection and use of technology applications. As a reminder, as a helping professional, technology is not a replacement for our client relationships and connections. Our training in counseling theories, techniques, and practice serve as the catalyst for our connection with our clients—not the type of technology used.

Technology can serve as a source of support and access to reach our populations of interest, rather than the end all and be all as we work with our clients and students. An exploration of the impact of technology on work highlights the need for workers to continue to develop technology skills to remain competitive across fields.

REFERENCES

Bullock, M. L. (2018, August 27). *The career identity program: Helping students successfully chose their major.* NACADA. https://nacada.ksu.edu/Resources/Academic-Advising-Today/View-Articles/The-Career-Identity-Program-Helping-Students-Successfully-Choose-their-Major-and-Create-a-Purposeful-Career-Pathway.aspx

Burns, S. (2011, February 22). *What is Boolean search?* New York Public Library. https://www.nypl.org/blog/2011/02/22/what-boolean-search

Career Practitioner Conversations with NCDA. (2022, April 6). *The future of work.* https://ncda.buzzsprout.com/1963679/10390491-the-future-of-work

Fatehpour, Y. (2022, January 28). What is automation? A complete guide to automation. *eWeek.* https://www.eweek.com/enterprise-apps/what-is-automation/

GCFGlobal. (2022a). *How filter bubbles isolate you.* https://edu.gcfglobal.org/en/digital-media-literacy/how-filter-bubbles-isolate-you/1/

GCFGlobal. (2022b). *Understanding virtual reality and augmented reality.* https://edu.gcfglobal.org/en/thenow/understanding-virtual-reality-and-augmented-reality/1/

IBM Cloud Education. (2020, June 3). *What is artificial intelligence?* IBM Cloud Learn Hub. https://www.ibm.com/cloud/learn/what-is-artificial-intelligence

Johnson, J. (2022, March 9). *Google: Statistics and facts.* Statista. https://www.statista.com/topics/1001/google/#dossierKeyfigures

La Duke, P. (2021, November 29). Preparing for the future of work: Dr. Melissa Venable of Red Ventures Education on the top five trends to watch in the future of

work. *Authority Magazine.* https://medium.com/authority-magazine/preparing
-for-the-future-of-work-dr-melissa-venable-of-bestcolleges-on-the-top-five
-trends-to-watc-10e41e6450e1

Larson, L. (2022, May 18). *Impacts of the COVID-19 Pandemic on college students: Challenges, coping strategies, and next steps.* Presentation for the NC State University Wellness Advisory Committee. Raleigh, NC.

Maurer, R. (2022, May 16). *BLS: For many employers, some remote expected to last.* Society for Human Resource Management. https://www.shrm.org/resourcesandtools/hr-topics/talent-acquisition/pages/many-employers-some-remote-work-expected
-to-last.aspx

National Career Development Association. (2015a). *Ethical use of social networking technologies in career services.* https://www.ncda.org/aws/NCDA/asset_manager/get_file/110167?ver=53186

National Career Development Association. (2015b). *NCDA code of ethics.* https://www.ncda.org/aws/NCDA/asset_manager/get_file/3395?ver=738700

Parker, K., Horowitz, J. M., & Minkin, R. (2022, February 16). *COVID-19 pandemic continues to reshape work in America.* Pew Research Center. https://www.pewresearch.org/social-trends/2022/02/16/covid-19-pandemic-continues-to-reshape
-work-in-america/

Price, C. (2021, September 23). 20 great search engines you can use instead of Google. *Search Engine Journal.* https://www.searchenginejournal.com/alternative-search
-engines/271409/#close

CHAPTER 9

CAREER AND MENTAL HEALTH: TOTAL WELLNESS

Erik Messinger, Angie C. Smith, and Katie Peterssen

LEARNING OBJECTIVES

By the end of this chapter, you will be able to:

- Review the relationship between **career** and **mental health**.
- Discuss the centrality of career and work in our lives and identities.
- Identify the relationship between mental health concerns and work/career.
- Explore concrete strategies counselors can use to engage in self-care.

WARM-UP EXERCISE

Reflect on a job you currently hold or have held in the past. What areas of the job brought you joy? Were there any parts of the job that caused you to pause and consider changing jobs due to challenges with coworkers, relationships, work-related tasks, supervisors, and so on? How did you navigate this experience? How will your own personal and professional experience inform the way you plan to counsel and work with your students and clients on career-related issues and concerns?

INTRODUCTION

Career counseling falls under the large umbrella of mental health, yet news of mental health appears to be covered only as part of public outcry or displeasure when a tragedy or injustice occurs. Much less attention is given to everyday people dealing with daily life stressors, inadequate support, and improper coping skills.

The relationship between career and mental health counseling is not new. To succeed in proper development, each individual should have access to proper career counseling. The field of career counseling is an ever-evolving area of the counseling profession with challenges that require constant adaptation and processing. In fact, counseling as a profession is rooted and originated from the career and vocational guidance movement. The counseling profession began when Frank Parsons (1909) began outlining a process for choosing a career, stating that choosing a career is more than simply deciding what one wants to do to earn a living.

THE RELATIONSHIP BETWEEN CAREER AND MENTAL HEALTH

Stoltz and Haas (2016) contend that counseling overall is based on a holistic pattern that emphasizes the development of the entire person. When it comes to mental health care in the United States, including career counseling, there is a significant deficit in services available. This deficit has led to barriers that prevent people from receiving services that should be a basic human right, and many who need services from the umbrella of mental health services are unaware of who provides these services and how to access them, thus preventing, delaying, or impeding residents (North Carolina Institute of Medicine Task Force on Mental Health and Substance Use, 2014). It has been reported that from 2009 to 2013, over half of the adults with various mental health concerns went without treatment (Substance Abuse and Mental Health Services Administration [SAMHSA], 2015).

While statistics on career counseling are hard to find, if the need for mental health counseling as a whole is not being met, we can safely assume there is even less career counseling occurring. It appears that for someone to receive any form of treatment or care, they must be ill in order for an institution or organization to help them become well (Grimmett et al., 2018). Yet in terms of career dissatisfaction, there is no objective way to state that a person is ill from their career, further indicating a need for proper and accessible career counseling.

While the process of obtaining any form of counseling can be confusing and intimidating, lack of health insurance is a major barrier for people to receive any form of career counseling. With so many individuals unsure of how to properly access mental health services, there are limited opportunities for community members to receive any form of career counseling. Even with efforts from the Affordable Care Act in 2014, some adults, unfortunately, will continue to be uninsured due to a few states' decision to decline federal funding to expand the Medicaid program (United States Department of Health and Human Services, 2015). This leads to a large gap for individual and quality career-counseling services.

THE RELATIONSHIP BETWEEN MENTAL HEALTH CONCERNS AND WORK/CAREER

When it comes to your career, mental health can impact performance in both positive and negative ways. As mental health concerns increase, clients may find themselves withdrawing from coworkers or limiting communication with others. Lerner and Henke (2008) found that depression can interfere with a person's ability to complete physical job tasks about 20% of the time and reduces cognitive performance about 35% of the time. The connection between mental health and career has a large ripple effect that career counselors must be aware of.

Trauma

Trauma has become a buzzword among both clinicians and clients. The Substance Abuse Mental Health Services Administration (SAMHSA; 2014) views **trauma** through three E's: events, experiences, and effects. "Individual trauma results from an event, series of events, or set of circumstances that is experienced by an individual as physically or emotionally harmful or life-threatening and that has lasting adverse effects on the individual's functioning and mental, physical, social, emotional, or spiritual well-being" (SAMHSA, 2014, p. 7).

The word *events* is related to physical or psychological harm or the threat of harm. This threat can occur once or over a period of time and is applied to all types of harms, such as physical violence or natural disasters. The "experience of events" is related to how an individual conceptualizes what is happening around them. One event may be traumatic for one person but may have no effect on another person who witnessed or was a part of the same event. The way people experience an event and assign meaning to that incident is often determined by their age, experiences, social supports, and cultural beliefs. "Effects" are the most critical component of trauma and gain the most attention. The effects of trauma vary greatly between individuals. For some, the effects of the trauma can occur immediately after the event or may have a delayed onset and not appear for a long time. The effects of trauma can also be of short-term or long-term duration (SAMHSA, 2014).

TRAUMA GLASSES

Unfortunately, counselor education does not include the skill of mind-reading, so how do we know, how can we tell, if trauma is factor in someone's life? In an article in *Faculty Focus,* Alana Sejdic recommends that we put on "trauma glasses" to help us see and interpret trauma more clearly (2022). Putting on trauma glasses gives counselors a fresh way of seeing how students' or clients' words or actions arise from a past trauma and perhaps also see a fresh way to support them better.

Adopting the four key assumptions in SAMHSA's (2014) trauma-informed approach is like putting on trauma glasses, as they help counselors define what trauma is and how it manifests. The four key assumptions, commonly referred to as the four R's, include:

■ realization of trauma and understanding its effect
■ recognition of the signs of trauma
■ understanding of how systems respond to trauma
■ resisting retraumatization of clients

The framework states (SAMHSA, 2014): A program, organization, or system that is trauma-informed realizes the widespread impact of trauma and understands the effects of trauma, and it plays a large role in mental health and substance use disorders. This connection between mental health and career is also seen in the career concerns brought up by clients in session.

Recognition is simply identifying the signs of trauma. For some people, careers and work environments may be contributing to their trauma. Response is ensuring that mental health counselors working from a trauma-informed lens provide a physically and psychologically safe environment. Response should be viewed as a top-down approach to ensure trust, fairness, and transparency. These practices all lead to resisting retraumatization and not triggering clients (SAMHSA, 2014).

PRINCIPLES OF THE APPROACH

Rounding out SAMHSA's (2014) framework are six principles of a trauma-informed approach, including safety; trustworthiness and transparency; peer support; collaboration and mutuality; empowerment; voice and choice; and cultural, historical, and gender issues. Safety is a high priority; all individuals within an organization or system must feel physically and psychologically safe. Trustworthiness and transparency ensure that decisions are made in a collaborative nature, with all parties appropriately informed and intentions always clear. Peer support is about showing survivors they are not alone in their trauma and can relate to others. Many find support within work communities, and their mental health needs should be highlighted. Collaboration and mutuality must be in place, so all involved with the healing process are properly informed and educated. An expectation of the principle of collaboration and mutuality is that everyone has a role when a trauma-informed approach is in place. Empowerment, voice, and choice play a vital role as a strength-based approach to trauma. With this principle, clients have a voice on how they want to work through trauma and determine what may be best for themselves in collaboration with the mental health professionals. It is important that clients feel heard and understood throughout the entire process, particularly related to work stressors.

Finally, cultural, historical, and gender issues are always recognized and valued. Many people have trauma historically stemming from this principle, and these values are supported as to not re-traumatize (SAMHSA, 2014).

ANXIETY AND DEPRESSION

From a young age, people are constantly being asked what they want to do when they grow up. For many of us, work becomes more than just a sense of income. Work identities can be intertwined into an individual's values, self-image, and self-worth. Jobs can even represent status and a major tenant of time and energy, along with the groundwork for skills, information, and experiences accumulated over a lifetime. It can also be a place where many friendships grow and develop.

Clients are often given inventories and surveys when seeking counseling on career decision-making and dissatisfaction. These clients may score in areas that indicate mental health conditions such as **anxiety** or **depression** (Saunders et al., 2000). People experiencing levels of depression usually demonstrate symptoms of impairment in cognitive functions related to memory, attention, and decision-making abilities, further enhancing career concerns (Woo & Keating, 2008). In a study by Walker and Peterson (2012), the authors found that dysfunctional career thoughts and occupational decisions were related to depression symptoms. This study highlights how depression is significantly associated with the decision-making process. Career counselors need to be aware of this process as they work with clients on career trajectories and career satisfaction.

Many people who are satisfied with their work tend to be satisfied with their lives (Duffy et al., 2013). Trauma can show up in the workplace in both large and small ways. SAMHA's trauma-informed framework provides the tools and resources necessary to enact a helping relationship through a trauma-informed lens. Counselors often find that people who seek counseling present issues that are commonly intertwined with their work. Work for clients can be the careers for which they receive a paycheck, but it can also be roles such as homemaker, stay-at-home parent, student, or volunteer. Career frustration, job stress, and discontent with one's life's work and roles are major preoccupations for many people and play a significant part of the work of counselors.

The novel coronavirus (COVID-19) pandemic has caused unprecedented employment disruptions worldwide. Career counselors are now faced with how to do effective career counseling in the world with COVID-19 and how to help clients manage these changes. Drosos et al. (2021) suggest the use of a holistic intervention model for unemployed individuals and for those facing career changes and challenges.

In this model, the authors focus on the following areas to assist with the ever-evolving career changes as a result from the pandemic. They suggest motivating clients through the development of client self-esteem and self-efficacy. They also suggest challenging dysfunctional thoughts and constructing new narratives for career goals. To help facilitate this process, tools such as the Career Construction Interview (Savickas, 2015) and the My Career Story workbook (Savickas & Hartung, 2012) can be used. Practical applications should also be explored, such as developing the client's self-knowledge (e.g., career-management skills, career values, career interests) while reviewing educational opportunities. Career counselors can also assist clients in learning job search techniques, developing self-presentation skills, developing a social network, and providing assistance for job applications and resumes. Finally, the client and counselor should work together to develop an action plan and support the client throughout the collaborative action plan for goals.

If you have ever felt disengaged with your work, felt unappreciated, had no motivation, or even felt bored with your job, you are aware of how that dissatisfaction can affect your life. This disengagement can lead to feelings of confusion over direction, feeling alone with no support, or can even promote a feeling that the future seems worthless. The term *enmeshment* is often used to describe a situation in which boundaries between people become blurred and individual identities lose importance (Koretz, 2019). Many clients feel this enmeshment as they spend so much time focusing on their career that other forms of self-care, family, or other responsibilities are worked around a career. Counselors help to discuss these values and feelings while offering support, encouragement, and even a structure to plan and make changes.

GRIEF AND RESILIENCE

Grief affects people in different ways. Simply stated, grief is the reaction to loss (DeSpelder & Strickland, 2009), and people can grieve the loss of a job, whether that job loss is sudden or planned. It is important that clients process the loss of a job and identify the grief they are experiencing. Grief can encompass physical, behavioral, and spiritual response. These responses and reactions can occur immediately after the loss of a job or be delayed; they may even be absent. Discussing the change and loss of career will be vital as counselors assist clients into the next career transition.

Resilience is a broadly defined term and can be thought of on a continuum that varies between individuals. With origins in developmental theory, resilience often refers to people from high-risk groups who have better outcomes than expected. They employ good coping skills and adaptations in the face of stressors and recover from trauma and traumatic experiences (Greene, 2012).

The use of resiliency theory can be used to guide the process of assessment, evaluation, and intervention when working with individuals who face various forms of risks and trauma. Even though resilience is often operationalized in multiple ways, most definitions appear to be based on two core concepts: adversity and positive adaptations.

People may come to counseling to discuss feelings or conflicts from experiencing job loss, a change in job, or even retirement. It is vital that people learn to make quality decisions about when and how they should initiate career changes along with coping with the associated feelings. As time progresses, individuals become established in their careers and are more secure, and taking new risks can become increasingly difficult, especially because career decision-making can influence an entire family system.

Counselors can assist by educating clients on how to make intelligent and thoughtful decisions. The process often involves learning to collect and assess useful information, generating alternative courses of action, exploring values, predicting potential consequences, initiating a plan of action, taking risks, and dealing with the aftershock of change. Counselors can also help to organize and cope with this process (see this article on Career Decision-Making Styles for more information: https://career.iresearchnet.com/career-development/career-decision-making-styles/).

As individuals, we all differ in our decision-making process. Career decision-making is usually a combination of weighing options, looking at alternatives, gathering information, and finally making a choice. Career decision-making models have become more diverse over the years as career counseling itself changed and developed.

Career taxonomies have largely been developed to assist in career decision-making. Krumbolt's taxonomy proposes five state-like styles: one being rational, which involves making decisions in a logical and systematic manner; fatalistic, which includes believing that one has little personal control; intuitive, which involves relying on nonspecific impressions; impulsive, **which** focuses on spontaneous, spur-of-the-moment choice-making; and dependent, which is about relying on the expectations or advice of others (Krumboltz, 1993).

In addition, Arroba suggested that individuals may use different decision-making styles depending on the decision needing to be made. With her classification, six state-specific styles are identified: logical, which involves the objective appraisal and selection; hesitant, which highlights procrastination or postponement of the decision; intuitive, which focuses on choices based on an inner feeling of rightness or inevitability; emotional, which includes choices based on subjective processes; no-thought, which states little objective consideration, such as a routine decision or in an impulsively chosen alternative; and compliant, which is the passive choice, based on expectations of others or even self-imposed expectations (Arroba, 1978).

SOCIOCULTURAL CONSIDERATIONS OF RESILIENCY THEORY

Resiliency theory has been termed as a U.S. concept, and its meaningfulness has been critiqued. While being an advocate for the use of resiliency theory with clients, Greene (2012) noted several implicit culture-imposed assumptions of the theory. One assumption with resiliency theory is that everyone can and should aim to "get ahead," with the implicit idea of surpassing others. This idea is problematic for collectivist cultures that seek to grow and heal as a group rather than as individuals. This assumption erroneously indicates that there is an open, fair, and accessible arena to get ahead of others where many races, genders, and cultures face challenges and barriers every day. These barriers are commonly seen in one's career.

There also appears to be an implicit idea that competition for getting ahead is structured like a game or sport where the individual can always regroup and re-enter the competition (Greene, 2012). For many people experiencing trauma and mental health challenges, most of the battle is taking the steps to begin the re-grouping process.

Counselor Considerations for Resiliency Theory

When using resiliency theory with clients, counselors should use an emic perspective rather than an etic perspective to approach resilience and positive adaptations from a culturally competent framework. When considering cultures and populations, an emic perspective is one that focuses on intrinsic culture distinctions that are meaningful to members of a specific culture or population. Simply stated, this is the "insider" perspective. In contrast, an emic view is the perspective of an outsider looking in.

DISASTERS AND CAREER IMPLICATIONS

People have varied reactions to disasters that can include physical, cognitive, emotional, and interpersonal responses. Common emotional reactions to disasters range from initial shock, fear, grief, and sadness (American Psychiatric Association, 2013). Individual reactions may be characterized by stage, ranging from the impacts, which could include losing a job, to the reconstruction of their lives, where individuals may feel they need to change jobs to meet their needs. As one might expect, for many people the experience of job loss or change due to disasters and changes in the world brings enormous distress and the feeling of being traumatized. Unemployment during challenging times can be viewed as an unexpected turn in career trajectory in which there is little to no preparation. The financial strain and lack of social support can be debilitating.

If there is ever a time where counselor's services are needed, it's during times of crisis and disaster. Career counseling is a valuable skill, and as laid off clients begin to use forced downtime to explore alternative career goals and even discover new skills or more satisfying interests. Counselors can also use hard times to teach clients new job-seeking skills while being mindful and realistic that new job opportunities may be limited as situations change and evolve.

HARASSMENT AND DISCRIMINATION

How we function in our jobs changes almost every year. As the world continues to change around us, workers are forced to adapt to meet new needs and demands. As change continues to occur rapidly, many people are likely to experience job elimination and unemployment because they are unable to adapt quickly to new expectations. Part of the role of counselors will be helping workers to cope and manage the stress and trauma of transition and dislocation to develop marketable skills and even prepare for shifts in working ideas and values.

One shift in the workplace has been women entering the career field in high numbers. Counselors must be aware of issues pertaining to dual-career families, sexual harassment, salary inequities, and even the stress of childcare for working parents. Sexual harassment examples are unfortunately widespread and can result in damages at both the individual and institutional levels. Sexual harassment and assault are widespread problems that cause pain, limit people's lives, and impact communities and society. Kearl (2018) reported that nationwide, 81% of women and 43% of men reported experiencing some form of sexual harassment or form of assault in their lifetime. Counselors must be able to assist people in responding to these issues as increased equality and opportunities are gained in the workplace. Additionally, a counselor needs to consider that women and immigrants are a large population entering the labor market, and these populations are often overrepresented in areas that experience the least amount of growth; they are also less prepared educationally for fast-growing career fields (Kottler & Shepard, 2014).

STRESS AND ITS EFFECTS ON CAREER COUNSELORS

Counseling can be mentally, emotionally, and even physically demanding for those in the profession, and there are high rates of burnout and compassion fatigue (Beaumont et al., 2016). Burnout is defined as "a syndrome composed of emotional exhaustion, depersonalization, and diminished personal accomplishment" (Clark et al., 2009, p. 580). Additionally, Clark et al. (2009) explored how burnout and level of stress influence career satisfaction, finding lower career satisfaction with higher burnout rates. Burnout isn't only a problem for counselors though; it is also linked to lower client involvement, decreased progress in sessions, and dissatisfaction with services (Beaumont et al., 2016).

To combat early career termination and burnout rates, counselor education programs are attempting to implement **self-care** strategies. The Council for Accreditation of Counseling and Related Educational Programs (CACREP, 2016) standards states that programs should foster professional and personal development so that students can learn "self-care strategies appropriate for the counselor role" (CACREP, 2016, para. 2). While self-care is a concept repeatedly discussed in the field as being important, there is no one correct way to operationalize this concept into a counselor education program or the general counseling profession.

Counselor Self-Care

Wellness is a well-known concept in the counseling field, yet there is minimal intentional wellness training in counselor education programs. With increasingly higher rates of burnout, wellness education is paramount to the retention rates of clinicians (Richardson et al., 2020). Counselor education programs mention counselor trainee self-care yet lack specific implementation of wellness initiatives to promote success, professional development, self-awareness, and overall personal wellness that can be translated to the professional world. Wellness theory has been consistently tested since its introduction in the counseling field. The 5F-Wel is known as the most valid wellness inventory to date (Bart et al., 2018). The theory, although having limitations, has important components that are helpful to implement into clinical practice. It has been stated that "well counselors are more likely to produce well clients" (Witmer & Young, 1996, p. 151). It is with this information that counselors incorporate concepts of self-care and identify why that concept is important. Teaching wellness at the earliest point of a counselor's academic career can be important to their overall development and satisfaction within the field. It is important for counselor educators to teach wellness, trainees to learn wellness, and clinicians to practice wellness. Using the 5F-Wel could create an influx in clinical implementation, giving an empirical look into a client's wellness. Overall, wellness theory and its counseling models provide a fundamental notion that balanced lives are the healthiest.

ADVOCATE FOR YOURSELF

Career counseling should involve encouraging clients to advocate for a job that can accommodate their wellness needs, including but not limited to time off, appropriate benefits, adherence to ethical standards, and realistic work demands. The same holds true for counselors. If our job does not allow us to be well for our clients, then we are subsequently in direct violation of the American Counseling Association (ACA) Code of Ethics. Section C of the ACA Code of Ethics (2014) states that "counselors engage in self-care activities to maintain and promote their own emotional, physical, mental, and spiritual well-being to best meet their professional responsibilities" (p. 8). The work of counselors is often rewarding, but it can come at cost. Counseling can be a stressful career and the idea of self-care and wellness has to be a top priority for counselors. The ACA views counselor self-care as a top priority and has compiled multiple resources to help counselors focus on themselves while helping others. For a list of resources, please see the self-care resource section on the ACA website, www.counseling.org/knowledge-center/mental-health-resources/self-care-resources-for-counselors.

BUILD COMMUNITY

It can be difficult to find community and support when doing this type of work. It is important that work professionals find others to consult with and find support. For those that work in systems that foster community, it is important to gain insight and validation from these individuals on clinical cases, imposter syndrome, and worries. Chen (2019) used the term institutional self-care to discuss how counselors can create a support system in their professional lives to promote wellness. Chen (2019) reported that a common way to feel support as a new professional is to create a "collaborative relationship with one's supervisor and colleagues" (p. 8). By creating this collaborative relationship, professionals can "feel secure, understood, and supported through personal disclosure and open consultation" (Chen, 2019, p. 8). This type of support comes from a supervisory relationship that can be formative in the first years of practice. Surguladze (2018) examined the relationship between social support, academic burnout, and clinical burnout and found results indicating that social support is a beneficial "buffer" for clinical burnout (Surguladze, 2018, p. v).

Set an Achievable Schedule

Counselors possess different stamina levels as far as how many clients they are willing to see in a day. It is important to know one's limits and end sessions at the appropriate time, which is usually 50-minutes per session. This allows 10 minutes between back-to-back appointments when able. Counseling is an expanding field with new advances constantly occurring. Counselors need to mold schedules to fit their needs and wellness to continue this important work. For example, school counselors may have limited time with students, and brief sessions may be more common than longer sessions due to the nature of the setting and availability of students between classes during the day. Counselors may also provide group sessions around a specific topic and incorporate individual and group counseling. Group sessions will require a different level of stamina and preparation compared to individual sessions. Some counselors may focus only on group counseling, while others focus solely on individual sessions. Counseling stamina takes time to build, thus it is vital that counselors take inventory of their own career journeys and progression to continue important work sessions. Take breaks when needed, and find the things that give you the energy to continue this work.

Prioritize Wellness in Supervision

Supervision can be expensive if it's not provided by the company or system a counselor works under. Despite the financial strain, counseling professionals grow and learn from their supervisors who set an example. It is important to choose a supervisor who models and prioritizes wellness. Supervisors who model wellness should be open to feedback from others. They should understand the critical impact of taking care of themselves through activities outside of the workplace and leaving client and supervisee concerns at work. Effective supervisors must also have strong leadership and mentoring skills, maintain professional boundaries with supervisees, practice in an ethical manner, and have a nonjudgmental attitude to complete this important work. As with clinical growth, it is also important to focus on wellness growth in counseling careers.

CASE STUDY

JACE

Jace is a 30-year-old married male who makes an appointment with you, presenting with a concern of depression after having to leave the military in his early 20s due to an ongoing hip injury. Though Jace was discharged a few years ago now, he still suffers from feelings of guilt and inadequacy because he could not handle military life. He had dreams of making a career out of the military and felt that was his calling in life. He has reported suicidal thoughts in the past but has never acted on these thoughts. Jace is now a stay-at-home dad and reports his son keeps him grounded. His wife works a full-time job supporting their family. She is currently pregnant with their second child.

Jace has been seeing a psychiatrist, and between therapy and medication, he is finally starting to feel stable and has been discussing working again. He has tried working for his parents' general store part-time but does not get along with some of the workers and feels that his parents let him work there out of pity. He would like to start a new career but is unsure what to do. He says he has lost his passion after feeling like he could not be successful in the military but has talked of taking some college classes. He also feels a lot of guilt and financial strain as they will have to find childcare for their two children if both he and his wife are working.

Jace feels conflicted about going back to work but frequently states that he is not happy with being a stay-at-home dad. He values and misses a connection with adults that he no longer has regularly. He appears to have a limited support system and most of his day-to-day function involves caring for his child and soon-to-be second child. You and Jace have started to explore values, but he often struggles to name and identify what is important to him.

Discussion Questions

1. What other information would you need to determine Jace's level of care?
2. Do you feel Jace is at a good place to start a new career and/or education journey?
3. From your perspective, what presenting issues do you recognize as Jace shares his story?
4. Jace is facing several difficulties—depression, worthlessness, unemployment, family stress, and ongoing physical pain. What issue(s) does he need to address first? Provide a rationale for your choice.
5. What type(s) of treatment would you recommend for Jace? Would this treatment affect his efforts in finding a career?

Almost every client you will see, no matter what the presenting concern may be, will have career concerns that are directly or indirectly related to the initial concerns. Career satisfaction is related to an individual's self-worth and life's meaning, and even if you do not specialize as a career counselor you will find yourself routinely assisting clients with the ongoing choices, values, and direction they make about what they do for careers and how they process those experiences.

The importance of career counseling will only increase with the impact and changes of the world around us. The counselor's role in an ever-changing society is to help individuals assimilate these effects of change, thereby allowing clients to develop to their fullest potential. As counselors take on these roles and continue to give a lot to their clients, it is of the utmost importance to continue to practice proper wellness and boundaries in the work that is so needed from counselors right now.

APPLYING A WELLNESS APPROACH: CAREER VALUES CARD SORT

When discussing possible careers or career changes with clients, values can be a great starting area to identify potential career choices that can help clients find fulfilling careers that are not retraumatizing and to provide a place to practice proper wellness and boundaries.

Begin by asking clients to define the term *value*. Say, "a value is an inner standard from which we receive the motivation to act as we do and by which we judge behavior (both our own and others). We all have a personal set of multiple values, but sometimes it can be hard to identify just which values we consider to be of the highest importance to us. These values can influence how you participate in multiple aspects of your life, such as family relationships, friendships, and work. Today I want to help you get a better understanding of what values you consider the most important to you and how they influence your performance in work."

Provide clients with a stack of value cards (for values card sort, see Exhibit 6.1). Tell them that you would like them to separate the values in three categories: very important to me, somewhat important to me, not at all important to me. However, there should be no more than 10 values in each category. Provide about 5 minutes for clients to go through the stack.

"Each of these cards has a different value defined on them. I want you to take each card and identify it as being either very important, somewhat important, or not at all important to you. However, do not place more than 10 cards in each category. When we are done with this step, I will ask you to do one more task with the cards." Provide clients about 5 to 10 minutes to sort their cards.

"Excellent. All of these sorts look great. Now, I would like you to arrange the cards that are in your 'very important to me' category in order from 1 to 10 with 1 being the value that is the absolute most important to you." Provide 3 to 5 minutes for clients to rearrange.

Follow-up discussion questions:

1. One important factor in what we value are the values of our friends, families, and society. How do your values differ from your family? From your friends? From your work environment?
2. Examine your top three values. Why did you choose those values as being the most important? How do they influence the way you behave within work environments with your peers and supervisors?
3. Think of a supervisor or leader who you look up to or respect. What do you think their most important value might be? What strengths or qualities do they have that you admire?
4. How our values are shown differs from setting to setting. How do you think your parents or family would describe your values?

5. What about your friends? Supervisors? What evidence do they have that would make them describe you in that way?

6. The values we hold may not always align with our actions. Some values are difficult to live up to, or other priorities get in the way.

7. Which of your most important values do you believe you could do a better job of showcasing with work? What changes would you need to make to accomplish this? What other values would you like to focus on in the future and why?

ETHICAL CORNER

In this section, the authors lead the reader through topical scenarios to surface common ethics questions and dilemmas faced by career professionals. They ask pertinent and personal questions to encourage reader reflection and insight into personal and professional ethics.

Azra Karajic Siwiec PhD, LPC, is a counselor educator employed by Capella University. She has been working in the counselor education field for over 14 years and has served as a committee member of the Ethics Committee of NCDA since 2015 and served as the chair of the Ethics Committee since 2017.

Sharon K. Anderson, PhD, is professor of counseling and career development at Colorado State University. Sharon has taught the master's level ethics course for counseling students for over 20 years, teaching and mentoring a multitude of students. She has coauthored or coedited four professional ethics books used by practitioners in counseling and coaching.

VIGNETTE

Sandi meets for lunch with her colleague, Isaiah. Isaiah shares that he is going through a divorce that is turning "nasty." On top of that, he recently experienced a loss with his father passing. As Isaiah shares these issues, Sandi recalls that Isaiah likes to go to the local bar before coming to the internship class. During lunch, Isaiah downed three beers. Sandi hasn't said anything to anyone, and she wonders if the internship instructor knows any of this information.

As they finish their lunch, Isaiah states, "I really am doing ok. I've kept my grades at A's, and I think I am excelling in internship. But I cannot wait to get done with school and be able to put this horrible year behind me." If Isaiah were your colleague, how would you approach the conversation during lunch? What if he were headed to his internship site after lunch and drinking three beers? What would you do? Consider how to bring ethical virtues, principles, and the ethics code into your responses. Role-play the conversation with a peer.

DIGGING INTO ETHICS

Post-COVID counseling has led to more widespread use of virtual counseling, where the client is in their natural surroundings as you conduct a counseling session. While it has made client access so much easier, it has also offered a lot of challenges. What if Isaiah had access to alcohol as he is home, and he was drinking during the session? Do you know this for certain because he has told you, or you have seen this be the case? What if he was driving and drinking? We have heard of both. How do you proceed regarding your ethical concerns and responsibilities?

9.1 PRACTITIONER'S PERSPECTIVE

Wesley Jackson Wade, MA, NCC, CCMHC, LCMHC, LCAS, worked as a career counselor for 7 years in the Career Development Center at North Carolina State University, where he served undergraduate and graduate students in the College of Sciences. While at North Carolina State University, Wade started two career-focused programs for students on the autism spectrum, for which he has received regional and national recognition, in addition to his involvement in training and development for new counselors entering the field of university career counseling and mental health counseling. He is currently a doctoral student at NCSU and counsels at Forward Counseling & Consulting.

As students walk into my office, one of the first things they see is a printed copy of my undergraduate transcript clipped to a magnet, sitting high up on a whiteboard behind my desk. This transcript is a tool of self-disclosure to affirm the students concerned about receiving a poor grade on an exam or having a low grade point average. For dramatic effect, I was going to put the transcript in a custom-made case behind a glass pane with the words, "Break Glass in Case of Emergency" in big bold font. I was even going have a tiny hammer chained to the side of the case. I use my transcript with students frequently, at least once per week, but I never bought the case with the glass pane and hammer.

In North Carolina, where I work as a college career counselor, salaries could range from approximately $38,000 to $53,000 per year (The UNC System, 2022), while the national average is slightly higher at roughly $58,000 per year (National Center for O*NET Development, 2022). All of this is to say the cost of replacing glass panes would far exceed the boundaries of my modest college career counselor salary.

Outside of financial costs, the scarcity of time is another reason I did not invest in the custom-made case for my transcript. College career counseling is typically a fast-paced and highly transactional environment where every minute during the academic year is critical. And, with the average student appointment being only 30 minutes, and the median ratio for student-to-career services professionals being 1,735 to 1 (National Association of Colleges and Employers, 2021), it is significantly difficult to sacrifice time for matters of creative presentation.

In addition to student appointments, many college career counselors also plan career fairs, provide workshops, cultivate relationships with key faculty and campus partners to better reach students, serve on advisory committees for student programs, and continuously revamp career resources to align with market trends and ever-changing student needs. For example, over a 5-year period, I worked as the sole full-time career counselor for approximately 4,100 undergraduate and graduate students pursuing degrees in areas such as statistics, math, chemistry, biology, and physics. During that time, I held over 1,600 student counseling appointments and conducted over 200 workshops with more than 4,000 student attendees in total.

It is also important to note two things: roughly 90% of a student career counselor's work occurs during the months of September, October, November, February, March, and April each academic year, and the ratio of student-to-career services professionals can vary widely from campus to campus, but there can be notable variations within an institution.

Reading these details about the pace, average salaries, volume of work, and student-to-career services professional ratios should be jarring to those investigating the career. It should prompt those wanting to enter this field, as well as those currently in the profession to ask, "Why work as a college career counselor?" I can only appropriately answer this question for myself anecdotally because hard statistics—including qualitative studies—do not fully allow for the intensely personal expressions needed to thoroughly answer this valid question. When casually conversing with other college career counselors on the topic of motivation, a theme I hear consistently is the desire "to be the person [we] needed when [we were] in college." For me, this is exactly why I have stayed in this profession for over 7 years.

The university where I work is the same university I attended for my bachelor's degree—a degree I struggled to earn and barely completed, as indicated by my cumulative grade point average of 2.26. This university is a large, public, predominantly White institution, and I am a Black man who is neurodivergent, specifically an "ADHDer" who also meets *Diagnostic and statistical manual of mental disorders* 5th edition (*DSM-5*) criteria for an unspecified learning condition or possibly dyslexia (American Psychiatric Association, 2013). People with my intersectionality were and still are, overwhelmingly pushed to the margins in these spaces. I learn and express myself differently, and I did not understand how to fully leverage my strengths as an undergraduate, which only further exacerbated the culminating weight of repeated racist incidents. To say the least, as an undergraduate I was depressed, anxious, and lacked a true sense of belonging.

Returning to the higher education setting to work as a career counselor, after a 9-year career in industry, felt as though I returned to my undergraduate campus to retrieve a version of myself I thought I lost forever. This means that every session, workshop, career fair, class presentation, newsletter, and outreach event I provide or participate in, is crafted for this student. Whether intentionally curating diverse panels with speakers who have "messy" and nonlinear career trajectories, serving on the advisory board for a living and learning village dedicated to students who are Black men, or creating a career-focused program and career summit for autistic college students throughout North Carolina, my work centers the belief that a rising tide lifts all boats. To increase this tide, I must place a large percentage of my focus on those students pushed to the farthest margins; I have to be the person I needed when I was an undergraduate, and few things have ever filled me with as much joy as this pursuit. Even so, to serve in a role so closely aligned with one's identity and some of the largest personal barriers from one's own life makes balancing work and well-being challenging.

LICENSING AND THE PRACTICAL USE OF THEORY

Having a license to practice counseling is not a requirement for my position, though I am a licensed clinical mental health counselor (LCMHC) and a licensed clinical addictions specialist (LCAS). I routinely incorporate counseling theories and techniques into my work with students, as well as my personal reflective work, including reality therapy and the WDEP (wants, doing, evaluation, planning) model, relational cultural theory, cognitive behavioral therapy, and motivational interviewing. When meeting with students, I challenge them to identify and define their values and vision for a fulfilling life. The details they share are typically not work-related and almost always mention valuing diversity, autonomy, having time for leisure, and the ability to maintain a connection with family and friends. This tends to remove work and career as the primary focus of a fulfilling life and repositions it as one aspect of a fulfilling life that has the power to consume your values and vision if left unchecked.

As a Black man who is also openly ADHD and who works in career services at a predominantly White university, there are a myriad of students at the margins who feel seen by my presence. Of course, this is something I embrace but also refuse to leave unchecked. The enjoyment of investing extra time with these students can easily result in me overextending myself, which in turn reduces my capacity for the most important roles in my life: husband, father, brother, son, and friend. And this is where I figuratively break the emergency glass pane for myself, removing my undergraduate transcript from the whiteboard, and place it side-by-side with my master's and doctoral transcripts. If someone told the undergraduate version of myself that after working 9 years in industry, I would go to graduate school and earn two master's degrees, then return to the university where I barely completed my bachelor's degree and begin working as a full-time career counselor, all while pursuing a PhD at the same university, my response would have been: "How? What's a career counselor? And what's next?" To which I can only respond, "Because many people took the time to invest in me, so I am currently investing in others, and what's next are my two children waiting for me at home."

9.2 PRACTITIONER'S PERSPECTIVE

Cindy Haeck, MEd, LCMHC, NCC, CCC, is a career coach, counselor, and college advising professional with more than 20 years of experience. Additionally, Cindy is a licensed professional counselor (LPC) in Michigan, Global Career Development Facilitator (GCDF), and Board Certified Coach (BCC).

One of my favorite career theorists, John Krumboltz, coined the term "planned happenstance." It asks you to focus less on having specific plans for your future and more on finding opportunities in unplanned events, and this is probably one of the best descriptions of how I moved into the career-counseling space.

I can still remember our high school counselor suggesting my options of nurse, teacher, or secretary upon graduation and wondering, "but what about . . .?" I earned an undergraduate degree in psychology because I loved learning about how people think. Then, after a string of seemingly unrelated jobs and occupations—waitress, lifeguard, bank teller, florist, preschool teacher, teaching assistant, administrative assistant, and community volunteer—all woven into parenting, I explored an opportunity to attend North Carolina State University's graduate counseling program. One of the middle-school counselors I was working with at the time encouraged me and was a great mentor in the process. As an adult learner, I found every course inspiring and thought-provoking but was hooked on career counseling after taking Dr. Larry Jones's course! All my previous experiences, including those in high school, were starting to weave into a beautiful work/life tapestry.

Over the past decades, I've worked as a professional counselor, academic advisor, and career development coordinator on great educational teams in both high schools and community colleges. I've improved my skills every day, not only from other professionals but also from the students I've served. As a "trailing spouse," I've lived in several places, and this required relicensure and additional training, but I gained more empathy for jobseekers. I had to walk those early steps to arrive at the career that I have with an innate passion for helping others discover their strengths, abilities, values, and interests and establish meaningful life goals.

I've been privileged to work with high school and community college students, as well as at a nonprofit center and with private practice clients. Though all were enjoyable, I particularly liked the diverse experiences I had at the community college. Some students were beginning college and learning to navigate the landscape and language of higher education. They were most engaged in career decisions that would guide their academic trajectory. Many were learning to make these decisions for themselves, despite what parents/guardians, family, or friends suggested. At the same time at the community college, I helped to develop creative programming for adults in transition due to economic shifts. So many found themselves in an unenviable position of having to retool their skillsets and develop a new career plan after decades of employment. Supporting their work through grief and loss was as important as a career and occupational exploration.

Regardless of the setting, each person is creating their own life story based on their priorities and experiences. Whether my clients are first-time college students, career transitioners, or new mothers struggling to find work/life balance, I have always felt my role is to help them find their inner voice and support their inquiry and exploration to make an informed choice. Honoring who they are by creating a nonjudgmental, sacred space often gave them the confidence to launch into their next chapter.

My own early experiences, as well as witnessing discriminatory practices against women in the workplace, influenced my interest in working with young adults making educational and occupational decisions. Helping them learn a decision-making process that they'll use over and over in their life span has been gratifying. Supporting each student, whether related to personal development, career or college exploration, empowerment in their workplace, and goal setting never feels like work to me.

At the community college, I found myself wearing many hats, yet meeting the needs of students and addressing their presenting issues was primary. The world of work is ever changing; no 2 days are alike, and you will never be bored! Many community colleges seem to be understaffed for the level of responsibility that employees have. With that said, you can develop wonderfully creative solutions to accomplishing department goals.

Beyond meeting student needs, advocacy, whether with administration or institutional policy was also an important part of our role in career development. Helping to develop an online/hybrid career exploration course, materials, and workshops to ensure equitable access, has also been important over the years. Consulting with faculty about the intersection of college-to-career–related topics has been useful to integrate services. Outreach to employers—whether bringing them into the classrooms, supporting workshops/events, developing internships opportunities and more, is also a major part of a career counselor role.

I truly enjoyed working with young adults. Each student was different in many ways, which made my role extremely exciting. I learned to meet them where they were and walk in the direction they had explored to be the best for them. Routinely, I'd remind them that it was fine to pivot and change their plan if they needed to. New information brings new opportunities.

I've recently moved from working in higher education to private practice. I'm in the midst of redefining my direction in retirement. Having worked in education for several decades, there have been philosophical changes I found myself at odds with. Budgets and finances were outweighing student development, and the landscape of higher education was feeling restrictive and slow to change. But I wouldn't trade any of my experiences and still encourage others who want to work in education to do so because it is a wonderful place to make a difference.

The people who are best suited to this role are people who are interested in working with other people—both individually and in groups. Interests in research, continuous learning, listening, and communicating, combined with patience, creativity, and appreciating diversity, have been useful to me over time. Comfort with outreach and advocacy would serve potential career counselors well.

PROFESSIONAL ETHICS

I maintain my professional standards and ethics by routinely reviewing and consulting with written ethics statements, as they must guide how you work with students or other clients. The National Career Development Association and ACA, as well as state licensing bodies, all demand awareness of laws and ethics.

At the community college, understanding the Family Educational Rights and Privacy Act (FERPA) is essential. Many students are coming from K–12 schools where parents have access to all student information. When students arrive on campus, they have a choice about allowing parents access, and this becomes an issue of confidentiality in practice.

WORK AND MENTAL HEALTH

Appreciating the holistic nature of our lives helps me to remember that I can't put "life" into little cubbies. Work influences family. Health and wellness influences work. What I have discovered over time is that we are wired to sense imbalance and need to devote time to discover where it is rooted. This holds true while working with clients of any age. The client's presenting issues aren't necessarily the only or most immediate need.

Dr. Larry Jones, Emeritus at North Carolina State University, shared with me sage advice: it's hard to separate "career" from "life" counseling—there is tremendous overlap. A client who presents with job dissatisfaction may be experiencing health concerns. A student failing their classes may be experiencing poor goal identification as they are pursuing the dream their parents have for them rather than their own dream. Our professional role is self-reflective inquiry and to "guide from the side" rather than offer solutions.

Personally, as a career counselor, I have discovered the importance of work/ life balance. Many who go into counseling/career counseling professions would describe themselves as "helpers." The challenge is to understand the old airline adage that you must put your oxygen mask on first before you can help anyone else.

Currently, my personal self-care focuses on the foundation of quality sleep, nutrition, exercise, and relationships—admittedly this hasn't always been true. I now appreciate my yoga practice, walks, and simple breath work. I create down-time and have lost the need to fill each day with "to do's." For me, when life feels unbalanced, I assess this foundation first. From there I can build my interests to learn, grow, and live with intention. Learning how to define what is important—both in work and personally—has helped me to use my energy in a direction I find fulfilling. Though I've found podcasts, books, and apps that may offer me new insights, I prefer to socially connect with friends over coffee or a meal to reenergize.

ROLE INTEGRATION

Taking time to first identify all the "roles" we inherit or take on is a great exercise of self-awareness. I think we show up differently based on our roles, and thus we are fluid beings. Earlier in my career, I discovered balancing so many roles without an understanding of personal wellness often left me feeling depleted. My "caring" personal quality that drew me to counseling was playing out in other roles, and the well can run dry if you're only giving.

I attended a parenting conference with other stretched parents, and one line of the keynote speakers' address, "You can have it all . . . but perhaps not all at once," was my game changer. Learning to "let go of" and not "take on" via the learned skills of prioritizing and setting boundaries has been one of the best life lessons for me personally and professionally. I've identified the values most important to me (thanks to Dick Knowdell), which are now my litmus test of where my energy flows.

TRAITS OF CAREER COUNSELORS

There are a variety of required qualifications for career counselors, coaches, and advisors, depending on the institution. Most community colleges require a 4-year social science/business degree with additional certifications (GCDF) at a minimum. To advance, a master's degree or higher and additional specialty certifications would be suggested, particularly if transitioning to university-level institutions.

I began my journey pursuing licensure (LCMHC/LPC) after finishing a CACREP accredited graduate degree in counseling. Taking the National Certification Corporation exam was an initial step in the process. Taking the GCDF course in Michigan from an excellent facilitator, Judith Hoppin, was one of the most practical and helpful courses that has allowed me to obtain the NCDA/CCC (Certified Career Counseling) credential. I am routinely earning additional continuing education units by attending state or national conferences, workshops, seminars, or college courses to update and broaden my content knowledge, as well as maintain licensure. Though there is considerable advocacy at this time for licensure reciprocity, you would be advised to check all state requirements through their respective boards.

In Student Voices, students offer a unique viewpoint as they begin in the career-counseling field. Here, students share their thoughts and reflections about the career-counseling profession and offer personal takeaways.

NICHOLAS VOGEL

I have a MEd from North Carolina State University, and I am currently working as a mental health counselor at William Peace University.

As students graduate from high school or college, the question "So what now?" rings around in their heads as loud as a clock tower chime on the hour. The question can taunt a mind with self-doubt and fear of the wide future in front of them. Working with college students has taught me just how powerful self-doubt and imposter syndrome can be when branching out after the college experience.

Choosing a path can feel like leaping into a black hole, but it is more like leaping onto a canvas and learning what you want to make of it and how to do so. It is a time of opportunity and exploration, to finally do what brings joy, and how to make a living of it. Pursuing a mental health career while also helping clients navigate their own careers has shown me how much our career paths guide our lives. There is tremendous excitement when one learns they have the freedom to pursue what fulfills them.

At the core of my professional degree and career pursuit is a balance of embracing the freedom to choose my career path while also using my training to provide mental health counseling to those in need. Helping others reach their first career goals has taught me the importance of being happy with what I am doing and how to accommodate what I am earning. After all, it is often how the colors blend and come together to create a piece that one can look back on and be proud of what they created for themselves—no matter what others think.

COUNSELING SKILLS CONNECTION

Career counselors must often set distinct boundaries between career counseling and clinical mental health treatment. At the beginning of a counseling relationship, career counselors should review the scope of the work that they can do with a client and describe how and when they will refer a client to a clinical mental health practitioner. For licensed counselors, this will likely be covered in the professional disclosure statement. Career counselors may treat or work with a client experiencing mental health disorders within the limited context of career development. Root causes, underlying trauma, etc., which may have created the clients' symptoms, are beyond the scope of career counselors, though the symptoms themselves may be directly impacting a client's career or work life. Consult a certified colleague if you have any concerns about whether or how to refer a client.

Career practitioners should prepare a list of local mental health practitioners and organizations that support mental health. In some cases, career practitioners may work in tandem with a clinical mental health provider and seek client approval to discuss the client's case. This can offer a great opportunity for a career counselor to support the clinical work and apply techniques that align with the client's needs. At times, a client may need to work with a clinical mental health counselor for a period of time before career counseling progresses.

MINDFUL MOMENT

Practice gratitude by creating your own gratitude cards.
  Supplies: Paper and pen
  Instructions: Using small pieces of paper, write down a favorite quote, saying, or something that you are grateful for. Store your cards in a small box or jar and keep it in a visible location, a place you frequent. Whenever you need a pick-me-up, take a relaxing belly breath and read one or two of your cards.

TECH TOOLS

Mental health and mindfulness apps are now readily available across multiple platforms' app stores. For many, apps provide easy-to-use guides and remind us to practice self-care with more consistency. Career counselors can suggest apps to help clients track their moods, reduce stress, encourage positive thinking, and more (Braun, 2022). Healthline provides a great review of some of the leading apps with evidence-based frameworks. Headspace, Calm, and MindShift CBT are three leading apps highlighted by Braun (2022) that you may want to try!

  Not all mental health apps are safe or effective; be cautious when selecting or promoting mental health apps.

REFLECTION ACTIVITY

Mental health and career satisfaction intersect heavily. What relaxation techniques can you teach clients that reduce the stress of being out of work or looking for jobs in a changing market and world?

  Explore with current or potential clients where they make meaning and where their identity comes from. How can this help clients to differentiate the meaning that comes from a career versus family and other important life events? How can you facilitate the expression of grief and loss as clients come to terms with the reality of career loss and change? How can you monitor your own resilience and self-care to prevent burnout? Working with clients who have lost their jobs means managing complex issues, both psychological and societal, which can feel overwhelming to clinicians. Counselor wellness is just as important as client wellness. How can you instill hope in your clients handling career concerns along with mental health concerns? Remind clients that a crisis by definition comes to an end, and out of a crisis can come new opportunities for both career pursuits and personal growth.

END-OF-CHAPTER RESOURCES

SUMMARY

The link between career and mental health is evident in our own lives as well as those of our students and clients. Being mindful of how trauma presents in career-counseling spaces related to working environments and one's personal life is imperative and essential in our own lives and also among individuals with whom we are working in schools, agencies, universities, and communities. As counselors, a few key elements to consider as we move through the counseling profession include the following: (a) ensuring that we are practicing self-care, (b) obtaining adequate supervision and consultation, and (c) focusing on holistic wellness for ourselves and our clients/students. Utilizing career-counseling and wellness models to support the development and growth of our clients allows clients to not only maintain wellness but also work toward thriving in their professional and personal lives.

REFERENCES

American Counseling Association. (2014). *The ACA code of ethics.* Author.

American Psychiatric Association. (2013). *Diagnostic and statistical manual of mental disorders* (5th ed.). https://doi.org/10.1176/appi.books.9780890425596

Arroba, T. Y. (1978). Decision-making style as a function of occupational group, decision content and perceived importance. *Journal of Occupational Psychology, 51,* 219–226. https://doi.org/10.1111/j.2044-8325.1978.tb00418.x

Bart, R., Ishak, W., Ganjian, S., Jaffer, K., Abedelmesseh, M., & Hanna, S. (2018). The assessment and measurement of wellness in the clinical medical setting: A systematic review. *Innovations in Clinical Neuroscience, 15*(9), 14–23. PMID: 30588362.

Beaumont, E., Durkin, M., Hollins Martin, C. J., & Carson, J. (2016). Measuring relationships between self-compassion, compassion fatigue, burnout and well-being in student counselors and student cognitive behavioral psychotherapists: A quantitative survey. *Counseling & Psychotherapy Research, 16*(1), 15–23. https://doi.org/10.1002/capr.12054

Braun, A. (2022, April 27). *13 of the best mental health apps to use in 2022.* Healthline. https://www.healthline.com/health/mental-health/mental-health-apps#fa-qs

Chen, C. (2019). *The experience of workplace emotional distress and practice of self-care in novice counsellors.* Dissertations & Theses at Ottawa University. https://doi.org/10.20381/ruor-24150

Clark, H. K., Murdock, N. L., & Koetting, K. (2009). Predicting burnout and career choice satisfaction in counseling psychology graduate students. *The Counseling Psychologist, 37*(4), 580–606. https://doi.org/10.1177/0011000008319985

Council for Accreditation of Counseling and Related Educational Programs. (2016). *Section five: Entry level specialty areas-clinical mental health counseling.* www.cacrep-.org/section-5-entry-level-specialty-areas-clinical-mental-health-counseling/

DeSpelder, L. A., & Strickland, A. L. (2009). *The last dance: Encountering death and dying.* McGraw-Hill Education.

Drosos, N., Theodoroulakis, M., Alexander-Stamatios, A., & Rajter, I. V. (2021). Career services in the post-COVID-19 era: A paradigm for career counseling unemployed individuals. *Journal of Employment Counseling, 58*, 36–48. https://doi.org/10.1002/joec.12156

Duffy, R. D., Allan, B. A., Autin, K. L., & Bott, E. M. (2013). Calling and life satisfaction: It's not about having it, it's about living it. *Journal of Counseling Psychology, 60*(1), 42–52. https://doi.org/10.1037/a0030635

Greene, R. (2012). *Resiliency: An integrated approach to practice, policy, and research.* National Association of Social Workers.

Grimmett, M. A., Lupton-Smith, H., Beckwith, A., Englert, M., & Messinger, E. (2018). The community counseling, education, and research center (CCERC) model: Addressing community mental health needs through engagement scholarship. *Journal of Higher Education Outreach and Engagement, 22*(3), 201–230. https://openjournals.libs.uga.edu/jheoe/article/view/1407/1404

Kearl, H. (2018). *The facts behind the #metoo movement: A national study on sexual harassment and assault.* Stop Street Harassment.

Koretz, J. (2019). What happens when your career becomes your whole identity. *Harvard Business Review.* https://hbr.org/2019/12/what-happens-when-your-career-becomes-your-whole-identity

Kottler, J. A., & Shepard, D. S. (2014). *Introduction to counseling: Voices from the field* (8th ed.). Cengage Learning.

Krumboltz, J. D. (1993). Integrating career and personal counseling. *Career Development Quarterly, 42*, 143–148. https://doi.org/10.1002/j.2161-0045.1993.tb00427.x

Lerner, D., & Henke, R. M. (2008). What does research tell us about depression, job performance, and work productivity? *Journal of Occupational & Environmental Medicine, 50*(4), 401–410. https://doi.org/10.1097/jom.0b013e31816bae50

National Association of Colleges and Employers. (2021). *NACE 2020–21 career services benchmark report: Executive summary.* https://www.naceweb.org/uploadedfiles/files/2021/publication/executive-summary/2021-nace-career-services-benchmarks-executive-summary.pdf

National Center for O*NET Development. (2022). *National wages: 21-1012.00—Educational, guidance, and career counselors and advisors.* O*NET OnLine. https://www.onetonline.org/link/localwages/21-1012.00?st=&g=Go

North Carolina Institute of Medicine, Task Force on Mental Health and Substance Use. (2014). Transforming North Carolina's mental health and substance use systems: A report from the NCIOM Task Force on Mental Health and Substance Use. https://nciom.org/transforming-north-carolinas-mental-health-and-substance-use-systems-a-report-from-the-nciom-task-force-on-mental-health-and-substance-use/

Parsons, F. (1909). *Choosing a vocation.* Houghton Mifflin.

Richardson, C. M. E., Trusty, W. T., & George, K. A. (2020). Trainee wellness: self-critical perfectionism, self-compassion, depression, and burnout among doctoral trainees in psychology. *Counselling Psychology Quarterly, 33*(2), 187–198. https://doi-org.proxy.lib.duke.edu/10.1080/09515070.2018.1509839

Saunders, D. E., Peterson, G. W., Sampson, J. P., Jr., & Reardon, R. C. (2000). Relation of depression and dysfunctional career thinking to career indecision. *Journal of Vocational Behavior, 56*, 288–298. https://doi.org/10.1006/jvbe.1999.1715

Savickas, M. L. (2015). *Life-design counseling manual.* Author.

Savickas, M. L., & Hartung, P. J. (2012). *My career story: An autobiographical workbook for life-career success.* Author. http://www.vocopher.com/CSI/CCI_workbook.pdf

Sejdic, A. (2022, July 25). *Add trauma glasses to your teacher toolkit.* Faculty Focus. https://www.facultyfocus.com/articles/effective-classroom-management/add-trauma-glasses-to-your-teacher-toolkit/

Stoltz, K. B., & Haas, K. J. (2016). Mental health or career counseling: A forced choice? No need! *Career Planning and Adult Development Journal, 32*(1), 43–53.

Substance Abuse and Mental Health Services Administration. (2014). *SAMHSA's concept of trauma and guidance for a trauma-informed approach.* HHS Publication No. (SMA) 14-4884. Author.

Substance Abuse and Mental Health Services Administration. (2015). *Behavioral health barometer: North Carolina, 2014.* HHS Publication No. SMA-15-4895NC. Author. https://www.samhsa.gov/data/sites/default/files/State_BHBarometers_2014_2/BHBarometer-NC.pdf

Surguladze, T. (2018). *The role of social support and demographic characteristics in academic and clinical burnout of mental health professionals in training.* Dissertation Abstracts International: Section B: The Sciences and Engineering. ProQuest Information & Learning.

The UNC System. (2022). *UNC system salary information database* (Updated December 2021) [Data set]. https://uncdm.northcarolina.edu/salaries/index.php

United States Department of Health and Human Services. (2015). *Key features of the affordable care act by year.* https://www.hhs.gov/healthcare/facts-and-features/key-features-of-aca-by-year/index.html#.

Walker, J. V., & Peterson, G. W. (2012). Career thoughts, indecision, and depression: Implications for mental health assessment in career counseling. *Journal of Career Assessment, 20*(4), 497–506. https://doi.org/10.1177/1069072712450010

Witmer, J. M., & Young, M. E. (1996). Preventing counselor impairment: A wellness approach. *Journal of Humanistic Education and Development, 34*, 141–155. https://doi.org/10.1002/j.2164-4683.1996.tb00338.x

Woo, S. M., & Keating, C. (2008). *Diagnosis and treatment of mental disorders across the lifespan.* Wiley.

CHAPTER 10

TEACHING AND PLANNING CAREER DEVELOPMENT

Stacy M. Van Horn, Katie Peterssen, and Angie C. Smith

LEARNING OBJECTIVES

By the end of this chapter, you will be able to:

- Review **teaching fundamentals,** including fostering a collaborative environment, encouraging active learning, communicating expectations, and respecting diversity.

- Generate ideas for teaching in an online environment while incorporating best practices.

- Outline career development **program planning,** including strategies for program development, implementation, and evaluation.

WARM-UP EXERCISE

Imagine you are entering your first course in a master's program. What elements would you prefer to be included in the class that would aid in your learning and development? For example, what key points would be useful for you to be included on the syllabus? How do you prefer to learn (i.e., in person, online, independently, within small groups)? What would you need to be successful? As a student, what characteristics would be most important for the facilitator or instructor to possess? As an instructor, what information and resources would be useful for you to learn in order to successfully prepare to facilitate student learning?

INTRODUCTION

This chapter reviews the elements that contribute to the teaching and planning of career development, including interactive and engaging teaching methods as well as how to use those methods in an online environment. Career counselors often teach or train groups on topics ranging from career decision-making, to resume writing, to navigating a job search. This section will focus on instructional strategies, including within an online environment, and career-development program planning.

The fundamentals of career development instruction include fostering collective environments, encouraging active learning spaces, communicating clear expectations, and respecting diversity inside and outside the classroom. Best practices for teaching online and building those fundamentals are offered and described in this chapter. As career development programs are developed, an example of a university program will be highlighted along with specific strategies for program creation, development, implementation, and evaluation.

TEACHING FUNDAMENTALS IN CAREER DEVELOPMENT COURSES

Professional behavior, pedagogic expertise, and compassionate modeling are necessary and transferable skills for up-and-coming career professionals who will be developing and leading career service programs and initiatives in career centers, starting a career development private practice, or working in any setting as a career practitioner. All methods, tips, tricks, and theories that one can use to develop a course on career development, one can also use to establish career development focused programs, workshops, and activities.

Planning, designing, and teaching a career development course, whether face to face or in an online environment, is a multifaceted process. It is important to use a variety of methods including lectures, discussions, reflections, group projects, presentations, and service-learning experiences to provide multiple avenues for all students to engage and contribute. This practice welcomes various learning styles and keeps students engaged and motivated, and it is important to offer multiple ways for students to show their knowledge and learning outcomes. Weaving moments of reflection, peer feedback, and collaboration into assignments helps students gain deeper insight, and disseminating information via videos and web links may promote student engagement and motivation (Cobia et al., 2011).

It is also important for instructors to be transparent by sharing their teaching philosophy and clearly communicating course expectations at the start of the semester (West et al., 2013). This includes telling students how various assignments, activities, experiences, evaluations, and assessments are intentional and meaningful and how they connect to the students' future work. Explaining the rationale is essential, especially in teaching career development, where students may not always see the benefit of the course content to their overall counseling training.

Personal Experience in the Classroom

I have learned to expect some resistance from students who question why career counseling is a required course. Students will gain the most from this learning experience if the course content is clearly connected to their future work with families, couples, and individuals. After reviewing the course requirements during the first week of class, I intentionally share how each of the assignments relates to working with future clients in various roles and within diverse settings. For example, students who are preparing to be school counselors can connect the importance of career and college readiness with their work with children, adolescents, and families. And students of clinical mental health and marriage, couple, and family therapy learn the value of working with people addressing job loss, self-esteem, and identity issues, along with family roles and relationships. It also helps students with majors other than counseling prepare to work in career-advising centers or with career-coaching practices.

Experiential Learning

Providing **experiential learning** outside the classroom promotes student self-reflection and self-awareness. Examples of experiential learning include volunteering at a high school career center, a vocational rehabilitation agency, a college advising office, or a university/college career center. Asking students to reflect on that experience and the impact they had on others using concepts they learned inside the classroom provides a deeper education, and meaningful reflection and discussions encourages critical thinking, which is essential in the helping professions. Service-learning experiences also provide students with a meaningful connection with course content because they can see firsthand how it applies to real-life situations (McGlothlin et al., 2013).

These experiences are helpful to both counselors in training and students in other majors. Providing students with opportunities to reflect on these out-of-class experiences is essential. They might include thought pieces presented at the start of class where the instructor requests students to pause and write down what was meaningful for them at their career site. It can also take the form of students journaling throughout the week about their experiences, or even integrate 1-minute papers at the end of class in which students connect concepts from readings to their experiences outside the classroom. Students can share these individually, or as I like to do, have them discuss in dyads and then share in the large group, pointing out themes to connect all experiences. I find this to be a way to model and stress the importance and significance of being a reflective practitioner in their future career development work.

Keeping It Current in Course Work

Of course, it is important for instructors to stay current in the content knowledge of the course, and incorporating current events connects concepts into class discussions and assignments. During COVID-19, my class examined the impact that the pandemic had on people and families and the health, socioeconomic, and educational inequities it brought to the surface. These discussions were then integrated into student reflections that were shared in small groups. It also connected key career concepts of the impact of culture and socioeconomic disparities and the psychological reactions to job loss.

Emmett & McAuliffe (2011) share that using relevant examples that connect with students' knowledge and experience are basic guidelines to successful lecturing. Pulling in stories from local, state, and national news, along with ongoing current events, can ignite student motivation and curiosity. This connection between concepts in their textbook with real-life events might also lead to increased student engagement and participation. I have found this to be true in providing a backdrop for students to connect events in their daily lives and experiences with what is being taught in the course. I especially find that with adult learners it is essential to pull out their past experiences and knowledge to take the conversation deeper.

One example comes to mind when discussing developmental career theory, such as Super's stages and the concept of minicycles (Super, 1980). I often have graduate students discuss their past work experiences and the transitions and times when they would have experienced continuous learning and pivoted to other career directions. These shifts align with how individuals transform throughout their life and re-enter various stages. This allows students to share experiences from their lives and create meaningful discussions with peers while at the same time linking to theoretical career concepts.

Reflective Practitioner as Instructor

It is so valuable to be a **reflective practitioner** when teaching career development. Personal reflection offers the instructor insight and awareness of classroom practices, such as student engagement, behaviors, attitudes, and perceptions. Writing a reflective commentary on your experiences as an instructor can provide knowledge of overall student learning and allow for improved personal and professional insight (Savory et al., 2007).

PERSONAL EXPERIENCE: REFLECTION

Even though I have been teaching the career development course for over 10 years, there are aspects of the course that I am still modifying and adjusting to improve student learning and outcomes. For instance, I recently swapped a final career theory paper for a career-counseling video demonstration that incorporates career concepts and career theory.

This career-counseling video demonstration requires students to work in small groups to bring to life one career theory that they previously presented to the class. Students work together to demonstrate developmentally appropriate application of career-counseling skills, along with integrating knowledge of the chosen guiding career theory. The demonstration requires a clear presentation of the "counselor" and the "client(s)" focusing on the presenting issue using theory-based language and conducting the session from that theoretical perspective. Students are to include the "counselor" discussing the connections between work, mental wellness, personal and professional relationships and other life roles, and factors that impact the "client's" life. This demonstration requires a brief background of the "client" along with overall goals and objectives for this session as well as the use of either an informal or formal career assessment that is discussed as benefitting the "client." This is a culminating assignment for the semester and the intention is to show how career theory can be incorporated into practice with client(s).

TEACHING IN AN ONLINE ENVIRONMENT: BEST PRACTICES

When my traditional face-to-face career development class transitioned almost overnight to online delivery due to the COVID pandemic, I was forced to reimagine the entire learning environment, including all of my assignments, activities, and evaluations.

One of the best practices for teaching a career development course online is prioritizing a safe environment where students can build trust and a sense of community within the space. The instructor can facilitate this by setting clear expectations at the start of the semester, including the preferred ways of interacting and engaging with peers and the instructor. Ice breakers and "getting to know you" activities can be integrated into the beginning of a career course using discussion board posts, video journaling, wiki pages, and other web-conferencing tools (Smith & Salam, 2018).

Icebreaker Activities

On the first class meeting, I start with student introductions and ask each to create a name tent where, on the outside, is their name, and on the inside they are to write one piece of advice that they would give themselves about their career direction if they could go back in time. Another example of an icebreaker near the beginning of the semester ask students to draw their career journey using the metaphor of a road, including exit ramps, detours, type of road (highway or country road, speed limits, etc.). During the semester when we are covering career theory, I pull out quotes from each theorist representing the main approaches of career development (e.g., trait/factor typology, developmental, learning theory, social cognitive) and place them around the room. I ask students to stand in front of the quote that resonates most with their viewpoint of career development. This is an interesting icebreaker that helps students to disclose their personal views of human development and influences and brings together aspects and perspectives of career awareness and decision-making. This icebreaker activity leads to students selecting their career theory groups for the remainder of the semester. In wrapping up the semester and bringing closure to the class, I ask students to think about a time in their life when they would have benefitted from career assistance. I then ask them to think of three characteristics or qualities of the person who could have helped them best and then share them with the class. Then I ask them to reflect on if they have those characteristics/qualities that they can use with future clients, students, and families.

Leveraging Technology

Instructors must also determine which tools to use that align with the course objectives that also support their teaching philosophy and enhance student learning. The affordability of course-required tools is important to keep in mind (Jencius, 2013), including digital textbooks in lieu of physical books and using e-text links to videos and case studies.

Creatively using technology can help give students an interactive, engaging, and informative career development course. Creating collaborative and creative online assignments, such as tasking small groups to create a wiki page representing various career theories, blogging on a career topic or experience, creating digital stories aligning with an individual's career journey, and using discussion boards encourage students to connect and share with peers (McGlothlin et al., 2013). Another resource that can be used to create community and evoke large-group discussion online is Padlet or similar tools, which serve as an online whiteboard whereby instructors can add prompts and students can respond directly on the board asynchronously.

Teaching the career development course through an online modality can include experiential learning opportunities and support experiences for reflection, sharing, and collaboration with peers. Students can also engage with online interactive tools, such as Kahoot and Quizlet, to review career-counseling content and prepare for upcoming course assessments or national examinations for licensure and/or programmatic requirements (e.g., NBCC, CPCE).

A great, in-depth, step-by-step guide for designing a career development course for an online environment is *Developing Online Learning in the Helping Professions* by Angela Smith, Jeffrey Warren, Siu-Man Raymond Ting, and Jocelyn Taliaferro. This practical resource touches on the basics of creating an online community and engaging students using online tools and strategies, and it addresses varying online delivery models, including asynchronous learning. The authors also address the challenges and potential obstacles, including fear, that hold instructors back from effective online teaching and learning, and they integrate tips from diverse instructors within the field. While the original audience for this book was instructors who are developing university courses for credit, many of the tactics and tools they offer are applicable to developing an effective online career-development seminar or program.

CAREER DEVELOPMENT COURSE PLANNING

Career Activities

I include the Career Lifeline and the Career Genogram in my career development course, and they are great tools for any career development seminar or program. Instructors, faculty, and practitioners should carefully select activities that align with accreditation and department or organizational standards. Both of the following assignments align with Council for Accreditation of Counseling and Related Educational Programs (CACREP, 2016) Section 5: Career Counseling Standards B.

CAREER LIFELINE ASSIGNMENT

Students will create their personal career lifeline that describes their work experience, starting with their earliest memory of paid or unpaid work to the present. Students will chart on a timeline each job, chore, and work experience, and list the specific responsibilities and skills learned for each experience. Then, students will classify each experience as a peak or valley and give a brief reason why. Extend the lifeline to include at least five career or life goals that you have for 5 years from now and another five career or life goals you might have 10 years from now.

Reflection Questions for Individuals or Small-Group Discussion

- Examine your personal patterns of peaks and valleys; did you notice similarities or differences? Do they connect to your career assessment results (e.g., Self-Directed Search, Holland Typologies, interest inventories)?

- In what ways did you increase in self-awareness in relating back to your skills and responsibilities?
- Were there any crises, trauma, or other experiences across your life span that may have impacted future decisions on your lifeline?
- Was it challenging to create goals for 5 and 10 years in the future? If so, explain why.

Questions for Large-Group Discussion

Reflect on your early, middle, and late childhood along with early and late adolescent experiences on your lifeline and discuss the connections you see to stages and concepts in developmental career theory (e.g., Super and Gottfredson). What was it like to go back to that time in your life? What were the most challenging, surprising, or revealing aspects of this assignment?

CAREER GENOGRAM ACTIVITY

Students will review examples of family genograms, and then create a three-generational career genogram that highlight each family member and their careers, jobs, talents, personalities, values, aptitudes, disabilities, interests, hobbies, life experiences, challenges, and strengths.

Reflection Questions for Individuals or Small-Group Discussion

- What behaviors were reinforced or discouraged for males? Females?
- What were the most significant values communicated verbally and nonverbally?
- How does the family address work and leisure and family interrelationships?
- Do any career patterns emerge as you look at the family structure?
- Examine gender roles, cultural impact, the significance of education, expectations, barriers, and definitions of success and failure in your family.
- Who has had the most significant influence? What impact?

Questions for Large Group Discussions

Reflecting on the stages of an individual's life, where are family members in their cognitive, social-emotional, physical, and career development? What were the most challenging, surprising, or revealing aspects of this assignment?

PERSONAL REFLECTION AS FUTURE RESOURCE

Career professionals in training can also use personal reflection on their own career journeys as a resource for future career development clients. The following are sample questions that both counselors-in-training and students in other majors can reflect upon as they complete a career development course:

- What are some ways that people's experiences influence their construction of a career?
- In what ways have you been challenged or impacted by the concepts and assignment in this course?
- How will you use career theory in working with future clients or students?

- How can elements of career theory and concepts in counseling be effectively woven into career development programs?
- In what ways can you use occupational information to serve individuals, couples, families, and students in your future work?

Implementation

There are a lot of things to consider when implementing a career development course, including **teaching modality**, assignments, and experiences both inside and outside of the classroom "walls." When the COVID pandemic arrived, many programs were required to pivot to delivering courses remotely using digital technology. The way the course was taught shifted from face to face (in person), to distance learning via virtual platforms, and this shift can often alter how activities are conducted due to the physical setting and availability of materials. For example, a fishbowl demonstration, role-play, or small group discussion would translate to a breakout room and Zoom recording.

Employing case studies, reflecting journals, and service-learning experiences that integrate relevant standards can create meaning for students. I find that students are much more engaged and attentive when they can express themselves in ways other than through papers and presentations.

Knowledge and Skill Evaluation

CACREP standards are adopted by many graduate counseling programs to determine what to evaluate. The National Association of Colleges and Employers (NACE) sets competencies that provide a framework for career readiness, namely identifying "what is needed to launch and develop a successful career" (2022, para. 7). Similarly, the American School Counselor Association (ASCA) defines career development as one of three key domains in which school counselors support and foster growth in their students, outlines the school counselor's role in career development, and defines student standards (2021). Each of these sets of **standards** describes the knowledge and skills students should be demonstrating, and they often impact the evidence collected through assessments and evaluations that show mastery of required knowledge and demonstrated skills.

Individual courses, as well as larger programs, must be prepared to be evaluated by both internal and external stakeholders. With a graduate counseling program, a **program evaluation** is often focused on graduation and alumni surveys examining what graduates will know and be able to do after completing their degree program. Programs integrate both formative and summative assessments to capture student learning outcomes. For instance, in my counselor education program we use a formative assessment that focuses on wellness. This consists of students creating a wellness plan (knowledge) during their Introduction to Counseling course, which is their first deep dive into challenges of work–life balance and counselor burnout. Graduate students review their wellness plans again in the Techniques of Counseling course the next semester. The summative assessment takes place during students' final clinical experience (internship), where they are tasked with successfully demonstrating (practice) wellness and balance with clients and students. Instructors of career development courses at any level must develop an assessment plan that aligns with relevant standards and demonstrates student learning or skill development.

CAREER DEVELOPMENT PROGRAM PLANNING

Career counselors' roles frequently require a proactive approach to **program development**. Particularly in education and community-based work settings, career counselors create and deliver psycho-educational workshops, seminars, and activities to engage and enrich the career development of their students or clients. These programs are frequently designed to serve students and clients in a group environment. Examples of such programs include facilitating mock interviews, hosting a career or education fair, delivering a career exploration workshop, facilitating a career assessment interpretation as a group, and more.

Student Learning Objectives

The focus on student outcomes emphasizes the change that we desire to create as a result of our teaching or programming. Keeling and Underhile (2007) state that **student learning objectives** (SLOs) define the goals of a particular learning experience (activity, workshop, course, etc.). It should describe what any participant "should be able to do, know, or value as a result of engaging in that learning experience" (Keeling & Underhile, 2007, p. 3). SLOs provide a foundation for strategically curated content and planned activities. Rarely do we have enough time to deliver content on everything that we know our students or clients need, so teachers must be intentional about how time is spent and ensure alignment with relevant organization, state, or national standards (Forehand, 2005). SLOs should be reflective of and be developed in the context of larger program, department, or organizational learning goals.

Writing learning objective statements can feel a bit tricky at first. Using a taxonomy of learning is helpful as you consider what your students or clients should be able to do. *Taxonomy for Learning, Teaching, and Assessing: A Revision of Bloom's Taxonomy of Educational Objectives* by Anderson et al. (2001) is one tool that can be used to analyze and design learning activities (Figure 10.1). This revised taxonomy provides verbs or "action words [which] describe the cognitive processes by which thinkers encounter and work with knowledge" (Armstrong, 2000, para. 8).

In the 2008 guide, *Basic Tips for Writing Learning Outcomes; Outcomes Checklist*, the University of North Carolina Greensboro (n.d.) provides the following suggestions for writing learning outcomes:

1. Differentiate between learning outcomes, satisfaction measures, **program evaluation**, and process measures (number of attendees).
2. Focus on smaller number of priorities: quality over quantity.
3. The less specific an outcome is, the more difficult it is to measure.

FIGURE 10.1 Bloom's Taxonomy.

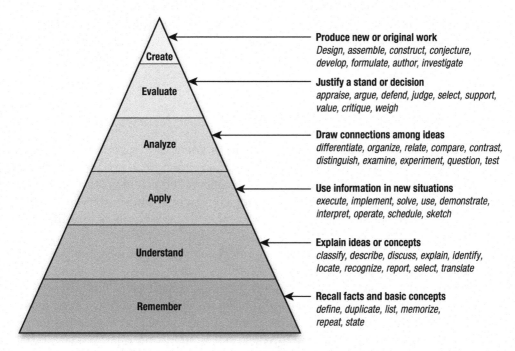

Source: Provided with permission from Vanderbilt University Center for Teaching. (2020). *Bloom's revised taxonomy.* Wikimedia Commons. Retrieved June 27, 2022, from https://commons .wikimedia.org/wiki/File:Bloom%27s_Revised_Taxonomy.jpg

4. Keep outcomes simple and without a multitude of variables and behaviors that are confusing and will confound your results.
5. Think about and build in the method of assessment as you develop learning outcomes. Effective teaching, career development or not, requires organized objectives with clearly aligned instruction and evaluation (Anderson et al., 2001).

Implementation

Program or course implementation in career development demands teaching, counseling, and program and event management skills. Career development is highly personal. Counseling skills will help build relationships with your students and facilitate difficult conversations. Programming and event management skills are necessary for career counselors who often have to manage a budget, volunteers, supplies, and so on while also developing and delivering program content. Counselors-in-training should gain experience managing an event or program, including writing communications, creating marketing materials, developing learning objectives and content, and coordinating space and technology.

Career counselors must be mindful of the multiple roles in which they may interact with a student or client and maintain appropriate boundaries. For example, a career counselor who is in a faculty or instructor role has power as an academic evaluator and likely access to student information that a career counselor operating in a career development center may not have. It is common for career development course instructors to also have students request career-counseling appointments beyond the scope of the course content. National Career Development Association (NCDA) ethical guidelines instruct career educators to minimize possible conflicts between professional roles and to explain to students the limitations associated with each role (2015).

Evaluation and Assessment

Specific, measurable program outcomes and student learning outcomes offer you an opportunity to intentionally evaluate your program. To assess the effectiveness of a program, begin by answering these questions: Did this program achieve your goals? How did participants learn, change, or grow as a result of your teaching or activity? What should participants know or be able to do as a result of this program?

It is critical in many career development settings to demonstrate the impact and gains from your programming. Within educational systems, measuring and recording the impact of career-planning programs can even affect the accreditation of the institution; career centers and other units within higher education institutions undergo a comprehensive program review focused on evaluating its programming over a period of 4 to 6 years. Also, funding and resources may be tied to career outcomes, student or client satisfaction, and other key performance indicators. Establishing clear objectives that align with the mission of the organization provides the foundation necessary to articulate your impact and value as a career counselor or career development team.

As you develop your assessment skill set, I recommend learning more about direct and indirect measures, providing feedback, and aligning assessment goals with institutional or organizational priorities. For example, you may offer a rubric to be completed by employers to evaluate students' interview skills after conducting mock interviews. Or, the Student Career Construction Inventory (SCCI) may be used, in part, to evaluate the impact of a multipart program on students' career development and activities (Savickas & Porfeli, 2011). You might also use a writing assignment with a rubric for scoring to evaluate the ability to articulate a clear career goal.

ASSESSMENT PLAN CHECKLIST

For each program you develop, use this checklist to guide your assessment planning (Exhibit 10.1).

INTEGRATED LEARNING EXPERIENCE

In my career development course, I created an integrated learning experience similar to service learning. This semester-long assignment is effective for both counselors-in-training and noncounselors who may want experiences in the career -coaching and advising field, rather than in a counseling setting. This opportunity allows students to meaningfully connect with experts in their career field

EXHIBIT 10.1 ASSESSMENT PLAN CHECKLIST

Learning Outcomes	Yes	No
An appropriate number of learning outcomes are identified (typically 3–5).		
Learning outcomes are detailed and specific.		
Learning outcomes are directly measurable.		
Learning outcomes align with department, organization, or unit goals.		
Learning outcomes begin with action verbs and are action-oriented.		
An activity or instruction can be developed and delivered to enable students or clients to learn the outcome.		
Target		
Performance criteria are set for each outcome.		
Performance criteria are developmentally appropriate.		
Assessment Instrument		
Assessment type (e.g., survey), is developmentally appropriate and reasonable.		
Unnecessary questions or prompts have been removed from the assessment. The assessment is as concise as possible.		
Assessment clearly indicates whether responses are confidential, anonymous, etc.		
Assessment measure(s) are identified and clearly specified for every outcome.		
Direct measures of student learning are prioritized.		
Data		
Scoring procedures are identified for each measure.		
Where data will be collected is identified and evaluated for confidentiality as needed.		
How clients or students will be selected is identified (sample vs. all participants).		
How and where data will be shared is identified.		

through diverse educational experiences. Students who participate get real-world experiences while receiving mentoring throughout the course at their selected career site. Students are intentional in constructing their own learning goals for this out-of-class experience, and reflection is built-in throughout the course so that the students gain self-awareness and recognize their own growth and development.

Working alongside career practitioners provides students access to populations with differing needs. For instance, graduate students who spend time in a middle or high school are exposed to the career needs of undocumented students, students with various exceptionalities, homeless students, and marginalized or at-risk students. Some graduate students spend time with adults with disabilities in vocational rehabilitation agencies or create workshops in university/college career centers for undergraduates who are first-generation college students. These experiences enable graduate students to link what they have learned in their readings and classroom discussions with populations in the real world. These experiences outside the classroom all align with the CACREP (2016) Career Counseling Standards.

Career service professionals can develop similar experiential learning opportunities for students or clients across the life span to explore various career pathways and opportunities that will expand their vision for what is possible. Career shadowing, short internships, in-depth informational interviews, and volunteer programs can give career seekers a hands-on and close-up look at various careers, companies, and organizations without a longer term commitment.

ESTABLISHING BOUNDARIES

Establishing and maintaining **boundaries** between faculty and students and career-counseling professionals and their clients is important yet often overlooked. There are many perspectives on how much a teacher or professional should self-disclose, and it is always important to remember to focus on what is in the best interest of our students and clients. I like to consider if or how what I am thinking about sharing may impact their learning.

This reminds me of the career development class I was teaching in the fall of 2016. It was the day after the 2016 presidential election, and Donald Trump was officially announced as the 45th U.S. President. Graduate students had varied reactions, from angry and depressed to excited and delighted. I could tell that many students wanted to discuss their feelings, thoughts, and how this impacted them. I also knew I had to be careful how I addressed the various tones and moods in the class, as well as how I would determine what to self-disclose about my own emotions. I reflected on what would be best to model for my students and how I could seize this opportunity to navigate a complicated discussion that was inclusive and respectful where everyone felt heard. It was not about my opinion of the election, but rather how can students process their feelings while still valuing each other and how this can mirror aspects they will confront in their future workplace.

Schwartz (2011) addresses additional considerations for setting boundaries for professors, which is also a good practice for professionals, that consist of articulating clearly defined limits, not gossiping, not venting, and not talking about other people, clients, or contacts negatively. This happens more than you think, and there have been times when I have entered a classroom before instruction begins and students are complaining about another professor's assignment or teaching style. I have witnessed faculty join in and commiserate with students about their experience. I often handle that situation by disrupting the conversation by asking questions about something unrelated to the discussion, usually involving a recent sports or entertainment event to shift everyone's focus. Ideally, professors and career professionals strive to maintain authenticity and find balance between an appropriate level of caring and compassion while maintaining their role as a teacher and evaluator (Schwartz, 2011).

Online teaching and career counseling can also be challenging in that it has unlimited boundaries, which can lead to undefined work–life balance (Hanson & Gray, 2018). For instance, lack of clearly defined work hours paired with online availability (email, text, social media, etc.), can create a culture and expectation of being accessible all the time. One way that helps to protect non-work time is to engage with students and clients through returning emails and maintaining virtual office hours and sticking to them (Hanson & Gray, 2018). Establishing and modeling appropriate work and interpersonal boundaries is necessary for professionals, students, and clients.

ETHICAL CORNER

In this section, the authors lead the reader through topical scenarios to surface common ethics questions and dilemmas faced by career professionals. They ask pertinent and personal questions to encourage reader reflection and insight into personal and professional ethics.

Azra Karajic Siwiec, PhD, LPC, is a counselor educator employed by Capella University. She has been working in the counselor education field for over 14 years and has served as a committee member of the Ethics Committee of NCDA since 2015 and served as the chair of the Ethics Committee since 2017.

Sharon K. Anderson, PhD, is professor of counseling and career development at Colorado State University. Sharon has taught the master's level ethics course for counseling students for over 20 years, teaching and mentoring a multitude of students. She has coauthored or coedited four professional ethics books used by practitioners in counseling and coaching.

VIGNETTE

Some of Sandi's friends are teachers who work in kindergarten through second grade. One of her friends recommends that Sandi organize a career development training event for the 40 teachers in the building. The school asks Sandi to complete a requisition form addressing her needs as well as how much she needs to be paid. Sandi considers this offer and puts together a requisition. She charges a minimal fee and later recognizes that she needs to make copies for all the teachers. She begins to realize the training event and the time she is spending to put it together deserves more compensation than she requested. Sandi feels frustrated and is thinking about canceling the training or scaling it back so that it is less work.

Sandi comes to you to share her frustration and asks for your opinion. What are some ethical implications of Sandi's potential actions: canceling or scaling back the training. What questions would you encourage Sandi to consider as she makes her decision? Think about how to bring in ethical virtues, principles, and the code of ethics as you address these questions. What would you want to consider if you were in her situation and making decisions?

DIGGING INTO ETHICS

As professionals we often hear the term "dual relationships" as it is one of the more common issues counselors deal with in their work. If you are hosting an event and notice that a current client that is looking for a job outside the school district is in the audience, how do you proceed? Consult the code of ethics. Does it offer any direction?

10.1 PRACTITIONER'S PERSPECTIVE

Christy Dunston, MEd, serves as the associate director for Career Counseling Programs at North Carolina Agricultural and Technical State University. Christy has worked in career services for over 10 years. She is a member and has held leadership roles in the North Carolina Career Development Association.

I chose this work through a bit of luck, maybe even happenstance. During my senior year of college, I was a student teacher at an elementary school. While teaching I observed the guidance counselor and her interactions with the students. When I spoke with the guidance counselor about her job and duties, she recommended that I teach for a while before returning to school to become a guidance counselor.

However, while teaching, I had a change of heart about the type of counseling I wanted to practice. I thought back to my sophomore year of college when I went to the career center to help me figure out what I wanted to do postgraduation, and that meeting helped me hone my interests and provided career options for me to explore. I remember being a college student that needed help, and I am thankful for the administrators and professors that provided that assistance to me.

It clicked! I realized that I want to help people figure out what they would like to do for their careers, and I made my decision to go into career counseling. In graduate school, I interned at a local university, which helped me understand the complexities of the college experience and solidified my career decision. I have been working in career services for over 10 years now.

I work with both undergraduate and graduate students who are tech savvy, creative, knowledgeable, open to feedback, and willing to discuss what does and doesn't interest them. I learn something new from these students every time I have the opportunity to speak with them about what they are learning in class or about the internships they have completed.

Even though college students are adults, they still need assistance. People do not know what they do not know, and I am here to help them with what they do not know. My team assists mainly with building resumes, conducting mock interviews, and preparing students for internships and full-time work. We also put together special career and professional development programs and events for students, and during these events, students have an opportunity to learn directly from employers.

In the past, I taught a career exploration course for first-year and sophomore students, and I also taught a job-searching course for juniors and seniors. The career exploration course helped students understand their major and corresponding career options. In the course, they took career assessments, such as the Strong Interest Inventory and MBTI, and they conducted informational interviews. In the job search course, I focused on preparing students for life postgraduation. They had to attend a career fair, create a LinkedIn account, and conduct a mock interview. I also had students write a career motto at the end of the course to help them think about the bigger picture for their career goals, not just a job title or company, but rather the values associated with what they wanted to do. Currently, I facilitate career and professional development programming such as cover letter writing, interviewing, salary negotiation, and networking.

When I first started as a career counselor I wanted so much to give the right response and say the right thing because I wanted to provide a great session. Then, I realized that I will not always get it right and every session will not be great, so I had to do some reflection on what I did right and ways I can improve. This meant reading student evaluations and asking my supervisor for feedback. Of course, these are not always easy tasks to do, but they were helpful in my early career and now. Learning that it is okay to say "I don't have an answer right now, but I can get back to you" took so much pressure off of me because there is no way you can know everything. Also, I do not think customer service is spoken about enough. We must provide excellent customer service because how you speak to students may determine if they tell their friends to visit the office or to stay away.

It really makes my day when a student states that I helped them with what they came in to see me about, knowing that I was able to help someone and provide them with great service. I have a small stack of thank you cards from students that I have received over the years. From time to time, when I have a hard day or week, I will pull them out and read them. This may seem simple, but I enjoy working with people and helping them in whatever way that I can. It is the little things that keep me going.

TRAITS OF CAREER COUNSELORS

In this field, it is important to be someone who is open to all possibilities. A person that thrives in this role has to actively listen, be empathetic, and be okay with the gray areas and with silence. Practicing cultural awareness, understanding bias, and being a continual learner, are also key characteristics of someone who will thrive in this role.

PROFESSIONAL ETHICS

Protecting student privacy is important, and I follow the guidelines set before me to keep me and the students within the bounds of ethics. I do not disclose personal student information to anyone outside of the office, and all of our notes are confidential within the office. If a student is in distress, I follow the procedures, policies, and protocols that are set by the university.

WORDS OF ADVICE

Be patient with yourself. When making a presentation, practice it to understand pacing and timing, and have fun. These are good skills and practices to have for facilitation. Here are a few key considerations I've learned for when I teach a course: knowing when to provide an example, setting boundaries for accepting and not accepting assignments, understanding when students "get it" and when they don't, and staying open to modifying everything when necessary. Watching other people facilitate can also assist with thinking about your presentation skills and ways you can improve.

10.2 PRACTITIONER'S PERSPECTIVE

Lori Nero Ghosal, EdD, PCC, has over 25 years of experience as a higher education professional, business professional, and career coach. She is a multicareer changer who worked as a project manager educational publishing, academic and career coaching in a research one university, and is currently a professional business and career coach and educational consultant with Inner Quest Coaching.

My career has been interspersed with stops and starts, re-education, and redirection. About every 10 years I get another degree or certification and a new career path! Yet my overall career focus has been human development, and each decade has focused more precisely on a specific area, building upon previous knowledge and streamlining my focus with each turn.

I have always been interested in cognitive and developmental psychology, so I thought I'd be a counselor. My first job after graduating college was working with emotionally disturbed teenagers. Soon, I felt defeated by the intensity of their problems and fighting against a system of limited resources. I realized I didn't feel called to work with severe mental health and sociological issues.

I then began working in an educational publishing company. This related to my interests as it drew on psychology, learning, and child development. I started in sales and quickly progressed to project management and program development, where I had the opportunity to work with educators, illustrators, and artists to bring educational concepts into hands-on materials for K–12 students. I enjoyed this work and grew professionally, yet after 10 years, I decided to retrain to work as an educator and counselor with college students, and I received master's and doctorate degrees in higher education.

I transitioned into working at the university where much of my focus has been on academic coaching with first-generation, low-socioeconomic status, and diverse populations. I help guide them in their academic path and support them through difficulties that might impact persistence, such as financial barriers, family and personal issues, physical and learning disabilities, as well as provide understanding how to navigate the university system.

I loved working with college students because that era in life is when they develop their individual identities. Students are independent for the first time in life, and their life decisions are their own. I enjoyed coaching and guiding students through this wonderful stage of life. Originally, I focused on helping these students stay in school, be successful, and graduate. I then transitioned into the career development center and worked with the general student population, especially first-year engineering students.

I codeveloped and led the Career Identity Program designed to serve first-year students on their career discernment and career pathway development. Ultimately, this program helped students create their own career and live life on their own terms. The Career Identity Program has grown to serve all first-year students at the university. I provided coaching to the students and trained faculty, staff, and advisors on coaching techniques and career development to support students in the program as well as their own students, who needed exploratory conversations on their career pathway development.

This program is a personal and professional development program based on identity development applied to career development. It helps students explore their values, sense of purpose, skills, and interests through interactive, hands-on workshops. The program is designed to help them determine their purpose-driven career path and the best major for them to provide a foundation for that purposeful career. Interspersed between the workshops, students work with a trained career coach to help them explore their individual needs and help them process their thinking gained through the group workshops.

This Career Identity Program is developmental in nature; it is activity-based and takes students through a series of self-exploration exercises to help them uncover and discern who they are and who they want to be in life. I believe that each of us knows deep down what is truly our sense of purpose, and that sense of purpose can be buried deep under a stack of societal messages and expectations that we are socialized to believe, such as needing to be an engineer because we are good at math and science or becoming a doctor because that is our parents' dream. International students often are expected to be in one of these fields because it is the only respected career in their home country.

One of my activities is to have students complete a life mind map. I lead them through a discussion on their personal and professional values to begin to open their minds to what is important to them and to begin to hear their own voice. Then, we move into a short visualization exercise where we time travel to a point in their future (age 35), where they have set up their life exactly the way they want it with their education completed, their personal life is exactly what they want, and they are living as their best selves in their ideal career.

At this point I ask them to experience what they see, hear, feel, and do in their life and in their work. What does it look like? Who are they working with? What are they doing? What is the purpose of what they are doing? What are others around them doing? I let them enjoy this for 5 minutes of silent visualization. If they can't or don't believe that they have it or can achieve it, I ask them to trust that they have it and just let the images flow. Then I ask them to open their eyes and draw on paper everything that came to their mind's eye. They can use words, symbols, pictures, or color to express connections among different aspects of their lives. I ask them not to analyze or judge, just let their creativity flow. I give them 20 minutes to do this and then lead them through how to analyze, identify themes, edit, and expand all of it into more practical details and put it into their mind map. Afterward, they pair up and share with their partner.

Students gain so much from this experience because it allows their own inner voice to truly emerge, and they realize what they've always wanted, or at least aspects of what they want in their life. This is a great exercise to move them forward in their individuality. I follow up this activity with a one-on-one coaching session to delve even deeper and coach them in how to process it.

These last 6 years in my career have been especially fulfilling as I have been able to work deeply with students in their self-discovery and focus that toward a fulfilling life through creating a fulfilling career path. I have enjoyed my work in teaching faculty, staff, and advisors on these strategies and coaching techniques to complement and assist them in expanding their academic advising meetings. However, as my career identity is constantly growing, I have decided to retire from the university and transition into my private coaching practice where I consult with higher education institutions and work with professionals who are looking to make a major career change from the ordinary to the extraordinary.

Part of this is working on clients' self-understanding so they can grow into their best selves and create a culture of support, respect, and synergy within their roles. It is clear that early-, mid-, and late-career professionals all need this type of guidance, support, strategies, and clarity of thinking to create their own fulfilling careers. We spend so much of our time and energy in our careers that it naturally flows into a purposeful life, a sense of fulfillment and happiness.

TRAITS OF CAREER COUNSELORS

Graduates of college counseling and higher education administration programs have the fundamental interests, empathy, and thought processes for career development work in higher education. The most important personal or character aspect of the Career Identity Program is the ability to support students holistically using coaching skills. Coaching is about helping students make their own decisions after deep introspection and self-exploration, and it helps them make very individualized decisions. It is a departure from the conventional advisement model. This work requires a sense of open inquiry, the ability to explore and be creative, and to have a deep insight into what students may be experiencing while at college, without teaching, advising, or telling a student what to do. Rather, it provides for an open, accepting, exploratory conversation where the student feels safe and supported to dig deep and connect with their inner self.

PROFESSIONAL ETHICS

The university is clear on legal and ethical standards including confidentiality (Family Educational Rights and Privacy Act [FERPA]) and offers training on identifying concerning behaviors such as suicide prevention and assistance, supporting underrepresented students, and cultural awareness. It is important to know your limitations and when to refer students to other resources that can best serve them. There have been several instances where I reached out to the university or community organizations for support for the student. Some of these include referring students to the counseling center and to the office of Student Behavioral Case Management.

Student Voices

In Student Voices, students offer a unique viewpoint as they begin in the career-counseling field. Here, students share their thoughts and reflections about the career-counseling profession and offer personal takeaways.

PATRICK STEPHENSON

Patrick Stephenson, MEd, is a residence life coordinator at North Carolina State University (NCSU). He works with the Engineering Living and Learning Village, supporting students' academic and professional development during their time with University Housing. He

(continued)

completed a practicum and internship with the College of Agriculture and Life Sciences Career Counseling Office, also at NCSU.

When I first started my counseling program, my aspiration was to secure a position working with college students in a way that supported their growth and development. I wanted to help them recognize the amazing potential that they have and apply it to whatever they strive to achieve moving forward. My very first course, Orientation to Professional Counseling, Identity, and Ethics, surveyed various counseling specialties, and as I learned more about career counseling, it resonated with me and the way I wanted to work with and support students professionally.

With career counseling as my goal, I remember feeling some concern during my theories and techniques courses about how what I was learning would apply to the specialty I'd selected and what I was aiming to do professionally. Those courses seemed geared more toward supporting individuals in navigating emotional issues and distress and did not seem to align with what I knew at the time about the more technical, instructional, and educational aspects of career counseling. When I started my practicum experience the next semester, my concerns were reinforced; as I was training in my new position, I learned the basics of resume and cover letter review, interviewing preparation, major and career exploration, and so on, without any mention of motivations, emotional development, or any other connections to my previous semester's coursework. I continued to feel this disconnect until I started getting repeat students through my practicum work.

During most of my initial sessions with students, many seemed to be interested only in navigating the more technical aspects of career exploration, preparation, and development. As I developed rapport with them and they returned for subsequent sessions, I began to see a different side of career counseling. Students started opening up about their anxieties about navigating an unknown future, the pressures they felt from familial expectations, and their fears of not being successful. This crystallized for me that at its root, career counseling is about supporting individuals and providing guidance and a safe space to help students navigate and find ways to mitigate and resolve their problems.

COUNSELING SKILLS CONNECTION

In our current context as instructors, we include teaching from a trauma-informed perspective (Imad, 2022). It is vitally important to create nonjudgmental, safe, and inclusive spaces for learners to develop, bring their authentic selves, grow, and thrive. Creating a trauma-informed space can include checking in with students, exploring self-care strategies, and offering opportunities for students to learn about resources beyond the classroom.

A suggestion for instructors is to share at your comfort level a small bit of information about yourself. For example, instructors may highlight their favorite movies, books, music, plants, family pets, and so on, to help provide connections outside of classroom content and learn about one another. Instructors can use a person-centered approach to take the opportunity to plan and create an instructional environment that fosters a feeling of belonging.

MINDFUL MOMENT

If you identify as a student or learner, ascertain the type of learning environment that enhances your learning experience. What is included in this space? What is the ideal environment for optimal learning for you? How might you support or contribute to a welcoming learning environment for your peers?

If you identify as a teacher, counselor educator, or facilitator of learning, brainstorm ways you can create a learning environment, in person or online, to exude feelings of calm, support, and safety and to create a welcoming place for learners to engage, learn, and practice skills.

TECH TOOLS

There are a multitude of technical tools to enhance student learning and engagement that can be used in person and online. A few technology tools instructors can use to invite students and learners to share information in a group setting include the following platforms: Padlet, PollEverywhere, Mentimeter, and VoiceThread.

REFLECTION ACTIVITY

Reflect on your own experience as a learner: When did you feel most comfortable? When did you notice a diversity of voices being included? What did the instructor do to create those spaces?

After reading the variety of ways to engage in learning career-counseling content and practices, reflect upon your own experiences as a learner. As a student or learner consider the following questions:

■ What content resonates with you the most?

■ When did you feel most comfortable?

■ When did you notice a diversity of voices being included in the content shared?

■ What did the instructor do to create a welcoming, safe space for all learners?

■ If you were to teach a career-counseling course, what elements would you include in your course for your students and participants?

END-OF-CHAPTER RESOURCES

SUMMARY

Career development instructors within any setting can create a welcoming, safe, and caring environment to engage students and clients. It is important to keep in mind to select appropriate and affordable tools that meet the program or course's goals and also support the student and client. Developing clear, specific, and measurable learning objectives for the program or course intentionally creates a foundation to build a curriculum on and activities that foster change. From the classroom to the community, we can implement effective experiential opportunities and helpful, standards-based education to assist students and clients discover and reach their career goals.

REFERENCES

American School Counselor Association. (2021). *ASCA student standards: Mindsets and behaviors for student success*. Author.

Anderson, L. W., Krathwohl, D. R., Bloom, B. S., & Benjamin, S. (2001). *A taxonomy for learning, teaching, and assessing: A revision of Bloom's taxonomy of educational objectives*. Longman.

Armstrong, P. (2010). *Bloom's taxonomy*. Vanderbilt University Center for Teaching. https://cft.vanderbilt.edu/guides-sub-pages/blooms-taxonomy/

Cobia, D., Carney, J., & Shannon, D. (2011). What do students know and what can they do? Assessing competence in counselor education. In G. McAuliffe & K. Erikson (Eds.), *Handbook of counselor preparation: Constructivist, developmental, and experiential approaches* (pp. 367–376). Association for Counselor Education and Supervision (ACES).

Council for Accreditation of Counseling and Related Educational Programs. (2016). *2016 CACREP standards*. https://www.cacrep.org/for-programs/2016-cacrep -standards/

Emmett, J., & McAuliffe, G. (2011). Teaching career development. In J. McAuliffe & K. Eriksen (Eds.), *Handbook of counselor preparation: Constructivist, developmental, and experiential approaches* (pp. 209–227). Association for Counselor Education and Supervision.

Forehand, M. (2005). Bloom's taxonomy: Original and revised. In M. Orey (Ed.), *Emerging perspectives on learning, teaching, and technology*. https://www .researchgate.net/profile/Kakali-Bhattacharya/publication/302947319 _Piaget_and_cognitive_development/links/60730722a6fdcc5f779c8716/Piag- et-and-cognitive-development.pdf

Hanson, B., & Gray, E. (2018). Creating boundaries within the ubiquitous online classroom. *Journal of Educators Online, 15*(3), 1–21. https://doi.org/10.9743/ JEO.2018.15.3.2

Imad, M. (2022). Trauma-informed education for wholeness: Strategies for faculty & advisors. *New Directions for Student Services, 177*, 39–47. http://dx.doi.org.oh0209 .oplin.org/10.1002/ss.20413

Jencius, M. (2013). Using technology in teaching. In J. West, D. Bubenzer, J. Cox, & J. McGlothlin (Eds.), *Teaching in counselor education: Engaging students in learning* (pp. 81–95). Association for Counselor Education and Supervision.

Keeling, R. P., & Underhile, R. (2007). *Putting learning reconsidered into practice: Developing and assessing student learning outcomes.* https://sa.uncg.edu/assessment/wp-content/uploads/learning_reconsidered_institute_workshop.pdf

McGlothlin, J., VanWinkle, D., & George, K. (2013). Using out-of-class learning activities. In J. West, D. Bubenzer, J. Cox, & J. McGlothlin (Eds.), *Teaching in counselor education: Engaging students in learning* (pp. 67–79). Association for Counselor Education and Supervision.

National Association of Colleges and Employers. (2022). *What is career readiness?* https://www.naceweb.org/career-readiness/competencies/career-readiness-defined/

National Career Development Association. (2015). *NCDA Code of Ethics.* https://www.ncda.org/aws/NCDA/asset_manager/get_file/3395

Savickas, M. L., & Porfeli, E. J. (2011). *Student career construction inventory.* http://www.vocopher.com/ms/scci/SCCI_Master.pdf

Savory, P., Burnett, A., & Goodburn, A. (2007). *Inquiry into the college classroom: A journey toward scholarly teaching.* Anker Publishing.

Schwartz, H. L. (2011). From the classroom to the coffee shop: Graduate students and professors effectively navigate interpersonal boundaries. *International Journal of Teaching and Learning in Higher Education, 23*(3), 363–372.

Smith, V., & Salam, J. (2018). Building community through intentional design: A course model. In A. Smith, J. Warren, R. Ting, & J. Taliaferro (Eds.), *Developing online learning in the helping professions: Online, blended, and hybrid models* (pp. 155–167). Springer Publishing Company.

Super, D. E. (1980). A life-span, life-space approach to career development. *Journal of Vocational Behavior, 16,* 282–298. https://doi.org/10.1016/0001-8791(80)90056-1

The University of North Carolina at Greensboro. (n.d.). *Basic tips for writing learning outcomes: Outcomes checklist.* Division of Student Affairs. https://sa.uncg.edu/assessment/wp-content/uploads/outcomes_checklist.pdf

West, J., Bubenzer, D., & Gimenez-Hinkle, M. (2013). Considering and articulating one's beliefs about teaching. In J. West, D. Bubenzer, J. Cox, & J. McGlothlin (Eds.), *Teaching in counselor education: Engaging students in learning* (pp. 1–11). Association for Counselor Education and Supervision.

CHAPTER 11

CAREER-COUNSELING SETTINGS ACROSS A LIFE SPAN

Helen Lupton-Smith, Katie Peterssen,
and Angie C. Smith

LEARNING OBJECTIVES

By the end of this chapter, you will be able to:

- Compare and differentiate between career-counseling **settings** and roles within those settings.
- Describe current trends influencing career-counseling settings.
- Evaluate career-counseling settings, identifying which settings fit best with your values, strengths, and interests.

WARM-UP EXERCISE

Consider your own career identity. What settings appeal to your values, strengths, and interests? What characteristics would be appealing to you in a work setting? Consider location to home, remote work, small or large organization, etc. List the types of settings you would like to explore and investigate further. List individuals you may know or like to network with who are connected to these settings. List three questions you would like to ask regarding working in your desired setting(s).

INTRODUCTION

Career-counseling skills and practices exist in a variety of settings that begin in elementary school and span through adulthood. Career counselors offer practical tools and resources to clients, students, and other professionals who seek career options, career transitions, and much more. The contributors in this chapter highlight a variety of settings where career counseling takes place and encourage the reader to consider a variety of settings to create a more comprehensive and personalized list. This chapter describes multiple career-counseling settings in K–12, higher education, and adulthood. The options for those exploring jobs in career counseling are highlighted as well as current trends, roles, and resources in the field.

AN OVERVIEW OF CAREER-COUNSELING SETTINGS

Career counselors and those with a background in career development may work in a variety of roles across their career life span, including assisting students in **schools** and **higher education** institutions as well as a range of **settings** for helping adults, including in industry, **private practice**, outplacement, government agencies, and corporate recruitment (Cherry, 2020; Sokanu Interactive Inc., 2022).

Career-Counseling Settings in K–12

The career-counseling professional has a crucial role in **schools** from kindergarten through 12th grade, and there are many options to explore, including school offices, community agencies, nonprofit programs, and vital online resources that assist with the career needs of youth. These professionals work with individual students, groups, clubs, and classrooms, and they are often involved with job and internship preparation, college readiness, and career development (Market Data Retrieval, 2022).

Tip: K–12 Roles in Career Counseling

- School counselor
- College counselor
- Assistant/associate director of college counseling
- Career and technical education teacher (CTE)
- Student services coordinator
- Youth talent development specialist
- Student life specialist
- Career development coordinator (CDC)
- School to work director

Career Counseling in Elementary and Middle School

Career development is a critical part of the growth and development of elementary and middle-school students, and school counselors are well-positioned to assist students in this area. Life career planning begins in the elementary school years (Magnuson & Starr, 2000), and school counselors can offer students a wide range of exploration opportunities, such as a school-wide career day and field trips with follow-up discussions, as a career awareness strategy (Beale & Williams, 2000).

There are specific strategies for middle-school students, and some of these strategies include infusing career-related topics into the curriculum, making available computer-based career-planning systems, using career portfolios, and offering interest assessments and work-based learning activities (Luzzo & MacGregor, 2001). This is a great time in life to try job shadowing and develop mentoring relationships.

PERSONAL EXAMPLE: ELEMENTARY SCHOOL CAREER FAIR

I coordinated a career fair at my child's elementary school in a volunteer capacity as a parent who is a career-counseling professional. The career fair team recruited parents and alumni to represent their careers at booths for the students to visit and ask questions, and we deliberately sought out stereotype-defying career representatives to inspire the students. I saw for myself that it is paramount for elementary students to get exposure to and explore various career fields. A career fair with guided reflection may really help with career development even in young, elementary-aged children (Beale & Williams, 2000).

Career Counseling in High School

Traditional career education at the secondary level consists of academic, aptitude, skills, and interest assessments, and sometimes personality assessments, that assist students in matching their career goals with their interests and skills. In high school, students often choose between two tracts: school to work or school to college. Career-development professionals help students get ready for whatever path they choose by help them be prepared with the key learning skills necessary to succeed in either college courses and/or possessing the knowledge, skills, and techniques to begin studying a career (Conley, 2010). Career counselors who focus specifically on college readiness assist students with acquiring information about college, college admissions, financial aid; submitting applications to college; and enrolling in college (Cabrera & La Nasa, 2000; Poynton & Lapan, 2017).

Outside of the school system, there are both public and private career centers for adolescents. For example, the U.S. Department of Labor, Employment, and Training Administration sponsors two resources to assist adolescents in identifying their career direction. First, the CareerOneStop website (www.careeronestop .org/) provides career exploration help (i.e., job search tools, resume building, and interview resources), and up-to-date information on job salary and benefits. It also lists available education and training opportunities. Second, the American Job Centers (AJCs), also known as One-Stop Centers, provide job referrals, counseling, and other supportive services to help with both job search and finding the location of training and education resources.

PERSONAL EXPERIENCE: PUBLIC AGENCY CAREER-COUNSELING EXPERIENCE WITH TEENAGERS

My first job out of college was as an employee with Volunteers in Service to America (VISTA). I worked on a grant at a counseling **agency** that serves teenagers in a city in the southeast. The grant funded a youth employment program serving Black teenagers (aged 16–19), from low-income areas. As part of the program, counseling staff would pick up the teenagers every day and bring them to the **agency** for a 2-week job readiness class. Then we would help place the teens in jobs and conduct job development. We would meet weekly for aftercare to discuss any concerns that arose with their jobs. It was a rewarding and growth-inducing experience for both the teens and our staff.

Career Counseling in Higher Education

Career counseling in colleges and universities has transformed from just being a center that places graduating students into full-time jobs to a comprehensive college and career-planning center that serves freshmen through alumni throughout their careers (Herr et al., 1993). And there are many roles for professionals with a career- counseling and development background in this setting. Today, it isn't unusual for a **university** to have a central career center while also having decentralized offices located within specific majors and colleges to help only those students in their particular specialties (Scott et al., 2018).

Career centers on campus are often called Career Services, Career Life Planning, and Career Development Centers. Career service staff frequently engage with alumni and employers to place students in jobs or internships. They also handle on-campus interviews for internships and jobs, set up classroom presentations, assist with job fairs, conduct career assessments with students, facilitate group counseling with a career focus, assist with the job searching process (resume preparation, cover letter writing, and interviewing skills), and assist students in applying to graduate school (Herr et al., 1993).

Tip: Higher Education Roles in Career Counseling

- Director of career and academic development
- Assistant/associate director of career services
- Career advisor or career coach
- Apprenticeships program manager
- Assistant director of experiential learning and student success
- Assistant/associate director of employer relations
- Program director, student employment
- TRIO counselor
- Faculty: Career-counseling course instructor
- Dean, executive, and administrative roles related to career and workforce development
- Career access and equity advisor
- Recruiter

CURRENT TRENDS IN CAREER COUNSELING IN EDUCATION

Research and literature in career counseling have identified populations of underserved students and communities, and these are new areas where there is room for growth in the field. These areas include career services for students in rural communities and students who feel conflicted about whether they should stay at home in their communities or leave home to pursue college and career aspirations (Azano, 2014). The economic decline in many rural areas across the country makes this a timely topic as some rural youth want to stay in their home communities (Seward & Gaesser, 2018). Other research has focused on meeting the career and college readiness of first-generation students, low-income students, and students of color who traditionally have been at risk of not having access to postsecondary education (Perna & Finney, 2014).

Career services on campus are chronically underused, and there are special populations who are at risk of having career development issues, such as nontraditional students, student athletes, first-generation college students, students with learning disabilities, ethnic minorities, and lesbian and gay students (Flores & Heppner, 2002; Krieger Cohen & Johnson, 2020; Luzzo & MacGregor, 2001). One of the challenges for career centers is getting the word out to students and alumni that the center exists to help them, and there is lots of room for new and fresh ideas on how to resolve this problem. Some research has recommended that career development be integrated into mainstream curricula to ensure that all students are reached (Bennett et al., 2016). Research has found that doing so promotes and normalizes the career-planning process and that low socioeconomic student's benefit from it (Doyle, 2011). In the future, there may be job opportunities in curricula integration and development.

A Career Assessment Tool

One of the tools that I find especially helpful is the Campbell Interest and Skill Survey (CISS), which I use with teens or young adults who are seeking direction with a career or major. CISS is a self-reported assessment of one's interests and skills in various occupations. I enjoy the one-on-one counseling and the assessment interpretation through examining my clients' interests and confidence in career fields. The assessment leads us into a discussion about what jobs to explore and which to avoid.

Career Counseling in Private Practice

Griffin et al. (2014) described the benefits of working in a private practice setting such as the opportunity to earn income and advance one's career; the ability to align one's needs, strengths, and vocational interests to demands; and the opportunity to manage one's own time to accommodate health and living necessities. Various publications have included the steps needed with operating one's own private practice, such as managing the financial aspect and maintaining insurance coverage through organizations such as the American Counseling Association or the National Career Development Association. Many career-counseling professionals may be drawn to the autonomy, creativity, and other perks that may come with owning one's own private practice. It is important for any practitioner entering private practice with a career-counseling focus to first understand licensure requirements for their state, including the education, supervision, examination, fees, etc., that will be needed to obtain licensure. Various career certifications are available and helpful for further specialization in assisting with clients' career concerns but may not be required to the same degree as licensure.

The National Career Development Association spells out the different credentials a practitioner who specializes in career counseling may obtain:

1. The Certified Career Services Provider (CCSP) is a credential qualifying individuals from an array of training backgrounds to deliver services and demonstrate core competency in the field of career services.

2. Certified Master of Career Services (CMCS) is a credential that recognizes highly experienced career services professionals. CMCS providers hold a minimum of a bachelor's degree combined with 5 to 7 years of career services experience as career coach, career counselor, career advisor, career consultant, executive coach, career development, human resources, talent development, leadership development, workforce development, training, resume writer, recruiter/talent acquisition, and/or university faculty.

3. Certified Career Counselor (CCC) is a credential that is intended for career counselors with an advanced degree (master's degree or higher) in counselor education, counseling psychology, rehabilitation counseling, or a closely related counseling degree, engaged primarily in a career-counseling practice or other career counseling–related services. The CCC credential is a recognition of two important factors in training and experience, including both counseling and a specialization in career development, theory, and practice. Finally, the Certified Clinical Supervisor of Career Counseling (CCSCC) is a credential intended for individuals who are trained for or experienced in the delivery of clinical supervision to career counselors and other practitioners who provide career services (National Career Development Association, 2022).

Career Counseling in Nonprofit Organizations

A nonprofit organization is a group organized for purposes other than generating a profit and in which no part of the organization's income is distributed to its members, directors, or officers. Nonprofit organizations include churches, public **schools**, public charities, public clinics and hospitals, political organizations, legal aid societies, volunteer services organizations, labor unions, professional associations, research institutes, museums, and some governmental agencies (Legal Information Institute, n.d.).

Most counseling nonprofits working with a specific population or community (veterans, substance abuse concerns, senior citizens, individuals who have a disability, children, afterschool academic programs, Boys and Girls Clubs, etc.) have a career component to services that may be more or less prominent as part of the overall services. Counselors in the nonprofit sector can expect to work with some of the country's most marginalized populations. Credentials of employees doing career-counseling work in nonprofit settings may range from full counseling licensure to career certification to on-the-job training. Local and national nonprofit organizations examples such as the Children's Defense Fund, the World Bank, Teach for America and others employ counselors who combine their skills in career counseling, mental health services, and mentorship with their passion for addressing social problems in their communities.

Counselors who work in the nonprofit sector are able to form deep and meaningful connections with their clients and members of the community, due to ongoing and lengthy contact. There are many examples of nonprofit career work. One example, a women's shelter called the Raphael House in Portland, Oregon, counsels women and children who have undergone trauma, and abuse. Broad interventions are used in aiding these domestic violence survivors including career counseling, mental health treatment, and access to resources. Another organization, Soldier

On, helps former veterans who may suffer from complex mental health issues due to wartime conflict or childhood trauma. Utilizing a number of resources, organizations like this provide services to veterans who may otherwise be debilitated by mental illness and seek to provide housing, job training, financial and marital counseling, addiction treatment, and monetary assistance. Easter Seals is an additional example of a nonprofit whose initiatives have a career component focusing on jobs, health, education, etc. for their clients (Wake Forest University, 2020).

Career-counseling roles in nonprofits may include a range of roles including training on how to get a job, keep a job, or exit a job; career development and assessment; resume writing; and interview skills. Some of these career-counseling aspects have been mentioned in other settings; however, catering to a specific population and the needs of that population could potentially include tasks such as providing clothes for the client's interviews or helping navigate transportation, etc. (Wake Forest University, 2020).

Career Counseling in Government Agencies

The 1960s and 1970s saw increased legislation due to higher unemployment instituting career-counseling programs in governmental agencies. Today, and in response to national and global events, government-sponsored programs are there to help unemployed and underemployed citizens and those who are employed but experiencing job dissatisfaction (Pope, 2011). A government or state agency is unique from the other **settings** discussed in this chapter in that it may be a permanent or semipermanent organization funded and initiated by the government that is responsible for the administration of a specific function or purpose or in response to a societal need. A government agency may be established by either a national or state government within a federal system (Definitions for Government Agency, n.d.).

The range and sheer number of job-training and career-development programs that are sponsored by government funds are extensive. Two of the largest government employment service programs in the United States, the Adult Worker and Dislocated Worker programs are examples of intensive career services that include one-on-one staff assistance: assessments, coaching, career counseling, and service referrals (McConnell et al., 2021).

Another government example, the Employment and Training Administration (ETA), part of the U.S. Department of Labor, demonstrates the range of employment qualifications for a career role in this type of setting. For example, the tasks of a role with a bachelor's degree might include coordinating unemployment insurance programs within the agency, compiling and analyzing research, and managing specific grant portfolios (U.S. Department of Labor, 2022).

Career Counseling in Corporations/Businesses

Also in the 1960s and 1970s, there was a movement in large companies to build their own career service centers. Career specialists would work with employees on their own career development, which made employees feel taken care of. These specialists might have had career certifications, bachelor's or master's degrees with a focus on career work, assessment, and career development skills (Pope, 2011). Businesses would also show investment in their employees through mentoring programs and opportunities for advancement.

In a recent poll (https://polldaddy.com/poll/9808716/) using the Kununu Workplace Happiness Index, users were asked to rank the most important workplace factors related to workplace satisfaction, aside from salary. The results showed that many are looking for career development, with 14% saying it's the most important workplace factor. Businesses such as Omni Systems were selected because of continual training to expand on abilities and capacity to grow in the company. Progressive Insurance offers nine employee resource groups, including the Network of Empowered Women and the Disabilities Awareness Network. Career development is what employees like most about Berkshire Hathaway. Many of Berkshire Hathaway's businesses provide continued training and group networking events. On Kaiser Permanente's career-planning website (www .kpcareerplanning.org/prd/index.php), they offer a toolkit for career assessment, career-counseling services, roadmaps of established career paths, courses to learn critical skills, and tuition reimbursement opportunities. Other companies, such as Wawa and Geico, prioritize career-development training classes and workshops to help employees build skills. Businesses are another exciting setting where career counselors can help employees continue to grow and maximize their potential (Martis, n.d.).

Career Counseling With Adults

Professional careers in career counseling with adult clients are vast and diverse. These jobs occur in industries, **private practice**, outplacement, government agencies, and corporate recruitment (Cherry, 2020; Sokanu Interactive Inc., 2022). Adults who seek career counseling may be facing finding a job or retaining one, job stress or job loss, organizational restructuring at work, or downsizing—or they may want to improve their job satisfaction and career counseling assists them with remediation (Stoltz-Loike, 1996). Some companies are starting to engage in proactive initiatives to recruit, support, and develop their employees via corporate career centers that generally exist in the same building as the company. Their goal is to retain employees and increase their productivity while helping employees develop career plans and get the training and skills they need to reach their goals (Ludden, 2001).

Tip: Roles in Career Counseling With Adults

Corporate and Private Sector Roles

- Program director, training, and workforce development
- EAP embedded counselor
- Human resources specialist/partner/manager
- Recruiting/talent acquisition manager
- Organizational development specialist
- Director, employee relations, and career development

Government and Public Agency Roles

- Training manager, economic and workforce development
- Career counselor/coach
- Employment specialist
- Client coordinator, adult workforce development
- Program director, training and workforce development
- Workforce development specialist
- Vocational rehabilitation counselor
- Employment development specialist
- Military and family life counselor
- Transition assistance advisor
- College and career readiness coordinator

CURRENT TRENDS IN CAREER COUNSELING FOR ADULTS

Career-counseling research has identified populations and social groups who need extensive and intentional assistance, including women, low-wage workers, unemployed people, and people with disabilities (Drosos et al., 2021). Career-counseling jobs in agencies, nonprofit organizations, and private practice that help underserved populations may be expanding.

It is also increasingly important for career counselors to explore social justice issues as career professionals, including helping clients cope with bias in their job search or workplace and ensuring that underserved communities are reached. There is also a growing trend in diversity, equity, and inclusion (DEI) work as companies embrace diversity and expand their hiring practices. The National Career Development Association's Social Justice web page offers resources and current initiatives on social justice and DEI for career development professionals that may be useful in this pursuit (www.ncda.org/aws/NCDA/pt/sp/social_justice).

Tech-savvy career counselors will also likely be in demand as research has indicated that many adults need to expand their technology skills to join and advance in the workplace (Drosos et al., 2021). Also, as a result of the COVID-19 pandemic, career counselors in most settings have increasingly used technology to meet with clients via telephone, web, and video chat services. New career professionals will need to be prepared to serve clients and work in person, remotely, and in hybrid formats.

BEYOND THE UNITED STATES: LOOKING AT CAREER-COUNSELING ROLES AROUND THE WORLD

When looking at career counseling and implications for career-counseling roles around the world, there are definitely some themes that seem to emerge across countries and internationally. First, there is an increase in the number of older people in the workforce globally. The World Health Organization Global Report on Ageism was released during the pandemic with responses from 15 different countries and found that both older and younger workers are more disadvantaged in the workplace and ageism is more likely to occur in certain professions or **industry** sectors—such as high tech or hospitality. These findings have strong implications for career counselors worldwide and populations that may be more vulnerable to job and career satisfaction.

Closely aligned with this is the work of the International Organization for Standardization (ISO) Technical Committee on "Ageing Societies" that is developing an international standard for Age Inclusive Workforces. The standard is being developed by experts from 20 countries. The new standard will provide recommendations for the provision and/or maintenance of quality, meaningful work that empowers workers of all ages to be productive and add value to the employing organizations.

Specific examples of solutions provided have included:

1. Development of new business models (e.g., sharing of workers across different sectors);
2. Encouraging senior entrepreneurship and business stimulation through policy, programs, and funding opportunities;
3. Provision of increased digital training and upskilling;
4. Job redesign and task shifting to reduce exposure to COVID-19 risk; and
5. Flexible working environments, including remote work and flexible hours (Pit et al., 2021).

Additionally and thematically, there are still gender inequalities worldwide in the area of work. World statistics suggest that women work more hours but still hold a lower income than men (Albrecht et al., 2018; International Labour Organization, 2018). Regarding international resources and programming, there are also growing opportunities in career services across the world. The Network for Innovation in Career Guidance and Counseling in Europe is a good resource to find information on careers, licensing, and ethics standards in Europe.

Considering universities and career planning, Career Guidance and Counseling (CGC) is an essential part of universities in many countries around the world. Countries including France, Germany, UK, Greece, Italy, Austria, Norway, and Finland are continuously working to enhance their CGC services (Sultana, 2004). Many world-renowned universities (e.g., Stanford University, the University of Melbourne, and the University of Oxford) have specifically designed career centers for helping students with career-related matters. Diverse services are available for students, including one-to-one sessions, group sessions, job fairs, career seminars, career assessments, career workshops, internship opportunities, job opportunities, job hunting, curriculum vitae (CV) writing, and **industry**-academia linkages (Yoon et al., 2018).

ETHICAL CORNER

In this section, the authors lead the reader through topical scenarios to surface common ethics questions and dilemmas faced by career professionals. They ask pertinent and personal questions to encourage reader reflection and insight into personal and professional ethics.

Azra Karajic Siwiec PhD, LPC, is a counselor educator employed by Capella University. She has been working in the counselor education field for over 14 years and has served as a committee member of the Ethics Committee of NCDA since 2015 and as the chair of the Ethics Committee since 2017.

Sharon K. Anderson, PhD, is professor of counseling and career development at Colorado State University. Sharon has taught the master's level ethics course for counseling students for 20-plus years, teaching/mentoring a multitude of students, and has coauthored or coedited four professional ethics books used by practitioners in counseling and coaching.

VIGNETTE

Sandi has been offered two positions. One position is an opportunity to work in a college career center offering services to college students. The other is in a community mental health agency that is trying to bolster its back-to-work program for people who have lost their jobs and who have also used mental health services at the agency. Sandi is trying to assess which is the better match for her. What are some of the questions you would encourage Sandi to think through? What would you encourage her to consider when it comes to ethical issues and match with the job opportunity?

DIGGING INTO ETHICS

Review the theories and settings we have covered thus far in the text. What are the factors, theoretical orientations, and/or settings Sandi uses as she makes a career decision?

11.1 PRACTITIONER'S PERSPECTIVE

CAREER COUNSELING IN HIGHER EDUCATION

Megan Kadrmas is a Nationally Certified Counselor with a MEd in College Counseling and Student Development. She supports students in higher education settings as they transition from college to career.

While attending graduate school at North Carolina State University, I explored several counseling roles in student affairs. I worked in the areas of student conduct, academic advising, admissions, and within two specialized career service centers on campus. While I enjoyed the other opportunities, I felt a spark with career services. I love that within a 30-minute session, students' entire outlook on their career development can completely change. I enjoy the challenge of finding the students who may not know about our services to help them begin the process of getting ready to find happiness and their version of success in their careers.

I currently work with undergraduate and graduate students in business school. The majority of our students are 22 to 24 years old, and I have the privilege of working with many veterans, transfer students, and students returning to college to begin another life journey. George Mason University has a strong partnership with the local community college and has a large transfer-student population as well as students dual-enrolled through both campuses. From the start of graduate school, I wanted to focus my efforts on the community college setting because I love working with their diversity of students and their backgrounds. Working on the other end of their transfer journey, I get to assist students with solidifying and reevaluating their career goals.

I started at GMU in March of 2021 as a career consultant, and I recently was promoted to experiential learning manager. Consultants focus primarily on one-on-one appointments and assist students in our business foundation classes, which include preparing resumes and conducting practice interviews. As an experiential learning manager, I still work one on one with students, but I am now responsible for the career service outreach to the overall School of Business. I oversee workshops, create online learning materials, and teach our Internship for Credit course. I also prepare students for unique connections with our alumni, employers, and board members by managing our mentorship program.

Over the last 3 years, I've realized that students may not attend Career Service Center events because they don't know they exist, or the programs are inaccessible to them. I've honed in on the importance of adapting our programs and services to fit the needs of our students.

TRAITS OF CAREER COUNSELORS

The most important characteristic for work in Career Services on campus is a passion for helping others, as well as empathy and understanding of different perspectives. Many students enter the office thinking they're just in for a resume-review assignment, and that session could turn into a huge unpacking of concerns for their future.

I'll continue to work in career service centers working with specific programs and populations as I like working with students individually and through larger programming efforts. The students are what make my job enjoyable, and now, as my first group starts to graduate and promote to their first "real" jobs, I love getting to see them succeed on their own terms and knowing our work together was the catalyst for where they are today.

CAREER SERVICE IN THE SCHOOL OF BUSINESS

There are various majors with different career goals housed within the School of Business, which always makes for interesting conversations and exploration. Accounting and finance students commonly have a path and a plan in hand when they come to the office and just need help finding the missing pieces to reach that goal. On the other hand, management and marketing students have so many options that we often work together to narrow down their options and set more focused goals in their internship and career searches. The programs that blend technology and business are especially interesting because while they are in the business school, they have heavy components of computer and data science, and a big part of my role in career services is to make sure that they have the training and certifications needed to compete against students coming from programs with a more analytic background. I have found that when working with students from different populations within a similar program, it is critical to remember to see each student as an individual and actively listen to support their unique goals rather than reinforce the commonalities found among peers in their academic programs. I have also found it incredibly beneficial to both me and my students to always maintain a diverse knowledge bank across all industries to be the most helpful in supporting their individualized career development journeys.

CAREER SERVICES FOR GRADUATE ENGINEERING STUDENTS

I have also worked in career service with graduate-level engineering students, where a majority were international students. In this role, I saw how mental health and career services work hand-in-hand, especially during the COVID-19 pandemic throughout 2020. In addition to a rigorous course load, the pandemic threatened the opportunity for many international students to travel home. Our larger-scale programming became focused heavily on weaving self-care techniques into the career development process to best support our students. Working with students in this setting during this particular time gave us not only an opportunity to focus more on values related to career goals for each of our students while they were still in graduate school but also gave the foresight into what change was to be expected in the workforce as students began to discuss negotiables beyond salary, such as permanent remote work, for the first time in our sessions and programming.

CAREER SERVICE WITH FIRST-GENERATION STUDENTS IN AGRICULTURE AND LIFE SCIENCE PROGRAMS

My experience with first-generation students came from my work with agriculture and life science students. Many of these students came from rural North Carolina and had either grown up in agriculture and had the expectation that they would continue the family business one day. Because these students already had a career projection lined up and secured, we got to focus more on work–life balance conversations and their goals for themselves as a leader based on their understanding of what their future would look like from years of generational shadowing.

NONPROFIT WORKFORCE DEVELOPMENT PROGRAM FOR TEENAGERS AND YOUNG ADULTS

When I participated in the nonprofit workforce development setting, our work was focused primarily on education and sharing resources and internship opportunities with students. We served as a liaison between the community and the students. Our nonprofit provided free college and career readiness resources, but we were not to work one on one with students. We were solely there to promote the resources and encourage them to do the exploration on their own.

PROFESSIONAL ETHICS

When working with college students, there are important boundaries and ethical standards to keep in mind. One must be cautious in the conversations you're having with the people you are helping. Also, it is critical to set the expectations from the beginning that I am there to help a student find a job and not place them in a job or get a job for them. I never make promises and choose my words carefully, using words like "I can assist you" or "I can help you" or "I would suggest/recommend." When students want answers, not assistance, I reframe the discussion with phrases such as "What do you think is the next best move?" It's imperative to set the boundary firmly and early that you are their coach, but you can't play or win the game for them.

SETTING BOUNDARIES AWAY FROM WORK

Almost everyone has a career, and the line between my work in career development and my other roles in life can get blurry. I've had to set boundaries to not be overworked as the "off-duty career counselor" for friends and family. Boundaries, I think, are a challenge. Just the other day I was getting my nails done and it turned into a full-blown career-counseling session as I helped the nail technician with her job search strategy in accounting! In hindsight, I should have probably set a firmer boundary with my self-care time, but I think that's a boundary most of us with a helper's heart would have had a hard time setting in the moment.

I recently caught myself in a dilemma where a friend who had spent days working on a new resume was excited to show it to me. After looking at it, I would have completely reworked it. I had to remember that my friend wasn't coming to me as a career counselor but as a friend who was excited about this accomplishment. It was important to ask if my friend wanted assistance rather than just handing out unasked for assistance.

ADVICE FOR FUTURE HIGHER EDUCATION CAREER SERVICE PROFESSIONALS

It's important for counselors in training to know that you're going to put a lot out there to help others, and it is rewarding to hear from students that they achieved their goals and couldn't have done it without you. So, save those emails for a rainy day. Trust me!

Also, depending on where you work, the salaries you're helping students earn could be two or three times your own salary. You have to be able to shake that off and remember the skills you're teaching them about negotiations to advocate for yourself the next time you discuss your own salary. In general, remember to take a pause to career counsel yourself from time to time to make sure you're still finding joy in what you do.

Also, in the smaller settings of career service centers within individual colleges or academic programs, get to know the team before accepting the job. Many positions are on very small teams, and we operate with a tight budget. We wear many hats—or all the hats—to keep the office running. In an office of two, it's extremely important that you work well together. That team member is not just your boss but could be your mentor, advocate, and even mentee if you form the right relationship. As a smaller unit, collaboration is going to be key; get to know the academic advising team, the communications office, the faculty your students talk about, and the student services office.

11.2 PRACTITIONER'S PERSPECTIVE

CAREER COUNSELING IN PRIVATE PRACTICE

Megan Collins Myers is a licensed counselor and career coach working in her own private practice, Myers Career Coaching LLC, where she supports people in career exploration and through mental health challenges. She also works for a group mental health private practice.

I became interested in the career-counseling profession when I used the Career Center at North Carolina State University during my undergraduate years to research my career options. As an undergraduate, I became a Career Ambassador for NCSU, which is a group of students who help other students in their career paths and in finding jobs or internships. When I graduated, I worked in Human Resources, specifically in recruiting, and I stayed on that career path for 6 years. Then I realized that I wanted more autonomy in my work, and I wanted to help individuals on a deeper level beyond what I could do as a recruiter. I later went back to school for a Master of Science in Clinical Mental Health Counseling, and I completed several informational interviews to determine what area of counseling was the right fit for me and to see if I wanted to work in a university, a private practice, or for an organization. It took some trial and error with my career; eventually, I moved into a portfolio career working in career coaching, career counseling, and mental health counseling.

THE PORTFOLIO CAREER

I enjoy the support I receive in a group private practice and the autonomy that private practice allows. I can set my own schedule in the group private practice, which also allows me to dabble in a portfolio career. I work three jobs: Career Counselor/Mental Health Counselor at a Counseling Group private practice, Career Coach/Owner at my own career coaching company, and a contract career coach for a large online career coaching program.

I operate in two separate modalities—career *counseling* and career *coaching*—and practice these modalities under different companies. There is a lot of mental health work in career counseling, and I bill insurance for that work. (If I wasn't billing insurance for that work I would have more flexibility in my approach, the primary focus of the work is mental health.) Career *coaching* is all private pay and coaching is not billable to insurance at this point. This work is future-focused, and I take a more directive method in providing concrete steps for people to research and reflect on their careers. I do not provide mental health counseling in career coaching because that would violate the American Counseling Association ethical code.

There is a difference between a career coach and a career counselor, and I would encourage counselors in training to research the difference. I am licensed to treat mental health issues, and there is such a high need for mental health counseling right now, that it has helped me supplement my income in an area I enjoy. Due to the fact that insurance covers mental health counseling, it takes less marketing and effort to acquire long-term counseling clients versus coaching clients.

CAREER COUNSELING IN PRIVATE PRACTICE

My clients are typically mid-level in their career and looking for mental health and career exploration support. My clients may be feeling decision-paralysis in their career due to anxiety or negative self-thoughts. There is a lot of overlap between clinical mental health counseling and career counseling in the early stages of career transition and exploration because the person's mindset, past experiences, trauma, and upbringing play a big part in their understanding of their own strengths and their career decision-making process. I explore how common diagnoses, like depression and anxiety, impact the career thought process.

In the counseling space, I focus on how a person's career impacts life holistically, and work with people who are focusing on mindset work and self-exploration versus action steps in the job search. Career counseling in a clinical setting (requiring a counseling license), enables me to combine my passion for mental health counseling and my interest in supporting people in career development.

My setting is unique in that I am able to combine mental health counseling and career exploration to help people with processing trauma, reframing their thoughts, and pursuing clarity within their career. I employ cognitive behavioral therapy to explore how thoughts impact our sense of self, our confidence, and our ability to make decisions. Another piece of my work is reflecting on clients' strengths and values and helping clients understand what strengths and values are important to them in their career. It also involves sharing with a client how to research and reflect on career-related information.

THE BUSINESS SIDE OF PRIVATE PRACTICE

In career counseling in the private sector, you must work to build a client caseload yourself. If you loathe sales and marketing, you might want to hire someone to help with this because career counseling in the private sector involves a lot of marketing and brand building in your community. I find career coaching and private pay career counseling require a great deal of marketing and branding. However, counseling requires less because it is covered by insurance. There is actually a shortage of private practice counselors right now and many have a waitlist for clients due to the number of people needing mental health support. When I see someone for mental health counseling and career counseling combined it doesn't take much marketing effort, but when I see a career coaching client it takes a lot more marketing effort.

At the university, the clients are the students, and your financial well-being does not hinge on growing your business. My values in my career led me to private practice because I deeply value flexibility, autonomy, creativity, and service. Salaries and pay differ across different career-counseling fields; I am paid per client that I see, versus a yearly salary.

PROFESSIONAL ETHICS

I must follow the American Counseling Association Code of Ethics and stay HIPPA (Health Insurance Portability and Accountability Act) compliant when I'm operating as a career counselor with a counseling license (LCMHC-A). In this setting, I must maintain strict confidentiality and privacy and set clear boundaries with my clients. In my career coaching, I practice business ethics and maintain strict confidentiality; however, I am not legally bound to HIPPA, so I have more flexibility. For example, I can use Google Docs to store client information, whereas in the counseling setting I cannot do that due to HIPPA.

Social justice issues are apparent in private practice as it presents socioeconomic barriers to some people, and I wish there were ways to offer more equity in private practice. I'm still exploring ways to solve this issue through offering online courses or other modalities as the online coaching space shifts and changes.

SELF-CARE IN A PRIVATE PRACTICE SETTING

I am very extroverted, and I see about 15 to 20 clients every week, one-on-one. However, I'm finding that 10 to 15 clients fit better within my comfort zone and allow more time for creative projects outside of counseling. Be aware that burnout is a possibility, and it's vital to know what your threshold is for working with people one-on-one. If you need to supplement your income, consider a portfolio career (a career that encompasses related jobs). This also allows you to build in other aspects that might feel important to you (for example, project-based work or resume editing). In private practice, you might have less diversity within your workload unless you are creative, whereas at a university you might have time to develop programs as well as time to see people one-on-one.

11.3 PRACTITIONER'S PERSPECTIVE

CAREER COUNSELING IN A NONPROFIT AGENCY

Emily Gomez, MS, CCC, is the program manager of the Federal Sector at Hire Heroes USA. She is a career practitioner committed to preparing and supporting clients in all stages of their career transition. Her 10-plus years of experience are enhanced by a master's degree in career counseling from Sacramento State University and several industry-leading certifications.

In college, I had plans to be a forensic pathologist, but it turns out chemistry and biology weren't my strengths. I adjusted my path toward forensic anthropology as I enjoyed the historical and cultural aspects involved in the approach. While in graduate school, after designing a qualitative research project about student motivations and major choice, I began to explore other options that combined anthropology and this newfound interest involving career and educational planning. It was frustrating to again experience these feelings of mismatch, and I knew I needed to talk to someone and brainstorm options. I called my cousin, a marriage and family therapist, and shared my thoughts with her. She responded, "You've just described one of the roles of a career counselor." I had no idea this job existed! Once again, I changed my path, and I ended up in a great graduate program and then rotated through a few internships. My first full-time position was in a career development center at a research university. In this setting, I gained exposure to many client scenarios and assisted undergraduate, graduate, and transfer students. The pay wasn't great, but I made a lot of great connections and took advantage of every professional development opportunity.

CAREER SERVICES FOR THE MILITARY-AFFILIATED

After 3 years of working in higher education, I secured a position working remotely for a nonprofit agency that provides no-cost career support to military-affiliated job seekers. Our clients are military spouses, active duty military in transition, and veterans who are seeking employment guidance in the civilian workplace, and I oversee a special program that advises clients who seek employment in the federal government. I began supporting student veterans while in higher education and found that I enjoy supporting this population of job seekers. I take a lot of pride in helping clients navigate an often difficult transition and have found there is a real need in the career-development space for resources catering to service members and their families. Luckily, there are foundations and other funders who believe in our mission, and they help us provide a social good through their financial support.

People who work in the nonprofit world often take on many roles, and as a program manager, I supervise full-time staff that delivers one-on-one career support and oversee resource development, service delivery options, and reporting. Our program is grant funded, and there are key metrics in the grant that must be met, including the number of clients helped and those who were a confirmed hire. Part of my job also involves developing resources such as handouts and virtual services, including workshops and self-paced learning. I am also a staff trainer and work with employees in completing career-related certifications.

REMOTE WORK IN CAREER SERVICE

The nonprofit agency is a fully remote organization, and we take advantage of technology to help our teams meet and engage virtually as well as enable our clients to receive support wherever they are. Most of our support services are delivered virtually, although we may host some in-person workshops based on need or a funding requirement. We have clients in many time zones and locations, and this approach gives everyone independence in their schedule. Our team works during normal business hours for our time zone, but we can flex our hours if needed. This flexibility allows us to retain a lot of employees who might otherwise have needed to resign when faced with a move or other geographic impact.

To thrive in a remote counseling role, it's important to be able to block out distractions and pay attention to details. It's important to build in time to get up and move around, as it is so easy to remain in a seated position. We tend to block-schedule time to review resumes, meet with clients, and teach in larger virtual classrooms. This schedule blocking helps us to not multitask and minimizes interruptions. I try to schedule everything and use a calendar to keep track of tasks.

PROFESSIONAL ETHICS

Many clients require additional support beyond my scope of practice. For example, I may have clients who suffer from suicidal ideation or need financial support, housing assistance, or educational guidance. To maintain professional standards, it is critical that I refer clients who have needs outside of career counseling to our partner organizations in lieu of assisting them myself or letting their needs go unmet. To help with providing referrals to clients who may need additional support, our organization added a Training and Referral Partners role that stewards relationships with partners that offer add-on support for free or low-cost. This enhancement has allowed us to better track those who request additional support and maintain current points of contact for those partners.

Because we do not offer therapy or mental health support, we are not subject to HIPPA, and all of our notes, client information, and documents can be stored in customer relationship-management technology and within our organization's Google Drive. Each of these systems requires authentication, and clients are provided directions on what documentation is needed throughout the process. Many military documents contain personal information, so we direct our clients in removing or sanitizing materials prior to uploading them into our systems. Our registration system allows clients to both upload and remove documents from their accounts; this is helpful because clients are able to share documents within this system and do not have to send everything via email. We retain client release forms to ensure that a client is aware that their feedback or background may be shared with a funder or used for marketing or other reporting purposes. Since our grant funders require us to serve only eligible clients (i.e., military members and their spouses), we do retain proof of service for audit purposes.

WORK–LIFE BALANCE AND REMOTE WORK

The flexibility of working from home or in a co-working space allows me to support clients while accommodating other life commitments. I am a new parent, and I'm still navigating how to balance my career and other life roles, though the ability to flex my working hours to accommodate motherhood has made the transition much easier. The ability to step away from the computer to attend to my new baby and make up the time later is helpful and might be more difficult to navigate in an in-person work setting.

The remote workplace has also allowed our family to take short trips to recharge; we can both work during the day and explore in the evening or weekend. These little benefits with scheduling have made a huge impact in my quest for work–life balance. However, this setting isn't for everyone. I enjoy the autonomy and flexibility, but some counselors may not thrive in a virtual or remote environment and may prefer a more structured calendar. It can be tiring to sit on conference call after conference call, but using technologies such as a whiteboard or other brainstorming tools can help mimic some in-person interactions. I also have room within my home for a dedicated workspace and I know that not all have that luxury. Finally, working for a nonprofit agency may mean that healthcare, retirement, and other benefits may not be as competitive as larger employers or other state or government settings.

Student Voices

In Student Voices, students offer a unique viewpoint as they begin in the career-counseling field. Here, students share their thoughts and reflections about the career-counseling profession and offer personal takeaways.

SHEENA KELLY, MS, APC NCC

> Sheena graduated from Walden University with an MS in marriage couples and family counseling. Sheena is pursuing her LPC certification in Georgia and her LCMHC certification in North Carolina while working with individuals, couples, and families in a therapeutic setting.

I worked in a private practice setting in Atlanta, Georgia, for both my practicum and internship, and my responsibilities included taking client calls, prospective client follow-up, and taking payments, as well as seeing my clients for treatment and handling those notes. I worked in a smaller office with two fully licensed therapists, and I was the only intern at the practice.

A significant number of our clients were children, and I aided them with getting through a divorce, performance anxiety, or social anxiety. The practice was also close to a military base, and so many military personnel were referred to the office. We served a population with a lot of trauma or compassion fatigue, such as the military, firefighters, EMTs, and police officers. My supervisor was trained in EMDR and in trauma, so he ensured the practice had contracts with the city of Atlanta and the Lockheed Martin base.

My advice for students is to find a practicum or internship setting that provides them with an array of clients; diversity gives a clinician a better understanding of the type of client they align with. It's also a good idea to do the research on your own—make sure you know your state licensing requirements and what you have to do to reach your goals. Don't be afraid to ask questions of your site to ensure that your boxes are checked and everything signed before completion.

CONNOR BRADY

> Connor Brady is a higher education professional at North Carolina State University. While working primarily in a residence-life setting, Connor's background also includes 14 years in the nonprofit sector serving a youth leadership organization. Connor is a PhD student in the Higher Education Administration program at North Carolina State University.

For the past 6 years, I have served as a residence life coordinator within a residential-life setting. While this is not the traditional counseling setting, nor am I considered a counselor in the traditional sense, I've found that helping skills are a regular and important part of the work that I do. It is often said that residential life sees students at their best, not so best, and everything in between. There could be no more accurate statement.

I primarily serve first-year undergraduate students in a high-achieving student community. As students with an honors affiliation, they were at the top of their class in high school, yet now find themselves in a community of students who were also at the top of their class. This creates competition, either directly or indirectly, and often results in imposter syndrome and a high-stress atmosphere. One of the things I appreciate about my role in this particular area of campus is the opportunity to provide programming outlets to de-stress.

(continued)

My role oversees a large number of students living on campus in residence life and often uses professional counselors as well as career counselors to assist in our programming efforts. What I appreciate about this particular arrangement is that I am able to build bridges with these partners on campus and bring these services to where students are: their homes on campus. Many students, particularly first-generation students, are either unaware of these resources or are hesitant to visit them. Bringing our partners to the students has heightened awareness as well as created a low-stress first meeting.

What I appreciate most about my setting in residence life is the opportunity to serve as a connector to campus and all that it offers our students. With that in mind, I would recommend that anyone serving in residence life be prepared to soak up as much knowledge and information as possible. Make connections. Find opportunities for your own professional development, but as you do, ask yourself if those opportunities can also benefit the students you serve. As a now-seasoned professional, I'm grateful for the opportunities I've had on my own campus to learn as much as possible about the things that await my students and share those as often as possible!

COUNSELING SKILLS CONNECTION

As you reflect on the environment or the setting in which you are interested in providing counseling services, it is vital to consider a variety of factors and specific logistics (i.e., time, available space, modalities), related to the type or location of the practice.

Different work environments and client populations will require counselors to select appropriate theories and interventions. For example, if you are located in a setting where students or clients are required to work with you (i.e., mandatory reporting), the interventions and approaches will need to mirror the client's affect. Similarly, if the model of your workplace is that you only have 30-minute appointments available with adult clients, approaching the appointment with a theory that emphasizes their early childhood may not be appropriate. You may want to explore a theory such as solution-focused brief therapy instead. In a college setting, college counselors working in a counseling center with students experiencing stress, childhood trauma, relationship issues, and academic challenges may use an eclectic theoretical framework that may include a trauma-informed approach, among other theories related to working with young adults. Group counseling can be effective across the life span and in multiple settings, including agencies, K–12 schools, colleges and universities, private practices, etc.

Integration Activity

1. Reflect on the life span stage that you would prefer to work with in a career capacity: children, adolescents, young adulthood, or adults.
2. Refer back to the age-related section in the chapter and list the settings and/or job titles listed in that section that appeals to you. For example, if you want to work with teens, list the job titles and settings available in which you could see yourself working.

3. Narrow down your top three specific job titles and conduct informational interviews with professionals who are working in those specific roles. The interviews can be in person, virtual, or by phone. Ask questions that will give you the information you need to know about the role and setting. You may want to ask what the qualifications are for the job as well as the responsibilities. You could also ask the person you are interviewing what they enjoy and don't enjoy in the role.

4. Write about what you learned from the information you gathered and how it influences your career path.

MINDFUL MOMENT

Think about a time when you felt most successful. What talents were you using? Who were you working with or for? Now think about a time when you felt most supported or had a strong sense of belonging. What type of environment were you in? What qualities existed within the organization or group? These reflections may provide insight into the qualities and characteristics of a setting that is satisfying and supportive for you.

TECH TOOLS

A variety of job search engines and specialty websites exist for job-seeking career development professionals. Professional associations, both national and regional, often offer job boards tailored for members. Some career-counseling settings require testing, certification, or licensure in addition to a related graduate degree. For example, K–12 school counselors in many states are required to pass the Praxis Professional School Counselors (5,421) test, and government and agency roles often require the National Certified Counselor (NCC) credential from the National Board for Certified Counselors (NBCC).

REFLECTION ACTIVITY

Take a moment to consider all of the different options available to career counseling and development practitioners. After researching the role responsibilities and types of qualifications that are needed for your preferred jobs, reflect on your own strengths, interests, and confidence. As you reflect, be intentional about matching your interests with the contribution and impact you want to make. What do you think is your most optimal setting to work in as a career counselor? What is your least optimal? Please elaborate. What surprised you the most after reading the content of this chapter? What was your most exciting takeaway from this chapter?

END-OF-CHAPTER RESOURCES

SUMMARY

Regardless of the setting, career counselors are charged with supporting a diverse population of clients throughout their life span. Career counselors have an opportunity to work in a wide variety of settings or work environments. Current trends in technological advancement will have a direct impact on the nature of career- counseling work in all environments. As indicated through the practitioner's perspectives, it is evident that each setting brings unique benefits and challenges. Career development professionals joining the field will need to reflect on their values, strengths, and interests to determine which setting best aligns with both short- and long-term career goals.

REFERENCES

Albrecht, J., Bronson, M. A., Thoursie, P. S., & Vroman, S. (2018). The career dynamics of high-skilled women and men: Evidence from Sweden. *European Economic Review, 105*, 83–102. https://doi.org/10.1016/j.euroecorev.2018.03.012

Azano, A. P. (2014). Gifted rural students. In J. Plucker & C. Callahan (Eds.), *Critical issues and practices in gifted education* (2nd ed., pp. 297–304). Prufrock Press.

Beale, A. V., & Williams, J. C. (2000). The anatomy of an elementary school career day. *Journal of Career Development, 26*(3), 205–213. https://doi.org/10.1177/089484530002600304

Bennett, D., Richardson, S., & MacKinnon, P. (2016). *Enacting strategies for graduate employability: How universities can best support students to develop generic skills.* Australian Government Office for Learning and Teaching.

Cabrera, A. F., & La Nasa, S. M. (2000). Understanding the college-choice process. *New Directions for Institutional Research, 2000*(107), 5–22. https://doi.org/10.1002/ir.10701

Cherry, K. (2020, March 9). *Career counseling job profile.* Verywell Mind. https://www.verywellmind.com/career-counselor-2795645

Conley, D. T. (2010). *College and career ready: Helping all students succeed beyond high school.* Jossey-Bass.

Definitions. (n.d.). *Definitions for government agency.* https://www.definitions.net/definition/government+agency

Doyle, E. (2011). Career development needs of low socio-economic status university students. *Australian Journal of Career Development, 20*(3), 56–65. https://doi.org/10.1177/103841621102000309

Drosos, N., Theodoroulakis, M., Antoniou, A. S., & Rajter, I. C. (2021). Career services in the post-COVID-19 era: A paradigm for career counseling unemployed individuals. *Journal of Employment Counseling, 58*(1), 36–48. https://doi.org/10.1002/joec.12156

Flores, L. Y., & Heppner, M. J. (2002). Multicultural career counseling: Ten essentials for training. *Journal of Career Development, 28*(3), 181–202. https://doi.org/10.1177/08948453020280030

Griffin, C., Hammis, D., Keeton, B., & Sullivan, M. (2014). *Making self-employment work for people with disabilities* (2nd ed.). Paul H. Brookes.

Herr, E. L, Rayman, J. R., & Garis, J.W. (1993). *Handbook for the college and university career center*. Greenwood Press.

International Labour Organization. (2018). *World employment social outlook*. International Labour Office.

Krieger Cohen, P. E., & Johnson, A. T. (2020). Career counselors self-disclosing to first-generation college students: A grounded theory study. *Journal of Career Development, 49(3)*. https://doi.org/10.1177/0894845320941251

Legal Information Institute. (n.d.). *Non-profit organizations*. Legal Information Institute. https://www.law.cornell.edu/wex/non-profit_organizations

Ludden, L. (2001, December 10). Corporate career centers have much to offer. (Re: Career Development). *Indianapolis Business Journal, 22*(39), 35A.

Luzzo, D. A., & MacGregor, M. W. (2001). Practice and research in career counseling and development—2000. *The Career Development Quarterly, 50*(2), 98–139. https://doi.org/10.1002/j.2161-0045.2001.tb00978.x

Magnuson, C. S., & Starr, M. F. (2000). How early is too early to begin life career planning? The importance of the elementary school years. *Journal of Career Development, 27*(2), 89–101. https://doi.org/10.1023/A:1007844500034

Market Data Retrieval. (2022). *Education*. MDR. https://www.mdreducation.com/pdfs/MDR_Ed_catalog.pdf

Martis, L. (n.d.). *Top 10 companies for career development*. Monster Career Advice. https://www.monster.com/career-advice/article/career-development-companies

McConnell, S., Schochet, P.Z., Rotz, D., Fortson, K., Burkander, P. & Mastri, A. (2021). The effects of employment counseling on labor market outcomes for adults and dislocated workers: Evidence from a nationally representative experiment. *Journal of Policy Analysis and Management 40*(4): 1249–1287. https://doi.org/10.1002/pam.22305

National Career Development Association. (2022). *NCDA credentialing*. https://www.ncdacredentialing.org/aws/NCDA/pt/sp/credentialing_home_page

Perna, L. W., & Finney, J. E. (2014). *The attainment agenda: State policy leadership in higher education*. Johns Hopkins University Press.

Pit, S., Fisk, M., Freihaut, W., Akintude, F., Aloko, B., Berge, B., Burmeister, A., Ciacâru, A., Deller, J., Dulmage, R., Han, T. H., Hao, Q., Honeyman, P., Huber, P. C., Linner, T., Lundberg, S., Nwamara, M., Punpuing, K., Schramm, J., . . . Yap, J. C. H. (2021). COVID-19 and the aging workforce: Global perspectives on needs and solutions across 15 countries. *International Journal for Equity in Health, 20*, 1–22. https://doi.org/10.1186/s12939-021-01552-w

Pope, M. (2011). A brief history of career counseling in the United States. *The Career Development Quarterly, 48*(3), 194–211. https://doi.org/10.1002/j.2161-0045.2000.tb00286.x

Poynton, T. A., & Lapan, R. T. (2017). Aspirations, achievement, and school counselors' impact on the college transition. *Journal of Counseling and Development, 95*(4), 369–377. https://doi.org/10.1002/jcad.12152

Scott, D., Royal, C. W., Sutton, G., & Gifford, R. (2018). Career counseling centers at the college level. In D. A Scott & C. W. Royal (Eds.), *Career counseling: An anthology of relevant career counseling research* (pp. 247–265). Cognella, Inc.

Seward, K., & Gaesser, A. H. (2018). Career decision-making with gifted rural students: Considerations for school counselors and teachers. *Gifted Child Today, 41*(4), 217–225. https://doi.org/10.1177/1076217518786986

Sokanu Interactive Inc. (2022). *What does a career counselor do?* CareerExplorer. https://www.careerexplorer.com/careers/career-counselor/

Stoltz-Loike, M. (1996). Annual review: Practice and research in career development and counseling—1995. *The Career Development Quarterly, 45*(2), 99–140. https://doi.org/10.1002/j.2161-0045.1996.tb00262.x

Sultana, R. G. (2004). *Guidance policies in the knowledge economy: Trends, challenges and responses across Europe: A Cedefop synthesis report* (Cedefop Panorama series No. 85). Office for Official Publications of the European Commission. https://www.cedefop.europa.eu

U.S. Department of Labor. (2022, June 16). *Employment and training administration.* https://www.dol.gov/agencies/eta

Wake Forest University. (2020, July 17). *The rise of the non-profit: How counselors can help solve problems in Their Communities.* WFU Online Counseling. https://counseling.online.wfu.edu/blog/the-rise-of-the-non-profit-how-counselors-can-help-solve-problems-in-their-communities

Yoon, H. J., Hutchison, B., Maze, M., Pritchard, C., & Reiss, A. (2018). *International practices of career services, credentials, and training.* National Career Development Association.

CHAPTER 12

THE NUTS AND BOLTS OF CAREER COUNSELING: SKILLS FOR PRACTITIONERS

Samara Reynolds, Katie Peterssen, and Angie C. Smith

LEARNING OBJECTIVES

By the end of this chapter, you will be able to:

- Demonstrate practical skills for counseling clients in developing professional documents, interviewing, and conducting a job search.

- Examine considerations and resources for helping clients identify spaces and roles where they feel a sense of belonging.

- Describe relevant employment regulations and the role of human resources in the workplace.

WARM-UP EXERCISE

This chapter offers steps to success and how to build your career using nuts and bolts tools to craft your ideal future. In the career profession, we often use metaphors with our clients to evoke imagination and creativity. For this activity, let's envision we are exploring career options and considering our past, present, and future selves in incremental stages, beginning with our origins or foundation, much like building a house.

As you engage in this activity, we invite you reflect on your career history, current career experiences, and ideal future career preferences using the imagery of building a house. The following prompts will help to guide your exploration and thinking.

Past

Foundation: What key building blocks have you used to craft your career thus far?

Construction Team: Who has been on your "construction team" and who helped you along the way as you explored your career options?

Present

Toolbox: What tools do you need now to get started or to grow?

Level: What do you need to achieve or maintain balance? How are you caring for yourself in your career development process?

Future

Measuring Tape: How will you measure success?

Structure and Support Beams: Who are or could be your support beams, cheering you on and providing ideas or encouragement?

Entryway and Front Door: What doors of opportunity could you create? Which doors are already opened? Which are currently closed? How will you take steps forward either way?

Reflection: What feelings come up for you after exploring and creating your career "house"?

INTRODUCTION

Career counseling at the core is about connecting to and supporting our clients and students. Helping professionals seek to develop rapport and an authentic relationship with clients to better understand who they are and how they show up in the world. Practitioners, through education, professional development, and training learn **practical skills** to serve their populations of interest. Career counseling also requires practical skills to provide clients guidance and education on employment standards.

There are many "nuts and bolts" that are part of the practitioner's "tool belt," including **interviewing**, **resume writing**, **networking**, and **job searching**. How these tools are deployed depends on the students' or clients' presenting concern or issue(s).

PRACTICAL SKILLS TRAINING

Certain topics tend to be the catalyst for someone to schedule a first appointment with a career counselor, or these topics are touchstones in the process of finding one's next best opportunity. Knowing how to support people in these areas helps to create trust in the relationship and build client confidence. It also, ideally, allows clients to take important steps in their lives to support their own needs, fuel their personal growth, and open new doors to professional possibilities. There is already a large amount of information out there on how to do these tasks well, and some of them may seem simple. Yet, the value of having a trained career counselor in your corner cannot be overstated as you navigate the triumphs, rejections, progress, and unexpected turns that can present themselves throughout the career development process.

Resume Writing

Career counselors may be called upon to assist clients at any age or stage to write a resume, from high school or college students writing a professional resume for the first time all the way through career changes and people pursuing encore careers postretirement who need help refining new themes and making transferable skills shine.

Through the life stages, our clients' level of professional experience and types of roles they apply for may be vastly different, so much of the resume-writing process remains the same across the life span. Clients need support crafting a focused document that highlights their relevant skills, qualifications, and experiences that aligns with the job description so that they are invited to interview for the position. Resumes won't get clients the job, but they can get them an interview and the chance to tell their story more fully, allowing their personality and potential fit to come through beyond what is on the paper.

Many people treat resumes as a record of employment by listing everything they have done with descriptors that could have been lifted right from their original job posting instead of focusing on individual accomplishments and impact. Their resumes are too long, not easy to skim for keywords and themes, and do not effectively sell what they bring to the table. Career counselors help clients focus on a few main areas for resume success: content, format, and customization.

RESUME CONTENT

Many people start their resume writing or editing process prioritizing format—trying to make the resume look a certain way or fit into a certain number of pages—and they get so intimidated or exhausted by the process that they end up piecing together a subpar resume that is formulaic, generic, and doesn't tell an effective story about their goals or contributions. It is more effective to have a client first think about resume content and then, working together, get the right information into the right format for sending and sharing.

Even with this approach, it can be better to start with larger categories and casual questions and then build out the wording in a more professional, marketable way. As an example of this practice, for those just starting the professional resume-writing process or wanting to start from scratch for any reason, VCU Career Services at Virginia Commonwealth University in Richmond, Virginia, created a Resume Starter Worksheet (https://docs.google.com/document/d/1XxS7ezJw62qQBAi0guLgYJRMOvRcMwWsCoBg13SYOx8/edit?usp=sharing).

A great step to build confidence as well as start outlining resume structure is to ask clients to think about what they can remember of their experiences in the following categories:

- academic experiences
- paid work experiences
- unpaid work, volunteer, and/or community service experiences
- clubs, sports, and/or community organization involvement
- awards and scholarships, and
- technical skills.

They may have a lot, a little, or nothing at all to include in any of these categories, but the structure can provide space to think critically and broadly about what may make sense to include in a resume, instead of focusing only on what paid work experiences or exact degree they have. Once there is a foundation of content to work from, career counselors can ask their clients to elaborate and add details to this initial information. Questions that one may ask to discover more details include:

■ "This experience that you wrote down sounds interesting; tell me a bit about what you did there. What did you enjoy doing most and what did you learn?"

■ "This section on student and community organization involvement looks great. Were you an active member only, or did you serve on any committees or take on any specific leadership roles as part of your engagement?"

■ "I see your paid work experiences so far have been mostly customer service focused. I wonder how we can market that transferable skill to the [roles/programs] you are looking into now. How could you put those skills to use in another environment?"

■ "This is a great start to your list of technical skills. Are you missing anything on this list that you have seen on job descriptions and know about but may not have considered including? Are there specific technical skills you want to build intentionally to add to this list in the near future? If so, how could you do that?"

The next big step for resume writers is shifting how they think about their accomplishments from vague and pragmatic (e.g., "Entered information into spreadsheets"), to specific and results-focused (e.g., "Supported daily data management and weekly analysis for a team of 12 professionals via Microsoft Excel and Google Sheets, strategically improving customer experience and engagement."). This can be a challenging assignment for clients because thinking about their responsibilities and achievements in quantifiable terms and with strong action verbs can feel like bragging or stretching what they really did day to day at work. However, the goal in this exercise is to ensure that their skills and abilities are front and center as they aim to appeal to hiring managers and supervisors.

Here is a general formula for clients to use as a starting point for constructing meaningful bullet points (also known as "action statements") to describe their experiences, as highlighted in the VCU Career Services General Resume Guide (https://careers.vcu.edu/applying-and-interviewing/preparing-to-apply/resume-guides/):

Who—Who did you help in this role (the organization, clients, customers)? Who were you working with?

What—Describe in detail what you did. What were the results of your work? Use action verbs to start each statement that are ideally aligned with the job description you are applying to.

When—When did this work happen (daily, weekly, monthly)? Highlight the frequency of your actions to show productivity.

Where—Where did your responsibilities occur? Did you interact with people outside of the organization? Was travel involved?

Why and How—Why did you do the work? How did your job duties help or add value to the organization, clients, or customers? Be as specific as possible.

Tip: Action Statement Formula

Skill	+	What you did	+	Results/Outcomes
Action Verb	+	Job responsibility	+	How/Why

With this exercise, practice makes perfect. Clients will likely need your support as they test out describing their experiences in a more confident, targeted way. As you read the action steps they have drafted, you can ask the probing questions discussed earlier and encourage them to quantify their statements whenever possible by adding numbers to paint a clearer and more impactful picture. For example, stating that they "organized activities for campers" during a summer internship experience could be even stronger if written as "organized age-appropriate athletic and artistic activities for 75 children, ages 5 to 13, across 6 week-long camp sessions, promoting learning, growth, and teamwork." Listing figures, percentages, and other numbers throughout the resume (written as the numbers, even if under 10, unlike normal sentence structure), also helps draw the eye of the reader to key points across the page and keeps them interested, which is critical when your client may be one of many applicants under consideration for an open role.

RESUME FORMAT

Now you can move forward to the part of the process that feels easiest and most satisfying for client and counselor: formatting. Once a resume is formatted well, it can give your client more confidence in submitting the document and allow for easy reading for a search committee, recruiter, or hiring manager.

Here are some big-picture formatting themes and suggestions to aim for, adapted from the VCU Career Services Resume Guides:

- **Consistency:** Be consistent with font size and style, layout, and formatting.
- **Order and Organization:** Organize sections and content with the most relevant toward the top. Both education (institutions and degrees), and experiences (paid and unpaid), should be listed most recent to least recent in their respective sections.
- **Customization:** Tailor section headers when possible and relevant (e.g., Finance and Budgeting Experience; Community Organizing Experience).
- **Brevity:** Keep information brief and easy to skim as most recruiters and hiring managers spend less than 10 seconds looking over a resume in the first review.

Tip: Resume Formatting

- Page Limit: one page, maybe two for jobs in government, education, and nonprofits.
- Line Spacing: Single line (1.0). Customize the size of line spaces between sections.
- Margins: Set margins to 0.5" to 1.0".
- Fonts: 10 to 12 for the body, 12 to 16 for section headers. Use fonts that Applicant Tracking Systems can read: Arial, Georgia, Helvetica, Tahoma, Times New Roman, Trebuchet MS, and Verdana.
- Contact information: Put relevant contact information in the header using an 18 to 24 font.

Looking at sample resumes to identify interesting styles can be a helpful exercise for resume writers; however, sticking too closely to making a resume fancy, colorful, or design-heavy to get attention in the job search is not a great practice. Resumes are a great place to keep the look and feel simple so that the focus can be on the content, and both AI scanners and recruiters looking over hundreds of potential candidate submissions can find your client and move their application on to the next round in the hiring process.

Remind your client that a resume is a sales document—a snapshot of what they have done and what they can do, written with a specific audience in mind. It is meant to get them an interview so they can tell their story in a more complete way.

RESUME CUSTOMIZATION

Two questions that the VCU Resume Starter Guide exercise asks clients to consider are: "What types of jobs or opportunities are you hoping to use this resume to apply for over the next 6 months or so?" and "If someone were to quickly skim your resume looking for highlights and themes, what are three things you hope they notice or take away from reading your document? *These could be specific experiences you are most proud of, a relevant major or academic focus, or a theme that runs throughout.*"

These questions lead to the last major priority in resume writing: customizing it to fit a specific audience or job. The most effective resumes are going to be tailored to an audience or industry first and then matched with a certain position description via keywords. Once you have a foundational resume to work from, the next step will be helping your client create resumes based on the fields they would like to enter. Creating more specific resumes for different roles or fields can help boost confidence and provide focus, especially for those pursuing jobs or internships related to their field of interests for the first time and for career changers hoping to transfer their skills to a new industry. The client may group experiences or choose specific section headers to craft a "Marketing and Communications Roles" resume as well as a "Nonprofit and Education Sector" resume to use as opportunities arise. For a career changer, adding a "Qualifications Summary" or

"Professional Statement" at the top of a resume can really drill home the "how" and the "why" of their new pursuits and help shape the narrative in a way that empowers the client on their journey. Examples of these resume boosters can be found on VCU Career Services' Career Changer Resume Guide (https://docs.google .com/document/d/1i3Nv8EM2Tz1Gcp3R3WZYZuE_P8oXhl-XUturhhuTcwU/ edit?usp=sharing), with two different formats to consider.

BEYOND THE BASICS: RESUMES

All it takes is some thoughtful tweaks to personalize a resume, and there are some very practical steps that a career counselor can share for how to do so. The first thing to remember is that everything they need is in the job description itself; even though this seems like "playing the game" to get your resume noticed, the rules are spelled out clearly. Look for the words used early and often in the text of a job description to start. For example, perhaps the job description has "communication skills" in a general "responsibilities" section and also as one of the top items in the "required qualifications" section. Make sure the word "communication" can be found on your resume. This may mean swapping out similar language from the job description with terms originally used in one's resume. If an Applicant Tracking System scanner has been programmed to look for the words "lead," "leadership," "led," and "leading," but a client only lists that they have "managed," "handled," or "overseen" projects or people, they may not get pushed through to the next stage of review. Look at the words used in the top-five bullet points in any "required" qualifications, certifications, or responsibilities sections of the job description and prioritize those words if the client has those skills. You can even use a word cloud generator to compare what words are popping up most often in the job description and in your client's resume, comparing the two for alignment. This extra effort will ensure that your client and the hiring manager can find each other in a sea of applicants.

Tip: Simplify Resume Writing

Frequently, we find clients spending countless hours crafting, editing, and customizing resumes. It is so easy to get trapped in a cycle of resume editing and submitting online applications. In a process where clients often feel powerless, the action of writing and submitting can offer some satisfaction. *The 2-Hour Job Search* (Dalton, 2020) provides compelling evidence that the endless cycle of applying to jobs online is ineffective and unlikely to produce results. Research continues to show that the best chances of success in the job search come from networking. Even for a well-qualified client with a perfect, keyword-rich resume, the odds of making it through the human and digital filters to get to the interview stage are very low. Encourage clients to build a strong, well-written resume and then move on to other areas of the job search, that is, informational interviews and networking, which have a much higher value (Dalton, 2020). Clients who crave structure and an evidence-based framework may find great comfort and success in the time-limited, step-by-step instructions found in Dalton's *The 2-Hour Job Search* (2020).

Cover Letter Writing

A common source of anxiety for people in a job search is writing cover letters. People tend to dislike writing cover letters because they aren't sure what or how to write them, and this can lead to people sticking to a dry, generic format that feels disingenuous. Also, writing a cover letter takes more time than customizing a resume. However, cover letters can truly be a secret weapon, especially through online portals, and they are worth the time and effort it can take to thoughtfully craft one. Resumes and cover letters are meant to be complementary—resumes provide a snapshot of one's skills and experience and cover letters explain why they are applying for specific positions and the ways that their skills and experiences connect in meaningful ways to the job description at hand.

Cover letters help hiring managers get to know a candidate's personality, writing style, and genuine interest in the role. They connect the dots between resume content and why someone applied for the role in the first place. It can even provide an opportunity for applicants to proactively address areas of concerns head-on, telling their story their own way when it comes to things like gaps in employment, a lower-than-ideal grade point average, or applying for roles in a different geographic location than where they are currently living and working. Just like a resume, a cover letter alone won't get someone the job, but it can make a real difference in whether or not someone gets an interview. Most people don't write cover letters at all, or they write them poorly, so writing a customized cover letter with relevant content and in one's own voice can really set an applicant apart in a broad candidate pool. The VCU Career Services Cover Letter Guide (https://docs.google.com/document/d/1W1sKSECIuyKgC8V--1eCMPl39tQ9qkhjUEVgotM3EXE/edit?usp=sharing), provides guidelines for cover letter structure, format, and content.

In the current employment landscape, where applications are made online and processed electronically, some employers will require a cover letter while others will only require a resume for the application. It's a good idea to create a cover letter to have one on hand anyway to edit and adapt as necessary. Preparation is key, and career counselors can support clients by reviewing both resume and cover letter submissions.

BEYOND THE BASICS: COVER LETTER

Customization is key when considering the most impactful and easiest way to write a cover letter. Each letter should be directed toward a specific person. If the job description mentions who the role would report to by title or if the client can infer the department based on the position (e.g., a marketing coordinator may work in the Marketing/Communications Department), then the client can search the organization's website or LinkedIn to find the name of the person with the title mentioned in the description or leading a relevant department. Since gender can't be inferred, it may be best to address to the full name (e.g., Dear Samara Reynolds) or by doctoral degree (as Dr.). If your client can't find a name to whom to direct the letter, then using the job title is a decent alternative (e.g., Dear Operations Manager, or Dear Chief Information Officer). At the very least, one can put "Dear Hiring Manager" or "Dear Search Committee," but it makes a much better impression to direct the letter to a specific person or title.

While formatting is important for a cover letter, the content is really what makes or breaks it in closing the deal for an interview. Encourage your clients to keep it succinct, but also allow their genuine interest in the role and relevant experiences to shine. One last big tip for cover letters is to be sure to check spelling and grammar. Having a third party, such as their career counselor, read it with a fresh set of eyes for flow, impact, and errors is great. Instead of quickly submitting error-ridden or generic cover letters that are neither compelling nor effective in the application process, putting the effort into writing a thoughtful cover letter is worth it in order to get a fair shot at an opportunity. A little effort to customize can go a long way.

NETWORKING AND PROFESSIONAL RELATIONSHIP BUILDING

While the term itself can sometimes be nebulous or stir up feelings of imposter syndrome for new and experienced professionals alike, *networking*, or professional relationship building, is a critical career development skill. Networking is a great way for people to gain information and advice about a chosen career field, learn about opportunities, and find other people who want to actively support their success. The U.S. Bureau of Labor Statistics has cited that up to 85% of jobs are found through networking, so spending time honing this skill will be worthwhile for the long term (McIntyre, 2020).

Even if your clients are in high school or just starting in postsecondary education, they likely already have a bigger network of people who can support their career exploration and goal setting than they realize. Consider some of these groups as starting points for inventorying who they already know and can turn to along their career and academic journey: friends and family members, current and former work colleagues, classmates and peers, faculty and staff advisors, members of campus and community organizations they are a part of, and alumni of any schools or colleges they have attended. They may be pleasantly surprised at how being intentional about talking about their career interests to people they already know opens new doors to professional opportunities and contacts.

The best approach for networking is one of mutual benefit and genuine interest; your clients want to learn, and the person they're networking with wants to help. Ideally those roles may reverse one day as they stay connected over time. Great longer-term professional relationships can serve as references for new roles. Cheer one another on as moves are made and achievements are shared, make introductions to other people in their network, and provide mentorship and advice in different capacities. Even in the short term, it can feel really great to help someone achieve their goals and feel like a valued and appreciated part of their team. It also feels great to pay it forward in your profession as an advisor to someone who has reached out.

Networking Online

LINKEDIN

The internet is an easy place to start for people interested in networking to connect to people who can support their career exploration and job search process. When people think of networking, a primary resource that comes to mind is LinkedIn.

com. LinkedIn has been around since the early 2000s but has become increasingly popular and widespread as the platform moved away from being a professional Rolodex toward being a true social media platform and job search and job-posting site. It gives people the chance to connect around professional topics and opportunities and share stories, insights, and accomplishments. It is an effective way to search and apply for open positions in a variety of industries.

VIRTUAL INFORMATIONAL INTERVIEWS

One effective approach to networking virtually is to reach out to professionals to request a virtual informational interview. As highlighted on the VCU Career Services website (2021, para. 1):

an informational interview is a professional development tool you can use to learn more about a particular career. In this type of interview, you direct the questions to a person of your choice that is doing work in a field or industry that interests you. Informational interviews allow you to learn from another person's career path, discover how they gained experience in the field, and learn the strategies and advice they have for someone entering the field today.

Informational interviewing can, of course, also occur in person. Yet, a virtual interview via a virtual meeting platform, a phone call, or simply an email exchange may provide maximum benefit with minimal inconvenience, especially if your clients are reaching out to individuals outside of their geographic area, to someone they haven't met in person before, or they are hoping to align two busy schedules.

Once they find someone they'd like to ask for an informational interview, advise them to craft a brief and specific request. Thank you notes/emails should be sent after every informational interview, with follow-up plans in place, especially if the interviewee provided specific resource or contact recommendations or if they asked your client to stay in touch should they apply for anything within their organization.

Typically, informational interviews are interesting, inspiring, and confidence-boosting experiences, and they get easier with each interview conducted and lesson learned. Having your client set a goal to conduct a certain number of informational interviews in a certain time period and making a chart or other way to keep track of who they talked to, when, and with what follow-up items, can set them up for success in the long run of their professional endeavors.

NETWORKING IN PERSON

Engaging with others in person is the tried and true approach to building a professional network. Professional associations related to your client's industries of interest can be a great starting point in this realm. Associations often host in-person training sessions, conferences, workshops, speakers, and lectures, and they sometimes host happy hours that are focused on building connections in real time. Students and new professionals can often get discounted rates for attending professional conferences or joining as members, which is a fantastic way to dip a toe into different organizations to find their ideal fit.

Outside of industry-specific opportunities, the local Chambers of Commerce, community-based organizations, or college or university alumni will often host networking events organized around specific topics or causes or to connect people who share something in common (e.g., young professionals, parents and families, alumni in a specific class-year range). Sometimes they may be highlighting a local business or neighborhood and can even have a learning or service focus. Most of these events are low-cost or free.

Career counselors can encourage clients to think of networking as making new friends instead of feeling like they must have a goal in mind for the connection or see immediate results professionally for the relationship to be worthwhile. Often, former classmates and coworkers, people from religious and community spaces, and even family members and friends can be wonderful future allies in professional situations, so networking can be considered a lifelong, natural process that, when given some thought and intention, can be one of the most effective professional tools and techniques for your client to use.

JOB SEARCH STRATEGIES

As clients prepare for the job search, ideally they have already begun writing resumes and cover letters and have started to network to create a more focused search process. Even with this preparation, the job search can be daunting, especially considering why they may be looking for new employment, what is at stake, and the personal impact of a role that they may or may not secure.

In this chapter, we are focusing on searches for full-time jobs, although clients may be considering other opportunities when working with a career counselor, including internships, part-time jobs, contract or seasonal work, volunteer positions, organizational leadership roles, and entrepreneurial ventures.

Engaging in Reflection

Reflecting on personal interests, skills, values, and priorities before getting too caught up in applying and interviewing is an important step in any job search process to ensure that the positions that one may apply for are a good fit for one's preferences, personality, or goals. You may want to have clients engage with resources such as a values card sort, motivated skills checklist, or other assessment as part of the reflection process.

Being mindful of the influences that clients bring into the job search process, consciously or unconsciously, can provide clarity on what they want and why and what they may be missing based on lack of exposure or support. The Career Genogram (https://docs.google.com/document/d/1yBDefA-xaHXjJqsKHw BnRVV2jLJa7H7yKTuN3nEDYiI/edit?usp=sharing) used by VCU Career Services can be particularly useful in "providing a visual picture of career influences, revealing career-related patterns and themes from one's family system, encouraging reflection on family influences, and exploring how family and heritage influence an individual's career decision-making" (VCU Career Services, n.d., para. 1). Once your clients have had a chance to think about their motivations and interests, they can approach the job search with additional clarity and purpose.

Getting Organized

Often the job search can feel overwhelming for clients, with too many possibilities and an intimidating set of to-do's that could lead to a big decision at best and rejection at worst. Getting organized can be an excellent way to make a job search feel more manageable and empower your clients. One helpful tool is to make a spreadsheet to track organizations of interest, specific jobs they have applied to (and when), networking contacts and follow-up plans, and associated tasks or results. This tactic can ensure that, if they are applying widely, they aren't just throwing applications into the void, and if they get interviews, they can recall details of the role and prepare accordingly.

Coming up with systems, timelines, and processes will help provide structure and stability, and ideally confidence and success, as they move through the job search over a series of weeks or months. The average job search takes at least 6 months of active search, application, and follow-up, so dividing it into manageable pieces can keep the overwhelmed feeling at bay during the journey (Doyle, 2020).

Finding Opportunities

ONLINE RESOURCES

Often, when people think about job searching, their mind goes to applying to postings online. This is certainly an easy strategy to start with. An online approach that may be most fruitful is starting from a more focused search and expanding to a broader area. If there are certain organizations they are interested in working for, they can start by looking at those websites to find a "careers" or "jobs" page with active postings. Once they find something they are interested in, they can add it to the spreadsheet and set a timeline for applying. While some postings will make deadlines/closing dates clear, others don't share that information, and it is up to the candidate to infer from either the original posting date (knowing many jobs are posted for 2 to 4 weeks before application review begins) or to just apply as soon as possible.

A next step is checking out your client's alma mater website, if they attended college, because sites such as Handshake, Symplicity, Purple Briefcase, and others allow employers to post opportunities to colleges and universities where they have a relationship and actively want to recruit. While many of the postings on these sites will be geared toward entry-level roles for those out of college for less than 5 years, organizations may mark postings for "alumni only" that may be midcareer or higher, as well.

A next great source for finding job opportunities is through professional association listservs and job boards. Many professional associations have state, regional, and nationwide chapters, each with the opportunity for members to post jobs to share within the network. There may be a cost to joining a professional association, but it could be worth the investment for the job search process—and there may be discounts for students.

If your client decides to check out a larger job search site or platform, including casting a wider net geographically and organizationally, using field-specific posting sites are a step in the right direction. Idealist.org is a source for opportunities in the nonprofit sector, USAJobs.gov is the place to start for federal government positions across agencies, and higheredjobs.com promotes staff and faculty postings from colleges and universities across the country. If they want to go bigger, LinkedIn.com is a good place to spend some time, as mentioned earlier, since posts are linked to an organization or individual profile, and often there is a cost to post for a finite amount of time.

A final stop for online job searching should be megasites such as Indeed.com, which will certainly have the largest number of job ideas and potential opportunities, but it is also a huge platform with both paid postings (which are ideal) and posts pulled from across the internet from other sites. It can be less clear what happens to an application once it is submitted, unless it is linked back to an organization's internal application portal. Indeed.com gives a broad sense of what organizations are hiring and what keywords to use when searching and preparing materials, and it allows for search alert emails, as well. It may be most helpful to use Indeed.com to find contacts on LinkedIn or go to individual organization "careers" pages to see what job posts are still live.

There is a wide world of websites that can be helpful in a job search, yet career counselors can be supportive in helping their clients set strategy and use their time effectively rather than just default to Googling for jobs and feeling overwhelmed.

INTERPERSONAL STRATEGIES

While job searching online often feels like the easiest and most accessible option, it is rarely the most effective or confidence-boosting. A as stated previously, but it is worth repeating, research suggests that up to 85% of jobs are filled through networking and at least 70% of jobs are not ever listed (Adler, 2016; Belli, 2017). Truly, the best job search includes multiple approaches, tackling this major task from various angles. This Job and Internship Search worksheet (https://docs.google.com/document/d/1C9tFDafsx3yKZmGxETHa0jYfVIvOhXwTc0PC2wpCrMk/edit?usp=sharing) from VCU Career Services may help your clients reflect on what they have done in support of their job search, what they still want and need to do, where they are willing to be flexible, and what next step is the highest priority.

Interpersonal strategies add more people to your client's job search team, and it can be great to have that extra encouragement and eyes and ears to the ground for job openings. Interpersonal engagement can also be a virtual experience, especially if the client is interested in a smaller company where contact information for leaders and department heads is readily available on the website. Sending a well-worded email, which is essentially a cover letter-style letter of intent regarding one's interest in the organization and specific roles, can open doors to opportunities that may not yet be posted online.

Lastly, clients presenting themselves as experts and change makers in specific areas is a less-direct but equally effective strategy for hearing about new professional opportunities. Clients can present at a conference, write an article for a professional association journal, post a thought-provoking post or relevant accomplishment on LinkedIn or other social networking sites, or take on a leadership role in a community organization or workplace committee. Sometimes our actions will speak loudest, and showing up authentically to share expertise in areas related to their professional interests can get job searchers noticed by the right people and bring opportunities their way.

Beyond the Basics: Applying With Confidence

Once your clients have found opportunities they would like to pursue, it is important to conduct a gap analysis. A **career gap analysis** provides a framework to evaluate your skills and qualifications in comparison with the requirements of your desired role (Career Vision, n.d.). Steps referenced in the VCU Career Services version of this tool include the following:

1. Find a job description of interest and either print it out or copy and paste it into a document.

2. Highlight the required qualifications, desired qualifications, and major responsibilities mentioned in the job description.

3. Create a chart and title the first column "Qualifications" and then list each of the qualifications in separate rows below it. In the second column, write out examples of how you can meet or could easily transfer skills to each qualification based on your experiences. If you cannot identify an example, leave that space blank. See an example Gap Analysis chart (https://docs.google .com/spreadsheets/d/1i37c2Pg8a6FIgNWQ_rpJukg5MpvAOKSKTrmM sD4u5fg/edit?usp=sharing) linked on the VCU Career Services website.

4. Create a third column labeled "Score," and evaluate yourself and your answers, scoring each line item from zero to five, with zero points for no relevant experience and five points for significant relevant experience in that area. As is true in real life, the more relevant examples you have to share or the more significant your accomplishments in areas related to the job description, the higher the evaluation you will receive from a recruiter or hiring manager.

In the areas where your clients scored lower, ask if there are things they could do today or in the future to improve those skills, build that type of experience, or better articulate the transferability of what you have already accomplished. Of course, clients shouldn't rule themselves out from a position completely if they don't have high scores, but these areas highlight where they can grow and what to be ready to talk about in an interview.

Clients should be mindful of application deadlines, track any application details on their job search spreadsheet, and possibly save a copy of the job description for future interview preparation. Clients should follow specific directions given on the job application, especially if there is a request to attach other items such as a writing sample, e-portfolio link, or reference list.

Professional References

A strong set of professional references is an important part of any job search process, and you can support your client in thinking through who may be their best champions and cheerleaders. A great reference can help close the deal and bring an offer their way. Professional references should be as they sound—professionals who can vouch for your clients' performance and character in a career-related setting. For many, this will mean current or past supervisors, colleagues, or collaborators, and sometimes even direct reports. For college students or recent graduates, and especially if the role is closely related to their area of study, course instructors and faculty advisors can serve as strong references, especially if there was a relationship and not just high academic marks in a particular class.

It is a good idea for clients to confirm with the people that they would like to have on their reference list that those people are open to supporting them and are aware that they are being added to the references. Lastly, when clients are finalists for a position of interest, it is important to tell their references that a call may be coming their way soon and to confirm that they would still be ready and available to respond. Being proactive on this front ensures that your client has the best possible professionals in their corner and at the ready, with the right contact information, as they move through the hiring process.

FOLLOWING UP

One of the most critical pieces of the job search puzzle is following up on applications and conversations in the job search. It is easy to add another column to the spreadsheet for when and how clients will follow up, which is typically done 2 weeks after an application or position closing, whichever comes later. When a candidate follows up, it shows that they really want the job and are being proactive, taking the time and putting in the effort to show they care and that they can communicate professionally. It is a great way to stand out in a sea of candidates or even be put back into the pool for consideration if the client had been screened out by applicant tracking systems. Even if clients follow up on an application and are told that the organization has decided not to move them forward in the process or they have already selected someone else, that closure can be helpful, instead of putting hope and time into something that wasn't a good fit or that they didn't have a real shot at.

The job search process can take some time, and it is okay to pause to reflect and regroup if disappointments arise or certain strategies aren't yielding results. It is also important that clients celebrate all the small wins along the way: anytime they get a screening interview, a final-round interview, hear that their references are being checked, have an offer to deliberate, or even realize that something isn't a fit for them and they decline an invitation to move forward in a process or accept an offer. While it can take a number of months to find and secure the right opportunity, approaching the job search with energy, strategy, an open mind, and an organizational system can make this big life step a little less stressful and a lot more empowering for your client. Job searching is a lifelong skill that can be built, strengthened, and adapted as priorities, systems, tools, and markets change.

INTERVIEWING

Almost every job search will have a step in between application and offer deliberation: the interview. As highlighted on the VCU Career Services Interviewing page (VCU Career Services, 2022, para. 2):

[An] interview is [an] opportunity to share how your skills and experiences have prepared you to be successful in the role you seek, and an opportunity for the employer to sell you on the company. Interviews take practice. You're much more likely to see a good outcome if you prepare beforehand. Nearly all interviews contain two parts: questions about your

past experience and situation-based questions to gauge your fit for the position. Afterward, you'll be given the opportunity to ask questions of the interviewer.

This is a great encapsulation of why interviews are important, and it is the general flow of the interview that your candidate should prepare for, no matter the employer.

Interview Mediums

Interviews will typically occur in one of a few ways: in person, on the phone, or online/virtual. In-person interviews may be on-site at the employer organization, especially for a final-round discussion, or on campus for college and university recruiting (typically in a Career Center space or other neutral office space), or as part of a larger conference, career fair, or interview-specific event. Phone interviews are most often used during first-round screenings and are often shorter and allow for maximum flexibility for candidates to wear what they want, sit wherever they need to, and have notes out in front of them for the discussion. Online or virtual interviews often try to bridge the gap between the convenience and flexibility of phone interviews and the personal connection opportunities of an in-person interview. Regardless of the interview medium, there are advantages and challenges to each, and knowing the style will allow your clients to prepare accordingly, whether that's choosing an outfit they feel confident in, getting notes and questions together, or making sure they have good internet connection or phone reception to ensure a seamless experience and great first impression.

Responding to Interview Questions

There are a few classic categories that interview questions tend to fall into, such as general, behavioral, technical, or case, and each requires a different approach and type of preparation. Sample interview questions can be found on the VCU Career Services website under the Common Interview Questions section of the Interviewing page (https://careers.vcu.edu/applying-and-interviewing/interviewing/common -interview-questions/). "Tell me about yourself," or some variation of this question, is commonly used to open an interview. Clients of all ages frequently have difficulty delivering a concise, compelling response to this question. Building a client's confidence and skill in talking about themselves is a core role for career counselors. Role-playing exercises such as mock interviews can be particularly effective for interview preparation.

Preparing to Interview

The interview begins the moment candidates first engage with the recruiter or hiring manager, log onto the call, or step on-site at the employer's location. How candidates engage with people at all levels of an organization, how quickly and professionally they respond to outreach, and the care and organization they show in their preparation make a big difference. It is often said that how someone interviews is evidence of how they will do the job, so being proactive, conscientious, and kind are all great qualities to prove through action.

Focusing on a few key areas, including research, attire, and questions for the employer, helps applicants feel more confident heading into any upcoming interview. Researching the employer and reviewing the job description are two of the most important ways a candidate can show genuine interest in the position. If your clients are applying widely or interviewing often, it is especially important that they are able to distinguish the "why" behind each of their interview conversations; this is critical in making a positive impression and highlighting what they bring to the table.

Looking over an employer's website to review mission, vision, values, leadership and staff structure, recent projects, and proud accomplishments can provide language and information to use in the interview, including clarifying questions to ask. Reviewing the job description, including responsibilities for the position, required and desired skills, and other qualifications are important, as the words and concepts found there often make their way into interview questions. Similar to the gap analysis exercise mentioned earlier, coming up with examples of how your clients can do the required work will prepare them for questions that are likely to arise. This exercise may also raise important red flags regarding organizational fit or lead to important questions for them to ask themselves as they determine if they would accept an offer from that organization.

Professional attire can be a nuanced and sometimes a controversial topic (as referenced in the diversity considerations section), and what is appropriate to wear to an interview tends to vary by industry and by the preference of the interviewer. However, preparing an ensemble that your clients feel confident in can make a difference in the way they present themselves. VCU Career Services has compiled professional style guides based on people's preferred clothing and accessory styles as part of a larger Suit Yourself Closet program (https://careers.vcu.edu/resources/suit-yourself-professional-closet/) and initiative that offers free professional clothing and accessories to students throughout the year.

When the inevitable end-of-interview arrives and your client is asked, "What questions do you have for us," it is a good idea to have questions written down. Beyond being an interview tactic to make a good impression, asking questions will help your clients make a good decision should an offer come their way. Interviews are really a two-way street, with your client interviewing the organization and the people there to see if there are any red flags they may want to avoid or reasons why they think this could be a great place for them to work or not. Examples of good questions to ask interviewers can be found on both the Identity + Career page (https://careers.vcu.edu/about/identitycareer/) and the Common Interview Questions (https://careers.vcu.edu/applying-and-interviewing/interviewing/common-interview-questions/) page of the VCU Career Services website.

Following Up

After an interview, there will be two important follow-up steps: thank you notes and checking in regarding a decision. It is wise during the interview process for candidates to write down the names and titles of the people they interview with, including in larger group sessions, or those whom they haven't already communicated with via email. This way, they can look people up after the interview and send personalized thank you messages. While it takes extra time and effort to write thank you notes after an interview, it can go a long way in showing genuine interest in the position, especially if they make a personal reference to something said or observed during the interview that further confirms a sense of fit. It also gives clients a chance to address anything important that they didn't get to mention during the interview or a question they don't feel they answered well. Inserting key information into the thank you note can bridge the gap in thoughtful ways. An example of a professional thank you note/email can be found on the VCU Career Services webpage (https://careers.vcu.edu/applying-and-interviewing/interviewing/thank-you-notes-and-emails/).

DIVERSITY, EQUITY, AND INCLUSION CONSIDERATIONS

As a counselor, you will encounter clients with backgrounds, identities, and life experiences that are different from your own. Ideally, you will always be poised and prepared to help your client navigate challenges they may face in life in a way that honors their own perspectives, history, identity, and preferences. Yet issues of diversity, equity, and inclusion can arise in both common and surprising ways. Career counselors should be prepared to respond to client concerns and questions on these matters and be proactive and unbiased sources of support and resources.

Career counselors can help individuals understand their values and needs (both work-related and those impacted by their work life), prepare for various professional situations, and find organizations and colleagues that focus on creating space where they can grow, advance, and thrive. Following are some considerations to be mindful of as you counsel clients in career-related matters.

Navigating the Inherently Oppressive Concept of "Professionalism"

As your clients move through the career development process, some of the advice they receive, norms they observe, and biases they encounter will be related to the topic of **"professionalism."** In American society, tenets of professionalism guide everything from what someone should wear and how they should look in a work or interview setting, to how and with whom they should communicate in person or via correspondence, and generally how they move through professional spaces and try to make a positive impression. Some of the rules of professionalism are so well-worn and ingrained in workplace culture, human resources policies, and career-counseling rhetoric that those upholding these particular standards may never stop to think about where these ideals came from, who they are potentially harming or keeping distanced from opportunities, and who they are trying to keep comfortable and in a place of power. Leah Goodridge calls it out blatantly in the *UCLA Law Review* article, "Professionalism as a Racial Construct" (Goodridge, 2022, para. 1):

Professionalism is a standard with a set of beliefs about how one should operate in the workplace. While professionalism seemingly applies to everyone, it is used to widely police and regulate people of color in various ways including hair, tone, and food scents. Thus, it is not merely that there is a double standard in how professionalism applies: It is that the standard itself is based on a set of beliefs grounded in racial subordination and white supremacy.

Professionalism constructs are also primarily sexist in nature, marginalizing women and gender nonconforming and nonbinary individuals, especially in the realms of attire and communication. They can also lead to discrimination on the basis of religion, especially if a particular culture has norms on head coverings and facial hair that could be called distracting or "unprofessional" in a work setting. Consider some of the following common advice that career counselors around the country readily give and share in workshops and on websites through this critical, perhaps new-to-you lens:

- "Keep hair neat, clean, and well-kept."
- "Men's faces should be clean shaved or neatly kept with minimal facial hair."
- "Avoid wearing bright colors or patterns in an interview, as it can be distracting."
- "Women should wear skirts with black or nude pantyhose instead of pant-suits in the most conservative of finance and other business environments."
- "Eye contact is a sign of respect; here are some tricks to maintain eye contact if it is uncomfortable for you."
- "Go with the flow and follow the lead of your interviewer or organization leader when it comes to eating and drinking at professional networking and interview events."

Workplaces are filled with these types of messages, and they pop up in meetings and individual discussions, as well as dress codes and leave policies, promotion and annual review processes, and certainly interviews and hiring practices. As career counselors, our role is to change the type of advice we are providing, making sure our clients are aware of these standards so that they feel they have a choice in how they would like to navigate them or help change them. Having honest conversations with your client about the challenges and biases they may face can be important and empowering in their career development process, and you can help them engage in positive and identity-agnostic workplace behaviors, similar to those outlined in the updated Professionalism Career Competency defined by the National Association of Colleges and Employers (NACE, n.d., para. 6): "Professionalism: Knowing work environments differ greatly, understanding and demonstrating effective work habits, and acting in the interest of the larger community and workplace. Here are a few sample behaviors:

- Act equitably with integrity and accountability to self, others, and the organization.
- Maintain a positive personal brand in alignment with organizational and personal career values.
- Be present and prepared.
- Demonstrate dependability (e.g., report consistently for work or meetings).
- Prioritize and complete tasks to accomplish organizational goals.
- Consistently meet or exceed goals and expectations.
- Have an attention to detail, resulting in few if any errors in their work.
- Show a high level of dedication toward doing a good job."

In the ideal working world of the future, people would not be unfairly judged regarding their potential and performance based on how they wear their hair, the cut and style of their clothing, their piercings or tattoos, the tone of the voice, the perceived degree of agreeableness versus assertiveness, or if and how they speak up for themselves. In the years to come, as traditional standards of professionalism change and forward-thinking leaders help to broaden the term, the workplace will ideally become a space where people and their work can stand out for their contributions and care, regardless of appearance and style. For now, if we can acknowledge the harm these standards cause and be part of the fight for true diversity, equity, and inclusion at all stages of the recruitment, hiring, retention, and rewards process across work environments, we will be able to support the success of career-counseling clients of all backgrounds, abilities, and experiences.

Beyond the Basics: Finding Organizations That Value Diversity, Equity, and Inclusion

There are a number of organizations, job-posting sites, and web-based resources that clients can use to find organizations that value diversity, equity, and inclusion or have specific identity-affirming missions or initiatives. A list of some of these resources and sites can be found at the bottom of the Identity + Career webpage for VCU Career Services (https://careers.vcu.edu/about/identitycareer/). This is just a starting point, and your client may want to search for more organizations and platforms specific to who they are and what is important to them.

With a little research, there are some excellent resources for career counselors related to supporting clients with disabilities, those who identify as LGBTQIA+, and military veterans, to name a few. These websites and other news outlets, professional associations, social media pages, and college and university job-posting platforms, can also help your client locate internships, recruiting programs, affinity groups and other retention and advancement programs.

Clients may also ask specific questions during a networking or informational interview conversation at an employer organization or in a given industry, as well as during a formal interview. Empowering questions and topics your client can consider include some of the following, highlighted on the VCU Career Services site:

- Does this organization have affinity groups or opportunities for employees to develop networks and mentorships based on identity, if interested?
- How are team members rewarded and recognized? What does appreciation look like?
- How does this team handle differences of opinion or approach? Can you provide an example of healthy conflict management within this organization?
- How are ideas and feedback solicited, shared, and discussed within this organization?
- Who tends to be consulted, and how, before decisions are made within the organization?
- How is professional development encouraged and supported here (e.g., coaching, time, funding, suggesting opportunities, invitations to research or co-present)?

Asking to speak to someone who shares one or more of an individual's salient identities can be supremely helpful in distinguishing between marketing speak and what is really true within the day-to-day work of an organization, office, or team. Using alumni networks, personal or professional contacts (and their networks), or finding people on an employer's "About Us" or "Team Leadership" page can be a great place to find people and get authentic answers to important questions.

Identity Disclosure

Regardless of where your clients are in their career development or job search journey, they will inevitably face moments where they must decide when, if, and how to share more about who they are and what they need and value. The VCU Career Services Identity + Career webpage determines that deciding to disclose is a personal decision, and there are no clear guidelines on when and what to share even though these things directly impact careers. There are very few things that someone must legally share in an interview, though to find a supportive and flexible environment, there may be benefits to sharing elements of personal information to networking contacts or hiring managers. While it is up to the person to decide what is best, career counselors can provide guidance on specific situations and give clients the opportunity to practice disclosing before meetings and interviews.

Questions on identity and disclosure can arise at every stage of the job search process. A few examples of these dilemmas and decisions include:

- People who are unsure if they should include memberships or leadership roles in religious or politically affiliated organizations on their resume or mention their involvement in interviews for fear of discrimination, even if those experiences are central to their life and provide some of their best examples of communication, teamwork, service, or other qualifications and qualities.
- Transgender or gender nonconforming people deciding whether or not to put their name of use and/or pronouns on their resume, cover letter, application materials, or LinkedIn profile, as opposed to their legal or deadname, or risking being misgendered in an interview.
- Those for whom English is not their first language may worry that their accent, the way they spell or pronounce their name, any grammatical discrepancies on their materials, or other markers of difference may be held against them during the application or interview process.
- Those who are advanced in their careers or experience levels feel unsure if they should include years alongside their degrees or work experiences for fear of age-based discrimination.
- Not being sure if it is safe to mention having children, being married or single, or having a same-sex partner or spouse in a particular professional setting or situation. Deciding how to respond when someone makes a statement or asks a question based on assumptions regarding their personal life and priorities based on their known or perceived gender identity and sexuality.

- Concern that one's citizenship status may preclude them from getting an interview or job offer based on an organization's lack of updated information or advocacy related to the work Visa process, including curricular practical training and optional practical training policies and protocols.
- People of different racial and ethnic backgrounds wondering if the people they engage with professionally may make biased assumptions about their identity based only on visual or auditory cues like the color of their skin, the shape of their eyes, the way their name is spelled, or the presence or lack of an accent.
- People with disabilities, whether their disabilities are physical, cognitive, learning-related, or a combination, wondering when and how to request accommodations to participate fully in an interview process.

These are just a few of the present challenges in the working world, and career counselors need to be ready to listen to and validate concerns and proactively advocate for change. Your meetings should feel like a safe space for clients to share, process, and work through specific situations they may encounter or have dealt with in the job search.

Beyond the Basics: Providing Advice on Responding to Illegal Interview Questions

In the United States, it is illegal for potential employers to ask candidates about any of the following during the hiring process (U.S. Equal Employment Opportunity Commission, n.d.-a): marital or relationship status, current or future parental or caretaking responsibilities (including pregnancy), religious practices, political affiliation, race or ethnicity, nationality or citizenship, sexual orientation, age, disability/ability status, sex or gender identity expression, housing or living situation, and arrest record (for most employers).

As a career counselor, you can empower your clients to understand what they shouldn't be asked in the interview, even if there isn't malicious intent, and practice how they may want to answer questions or address comments on the specific identity markers listed earlier should they arise. If your client ends up being asked illegal questions during an interview and needs legal support on how to follow up if they believe they have been discriminated against in the hiring process, they may look to you for advice and referrals on how to pursue legal action against the employer organization or an individual hiring professional.

While sometimes well-intentioned, these questions can lead to discrimination in the recruitment and selection process. If your clients are asked about any of these topics during an interview, application process, or networking conversation, they can decline to answer, redirect to a related skill or competency they would like to highlight, or use it as an opportunity to disclose if they feel comfortable doing so. For example, if work–life balance is highly important to them, mentioning their family in the interview may give them a chance to see if there is value alignment with their potential supervisor or the organization more broadly.

EMPLOYMENT LAW AND THE ROLE OF HUMAN RESOURCES IN THE WORKPLACE

As noted in the previous section, federal laws "make it illegal to discriminate against a job applicant or an employee because of a person's race, color, religion, sex (including pregnancy, transgender status, and sexual orientation), national origin, age (40 or older), disability, or genetic information" (U.S. Equal Employment Opportunity Commission, n.d.-a, para. 8). The U.S. Equal Employment Opportunity Commission is charged with enforcing and investigating cases of employment discrimination (U.S. Equal Employment Opportunity Commission, n.d.-b).

In addition to federal guidelines, the Society of Human Resources Code of Ethics (2014) establishes fairness and justice as a core principle for professional practice. Human resources (HR) professionals manage and coordinate employment processes and are largely responsible for creating legal, equitable employment systems and policies. These include the creation of job announcements, recruitment strategies, promotions, pay, benefits, and discipline policies. Employers are required by law to provide reasonable accommodations to an employee with a disability, and HR staff are responsible for coordinating disability accommodations (U.S. Equal Employment Opportunity Commission, n.d.-a).

Employers are also subject to state and local employment regulations. In recent years, minimum wage and equal pay laws have gained significant traction (Deschenaux, 2019). HR professionals are tasked with training managers and other decision makers to ensure compliance, and this training extends to pay equity. Historically, it was common for employers to ask job applicants for their salary history. In recent years, 21 states have outlawed this practice, and employers may no longer ask prospective employees about their prior compensation (Gorman, 2022). Interestingly, recent research finds that employers have negative associations for those who refrain from disclosing prior compensation information, and applicants who disclosed salary history received offers 9% higher than those who did not disclose (Gorman, 2022). Deciding whether or not and how to disclose salary information and salary requirements are just a few of the nuances and challenges that career counselors must help clients navigate throughout the job search process.

HR professionals often initiate and coordinate affinity or employee resource groups that aim to foster a sense of community and create safe spaces for employees with shared identities to gather and connect. HR professionals and similar career professionals benefit from connection and networking with each other and serving as a support system both inside and outside the workplace. Organizations such as Society of Human Resource Management (SHRM) offer spaces in person and virtually to meet to discuss topics related to recruitment, hiring, HR roles and responsibilities, and employment law.

CAREER COUNSELING AS SOCIAL JUSTICE WORK

It is important for counselors in any specialty to know that questions and concerns related to career development or the workplace may arise as part of discussions about marriage and family, mental health and wellness, confidence and self-efficacy, and so much more. It is important that career counselors understand their engagement with clients to be social justice work because income and a person's general happiness in a job can have such a large impact on quality of life, the ability to support a family, and a sense of autonomy and self-worth. It is also important because our society has for so long held up standards of professionalism, means for learning about and obtaining professional opportunities, recruitment and promotion, and workplace cultures that are often biased against, if not outright closed off, to underrepresented and marginalized communities. Our job is to help break down barriers, boost social capital and confidence, share strategies for finding and securing new opportunities, and, overall, open doors for individuals to have the best chance of professional success.

While sometimes reviewing resumes and cover letters, conducting mock interviews, or sharing common job search resources can feel repetitive for career counselors, especially those working with a specific population, trust that the advice you are sharing with your clients is novel, interesting, and empowering to them, and you are changing lives and breaking generational cycles with your work.

EMPLOYER AND COMMUNITY RELATIONS AS PART OF A CAREER-COUNSELING TOOLKIT

The best career counselors today have a pulse on what is going on in the hiring and recruiting marketplace and develop relationships with employer partners across industries. Doing so will help you make timely suggestions and meaningful connections and help you guide your clients toward career success instead of providing only vague advice or outdated information as the world keeps changing. No matter where you work—in private practice, K–12 setting, higher education, a government agency—some amount of employer and community relations and keeping up with industry trends will be an important part of your job and your career-counseling toolkit. How this looks may differ by sector and role, but you can employ some of the same tactics when it comes to engaging in employer and community engagement for yourself. Here are a few tactics.

Use LinkedIn

LinkedIn is a great system for finding and connecting with recruiting professionals and organization leaders as well as engaging via posts and articles, comments and reactions, joining groups and following organizations, and browsing for job openings and general industry trends. Since so many companies, organizations, and recruiters use LinkedIn for networking or sourcing talent, it is easy to find people. Connecting on LinkedIn will allow you to stay in touch when you or a contact change organizations, as well.

Engage With Professional Associations

Professional associations provide a great bang for your buck when it comes to connecting with employers, community organizations, and recruiters. These associations may be an industry-specific organization your clients may be interested in, a broader career- and recruiting-related organization like the NACE, or one of its regional or state-based chapters. As an organization member, you will gain access to information about relevant conferences and training sessions, networking events, research articles and thought leaders, and policy and advocacy work. From there, one may take involvement to the next level by joining a committee, running for a board position, writing an article, or delivering a presentation or workshop; this can be a great way to network and collaborate within the organization.

Conduct Informational Interviews

Just as you would tell your clients, informational interviews are a fantastic low-stakes, casual opportunity for you to get an inside look into a particular industry or organization. Informational interviewing can create strong professional connections for you with employers and community partners, and potentially lead to ideas for collaboration, sponsorship, and other means for bridging the gap between the clients you are supporting and the hiring needs of your contacts' organizations. To connect, reach out via email or social media to set up time to talk and broaden your knowledge regarding how your clients can be successful in their field.

Network for Mutual Benefit

It should be clear that networking with employers and community organizations is absolutely beneficial for both parties as, ideally, you will help each other achieve your goals and open new doors to potential opportunities and talent pipelines. It may feel a bit strange at first, or too "business-like/sales-y" for career counselors, yet it helps to remember that the recruiters, hiring managers, and organization leaders are also just trying to be successful and build sustainable organizations with great collaborators. The more informed and well-connected you are with employers in your region and industry area, the better off your clients will be as they are looking for inspiration, guidance, and empathy while going through the job search process.

Set Goals and Get Organized

It is advisable to create a means of tracking your progress in your community relations strategy. Begin by collecting your own research and the names of organizations and industries your clients are interested in to come up with a list of 10 to 15 companies and organizations. Create a spreadsheet with columns for organization name, industry, contact name(s), date(s) of outreach, dates and details from any meetings, and follow-up plans and assignments. This will help you add structure and purpose to your process and expand your network intentionally while balancing employer and community relations with your other responsibilities.

Employer and community relations are skills that can be honed, and it is a good resource in your toolkit as a career counselor working in an ever-changing economy and world of work.

ETHICAL CORNER

In this section, the authors lead the reader through topical scenarios to surface common ethics questions and dilemmas faced by career professionals. They ask pertinent and personal questions to encourage reader reflection and insight into personal and professional ethics.

Azra Karajic Siwiec PhD, LPC, is a counselor educator employed by Capella University. She has been working in the counselor education field for over 14 years and has served as a committee member of the Ethics Committee of NCDA since 2015 and served as the chair of the Ethics Committee since 2017.

Sharon K. Anderson, PhD, is professor of counseling and career development at Colorado State University. Sharon has taught the master's level ethics course for counseling students for over 20 years, teaching and mentoring a multitude of students. She has coauthored or coedited four professional ethics books used by practitioners in counseling and coaching.

VIGNETTE

Sandi recognizes that resumes and mock interviews are quite important, but so is the social media presence when dealing with job searches and presentations. She speaks candidly with her clients about the need to "clean up" social media profiles and even offers several short trainings on the importance of "cleaning" a social media profile. Sandi gets called into her supervisor's office because a client has shared that the privacy they have on social media should not have been a topic that they discuss in session. What are your thoughts about this situation when you think about the ethical issues? How would you address the student's concern with the student if you were Sandi's supervisor? How would you address the student's concern with Sandi?

DIGGING INTO ETHICS

Consult ACA and NCDA code of ethics: Can you find any connection or guidance for the next steps in thinking through the student's concern with Sandi? See Appendix for ethical codes.

12.1 PRACTITIONER'S PERSPECTIVE

Ashley Pelham, MEd, NCC, is a first-generation college graduate and mother of two. She has made a career of helping others find their purpose, celebrate their passions, and do what they think is impossible. She is the assistant director of Alumni Engagement in the LEADR Program at University of California Davis.

I struggled when it came time in my graduate program to find a practicum site. I had a few interviews, but nothing took. An alum of the Counselor Education Program at North Carolina State University was in contact with my graduate program coordinator, and they just so happened to need an intern for the coming year. My graduate program coordinator connected me with the site supervisor, and we met.

During the meeting, she gave me a challenge. She asked me to review a few example resumes and mark what I thought needed to be changed. After I corrected those forms, she explained to me what she would have corrected and then agreed to have me as a practicum student but asked me to go home and completely rewrite my resume and bring it back the next week. I spent the next almost 18 months working exclusively with computer science graduate students, perfecting the art of the computer science resume and learning the culture and recruiting strategies in the field.

When I was hired into my internship, my daughter was 9 months old and I was 4 months pregnant with my son. The situation was not ideal, but it was my life—graduate student, working full time, and soon-to-be mom of two under 2. I was fortunate to have a husband who supported me in my endeavors, both financially and logistically. Having both of my children and taking no real time off to care for them made me feel like I was drowning and could never really catch my breath. I worked full time as an HR/payroll manager and kept up with my internship hours up until the month before my second child was born. I was intent on doing both as long as I could because I didn't want to feel like I was letting my employer and coworkers down.

One day at my internship site I felt like a was failing at everything—probably mostly due to pregnancy hormones, but also because I was stretched so thin that I wasn't giving my all to any part of my life. So there I sat, hysterically crying at my desk, being comforted by my internship supervisor, whom I had only known for a few months at that time. She made me realize that what I was doing was not good for anyone. I could not be successful in the things that really mattered if I was wasting energy on what didn't. The next day I gave my notice at my full-time position and immediately felt a weight lifted off my shoulders. It was no longer my job to run around and put out all the fires, it was my time to recalibrate and focus on my needs. Things got challenging again after my son was born, but I felt a renewed sense of purpose. I was doing this for him and his sister. I was working to give them the life I never had; a life of stability and awareness of the world around me.

A few months before graduation, I accepted a position with a local community college as a career specialist. It was a full-time role when I interviewed, but the manager decided to make it a contract when she called to offer it to me. I accepted because it was the only offer I had, and I was scared I wouldn't get another one. I had been to several in-person interviews and numerous Zoom and phone interviews but never made it to the second round. My anxiety would always get in the way. Working with first-generation students over the last few years, I have encountered dozens of job seekers with the same fear: what if I don't get another chance? I have learned that your first job will likely not be your last, and every position is an opportunity to learn and grow.

My first job out of graduate school was a very unpleasant experience that made me angry, sad, and bitter most days. I loved the students and the work I was doing, but the environment was not healthy. I felt very isolated and was desperate to find my way back to a supportive and caring space. My role as a mother to two small children only intensified my emotions and my drive to get to a better space, physically and emotionally. My position at the community college ended only 4 months after it began. I left that job feeling awful about myself and almost became resigned to forsaking my education and being a stay-at-home mom. Looking back on this experience now, I am grateful for the hardships I faced and getting a taste of the burden that so many working mothers bear.

A few months later, I got a call for my current position. I had interviewed for it almost 5 months earlier. The hiring manager explained that an unforeseeable issue had delayed the decision, but she still wanted to hire me. I accepted and moved my family back across the country to California.

The population I worked with in the LEADR Program is undergraduate, first-generation, underrepresented minorities in an engineering program. Many of my students have complicated home support systems. They sometimes struggle to ask for help as they are used to figuring things out on their own. A strong motivator for most of my students in pursuing engineering is to make a lot of money to support their parents. I am also a first-generation college graduate, so I understand the barriers and obstacles these students face, as I have dealt with them myself in one way or another.

I primarily worked with upper-division students in a career-focused capacity. Students were required to meet with me each quarter to ensure that they are on track academically and pursuing internships or research. I have a comparatively small population versus regular engineering program advisors, and my program uses high-touch advising to work with students on a holistic level and address personal and academic barriers to their success. We also host a yearly summer bridge program for incoming freshmen, monthly community events, and workshops.

In 2021, I joined the California Career Development Association and have attended an advising certificate program and career champions program designed for UC Davis staff.

TRAITS OF CAREER COUNSELORS

To successfully manage working in this role, you must be able to gain the trust and confidence of the students. Empathy is a must in this role, as well as good customer service skills, organization, and being able to work independently as well as with a team. You must also be great at juggling many things at once, and easily be able to solicit recruiters and employers to speak with your students. I manage employer relations for the program, and it is sometimes intimidating to cold-call employers. I rely on alumni of the program to build connections with employers and bring jobs and internship opportunities to my students.

PROFESSIONAL ETHICS

Maintaining confidentiality and appropriate boundaries with students is paramount. I have an open door policy with students, and they know they can trust me and that I will listen to them without judgment. I will often have students who reveal significant personal traumas from their past or present, and it is difficult to keep that information inside. Bearing the knowledge of these students' trauma impacts me more than I would like it to. Some days, the burden becomes too great, and I have to let myself take a break. I have never been someone to take mental health days or quit before the work is done, but I now know that if I don't pause and breathe, I am no good for myself, my family, or anyone else who depends on me for emotional support.

For the students, I make referrals to help them find appropriate solutions to their needs; I rely heavily on our campus tutoring center for students who are struggling academically and the student health center for students who need to address mental health concerns.

Students often invite me out to lunch and dinner or to community events with them. I definitely want to go and do these things. But I must remember that I am not their friend; I am their advisor, and as much as I care about them and enjoy being around them, I must maintain a sense of professionalism.

The thing that has had the greatest impact on the way I operate in this role is the influence and wisdom of my (deceased) program director. She was a phenomenal person and taught me more about life and how to connect with students in the time I knew her than I have learned through any other experience. A great mentor makes a world of difference.

12.2 PRACTITIONER'S PERSPECTIVE

Jane Matthews currently serves as associate director of employer relations in the Office of Career Planning at Meredith College, and prior to joining the team at Meredith, she served as a career counselor at North Carolina State University and held roles in both corporate recruiting and hospitality management. Jane is a Nationally Certified Counselor (NCC) and holds a MEd in counselor education (college counseling and student development) and a BA in communication, both from North Carolina State University.

My career path has not been linear. As an undergraduate, I had no idea what I wanted to do careerwise. After completing my undergraduate degree, I began managing the restaurant where I had worked in college. During that time, I realized that my interest in working with people had grown, and I moved into a talent acquisition role in the restaurant industry. It became clear that I wanted to help people identify a career in which they could use their talents. I also realized that I enjoyed working with college-aged students. I had been thinking about going into counseling, and, luckily, I found a job in the career center at a large research institution. Soon, I began graduate school to get a counseling degree and started my journey in higher education.

I work in the Office of Career Planning now, where I serve our students and alumni population. I enjoy being part of each student's unique journey of growth and identity clarification. In reflecting on my own nonlinear journey, I recognize how much it would have benefited me to work with someone in a career-counseling capacity.

I work at a small, private women's college, with a total student enrollment of about 2,000. My team is small, and as a result, we juggle many responsibilities. Unique to smaller colleges and universities, my role is dual in nature; I serve as a career counselor and also lead our team's employer relations strategy. I work with employers to develop recruiting relationships on campus and provide our students with access to internships and full-time opportunities.

The majority of our students are members of Gen-Z. They are curious, socially and environmentally conscious, and want to ensure a strong return on their investment in a college education. Flexibility is becoming increasingly important to this population in regard to career choice, work environment, and working hours.

My students, team, supervisor, and the sense of community that my institution provides keeps me here. I have a strong supervisor who supports and encourages our individual professional growth and development. This, combined with having the honor of helping our students navigate their career journeys, motivates me to continue working in the field of career development within higher education.

PROFESSIONAL ETHICS

As an NCC, I am bound by ethical guidelines set by the National Board of Certified Counselors (NBCC). I work on a college campus, so I am also bound by the Family Educational Rights and Privacy Act, which means I must maintain the confidentiality of student records and counseling notes. Sessions with students and alumni are considered confidential conversations unless the concern is raised regarding the safety of the client or other individuals. However, we are not considered an official confidential site on campus, like our counseling center or the chaplain's office. This can present challenges in terms of what students feel comfortable disclosing in our setting or in regard to what the term *confidential* means in our setting.

THEORIES, FRAMEWORKS, AND TECHNIQUES

I take a strengths-based approach to career counseling. I believe that helping students focus on what they naturally do well allows them to intentionally develop and apply those strengths to careers they are considering. I use a number of Gallup- and CliftonStrengths-based resources when working with students and alumni, and I also incorporate values-based conversations into my work. I'm also a big fan of informational interviews as a career exploration strategy and encourage every student with whom I work to have conversations with a variety of professionals early and often.

TRAITS OF CAREER COUNSELORS

Collegiate counselors should be caring, empathetic, and humble. They should be good listeners and astute observers. They also have to be willing to adapt to shifting cultural, economic, and workforce trends and they must be able to reimagine programming and career education delivery to meet those trends. Finally, it is important for career counselors to be transparent and authentic with clients to develop meaningful and rewarding relationships.

The ability to effectively communicate, in both verbal and written mediums, is fundamental. The ability to coach students and alumni on how to articulate their strengths, skills, and experiences in a clear and concise way (and the ability to do that ourselves!), is a key part of this job. I also believe that boundary setting is a critical skill as a counselor and a key part of self-care.

Involvement in professional associations has been instrumental in shaping my career. The best advice I received from colleagues upon finishing graduate school was to get involved in professional organizations, specifically the North Carolina

Career Development Association and the North Carolina Association of Colleges and Employers and their associated regional and national affiliations. I have been fortunate to serve on the executive boards in multiple leadership roles for both throughout my career, and I have received mentorship, expanded my leadership skills, and learned practical applications as a career counselor and employer relations professional as a result.

Student Voices

In Student Voices, students offer a unique viewpoint as they begin in the career-counseling field. Here, students share their thoughts and reflections about the career-counseling profession and offer personal takeaways.

LIAN CURRIE

Lian Currie is a MEd, LPC-R graduate from the Counselor Education Program at Virginia Commonwealth University (VCU). Lian is currently an academic advisor at VCU and a resident in counseling at the University of Richmond in the Counseling and Psychological Services (CAPS) office. Lian completed both her practicum and internship at the University of Richmond CAPS office.

While there is never a typical day in the life of a college counselor, I mostly work with students with issues of anxiety, depression, transitions, conflict resolution, and stress management. When I reflect back on the clients that I worked with during my time in practicum and internship, I can pinpoint a time with each client that we spent discussing their career goals at length. Whether students felt career factors contributed to presenting concerns or saw changes in career goals as part of the solution for their concerns, it was important for them to have a counselor who was prepared to discuss this openly.

The nature of college career counseling is that it is often brief and solution focused. Whether you work in student affairs, academic affairs, or even student health and college mental health counseling centers, the services professionals provide for students need to be quick and effective. When working with college students to tackle big topics on a limited timeline, counselors should focus on building rapport, setting goals, and exploring student's values. For career counselors, this is no different.

Basic counseling skills are indispensable when building rapport with students and clients, especially with limited time. Active listening, asking open-ended questions, using minimal encouragers, summarizing, and paraphrasing allow practitioners to quickly learn information about their client's concerns and goals. Taking the time to build and test the bonds between yourself and the client is a crucial step. Building rapport with students increases trust and, it is hoped, lets students know that your meetings are a place where they can share openly and take steps toward their goals.

Speaking of goals, goal setting with clients and students is an essential part of the counseling process, including career counseling. Students may be seeking counseling services for career exploration, strengths and values identification, career transitions, or something else entirely, but it is important to work in partnership with your client to identify goals for the counseling process. These goals should be SMART, meaning specific, measurable, attainable, realistic, and time-bound. Goal setting will help guide the counseling process but should also remain flexible as both counselor and client learn more about what is most salient for that client's life.

(continued)

Student Voices (*continued*)

Lastly, it is rare that I have a conversation with students about their career goals without also discussing values. A discussion or exercise that challenges the client to reflect on and identify the values that are most important to them is a good way to not only get the client involved in the counseling process but also to give the counselor a bit of insight into motivating factors for the client. A values card sort activity is also great for a client who is finding it difficult to express themselves verbally or a client who appreciates experiential activities.

No matter what setting you find yourself in, career conversations will happen. It is important for counselors to feel prepared to walk alongside their clients in this exploration and use activities and skills that give clients insight into their own wants and needs.

COUNSELING SKILLS CONNECTION

Career counselors conduct their work in a variety of settings, many of which make confidentiality challenging. Imagine hosting drop-in hours for career counseling in a public space such as a multipurpose room, cafe, or library. It is very difficult to maintain confidentiality in public spaces and areas with high foot traffic. Career conversations can quickly become quite personal as clients share employment histories and life experiences that have shaped decisions and trajectories. In such settings, counselors must select and apply appropriate theories or frameworks such as those that are brief and solution focused. We recommend beginning conversations openly, creating awareness around the limitations of confidentiality in the public space. Career counselors must be mindful of keeping their clients safe, including their story and personal history, and when necessary and possible, move sensitive conversations to a private space.

Clients with a history of trauma or adverse life experiences, or those experiencing symptoms of anxiety, depression, and other mental illness, may have more difficulty making career decisions and low career decision self-efficacy. This might look like a client who has difficulty envisioning goals for the future, summarizing skills they have developed in prior roles, choosing a major, and so on.

Career counselors may work in tandem with clinical mental health practitioners to elevate clients' confidence in their ability to successfully engage in tasks required to make a career choice. Using a feminist theoretical approach and discussing systemic issues that may be out of the client's locus of control may empower the client to own their story and increase agency.

MINDFUL MOMENT

This chapter is about tools and techniques. *Mindfulness Skills Workbook for Clinicians and Clients* (Burdick, 2013) is a wonderful book to add to your toolbox. Consider introducing manipulatives to reduce anxiety with your students or clients. For example, fidget toys, beads, Play-Doh, blocks, kinetic sand, and so on.

TECH TOOLS

Clients creating resumes for creative industries and roles may gravitate toward generating documents that feature stronger design elements, distancing themselves from more traditional resume formats. A note of caution: beautiful design does not always equal effective design. Encourage clients to focus on content first, then select or build a creative resume that drives attention to key qualifications. Canva.com is a free graphic design tool that provides creative resume templates. *Tip: As a career counselor you might also use Canva to create flyers, social media posts, slide decks, and more!*

REFLECTION ACTIVITY

Reflect on your own current or past job search processes. How did you feel as you developed your professional documents and navigated a job search? What parts of the process seemed easiest, and which were most challenging? After reading this chapter, what parts of the job search process had you not thought much about previously?

END-OF-CHAPTER RESOURCES

SUMMARY

Career counseling demands a large toolbox to educate, prepare, and support clients through different stages of the career development process. This chapter explored in depth some of the core components of the job search, such as building advocates through informational interviewing and networking, crafting tailored professional documents, and preparing for interviews. Career counselors support clients in exploring their identities and finding work environments in which they feel a sense of belonging, opportunity, and satisfaction. Among the many roles that a career counselor might fill, employer relations work narrows the gap between employers and job seekers, creating opportunities for education and reducing barriers to employment. Career counselors can advocate for and with clients, challenge systems that foster discriminatory practices, and empower clients to break cycles of underemployment.

REFERENCES

Adler, L. (2016, February 29). *New survey reveals 85% of all jobs are filled via networking*. LinkedIn Pulse. https://www.linkedin.com/pulse/new-survey-reveals-85-all-jobs-filled-via-networking-lou-adler/

Belli, G. (2017, April 10). At least 70% of jobs are not even listed—Here's how to up your chances of getting a great new gig. *Business Insider*. https://www.businessinsider.com/at-least-70-of-jobs-are-not-even-listed-heres-how-to-up-your-chances-of-getting-a-great-new-gig-2017-4

Burdick, D. (2013). *Mindfulness skills workbook for clinicians and clients: 111 tools, techniques, activities & worksheets*. PESI Publishing & Media.

Career Vision. (n.d.). *Use gap analysis as a career management tool*. The Ball Foundation. https://careervision.org/use-gap-analysis-career-management-tool/#:~:text=Career%20gap%20analysis%20enables%20you,plan%20to%20bridge%20the%20gaps

Dalton, S. (2020). *The 2-hour job search* (2nd ed.). Ten Speed Press.

Deschenaux, J. (2019, May 31). How to comply with new state and local laws. *HR Magazine*. https://www.shrm.org/hr-today/news/hr-magazine/summer2019/pages/how-to-comply-with-new-state-and-local-laws.aspx

Doyle, A. (June 29, 2020). *How long does it take to find a job*. The Balance Careers. https://www.thebalancecareers.com/how-long-does-it-take-to-find-a-job-2064245

Goodridge, L. (2022). Professionalism as a racial construct. *UCLA Law Review*. https://www.uclalawreview.org/professionalism-as-a-racial-construct/

Gorman, L. (2022, January 1). *How knowledge of salary history affects wage offers and hiring*. National Bureau of Economic Research. https://www.nber.org/digest-202201/how-knowledge-salary-history-affects-wage-offers-and-hiring#:~:text=The%20researchers%20conclude%20that%20employers,offer%2C%20conditional%20on%20a%20callback

McIntyre, M. (December 7, 2020). *85% of jobs are secured via networking: Here's how to do it right*. Business to Community. https://www.business2community.com/human-resources/85-of-jobs-are-secured-via-networking-heres-how-to-do-it-right-02368331

National Association of Colleges and Employers. (n.d.). *What is career readiness?* https://www.naceweb.org/career-readiness/competencies/career-readiness-defined/

Society of Human Resources. (2014, November 21). *Code of ethics*. https://www.shrm.org/about-shrm/pages/code-of-ethics.aspx

U.S. Equal Employment Opportunity Commission. (n.d.-a). *Prohibited employment policies/practices*. https://www.eeoc.gov/prohibited-employment-policiespractices

U.S. Equal Employment Opportunity Commission. (n.d.-b). *Overview*. https://www.eeoc.gov/overview

VCU Career Services. (n.d.). *Career genogram*. Richmond. https://careers.vcu.edu/media/vcu-careers/docs/CareerGenogram.pdf

VCU Career Services. (2021). Informational interviews. https://careers.vcu.edu/applying-and-interviewing/networking/interviews/

VCU Career Services. (2022). *Interviewing*. https://careers.vcu.edu/applying-and-interviewing/interviewing/

CHAPTER 13

CAREER PATHS IN COUNSELING

Carolyn D. Jones, Katie Peterssen, and Angie C. Smith

By the end of this chapter, you will be able to:

- Be aware of the varied pathways to becoming a career counselor and practitioner.
- Review specific career development roles and responsibilities among **counseling settings**.
- List opportunities for continuing education in career counseling.
- Name specific certifications, credentials, and training opportunities for professional growth within the profession.

WARM-UP EXERCISE

Brainstorm possible career paths you've considered as options throughout your life span. What career paths interest you the most? What jobs sounded appealing? What jobs would you never pursue and why? Now, consider the possibilities within your preferred profession of choice. What settings are appealing to you? What populations would you be most interested in supporting and working with in the community?

INTRODUCTION

This chapter focuses on **pathways** to becoming a career **counselor**, including recommendations for identifying practicum and internship sites and networking opportunities. We also look at changes and trends in the career-counseling field. There are many pathways within the career-counseling profession beyond the first job out of an academic **training** program. Opportunities for specialization and career changes are possible for career counselors in various seasons throughout their career within the field. We explore the many roles within the career field and offer a survey of career organizations, licensure, and **certifications**. The intersection of career and mental illness, multiculturalism, and diversity are also addressed.

BECOMING A CAREER COUNSELOR: PATHWAYS TO CAREER DEVELOPMENT ROLES

If you are deciding to pursue a career as a career **counselor**, consideration must be given to every aspect of the profession. These aspects include the pathways to becoming a career **practitioner**, key career development concepts, working with special populations, and **continuing education.**

Career Counseling as a Profession

The scope of services provided by career counselors is wide, and it includes individual and group counseling, assessment, coaching, advising, conflict resolution, career planning, job search skills **training**, student services, vocational guidance, rehabilitation, and retirement planning. Career counselors also help their clients to acquire career decision-making skills and offer assistance with on-the-job stress, interpersonal work-related conflict situations, and career transitions.

There are employment opportunities for practitioners within colleges, universities, schools, community agencies, corporate settings, organizations, associations, and government agencies. A practitioner may also be engaged in entrepreneurial work settings and provide consulting services, depending on the person's level of education, **credentials**, and experience.

Jobs for Career Counselors

SUCCESS COACH

A success **coach** serves as a liaison and advocate for people and families in the community. Success coaches are responsible for identifying the strengths, needs, and risks of participants and their families to assist them in developing short and long-term goals. This particular role may serve at a community-based agency, for example, the YMCA. In general, the minimum requirement for this type of position is a bachelor's degree.

CAREER SPECIALIST

A career specialist provides a comprehensive career development and management program for students and employers. This program contributes to the continued growth of internships and employment opportunities for students and alumni of a college or university. In general, the minimum requirement for this type of position is a master's degree or coaching certification.

TRAINING COORDINATOR

A **training** coordinator is responsible for the coordination and facilitation of training site supervisors, staff, and youth orientation. The position may last up to 16 weeks, depending on the number of hours worked per week. Generally, these positions are available at community agencies and summer youth programs, for example, summer camp. In general, the minimum requirement for this type of position is a bachelor's degree.

DIRECTOR OF CAREER SERVICES

A director of career services is responsible for planning, developing, and administering career-planning and career development programs for students and graduates in college settings. They oversee and manage the career placement process to ensure the campus achieves its placement goals and adheres to the professional standards and school policies in all aspects of student placement and academic partnerships. Usually, the minimum requirement for this position is a master's degree or coaching certification.

WORKFORCE SERVICES COORDINATOR

This position is responsible for providing a wide-ranging scope of services, including the following: career planning; work–life guidance; daily living support, housing, and money management education; health and self-care assistance; prosocial relationship development; intensive daily case management; and familial and crisis counseling. It may also lead psychoeducational life skills groups.

DIRECTOR OF WORKFORCE DEVELOPMENT

This position is responsible for all workforce development initiatives including programming and contract oversight, operations, administration, and project management. The position drives the overall strategy for the organization and is usually based at a community-based agency, for example, the YMCA. In general, the minimum requirement for this type of position is a bachelor's degree.

More information about these or similar roles can be found at O*Net, *Occupational Outlook Handbook (OOH)*, U.S. Department of Labor Career OneStop Toolkit, Indeed, and Career Builder.

Personal Experience

As a career development practitioner, my work in the field of career development focuses on the needs and concerns of the individual and builds the foundation for the development and implementation of other services, for example, organizational leadership training and team building. I assess the needs and concerns of my clients, and together we work toward developing a plan that is most advantageous for them as they navigate and orchestrate their career journey. The personal traits in a career counselor that are most strategic and helpful to career- counseling clients are knowledgeable, transparent, ethical, empathetic, and sincere.

CERTIFICATIONS, CREDENTIALS, AND TRAINING: PATHWAYS TO BECOMING A CAREER COUNSELOR

There are many career pathways to becoming a practitioner in career development, and the required educational levels and **credentials** vary by professional employment settings, including academic **credentials** (e.g., MA, MEd, PhD), state licensure (licensed professional counselor [LPC]), and certification (Certified Career Services Provider [CCSP]). There are also specific required professional competencies from the National Career Development Association (NCDA; https://ncda.org) and the Council for Accreditation of Counseling and Related Educational Programs (CACREP; cacrep.org).

The pathways to become a career development professional may include:

- degrees in higher education
- coaching certifications
- credentials that demonstrate knowledge in certain areas of the field
- state licensure
- continuing education classes with professional associations that offer professional development opportunities and training.

Minimum Competencies

Based on the guidelines for professional practice set forth by the NCDA (1997), professional career counselors must demonstrate minimum competencies in nine designated areas:

- *Career Development Theory:* Theory base and knowledge are considered.
- *Individual and Group Counseling Skills:* Individual and group counseling competencies are considered.
- *Individual/Group Assessment:* Individual or group assessment skills are considered.
- *Information/Resources/Technology:* Information/resource/technology knowledge and skills are considered.
- *Program Promotion, Management, and Implementation:* Skills necessary to develop, plan, implement, and manage comprehensive career development programs in a variety of settings are considered.
- *Coaching, Consultation, and Performance Improvement:* Knowledge and skills are considered essential in enabling individuals and organizations to impact effectively upon the career counseling and development process.
- *Supervision:* Knowledge and skills are considered essential in critically evaluating counselor performance, maintaining and improving professional skills, and seeking assistance for others when needed in career counseling.
- *Ethical/Legal Issues:* Information base and knowledge are essential for the ethical and legal practice of career counseling.
- *Research/Evaluation:* Knowledge and skills are considered essential in understanding and conducting research and evaluation in career counseling and development.

The National Career Development Association Code of Ethics

NCDA offers a code of ethics to guide career professionals in their daily interactions with clients. The NCDA Code of Ethics (the Code) outlines and defines parameters for professional behavior with the goal of protecting the public, the profession, and practitioners. The Code offers guidelines for informed ethical decision-making. As you consider possible courses of action, ask yourself, "Will I be embarrassed or concerned if someone knew that I did or said this?" (NCDA, 2015).

The Code is a guide and resource for career practitioners. While it offers a set of principles that can be applied to a wide range of settings and situations, it is not, nor can it be, comprehensive. If you are concerned about whether a particular practice is ethical, then you should not engage in that behavior without seeking competent advice. More succinctly, when in doubt—don't, at least not without professional consultation. Peer review isn't always going to give you perfect advice; but you can take comfort in knowing that you questioned your behavior before proceeding and allowed others to comment before taking action. There is safety and strength in the depth and breadth of opinions you seek before engaging in activity that may be untried or questionable.

The NCDA Code of Ethics serves five main purposes. The Code enables NCDA to clarify to current and future members, and to those served by their members, the nature of ethical responsibilities held in common by its members. It also supports the mission of NCDA. The Code establishes principles that define ethical behaviors and practices of association members and serves as an ethical guide designed to assist members in constructing a professional course of action that best serves those using career services while promoting the values of the career profession. Also, the Code serves as a guide for those receiving career services so that they may understand what to expect from working with a career professional as well as understand their rights and responsibilities as consumers of these services (2015).

Based on the *NCDA Policies and Procedure Manual*, The NCDA Ethics Committee is responsible for educating the membership as to the Association's Ethical Standards; making suggestions to the NCDA Board for modifications or development of ethics-related documents and procedures; responding to questions about ethical standards; investigating complaints of alleged violations of the ethical standards of ACA or NCDA if called on to do so by the ACA Ethics Committee or the NCDA Board; and referring complaints to ACA for adjudication, if necessary (2021).

Career development professionals acknowledge the following professional values as put forth by the NCDA Code of Ethics (2015):

■ Enhance career development throughout the life span.
■ Safeguard the integrity of the professional working relationship.
■ Practice in a competent and ethical manner.
■ Support the worth, dignity, potential, and uniqueness of everyone.
■ Honor diversity and promote social justice.
■ Advocate for clients as well as issues affecting social policies and legislation.

There are 12 professional competencies that are required for NCDA certification for the Global Career Development Facilitator and CCSP credentials. Knowledge and training in these core topics ensure that the work is being carried out with appropriate skill levels, transparency, and integrity (NCDA, n.d.). The 12 professional competencies are:

1. Helping Skills
2. Labor Market Information and Resources
3. Assessment

4. Diverse Populations
5. Ethical and Legal Issues
6. Career Development Models
7. Employability Skills
8. Training Clients and Peers
9. Program Management/Implementation
10. Promotion and Public Relations
11. Technology
12. Consultation.

CACREP is the accrediting body and developer of professional standards for the counseling profession. The CACREP website (www.cacrep.org/secion-5-entry-level-specialty-areas-career-counseling/) offers professional competencies for students training to be career counselors, including foundational knowledge (e.g., history and theory), contextual knowledge (e.g., unique needs of diverse populations, factors affecting clients' attitudes toward work, and decision-making), and practical skills (e.g., career assessment, strategies to assist clients in the job search, planning career development programs; Council for Accreditation of Counseling and Related Programs, 2016).

MENTAL ILLNESS

Mental health and mental illness are important aspects of any counseling profession. Therefore, we must consider the mental health concerns and issues of our career-counseling clients.

The stigma of mental illness is one of the major issues that negatively impacts career developments (Granello & Granello, 2000). Disclosing to a potential employer that one has a mental illness can be anxiety provoking due to the possibility that the other person may have discriminatory opinions about psychological issues. As such, it is important for job seekers at all stages in their career to consider whether it is necessary to disclose their psychological concerns to their employer.

To provide holistic service to my clients, my work must consider the intersection of mental health and career counseling. Krumboltz (1993, p. 143) asserts that "career problems are inextricably intertwined with personal problems and must be treated as such by professional counselors." Some people experienced mild to moderate mental health issues, and unfortunately, others suffer severe levels of distress. These issues present unique challenges to students, employees, job seekers, and retirees. As career development and mental health professionals, it is an essential ethical responsibility to foster collaboration in assisting these populations.

The potential internal turmoil that mentally distressed people suffer can make coping with the multitasking nature of the job search, both overwhelming and discouraging. According to Super's (1957) career development theory, there are five developmental tasks occurring during the exploratory stages of the career decision-making process: (1) concern with vocational choice, (2) increased vocational information, (3) increased consistency of vocational choice, (4) the crystallization of traits relevant to vocational choice, and (5) the increased wisdom of vocational preferences. Career counselors can create an organized and supportive environment for people who experience mental health issues to navigate these developmental tasks and to identify strengths and weaknesses that build job-related skills and can also be used to create stability in practical areas of life.

Psychotherapists recognize the impact that a well-organized, consistent, and skill-building career search can have on reducing the anxiety, hopelessness, and pessimism that is generated by unemployment. It is helpful when working with a client to identify where the client's actions have contributed to their work experiences and to then examine the thoughts and feelings that impact their behavior. This helps the client to define and ultimately redefine their career choices. It also offers insight on how to deal with potential employment challenges that are external to them using the strengths they have found from working with a career professional. It is beneficial to have emotional and mental support that validates one's experiences yet also assists the person in becoming aware of their own contribution to the presented issues, and then helping the client explore problem-solving options.

Collaboration between the psychotherapy and career-counseling departments is useful in creating consistent, supportive environments that validate their clients' experiences and help them in managing their symptoms while making strategic job search efforts in a paced and organized fashion. The integration of the work of career counselors and therapists offers proactive goals that include providing hope and a sense of control and empowerment for those whom we provide services (Jones & Jones, 2016).

For clients with mental health challenges, the following recommendations are alternative strategies when typical options for life planning and career decision-making are limited:

- Explore transitional careers during career counseling.
- Participate in talk therapy to explore new ways of managing stress and explore alternate life planning.
- Practice meditation and mindfulness to promote a sense of well-being and build resilience.
- Continue education and/or participation in training courses/programs.
- Explore financial planning and recovery training or assistance.
- Research community resources and social support options.
- Get involved with new or different work assignments on your current job.
- Engage in intentional distraction and socialization. Schedule meetings with family and friends.
- Increase engagement in healthy stress-relieving activities that are still safely/readily available.
- Positively respond to employers and employees by offering confidence builders and motivational activities in the workplace. Praise, positivity, and reassurance are key.

By working together with various career development practitioners and mental health providers we will be better able to create meaningful and effective responses and be more prepared to foster successful outcomes for our clients. It will be a challenge but well worth our efforts to offer viable solutions to respond to the needs of those we serve.

CAREER DEVELOPMENT, MULTICULTURALISM, AND DIVERSE POPULATIONS

As **practitioners**, career development work and services must be tailored to meet the unique needs of the population served. In particular, it's important for career counselors to be aware of one's attitudes toward the cultural differences in populations. Culture is the sum total of the lived experiences of a group of human beings to meet the biological and psychological needs of the individual and the group. It consists of the shared patterns of attitudes, values, customs, traditions, linguistic and nonverbal expressions, aesthetic judgments, and other characteristics learned by human beings as members of society and manifested in that society's institutions and artifacts.

To work within the scope of practice most effectively as a career **counselor**, the awareness must also include an understanding of multiculturalism, which is also included as a citation in the NCDA Code of Ethics (2015). Based on my understanding and professional experiences as a career **counselor**, multiculturalism can be defined as the process of understanding and appreciating one's own culture as well as the cultures of others. It stresses an appreciation of the cultural impact of differences, including race, ethnicity, gender, socioeconomic class, age, sexual/affectual orientation, religion, and mental or physical functioning.

To effectively consider factors, such as culture, one must be able to engage in metacognition: "the process of focusing on people's ongoing self-monitoring and self-control of their own thoughts" (Byars-Winston & Found, 2006). In other words, practitioners must actively incorporate their own cultural framework, values, and worldview in the counseling process. Multicultural competence includes conscientious, deliberate self-reflection on his or her cultural contexts of the counseling process (Byars-Winston & Found, 2006).

For example, when examining one's own sociocultural background, consider the following self-reflection questions:

■ What is my sociocultural background, that is, race, ethnicity, gender, religion, sexual orientation, socioeconomic class, mental functioning, physical functioning/appearance?

■ What aspects of my sociocultural background am I most comfortable with or proud of?

■ In what ways does my attitude toward my sociocultural background resemble or differ from my parents/guardian attitudes?

■ What aspects of my sociocultural background make me uncomfortable, if any? In what way(s) am I uncomfortable with them?

■ In what way(s) do I feel that these insights may impact my work as a career counselor with my clients?

According to the NCDA, multicultural career counseling and development for individual and group-counseling skills necessitates that a person is aware of his or her own cultural beliefs and assumptions and incorporates that awareness into decision-making about interactions with clients and students and other career professionals. The counselor must continue to develop group-counseling skills to respond appropriately to people from diverse populations and be cognizant when working with demographics to ensure appropriate respect and confidentiality are maintained (NCDA, 2009).

CONTINUING EDUCATION

Continuing education, which is ongoing educational professional development programs offered—and often required—in career counseling, is available through colleges, universities, and professional associations via conferences, courses, seminars, workshops, supervised practice, internships, presentations, and other training opportunities. Professional associations also provide updated and relevant information, training, and educational programs.

The NCDA provides professional development, publications, standards, and advocacy to practitioners and educators who inspire and empower individuals to achieve their career and life goals.

National Resume Writers Associations (NRWA), a nonprofit trade association for career professionals, increases the visibility of the industry, encourages ethical practices, promotes excellence, and raises industry standards through peer marketing and training.

The Professional Association of Resume Writers and Career Coaches (PARW) was founded in 1990 as the first association for career professionals. Its goal is to provide opportunities for career professionals to exchange information, enhance their skills, and demonstrate their commitment to providing high-quality professional services to today's job seekers.

Career Thought Leaders is an international organization focused on providing education, spotting trends, and driving innovation for career industry professionals worldwide. Through leading-edge thought leadership, pioneering training programs, and high-quality free content, they gather top industry professionals together to create a global community that listens, shares, learns, and leads so that all succeed.

The National Association of Colleges and Employers (NACE) empowers and connects the community of professionals who support, develop, and employ the college-educated workforce.

It is also important to stay up to date on the research and expanded knowledge that is available in books, journals, and relevant professional writing. The larger professional journals in the career-counseling field include the *Journal of Career Development, Journal of Career Assessment, Journal of Employment Counseling, Asia Pacific Career Development Journal, Journal of Employment Counseling,* and the *Journal of Vocational Behavior.*

The career development field has many thought leaders and experts that have provided the foundation for the work in the field. Career-counseling visionaries and theorists such as Parsons, Strong, Holland, and others provide early theoretical foundations for career counseling. They set the stage for Savickas, Gottfredson, Krumboltz and Vosvick, Cochran, and others to refine, reframe, and conceptualize themes introduced by early scholars. Spencer G. Niles (2003, para. 2) describes some of the more recent evolution of career-counseling theory in *Career Counselors Confront a Critical Crossroad: A Vision of the Future* "Gottfredson (1996) illustrated that children can benefit from developmentally appropriate career interventions but that these interventions are not being systematically provided. Krumboltz and Vosvick (1996) reminded career counselors that sometimes clients' beliefs about the world and about themselves impede their career development progress. Cochran (1997) helped clients find career meaning in their life stories.

Amundson (1998) encouraged career counselors to actively engage their clients in the career counseling process." Career counselors will often draw from a variety of career theories to support clients. Good, ethical practice demands that career counselors understand the theoretical underpinnings of their approach and the resources or tools they select.

CASE STUDY

Put your knowledge to the test: Review the following case study and reflect on the discussion in an individual or group setting.

MARIA

Maria, a Latina American, was one of the best tech employees in ABC Software Company. She and her supervisor have contacted you, the ABC Company EAP/ Company Career Coach, for assistance in facilitating the following situation:

Maria always had a positive attitude and was great with customers when they had problems. One day, Maria didn't show up for work until late morning. When her supervisor asked why she was late, she replied that a family member needed her help. The supervisor reprimanded her, put a note in her file, and was puzzled that Maria, who had been so reliable, did not feel more strongly about her obligation to the employer. Maria was hurt and disappointed that her supervisor did not automatically understand that one's family always comes first.

Discussion Questions
1. What do you consider to be the cultural dynamics involved in the supervisor's response to Maria?
2. What are the cultural differences at the core of Maria's confusion in this situation?
3. As the EAP career coach, what will you include in the counseling session conversation with Maria in response to her situation at work?
4. What recommendations would you make to the company to respond to employee concerns of this nature?

ETHICAL CORNER

In this section, the authors lead the reader through topical scenarios to surface common ethics questions and dilemmas faced by career professionals. They ask pertinent and personal questions to encourage reader reflection and insight into personal and professional ethics.

Azra Karajic Siwiec PhD, LPC, is a counselor educator employed by Capella University. She has been working in the counselor education field for over 14 years and has served as a committee member of the Ethics Committee of NCDA since 2015 and served as the chair of the Ethics Committee since 2017.

Sharon K. Anderson, PhD, is professor of counseling and career development at Colorado State University. Sharon has taught the master's level ethics course for counseling students for over 20 years, teaching and mentoring a multitude of students. She has coauthored or coedited four professional ethics books used by practitioners in counseling and coaching.

VIGNETTE

The program that Sandi is attending encourages students to network at their own practicum and internship site. As Sandi contemplates sites to contact, she wonders what type of questions to ask to get a sense of the ethical culture of the organization. If you were Sandi's practicum or internship instructor helping her secure her site, what questions would you encourage her to ask? What questions would you encourage her not to ask? What would you encourage her to notice when she is meeting potential supervisors and colleagues onsite?

Sandi landed the internship that all of her classmates were aiming for. She feels fortunate to get the position. Yet, a third of the way through the term, Sandi recognizes that supervision is sporadic—mostly a monologue from her supervisor—and ends early most of the time. How would you encourage Sandi to address her concerns? Who would you encourage her to talk with and why? What ethical issues concern you and you would like Sandi to address? When you address the ethical concerns, consider how you might state them when it comes to virtue ethics, principles ethics, and the parts of the code you believe are pertinent.

DIGGING INTO ETHICS

Over time, we as working professionals have recognized that learners in the counseling courses experience dissatisfaction at how "gray" ethical codes appear to be and that they do not offer a prescriptive way of doing things. Professional judgment and discernment become important in order to use the code(s) in the best way possible. To be cognizant of this requires independence and confidence in our own decision-making processes. How would you assess your professional judgment and discernment? Your confidence? Your willingness to seek consultation? Your ability to take correction and exhortation?

13.1 PRACTITIONER'S PERSPECTIVE

Damarcus Smith, EdD, CWDP, is an operations manager with Zeiders Enterprises Inc., which supports military spouses worldwide to achieve their career and academic goals. A veteran, Damarcus is passionate about seeing others achieve their goals and serving his community.

My first undergraduate professor was the director of the career center. I remained connected with her throughout my undergraduate career, and I came to appreciate the profession. After nearly a decade in the field of social services, I began working in higher education at a career center. Over the years, I was promoted into various positions in and out of the career center, but eventually returned to career counseling a few years ago and have rediscovered my passion for career counseling.

After working for various nonprofit organizations in social services, my life changed, and I needed a more structured work environment. The first opportunity available to me was working as a career specialist in a career center at a local community college, and I accepted the offer. Over the next few years, I was promoted to coordinator and eventually director of the career center. For the following 14 years, I followed the same trend with another organization, initially starting within the organization as a career coach and eventually leading a team of career coaches as a supervisor and manager.

I currently work with military spouses. The diversity of the population makes it the most rewarding and most challenging. At any given moment, I could be working with a recent high school graduate or a person with a doctoral degree seeking a career change. I served in the military and currently have a family member who is a military spouse, so I had noticed a gap in services provided to military spouses. In my search for a career change, I was pleased to find an organization that was seeking career counselors and was serving military spouses.

My passion for the population that I serve is what keeps me doing what I do. I love both the organization and the environment I work in. Both are extremely supportive and have provided me with a variety of opportunities to meet my professional goals while also giving me the opportunity to work with an often forgotten population. I am motivated by my desire to continue to make a difference in the lives of military families. I will continue to work in this field because I see the value in helping people achieve their academic and career goals. I also believe in the mission of the organization, and I have seen firsthand their sincere commitment to the population.

My job is very fast-paced and unpredictable at times. As in any career center environment, you have some insight into who you will be meeting with; however, the goals and needs of the person often change prior to or during appointments. What adds to this challenge, and is one of the most unique elements of my role, is that my role is completely remote and my clients span the globe.

TRAITS OF CAREER COUNSELORS

A person with a strong career development background is best suited for this environment. Though we have an extensive training program, a person would really benefit from having a solid foundation in career counseling to be adaptable to the diverse situations that arise. Personal characteristics that are important for a person in my role include traits such as being self-motivated, self-disciplined, structured, passionate, having a strong work ethic and strong communication skills, and having a willingness to learn.

In my position, it is required to have a master's degree in counseling, education, or in a closely related field. A national certification, such as the Nationally Certified Counselor or Certified Workforce Development Professional (CWDP) certifications, is also required. Additional credentials aren't required for advancement, but leadership experience is instead.

PROFESSIONAL ETHICS

As with most organizations, we have policies in place that provide guidelines and expectations for ethical behavior. I am also a member of the NACE and the National Association of Workforce Development Professionals, and they provide me with additional guidance on ethical behaviors and considerations.

ADVICE FOR STUDENT COUNSELORS ENTERING AN INTERNSHIP OR PRACTICUM

I offer student counselors two pieces of advice. First, when appropriate, ask the counselors who are supervising or training you this one question repeatedly throughout the process: Why? Asking why something was done or not done will expedite your learning curve. Secondly, find a mentor who is willing to share insight into how to navigate the field and how to overcome obstacles or barriers in the field.

13.2 PRACTITIONER'S PERSPECTIVE

Linda Whited, MS, is a Certified Career Counselor who works in higher education and in private practice with adults in transition. She seeks to help others make confident career decisions. She is a Nationally Certified Counselor with a degree in counseling from the University of North Carolina at Greensboro.

When I was a kid, I wanted to be a movie director and a journalist. When I got to college, I chose public relations and minored in communications. For me, those paths intersect because I just love stories. And I think passion is contagious; I tell people I could be persuaded to be a trash collector if I could spend time with one who loved the work. Rather than changing professions each time I heard someone passionately describe their job, I chose career counseling to help others in pursuit of their life's work.

I got a part-time job in my undergraduate studies conducting mock interviews, which exposed me to a career services office, and it planted the seed for me to get a graduate degree and start this work. I worked in a centralized career office at a regional public university for about 5 years, and then I worked at a private university specializing in graduate students while also starting my own private practice. I gained confidence in my work through professional development with NCDA and its state association.

Today, I work with adults in transition to help them make confident career decisions. In my first few years in a university career center, I supported business students in their internships, job searches, and career direction. Then I worked with all students which included a lot of adult learners, international students, and first-generation students, and this diversity was a great training ground. As I transitioned between settings, I grew in my ability to support graduate and Ph.D. students in their unique endeavors.

In my private practice, after I had my own children and made career changes, I chose to support women in transition, especially related to motherhood issues. My own transition to motherhood rocked my career trajectory. I made choices to align with my values, which were changing as my roles changed. This all gave me insight into the specific issues that women face regarding promotions, time off, maternity leaves, advocating for themselves, and needing flexibility. I have found Catalyst.org (www.catalyst.org/topics/working-parents/) and books like *How Women Rise* by Sally Helgesen, *The Confidence Code* by Katty Kay and *The Fifth Trimester: The Working Mom's Guide to Style, Sanity, and Success After Baby* by Lauren Smith Brody have been instrumental in helping me navigate these topics.

I've found that all the settings that I have worked in helped to broaden my knowledge, yet I am a good counselor because I'm an expert in the career development process—not in their particular career field. This allows me to work with most career issues across the life span.

To be hired in a university setting, I needed a master's degree and some experience with students, which I got in my counseling degree internship requirement. Also, the credentials offered via the NCDA have been helpful for me. I got my Certified Career Counselor credential, and it has given me the confidence to describe my skills and background to potential clients in my private practice. This credential is competency based and built my confidence in sharing my own professional standards with new clients. I recommend reviewing the qualifications for a credential through the National Career Development Association's (NCDA's) website (www.ncda.org/aws/NCDA/pt/sp/credentialing_home_page).

Watching clients have lightbulb moments keeps me in this field. I love how, in a short amount of time, I can help someone create something, increase their confidence in a decision, or breathe easier with new information regarding their career path or job search. So, what's a lightbulb moment? To me, it's when clients feel clearer on their next steps or have more confidence to go in the direction of their dreams. This happens often in the settings where I provide career counseling, and it is a gift to me. When a client has a lightbulb moment, I am reminded that this work is my calling. I can ask questions, provide resources, and equip people in ways that help them make their lives more meaningful. How cool is that?

Curiosity is a helpful trait to me as a career coach. Most of the time, people have the answers inside them and just need someone to help them get it out. I often say I majored in reframing. I learned how to ask questions and offer a new way of looking at a situation.

PROFESSIONAL ETHICS

I maintain ethical standards in my work through my credentials as a Nationally Certified Counselor and a Certified Career Counselor, which provide ethical codes that I adhere to. Having these credentials helps me to communicate my expertise and skills to future clients so they know what they are getting; I'm not a substitute for therapy, and I may refer clients back to a counselor if they present concerns that are keeping them stuck from making progress with me.

My advice for student counselors who are entering their internship or practicum experience is to look for ways to add value to the setting they are in. See if there's a project you can lead or help with that can be completed while you're there. It helps them, and you get something concrete to put on your resume.

13.3 PRACTITIONER'S PERSPECTIVE

Christin Taylor earned her master's degree in college counseling and student development from North Carolina State University (NCSU), where she currently serves as an academic advisor and lecturer in exploratory studies.

Prior to my undergraduate experience at NCSU, I had never considered pursuing a career in higher education. During my undergraduate years, I served as a student ambassador and peer career coach. These experiences exposed me to the functional areas of admissions and career services, and I began to realize my passion for working with college students in a higher education environment.

This was a major milestone in my career trajectory, and after graduation I decided to pursue a master's degree in College counseling and student development from NCSU's College of Education. During my graduate studies, I served as an academic advising graduate assistant in the Poole College of Management. I became increasingly interested in academic advising, and after graduation I secured a position as an academic advisor in the College of Education at NCSU. After 3 years, I transitioned to a new department, and I now serve as an academic advisor and lecturer in exploratory studies at NCSU. A master's degree is required for academic advising jobs at NCSU, preferably related to counseling, higher education, or a similar field.

In this role, I work with first-year undergraduate students who are undecided on their academic major. All students are at a different point in their exploration process. My goal is to help them increase their self-awareness and explore their options in order to make an informed decision and select a major that aligns with their future career goals. Many of my students live in the Exploratory Studies Village, which is a living–learning community right across the street from the Exploratory Studies office.

I have always enjoyed working with first-year college students because a person's first year of college is a time of major transition and new experiences. As an academic advisor, I have the opportunity to assist and guide students during this important transition. Working with exploratory studies students, I am exposed to all undergraduate majors, and I love the challenge of helping students find the academic major that is right for them.

My role is unique in that I am cross-trained on all majors across the university. Our students can matriculate into any major at NCSU; therefore, I must be knowledgeable and have an understanding of all programs on campus. Another unique aspect of my job is my role as a lecturer for University Studies Course 101 in the fall semester and University Studies Course 102 in the spring semester. All the students in my classes are my assigned advisees, which allows me to interact with my students on a weekly basis and foster a strong advising relationship. I serve as not only an academic advisor, but also a mentor, advocate, supporter, and teacher.

TRAITS OF CAREER COUNSELORS

To work in academic advising in higher education, one must possess a genuine interest in students and care for their development and well-being in college and beyond. A person should have basic counseling skills: active listening, rapport building, meeting students where they are, and genuine empathy for a student's experiences. Academic advisors work with a diverse population, and this makes cultural competence imperative. An advisor must have the awareness, knowledge, and skills to effectively advise and support students from all backgrounds.

As most higher education professionals would say, students are the reason that I work in this field. It is easy to burn out in a helping profession; however, interacting with students on a weekly basis reminds me of the importance of my role in a student's journey. I appreciate that every academic year and every semester brings its own energy, challenges, and learning opportunities. Working on a vibrant campus such as NCSU keeps me energized and motivated to continue in this profession. Meeting new students, maintaining relationships with past advisees, and watching my students grow and develop each semester is very fulfilling.

PROFESSIONAL ETHICS

There are many situations with students, families, and colleagues that require me to maintain legal and ethical standards in accordance with Family Educational Rights and Privacy Act (FERPA) and university regulations. I am most often faced with these challenges as it relates to communicating with parents and families of my students. When speaking with a parent or family member, I must ensure that NCSU has the student's consent before disclosing any information.

Student Voices

In Student Voices, students offer a unique viewpoint as they begin in the career-counseling field. Here, students share their thoughts and reflections about the career-counseling profession and offer personal takeaways.

GLORIA VANN DEBNAM

I graduated from the Master of Education—College Counseling and Student Development Program at NCSU in May 2021. I currently serve as a customized training coordinator within the Workforce Continuing Education Department at Wake Technical Community College. Also, I serve as a teacher/facilitator with the small-group ministry at church and as a volunteer with Dress for Success of the Triangle and the Lightner Y Achievers.

One might describe my pursuit of a master of education degree as a mid-career change. I have a strong desire to be in a position where I can guide and counsel young adults in an academic setting. I enjoy counseling, advising, and helping others, and people find it easy to talk to me about matters of the heart. Helping others find the resources they need is a trait I inherited from my late father; I enjoy making a referral for a service (i.e., medical, auto repair), helping someone find a home for unwanted items, or connecting people with a common interest. I enjoy teaching and facilitating small-group studies and workshops—activities that don't require assessing participant performance. My prayer is that my master of education degree, combined with my professional experience and a deep passion to help others, will lead to a satisfying career in counseling and student development.

My Christian faith is very important as it provides the lens through which I see and experience the world. My faith in God, as imparted by my parents and developed through years of church attendance and participation in Bible studies, serves as the foundation for my desire to help others. I believe God has gifted me with a warm personality and a love for others that allows many to feel safe around me and freely share aspects of their lives with me. I value the trust that people give, and I desire to listen empathically and share thoughtful guidance. Unfortunately, since graduating from the Master of Education Program, I have not yet had a full-time position where I work with young adults.

I have worked at Wake Technical Community College (WTCC) for the last 9 months with the Customized Training Program (CTP), and after the first 5 months, I realized that my work as a CTP training coordinator is not fulfilling. While I have appreciated learning about WTCC (i.e., campus locations, degree/certificate programs, community outreach), I have no direct contact with students.

(continued)

Student Voices (*continued*)

Admittedly, I accepted the coordinator position because, after searching for months, I was offered a position with a college I desired to work for, and it provided the highest salary of the three positions I was offered. So, a year after graduating, I am again searching for a full-time position. However, in my next search, I will do so with a determination to find my fit and not settle for just any position.

After talking with a few friends and LinkedIn connections, I am expanding my search outside the world of higher education. My goal is to work with young adults in a way that allows me to provide meaningful assistance to and advocate for populations that are misunderstood and overlooked as they seek to navigate life through their educational and career pursuits.

COUNSELING SKILLS CONNECTION

Realistically and honestly evaluate your skills and training as it relates to the profession and ethical practice. Review the ethical standards for NCDA and ACA that relate to your preferred setting. While reviewing the standards, we suggest that you complete a self-evaluation of your own counseling identity. This might include assessing your theoretical orientation, your values, multicultural skills, and existing biases.

Note your resources for consultation and referrals. Reach out to consult with peers and mentors to support your evaluation. Networking with professionals with a diversity of experiences and specialties may help you explore your own professional identity and lends to learning more about possibilities within the field. The ethical considerations and theoretical orientation may vary depending upon the setting in which you intend to practice. For example, a school-based counselor working with young children may have to employ a solution-focused brief therapy model, whereas a practitioner working with a similar population within a clinical setting may have more time and the option to use a more eclectic approach, drawing from multiple theories and techniques.

MINDFUL MOMENT

Practicing mindfulness during the workday creates the opportunity for enhanced focus and awareness. Hougaard and Carter (2016) encourage us to apply mindfulness when opening our email inboxes, an easy and frequent source of distraction: "Focus on what is important and maintain *awareness* of what is merely noise. To get a better start to your day, avoid checking your email first thing in the morning. Doing so will help you sidestep an onslaught of distractions and short-term problems during a period of exceptional focus and creativity" (Hougaard & Carter, 2016, para. 7).

TECH TOOLS

Career practitioners use a wide variety of technology tools, regardless of their work setting. Technology may be used to communicate with clients (e.g., email), provide service to clients (e.g., Zoom, Teams), securely host client notes (e.g., Vcita, TherapyNotes), catalog job postings (e.g., Handshake, GradLeaders), manage appointments (e.g., Calendly) and more. Don't forget about creative tools you may use to develop psychoeducational worksheets and marketing collateral (e.g., Canva). Counselors must build skills in navigating digital platforms. Seek technology training during internship and practicum experiences and ask professionals in different organizations which tools they use most frequently. Visit LinkedIn Learning to explore basic training on select tools, and dive into tutorials targeting beginners, which are available on individual software products.

REFLECTION ACTIVITY

What do you hope to contribute or change the lives of the people or groups with whom you will be working? How do your personal and work values contribute to your career choice and career trajectory? What aspects of your work–life balance do you think warrant consideration as you enter the field of career development. Reflect on thoughts you may have had that suggest biases you may have regarding multicultural populations. What helping skills do you contribute to working with your clients/constituents? Are you willing to work within the guidelines of the respective codes of ethics in the field? As you reflect on the field, what career pathways sound most interesting and appealing to you and why?

END-OF-CHAPTER RESOURCES

SUMMARY

Even as its own niche within the counseling profession, career counseling offers a wide variety of career opportunities within a range of work environments. This chapter highlighted some of the pathways and explored unique characteristics of each setting. Even within a setting, there are opportunities to lean into your strengths, interests, and values and find a niche that fits you. Career development roles demand counseling skills paired with program, people, and content management qualifications. Career counselors are encouraged to continuously develop and grow their skills through **continuing education**, **training**, and **certifications**. Professional associations such as NCDA offer a strong source to begin exploring training opportunities. The profession is diverse and welcoming; opportunities for growth abound! What areas of the field intrigue you most? Connect with professionals in the field to continue your exploration.

REFERENCES

Byars-Winston, A. M., & Found, N. A. (2006). Metacognition: Multicultural competence: Expanding the culturally appropriate career counseling model. *The Career Development Quarterly, 54*, 187–201. https://doi.org/10.1002/j.2161-0045.2006.tb00151.x

Council for Accreditation of Counseling and Related Educational Programs. (2016). *Section 5: Career counseling.* https://www.cacrep.org/section-5-entry-level-specialty-areas-career-counseling/

Granello, D. H., & Granello, P. (2000). Defining mental illness: The relationship between college student's beliefs about the definition of mental illness and tolerance. *Journal of College Counseling, 3*, 109–110. https://doi.org/10.1002/j.2161-1882.2000.tb00170.x

Hougaard, R., & Carter, J. (2016, April 11). *How to practice mindfulness throughout your work day.* Greater Good Magazine. https://greatergood.berkeley.edu/varticle/item/how_to_practice_mindfulness_throughout_your_work_day#:~:text=Mindful%20working%20means%20applying%20focus,mistakes%2C%20and%20even%20enhance%20creativity

Jones, C. D., & Jones, D. C. (2016, Fall). The integration of career counseling and psychotherapy. *Career Developments Magazine*, NCDA, 32.

Krumboltz, J. D. (1993). Integrating career and personal counseling. *The Career Development Quarterly, 42*, 143–148. https://doi.org/10.1002/j.2161-0045.1993.tb00427.x

National Career Development Association. (1997). *Career counseling competencies.* (Rev. ed.). Columbus, OH: Author.

National Career Development Association. (n.d.). *Career development competencies. broken arrow.* https://associationdatabase.com/aws/NCDA/asset_manager/get_file/631290?ver=0

National Career Development Association. (2009). *Minimum competencies for multicultural career counseling and development.* Author. https://www.ncda.org/aws/NCDA/asset_manager/get_file/26627?ver=50664

National Career Development Association. (2015). *Code of ethics.* Author.

Niles, S. G. (2003). Career counselors confront a critical crossroad: a vision for the future. *The Career Development Quarterly, 52*, 70–77. https://doi.org/10.1002/j.2161-0045.2003.tb00629.x

Super, D. E. (1957). *A psychology of careers.* Harper & Row.

CHAPTER 14

WORKFORCE TRENDS: THE FUTURE OF WORK

Raychelle Cassada Lohmann, Angie C. Smith, and Katie Peterssen

LEARNING OBJECTIVES

By the end of this chapter, you will be able to:

- Explore the trends in employment and career readiness.
- Review the crises (pandemics, disasters, racism) and their influence on career.
- Define the trends currently impacting the career field.
- Explore workforce trends in the profession of counseling.

WARM-UP EXERCISE

How do you define a trend? What trends do you remember from your childhood, adulthood, or even last year? Some examples of the types of trends you might recall include: (a) fashion, (b) popular television shows, (c) viral videos or other popular social media, and (d) music genres or specific songs.

Now, let's turn our attention to career trends. What career trends can you identify from the past? What jobs were sought after and popularized during different eras or decades (e.g., web development in the dot-com boom)? How about now? What career trends do you anticipate given our current context? How can we, as helping professionals, remain current and on trend in our own careers and within the profession?

INTRODUCTION

This chapter focuses on the future of work and explores **trends** influencing **employment**. We explore how companies are using technology to increase productivity and what employees want and demand from their employers. Finally, we review the impact of recent crises (public health, environmental, racial inequities, etc.) along with strategies for preparedness and **crisis** response.

The information presented in this chapter is not a deep dive into each of the areas covered; rather, it is an introduction to the emerging **trends** that counselors need to be aware of to address client needs. If you'd like to learn more about a specific topic discussed in this chapter, additional resources are provided after the chapter.

THE GREAT RESIGNATION AND THE AGE OF THE EMPLOYEE

The workplace is in a constant state of change. Unlike any other time in history, people are switching jobs, positions are being crowdsourced, freelancing services are increasing in popularity, and workplace flexibility is in high demand. Additionally, technology is revolutionizing the business sector, not just nationally but globally. Many workplace changes were emerging before the COVID-19 pandemic began in 2020, but the global response to the virus put the change pendulum into an accelerated motion. The long-term impact of the pandemic has permanently redesigned the landscape of the work environment.

In 2021 we witnessed a shift worldwide in which members of the workforce left their jobs in droves, citing low pay, lack of opportunity for advancement, and feeling disrespected at work as the reason for leaving (Pew Research Center, 2022). These workers desire to find a job that they feel appreciated for and that meets their needs. As counselors, we need to be aware of these shifting trends and be prepared to help our clients find an occupation that matches their values and skill sets, where they can find meaning and purpose while meeting the needs of the global labor market.

We must keep a close eye on the use of technology and data, such as big data, **artificial intelligence (AI)**, and automation. We will see more and more industries relying on technology to inform decision-making, and future workers will have to adjust to more automated work environments.

JOB SATISFACTION (CACREP 2.F.4.B.; 2.F.4.D.; 2.F.4.E.; 2.F.4.H.)

The typical American worker spends, on average, 90,000 hours at work in their lifetime (Pryce-Jones, 2010). Now that's a lot of time, especially if you're not content with your job. According to Pew Research Center (2016), nearly 51% of American workers align their identity to their job, so we can see how job satisfaction contributes to mental and physical well-being. The term *job satisfaction* refers to our contentment, motivation, and satisfaction with our jobs, and when we are happy doing our job, we are more motivated to perform well (Shobe, 2018) and are less likely to quit.

In a Gallup Poll, nearly 55% of U.S. workers get a sense of identity from their job. This percentage has consistently held the same since 1989 (Riffkin, 2021). Those who have pursued higher education are more apt to attach their identity to their work. In fact, nearly 70% of people with a college education report attaching their identity to their job compared to 45% of workers who don't hold a college degree (Riffkin, 2021). Stop and think about this number for a minute. Rather than a job being simply a means to earn money, we have attached our jobs to who we are as a person. Think about how this information will affect how you counsel people for tomorrow's workforce. Based on this data, the odds are that when you counsel adults, their career may be deeply embedded into their identity, so job satisfaction is of utmost importance.

Job satisfaction is linked to learning motivation, turnover rate, and overall performance (Robbins & Judge, 2022). As counselors, we must understand that our clients will feel better both inside and outside of work if they feel like they have a *good job*. This leads to the question, what is a good job? The Organization for Economic Cooperation and Development (2018) states that a good job exists in an environment in which high-quality jobs can thrive, workers are protected from labor market exclusion and risk, and adaptations are made to meet the future world of work. To be more precise, 10 dimensions of a good job have been identified, and these are level of pay, predictability and stability of pay, stability and predictability of hours, ability to work remotely, job security, employee benefits, career advancement, enjoyment of work, a sense of purpose, and the power to change unsatisfactory aspects of a job (Wigert, 2022).

Here are a few questions for you to consider for yourself and perhaps to ask your clients:

■ How do you define a good job?
■ Would you add another characteristic to the list? If so, what characteristic(s) would you include?

When workers are unhappy, they may leave their jobs. We saw this during the pandemic when there was a mass exodus from the workplace, a period of time that has been deemed The Great Resignation. In the March 2022 report, the U.S. Department of Labor, Bureau of Labor and Statistics released that nearly 4.5 million Americans quit their jobs in March 2022 (BLS, n.d.). Many of these people were switching occupations, leading to a reorganization or reshuffling of the workplace. Economists forecast that The Great Resignation is far from over. According to a 2022 Global Talent Trends report, today's employees are willing to walk away from jobs that don't meet their needs. According to Pew Research Center (2022), employees who quit a job in 2021 reported doing so because of low pay (63%), minimal to no opportunities for advancement (63%), and feeling disrespected at work (57%). These employees have taken a stance to let employers know that things need to change.

The era that we are living in has been called the *Age of the Employee* (Visier, n.d.), because employees are driving many workplace changes. Today's workers expect to feel appreciated and have autonomy and flexibility. The pressure from employees has companies reassessing ways to meet these new demands while increasing their productivity and employee retention rates. Companies must also recognize that their employees are their most valuable asset and then adapt the work environments to meet their needs. When we can find a good match between our desires, interests, and skills, it is a win-win situation for everyone.

TECHNOLOGY TRENDS (CACREP 2.F.4.C.; 2.F.4.D.)

Let's explore a little more about some of the most popular workforce trends in technology. As you read, think about how much technological change has occurred in your lifetime. Then conduct an internet search on cell phones in the 1990s, 2000s, and today. This little experiment will show you how far we've come in such a short amount of time.

The landscape of the workforce has changed significantly in the past few years. For starters, remote work has skyrocketed, and more workers than ever before are working from home or telecommuting. With employees being offsite, companies have to come up with clever ways to monitor employee performance while assessing accountability. The changing workforce patterns coupled with remote work can create challenges and opportunities for economic development (Soroui, 2021). For example, how do you get employees to connect if they aren't sharing a physical workspace? The conference room, in many cases, has been replaced by a social media platform (Evans, 2020; Karl et al., 2022; Peters, 2020; Thorp-Lancaster, 2020), and office water cooler talk has been replaced by emails, chats, and texts.

While working offsite has its perks, employers must think of outside-of-the-box ways to form a team mentality. More and more companies are trying to figure out ways to make telecommuting and remote work effective. As a result, companies such as Workplaceless offer companies e-courses and trainings to help them train employees and leaders in remote work skills, including effective asynchronous communication skills, and help companies foster a feeling of connection among employees. On top of the remote and hybrid work settings, many jobs are automated or driven by big data and AI. As counselors, how do we help prospective employers navigate these modern day changes?

Remote Work, Telecommuting and Connectivity, and Accountability

Employees want flexibility in their jobs. As a result, more and more employers offer viable options such as telecommuting and remote work. Remote work is defined as working outside the traditional company environment. Nowadays, many people who work remotely do so from home and report being just as productive, if not more so, at home as in the office, according to the Becker Friedman Institute for Economics at the University of Chicago (Barrero et al., 2021). About 30% of the 10,000 employees surveyed stated they were more productive and engaged working from home (Barrero et al., 2021). Furthermore, in a 2021 survey conducted by Owl Labs, 55% of employee respondents say they work more hours remotely than at the physical office, and 32% reported they would quit their job if they could not continue working remotely (Owl Labs, n.d.).

Nine to five jobs are becoming a way of the past. Instead, companies are increasing remote work options to retain employees with diverse skills (Soroui, 2021). Many employers ask employees to telecommute. Telecommuting is a hybrid work environment where an employee works both in the office and offsite remotely (Shabanpour et al., 2018). Both telecommuting and remote work allow employees to have more of a work–life balance. Research has shown that this flexibility in the workplace can increase employee morale and productivity, which in turn reduces organizational costs (Shabanpour et al., 2018). Both remote work and telecommuting are trends that are sure to continue.

Connectivity in the workforce refers to the connections employees form, allowing them to work toward a common goal and collaborate to get work done. Today, companies use innovative approaches, such as teleconferencing, to increase employee morale and connections while enhancing retention efforts. As a result, reliable teleconferencing platforms and software systems are a must today, more than at any other time in the past. These avenues are a means for companies to connect with employees and convey essential information. For example, in December 2019, before the massive shutdowns during the pandemic, the platform Zoom had about 10 million meeting participants each day. In April 2020, that number had increased to over 300 million (Evans, 2020). Other platforms, such as Google Meet™ and Microsoft Teams, also experienced surges in daily participants (Karl et al., 2022; Peters, 2020; Thorp-Lancaster, 2020).

This trend of video conferencing has proven to be cost-efficient and a viable way to communicate. With many employees joining meetings remotely, companies are saving money by not having to pay travel and other associated expenses. It is predicted that by 2024, only 25% of work-related meetings will take place in person (Standaert et al., 2021). Although video conferencing has revolutionized how companies do business nationally and internationally, it comes with some shortfalls, such as fatigue from online conferencing, eye strain, and information overload (Karl et al., 2022). Regardless, as more companies are using teleconferencing, you can bet that it's here to stay (Barrero et al., 2021; Karl et al., 2022; Standaert et al., 2021).

Accountability is defined as the need to defend or justify an employee's actions to an employer who has a potential reward or sanction power (Frink & Klimoski, 1998). Accountable employees adhere to and perform according to the company's mission, vision, and goals. Unfortunately, many employers grapple with management control issues relating to accountability with employees working remotely (Delfino & van der Kolk, 2021). For example, during the pandemic, some employers became more demanding of their employees, which resulted in tighter and constrained control, such as clocking in and out, monitoring the number of emails sent, and chat responses. However, these demanding monitoring antics are not popular with employees (Delfino & van der Kolk, 2021). Good leaders know that if you want to get the most out of your employees, either remotely or in the office, you need to establish an equitable work environment built on trust, autonomy, and accountability (Huffman, 2021).

Big Data, Artificial Intelligence, and Automation

Technological trends are continuing to dominate the workforce. Now more than ever, companies are using big data to inform decisions and AI and automation to reduce mundane job tasks while increasing performance. Big data is a term that describes large datasets collected to help improve business growth by allowing businesses to predict events, support AI, and increase automation (Pappas et al., 2018). Big data also helps inform decision-making management practices and allows for an edge over competitors (Pappas et al., 2018).

AI combines computer science algorithms with data sets to reproduce aspects of human intelligence through learning (Sestino & De Mauro, 2022). AI is the future and will have both business and human implications. The International Society of Automation (ISA; n.d., para. 2) defines automation as "the creation and application of technology to monitor and control the production and delivery of products and services." Automation decreases the need for humans to carry out mundane and repetitive tasks by increasing productivity using machines.

As our understanding of technology increases, we will see advancements involving the use of big data, AI, and automation; businesses will continue to rely on data to drive decisions, AI to provide information, and automation to deliver products at an accelerated rate. As counselors, we need to make sure that we know how these technological advancements impact the workforce. Today's workers must have some technical skills to remain competitive in the job market. Also, counselors will need to adapt to the future workforce trends. Remote and telecommuter work are even impacting the healthcare sector, with more and more practitioners offering telehealth services. For the counseling profession, this means we can offer more accessible services for the communities we serve.

PREPARING FOR THE FUTURE OF WORK
(CACREP 2.F.4.A.; 2.F.4.C.)

Today's employees must be adequately prepared to meet the demands of a globally competitive market, and some people will need to pursue postsecondary education to attain their career goals. Unfortunately, disparity exists in education. Only 25% of America's 1.2 million first-generation or low-income college students are predicted to earn a degree, get a job, or get a graduate-level education (Davis, 2021). As a nation, we must make sure that education is accessible because some careers will require advanced education.

The term most often used to describe the skills needed to enter the workforce is career readiness. According to the National Association of Colleges and Employers (NACE, 2021), career readiness "is a foundation from which to demonstrate requisite core competencies that broadly prepare the college-educated for success in the workplace and lifelong career management" (NACE, n.d., para. 1). The National Association of College and Employers (2021) identifies eight core competencies needed for career readiness or entry into the workforce. These competencies are:

1. Career and Self-Development—Developing awareness of strengths and weaknesses, exploring career opportunities, creating a plan and goals to pursue a career, and networking to build relationships within the workforce.
2. Communication—Effectively listening and expressing oneself through the exchange of written, nonverbal, and verbal language.
3. Critical Thinking—Gathering and analyzing information using logical reasoning skills to make good decisions.
4. Equity and Inclusion—Demonstrating cultural awareness, knowledge, and skills to increase cultural competence, engage in equitable practices, and work with diverse populations.

5. Leadership—Identifying and capitalizing on individual and team strengths to work toward goals within the organization.

6. Professionalism—Acting in the best interest of the workplace by demonstrating work habits that align with the organization and personal values. For example, being dependable, trustworthy, and consistently meeting or exceeding expectations.

7. Teamwork—Working collaboratively toward common goals while considering other perspectives.

8. Technology—Enhancing work performance ethically using technology.

According to the U.S. Chamber of Commerce Foundation, these eight career-readiness competencies will provide workers with a competitive edge during interviews and internships and in turn will help them become a more valuable employee (Johnson, 2016). Furthermore, an investment in career- readiness training can help underrepresented college students achieve better jobs and pursue higher education (Davis, 2021). As counselors, it is our role to help our clients know the skills they need outside of their education and training and prepare them for future work.

WORKPLACE DIVERSITY AND INCLUSION

The United States is projected to become a majority–minority nation for the first time in 2043, and by 2060 57% of the U.S. population will consist of racially ethnic minorities, according to data from the U.S. Census Bureau (U.S. Census Bureau Public Information Office, 2016). This data supports the notion that business leaders and organizations must create practical solutions to recruit, support, and retain a more diverse workforce. Therefore, diversity and inclusion are essential practices that extend beyond company policies and programs.

Although the terms diversity and inclusion are often linked together, they are not the same. Workplace diversity means the place of employment is made up of people from various ages, genders, ethnicities, religions, physical abilities, races, and other diverse demographics. Workplace inclusion is when the workplace provides employees with equitable access to opportunities and resources (O'Donovan, 2018). In an inclusive workplace, all employees, regardless of age, gender, race, religion, and so on, feel included in the environment. Inclusion in the workplace is likely the most critical key to retention. A diverse and inclusive workplace creates a cohesive, welcoming environment where employees are valued and accepted.

A diverse and inclusive workplace is beneficial to the business, too, including increased financial performance, increased employee creativity and innovation, a higher likelihood of recruiting a diverse talent pool, and higher employee retention (Bush, 2021). According to a Great Place to Work's research (Bush, 2021) on company culture, when employees trust that they and their colleagues will be treated fairly regardless of their race, gender, sexual orientation, or age, they are:

- 9.8 times more likely to look forward to going to work
- 6.3 times more likely to feel gratified in their work, and
- 5.4 times more likely to remain at their company.

The Boston Consulting Group's survey of employees in 1,700 companies, spanning Austria, Brazil, China, France, Germany, India, Switzerland, and the United States, found that work environments with management teams with diverse backgrounds and experiences earn 19% more revenue from innovation than do their less diverse competitors (Lorenzo et al., 2021). Seventy-five percent of employees surveyed at these companies also reported that workplace diversity is increasing within their organization (Lorenzo et al., 2021). Undoubtedly, workplace diversity and inclusion underscore the importance of having accepting and equitable work environments. As a result, diversity and inclusion will continue to shape business decisions within national and international markets as we move forward.

WORKFORCE TRENDS IN THE COUNSELING PROFESSION

According to the U.S. Bureau of Labor and Statistics (BLS, n.d.), the job growth of school and career counselors is projected to grow 11% from 2020 to 2030. Substance abuse, behavioral disorders, and clinical mental health counseling are expected to grow 23% between 2020 and 2030 (BLS, n.d.). All of these positions are at a higher than average job growth rate. For counselors-in-training, the job prospects look good.

Destigmatization of Mental Health

Just like in the other employment sectors discussed in this chapter, the profession of counseling is also feeling the impact of changing times. Nowadays more people are seeking professional mental health help. Celebrities and musicians (i.e., Prince Harry, Lady Gaga, Demi Lovato) and athletes (i.e., Michael Phelps, Naomi Osaka, Simone Biles) are coming forward and discussing their own struggles with anxiety, depression, and substance use, to name a few. As a society, the more open we are to discussing social and emotional issues the more we normalize mental health issues. Organizations and campaigns such as Lady Gaga's Born This Way Foundation and Dove's Real Beauty campaign are leading the way in conveying messages of help and support, embracing who we are both inside and out. As the importance of mental well-being becomes more accepted, there will be an increased need for counselors. Our growing profession is leading the way in helping people find purpose and meaning in their lives academically, occupationally, emotionally, and socially.

Telemental Health

The counseling profession has also been impacted by technological changes. The pandemic shutdown led to the increasing frequency of telemental health. Telemental health is rapidly increasing across the nation, and companies such as TalkSpace and BetterHelp are providing online mental health services through electronic interaction.

Tip: Counseling Compact

The Counseling Compact is an interstate contract among member U.S. states to allow licensed counselors to practice in other member states without needing multiple licenses. Member states agree that a state license is mutually recognized by other member states. As of August 2022, 16 states have become members, and six states have Compact legislation pending.

This compact is expected to remove barriers to practice for counselors and reduce long waiting times for clients. It will also improve continuity of care for clients, especially those who travel or move frequently for work or are in the military, and fill critical gaps in mental health care. In 2023, counselors will be able to apply to be a Compact counselor to receive the privilege to practice in person and via telehealth in each Compact-member state. For more information, visit https://counselingcompact.org/.

The National Board for Certified Counselors has developed a credential for the Board Certified-TeleMental Health Provider (BC-TMH) to help prepare clinicians for the rising demand of telehealth services. Telemental health is paving the way to make counseling more accessible to those who may not be able to access services. As society changes, just like the rest of the workforce sector, we as counselors need to meet the needs of our clients, and there is no way around it: technology is a means for doing so.

CASE STUDY

Apply your knowledge about workforce trends to help Amber navigate the difficult decision to change college majors.

AMBER

Amber is a 22-year-old Asian American full-time student who attends a local university. She is completing her second year in a pharmacy program. However, lately, she has not been happy in her studies and is considering switching majors to psychology. Amber has taken many psychology courses and has excelled in them. She had already planned on pursuing a graduate program in pharmacy and now is finding that she's interested in getting a master's degree in mental health counseling. Amber is conflicted about what to do because she knows her family will not approve of her decision. From the onset, her family has stated that Amber needs to go into a STEM-related career to do well and thrive in today's world.

There's also the financial issue to consider, because if Amber changes majors to one that her family doesn't approve of, she could lose their financial support. Amber has come to see you seeking help navigating through this decision. She knows if she presents this idea to her family, she will need facts and data to help support her decision. Does Amber follow her dream or continue to push herself into a career that will please her family?

As a counselor, work out an intervention plan for helping Amber with her dilemma. Consider the following questions in designing your intervention.

(continued)

CASE STUDY (*CONTINUED*)

Discussion Questions
1. What tools would you use to help Amber assess her interests, strengths, values, and abilities?
2. Culturally, what factors may Amber face by switching majors?
3. Financially, what barriers may arise?
4. What resources would you share with Amber so she could find information and data to present to her family?
5. Discuss the current labor market trends for advanced degree careers in pharmacy and psychology or counseling.
6. How can you use the information on job satisfaction to help Amber?
7. Exploring worldviews and culture, could it be beneficial to include the family, provided all parties agree, at some point in the career intervention?

In this chapter, we've examined emerging workforce trends. From automation to technological advancements, we are in a constant state of change. The COVID-19 pandemic was a staunch reminder that it's a small world after all, and we work best when we work together. Although oceans may separate us, we are connected and rely on one another, and one change can set off a ripple effect felt worldwide. For example, we witnessed employees taking a stand and walking out of their jobs, a phenomenon known as The Great Resignation, which serves as a reminder of the importance of finding a good job that aligns with our skills and values and provides a sense of satisfaction.

As counselors, it is essential that we stay up to date on the current and future workforce. During a session, it's not uncommon for our clients to bring up their jobs, as what we do for a living is a big part of our lives. Your clients may even be seeking you out because their jobs have caused angst, and they may not know how to navigate the next chapter of their lives. Counselors need to be equipped with current information and resources that will help our clients explore their options.

We also need to be engaged with state, national, and international organizations. Consider joining your state's Career Development Association, and better yet, join the National Career Development Association (NCDA), too! The pathway to finding a meaningful career is a journey, not a destination. The journey focuses just as much on self-awareness as it does on skill sets. What a privilege it is to help someone discover a career that helps them find meaning and purpose in what they do!

ETHICAL CORNER

In this section, the authors lead the reader through topical scenarios to surface common ethics questions and dilemmas faced by career professionals. They ask pertinent and personal questions to encourage reader reflection and insight into personal and professional ethics.

Azra Karajic Siwiec PhD, LPC, is a counselor educator employed by Capella University. She has been working in the counselor education field for over 14 years and has served as a committee member of the Ethics Committee of NCDA since 2015 and served as the chair of the Ethics Committee since 2017.

Sharon K. Anderson, PhD, is Professor of Counseling and Career Development at Colorado State University. Sharon has taught the master's level ethics course for counseling students for over 20 years, teaching and mentoring a multitude of students. She has coauthored or coedited four professional ethics books used by practitioners in counseling and coaching.

It is important for career professionals to balance ethical principles and draw upon ethical virtues. Check in with yourself: which ethical principles do you think about most often and why? Which ethical principles spend less time on your radar and why? What ethical virtues may need some attending to when you think about yourself as a career counselor in the future? What types of clients and issues might strike you as more difficult to work with and why? Do you see some places where the current ethics code may be lacking and need some updates based on what you have read in the chapter? How will you balance the principles, and which ones will be important to consider based on the work trends discussed in the chapter?

DIGGING INTO ETHICS

As a professional joining our profession, we welcome you. We also want you to recognize the fluidity of career and to consider your "transferability" of skills. How could you use your skills to connect to other tasks? For example, if you are excellent with billing, how can you use that to promote your own career? Also, if crisis management is your strong suit, how can you use that to develop a longer term vision for how you can amplify those skills and promote your career? Finally, how will you remain on the ethical course despite workforce trends imposing changes?

14.1 PRACTITIONER'S PERSPECTIVE

Teri Mills attended Indiana University Bloomington and earned a master of science in college student personnel administration. She is a dedicated professional who works to inspire others to discover their inner selves to live their best life. She worked at Duke University for twenty 20 in the career center designing programs and services to meet the needs of students and working with students through their professional development journey.

I chose career counseling when I was an undergraduate, knowing that I wanted to work with students in higher education. I did not yet know that I would be in career services, but I knew that I wanted to inspire and influence students in a special way. I began my career after graduate school, working as Director of Residence Life at Queens College in Charlotte, North Carolina, and I transitioned to the career center 3 years later.

I very much enjoyed the world of work and the connections to the outside world that career services could provide. I liked learning about the recruitment process, the many industries, and the current trends in hiring college graduates. It was fulfilling to help students with their journey to discover themselves and find their first adventure out of college.

I then left academia to follow my husband for his career. I surprisingly ended up taking a role as the training coordinator at a bank. It was only for a year due to another move for my husband's career, but what I learned from this role was invaluable. I found that I loved the teaching and training process and that I was good at it. Then I stayed home with my children for about 10 years, which was also a learning experience. I am confident that my time outside the workforce taught me much about myself and others. During this time, I started a niche catering business, became the queen of the PTA, and practically lived at my kids' school. (Talk about a helicopter parent!)

After 10 years, I got antsy and started to look for potential ways to get back to work. I was fortunate that someone at North Carolina State University hired me to work with a career program designed for football players. I also did some community professional development training. The person who hired me for these roles put me in touch with someone at Duke University, as there was a position open in the career center there. I started as a temporary counselor and secured a permanent position 5 months later—and never left.

Duke is where I grew up as a professional. In my 20 years at Duke, I did amazing work and met the most interesting people. I grew as a counselor and very much enjoyed inspiring students to discover their talents and interests so they could find fulfilling work and fulfilling life. One of my greatest experiences was working with the director of Financial Aid to develop a program called LAUNCH for first-generation sophomore women. There are many other programs that I was able to envision and bring to reality while I was at Duke.

During my 20 years at Duke, I worked with all populations of students. Undergraduate students are just experiencing the professional development process for the first time. They are all over the place with different levels of motivation, but it was fun to introduce them to the process and the possibilities. I found that they were motivated by having someone else "see them" and help them identify parts of themselves that they had not recognized as important.

Graduate students ask higher level questions, are more focused on their path, and often need more detailed information about the job search process. Although in many cases, the students were often interested in changing their professional course and that took some serious counseling.

I worked a great deal with first-generation and low-income students. I was able to provide some valuable resources to help them move forward in their professional development. They often need a different level of support to find resources, understand processes, and make connections. I also worked with student-athletes. They were very busy, so I tried to streamline the process for them. It was a pleasure to reassure them that they came to the table with a myriad of skills other students did not have. Oddly, working with these populations just happened serendipitously. I was lucky to recognize an opportunity to work with these different groups as they presented themselves. That is what kept me at Duke for so many years. I was able to add, switch, and experiment with different areas.

Working at Duke was unique in that it provided a great many resources other institutions did not. Students were typically supported at the highest level. If a student had a serious issue or needed some help, I was able to reach out to various partners to support students in different ways.

I am now retired, though I continue working with students on a contract basis at another institution. I have continued this work for so many years because:

■ It is ever-changing, you never stop learning.
■ It allowed me to try new strategies, programs, and ideas.

■ I thrive in developing relationships with others, and that never ends. I enjoy teaching others, the presentations gave me energy, and I found that students always took away something from each presentation.

The COVID pandemic changed my work significantly. It was very difficult (at least for me), to do virtual counseling, but I did get used to it. We found that we needed to create a great deal of digital content and make it widely accessible to students. I also dealt with more personal issues in my counseling sessions with students as we all tried to figure out how to manage in this new world. Many students needed to learn skills in adapting, pivoting, and being flexible (and staff did as well). Some students lost their internship and job offers, so this elevated a need for staff to assist the student in considering options and alternatives to their previous thinking. Employer recruiting also changed, with a great deal of uncertainty for everyone. We needed to increase communication and get creative to help students connect with employers.

TRAITS OF CAREER COUNSELORS

All kinds of people are suited to this work. The bottom line is that one must care about the welfare of another person and thrive in helping them design and develop their goals. It takes a village, as they say. I tried to hire people for roles in the career center who had strengths that I did not have so that all students could be served in the most effective way.

Someone doing this work must care about the students they serve. They must be good listeners and learners. It is essential that one has a learning mentality to keep up with the trends in the industry, research in the field, and patience!

PROFESSIONAL ETHICS

The first step to maintaining ethical and legal standards is by understanding what they are! There are guidelines one must follow in terms of counseling, confidentiality, and so on. For example, a student informed me that a professor borrowed money from her. It was critical for me to maintain confidentiality with this student who had not and did not want to tell anyone. She finally let me get the university involved, understanding that she did not want this to happen to another student. The case was resolved, although I was not involved in that resolution.

FUTURE TRENDS

In the future, I can imagine that much more work will be done virtually and digitally. Students will need to be increasingly savvy about virtual interviewing, connecting with employers, and networking to create leads. Students must prepare for jobs that don't exist yet. Career centers will need to imagine these jobs and help students find experiences to prepare for them.

The world of work will likely change quite a bit, too. Many employers will not rely on the college student pool for resources. Instead, they will begin to develop training programs for high school students and others and may not prioritize a college education. It will be very interesting to see how the field changes in the next 10 years. In my opinion, I believe that "counseling" will become much less of a priority, and information will take the lead. Students will need to seek out the information they need rather than rely on experts to provide it in person. It is likely that career centers will evolve as times change and may not exist in their current state, and there might be stronger partnerships with the alumni offices, other institutions, and resources that will connect students to jobs and employers.

I think the entire recruiting system will change. For example, career fairs will no longer take place in person. I am not certain how this will play out. Yet, students will need to reach out directly to employers, and employers will need to have a system in place to make this happen so they can find the talent they need. Diversity will take a much higher priority as well in the coming years. We will all need to check our biases and think more seriously about how we are meeting needs.

14.2 PRACTITIONER'S PERSPECTIVE

Stephen DeWitt is deputy executive director of the Association for Career and Technical Education (ACTE), the nation's largest not-for-profit association committed to the advancement of education that prepares youth and adults for successful careers. DeWitt began as the organizations' senior director of public policy and now leads efforts in content development, partnerships, and its outreach agenda.

I graduated with a bachelor of science degree in communications, and honestly, I did not have a clear vision of a career that I wanted to pursue. Following graduation, a friend who moved to Washington, DC, convinced me to move there too. Fast forward 35 years later, and my pursuit of public policy—a key aspect of my career—has, to a large extent, required the communications skills that my degree proclaims. Yet, had I sought more career counseling and been more intentional about a career path prior to acquiring my degree, I would have had a more direct trajectory to my career. It took a few years to find my way.

The ACTE is a national education organization, and I represent the interests of many people: educators, administrators, school personnel, and indirectly, the students those professionals serve. I'm often working to communicate public policy or services and benefits that the organization provides to education professionals, but I also work with a broad range of other partners, including policymakers, media professionals, and education company representatives.

My work in education policy is driven by an equity lens. I believe that everyone has the right to a quality education, more needs to be done to ensure an equitable and supportive learning environment for students of all ages, and the individuals serving students need our support. I view my work as centering on educational access and equity, which motivates me. Later in my career, my mission extended to the educators and other professionals who are making a difference in students' lives. This focus has helped me to stay interested.

Despite my being an education advocate, the reality is that my occupation and career are removed from directly serving students. I work on matters such as forming partnerships with like-minded organizations and those who might want to reach schools but have goals different from those of my organization. The danger of these multiple layers of priorities is that the focus can get murky at times. It requires me to occasionally step back to question the intent and purpose. I appreciate that challenge.

This career involves many facets, but people who work in public policy must have an understanding of the technical aspects of legislative procedures and hands-on, direct interaction and networking with people. The occupation is fast-paced on many days, and the nature of government is long waits followed by quick action. It's important to have patience, vision, and passion to make an impact.

PROFESSIONAL ETHICS

Within public policy, there is always compromise. But that has to be tempered because too much compromise can inhibit the goal of what I am trying to accomplish; it's a delicate balance, and each situation has to be evaluated on its own terms. For example, I've been involved in many federal budget deliberations. To develop our "ask," we consider what is palatable to legislators given the current political climate, even if we believe a greater funding amount is justified. It's important to think about how these decisions impact people, and that helps me to keep a balanced and ethical approach.

TEN-YEAR VISION

Over the next decade, I believe that my work will become more remote. Positions that were exclusively based in Washington, DC, are now open to talented people from around the nation. The virtual nature of work has impacted membership organizations such as mine, and I believe that trend will continue. Couple this with the changing nature of interest in "joining" a membership organization and competition from virtual entities that do not have similar overhead costs as my organization, and there will most definitely be change in some form.

For career counseling, the next 10 years will be pivotal as the workforce continues to evolve. Many employees are looking for work–life balance, remote or hybrid workplace environments, and more meaning in their careers. At the same time, workforce shortages are impacting employers. Career counseling has always focused on supporting individuals, but as a result of these changes, I believe it will become even more student/employee-centric, focusing on ways to better blend work with home life.

14.3 PRACTITIONER'S PERSPECTIVE

Cindy Broderius, MEd, NCC, served Duke University students and alumni for 10 years, first as a career counselor in the career center and later as a prehealth advisor in the Office of Health Professions Advising. As she begins a new chapter in retirement, Cindy anticipates finding opportunities to continue helping others discern next steps on their career journeys and in their personal lives, at whatever age and stage those individuals may be.

The current chapter of my career journey is a culmination of a lifetime of experiences and self-discovery. My journey began as a medical technologist in clinical microbiology laboratories where I discovered the value of transferable skills that I then invested in technical, leadership, teaching, and writing opportunities. I later reinvested those transferable skills in service to a faith-based community, where I discovered the value of "meeting people where they are" while assisting them in discovering their gifts and talents to invest in service to others.

A serendipitous meeting with a career counselor introduced me to the field, leading me to return to graduate school in my 50s to pursue a master's degree in counselor education. My goal was to assist college-age young adults in a process of self-discovery to discern where their own career journeys might lead them. My six-word personal statement, "passionate career counselor helping others become," encapsulates the guiding premise of my modus operandi.

My current service to college undergraduates and young alumni pursuing careers in the health professions has brought me full circle, so to speak, by focusing my counseling and advising on a population of students seeking to serve others in the healthcare arena. The students share characteristics of altruism, innovation, resilience, and dedication to their goals.

A significant portion of my current position involves providing application support to students who are in application cycles for health profession schools. My meetings with the applicants provide me the opportunity to offer ongoing career counseling as we reflect on experiences they've had and how they see those experiences contributing to their personal and professional development. Application support informs the ways that I counsel and advise younger students who are in the early stages of discerning who they are, what their interests are, and who they want to become.

TRAITS OF CAREER COUNSELORS

Someone best suited for this type of work enjoys the thrill of walking alongside students on their journey of "becoming." To thrive in this position, one would have qualities and characteristics that include insatiable curiosity, a love of learning, a relational and accessible manner in connecting, the ability to bring order out of an advisee's chaos, and a glass half-full perspective that offers critical encouragement in challenging times.

This passionate career counselor enjoys helping young adults figure out who they are and who they are becoming and receives great joy in partnering with them in the process of charting the next steps. The numerous opportunities to celebrate their accomplishments, from taking a single hard step to achieving their dream goal, provide motivation for continuing with this work!

THE FUTURE OF WORK IN CAREER COUNSELING

Technology will certainly play a role in career counseling in the future. Since March 2020, the beginning of the COVID pandemic, my work has been conducted entirely on a Zoom platform, and for the majority of this time, I have worked remotely. The pandemic hugely increased my health professions advisees' stress, anxiety, and concern for their futures—change has been a constant for them. We have collectively expanded our capacity for creative flexibility and adaptability; for example, well-established timelines and deadlines became more fluid as the status of the pandemic evolved.

Hockey player Wayne Gretzky said, "I skate to where the puck is going to be, not where it has been" (Kelly, 2021, para. 1). Changes we've navigated over the past 10 plus years of work, from the Great Recession to the COVID-19 pandemic, suggest the need for a nimble posture and an affinity for continual learning as types of work, workplaces, technology, and population demographics continue to change. I see future career counselors becoming even more finely attuned to the ever-changing trends of the workforce, guiding clients in successfully navigating those trends and developing an eye to see what may be ahead for them. John Krumboltz's planned happenstance learning theory (Krumboltz 2009) seems particularly appropriate as a framework for equipping clients with the self-knowledge, optimism, and confidence to imagine and implement new work opportunities for themselves.

As I prepare to retire from higher education, I see great opportunities for continuing career counseling and advising with young adults, but also with fellow Baby Boomers who may be seeking assistance in starting a new career chapter. While these populations are vastly different in so many ways, across the generations I find a common need to meet people where they are and help them listen to their lives as they chart next steps.

Student Voices

In Student Voices, students offer a unique viewpoint as they begin in the career-counseling field. Here, students share their thoughts and reflections about the career-counseling profession and offer personal takeaways.

KEVIN B. EASON

Kevin has worked within the nonprofit sector for nearly 25 years, focusing on increasing access to mental health services, human rights, civil liberties, and equity, diversity, and inclusion initiatives. Most recently, he spent a decade in leadership with one of the nation's largest civil liberties organizations before returning to graduate school, where he remains focused on helping empower LGBTQIA+ individuals, communities of color, and other minorities.

The presence of multiple pandemics has altered the types of needs addressed by career counseling and other counseling professions and will continue to do so well into the foreseeable future. In addition to the COVID-19 pandemic, many people have grappled with pandemics related to employment, housing, and food insecurities; healthcare disparities; civil unrest; and systemic racism. George Floyd's murder and seemingly endless accounts of police brutality continue to add to the nation's upheaval. While these pandemics undeniably impacted many people and their communities, they've disproportionately impacted minorities (particularly communities of color). These have had tremendous impacts on the economy and workforce.

Many Americans found themselves unemployed or working from home while juggling numerous responsibilities, such as providing childcare and at-home schooling due to school closures. As a result, in 2020, the Centers for Disease Control found that more Americans feel anxious and depressed, with 40.9% reporting at least one adverse mental or behavioral health concern (Czeisler et al., 2020). Many people have begun to reprioritize their families and biopsychosocial well-being and place less emphasis on meeting the prior demands of the workplace, and many have resigned from the workforce entirely.

(continued)

These impacts provide many opportunities for counselors and employers alike. Today, employees want to feel valued, heard, and appreciated. Workplace culture is becoming more and more critical and is often a primary factor people consider when deciding whether to stay at their jobs or within their careers. Employers should encourage a person-centric environment to increase job satisfaction and retain employees. Leadership styles should reflect these cultural shifts, and rather than enforcing strict hierarchies with a "top-down" approach, leadership should be seen as an opportunity to serve others, where focus is placed on opportunities for growth and development. Now more than ever, employers should consider providing comprehensive benefits packages that support individuals and their families and is inclusive of people of different genders (including access to transgender healthcare). Rather than simply focusing on providing "safe spaces," businesses and counselors should encourage the creation and use of Brave Spaces. Brave Spaces seek to "cultivate a productive dialogue where participants are encouraged to speak honestly and critically from their own experience toward the end of mutual learning and liberation" (Holman & Mejía, 2019, para. 5).

Career development and other counseling professional's role within these changes cannot be overstated. Counselors are now tasked with working with clients who have experienced a multitude of pandemics (COVID-19, **employment**, housing and food insecurities, healthcare disparities, civil unrest, etc.) that have often altered their priorities and career goals. Counselors should always advocate for their clients and encourage workplace policies and laws and regulations that protect employee rights and interests. We must also be prepared to work with clients who have experienced significant loss, including the loss of family, friends, their own health and well-being, and so on. Loss and grief impact their career trajectories and overall mental health.

I believe that to be best prepared, counselors should be knowledgeable about workplace and economic trends, understand **employment** needs and the market, and be prepared to help individuals overcome anxiety, depression, or grief that may restrict their career development and mental wellness. Multiple pandemics have forever changed the world, and part of our role as counseling professionals and employers is supporting individuals in adapting and thriving in these new environments.

ANGEL HATHAWAY RICHARDSON

Angel is a Licensed Clinical Mental Health Counseling student in the Clinical Mental Health Counseling Program at North Carolina Central University. She is also a special education teacher and is currently completing her counseling internship at Peaceful Waters Counseling and Wellness Center in Moyock, North Carolina.

As a special education teacher with 21 years of experience, as well as being a current clinical mental health counseling graduate student at NCCU, I see a variety of trends in the counseling field. Over the past couple of years, we have embarked on a new lifestyle of having to work through and around the COVID-19 pandemic. I have seen more families seeking assistance through face-to-face therapy as well as virtual teletherapy. Clinicians have been faced with an increased number of clients and work hours, and they have been faced

(*continued*)

Student Voices (*continued*)

with working with the needs of clients that may not be within their area of specialty or the population they normally encounter.

In the future, I anticipate that clinicians will have greater opportunities to expand their expertise, skills, knowledge, and experience to stay abreast on current counseling resources. A few certifications clinicians may want to explore include: play therapy, art therapy, eye movement dissociation and processing (EMDR), and thanatology certifications. Additionally, I would recommend training in the areas of grief, loss, and bereavement, and professional development in working with clients with disabilities. All clinicians may benefit from continuing education in progress notes, treatment plans, telehealth, and ethics. I also anticipate increases in affordable mental health professional development, certifications, and community resources. Another opportunity for career counselors to consider includes expanding community education regarding the stigma of mental health.

I see career counselors and the counseling profession being the driving force in helping individuals, families, and communities navigate and move forward from trauma, grief, unemployment, and other hardships. I'm looking forward to seeing the counseling profession grows along with new interventions and tools counselors will keep in their toolboxes.

COUNSELING SKILLS CONNECTION

As we consider future practice, research, and trends, exploration of topics such as trauma-informed counseling skills, disaster mental health, and grief counseling will become increasingly needed and prevalent. The need for evidence-based practice and research within the counseling profession continues to be a focus due to the increased levels of loss, trauma, and grief witnessed and experienced in our society and throughout the world. It is imperative for counselors-in-training to learn skills related to supporting clients in growth and healing. Given the increase in natural and other disasters and crises in the United States and internationally, disaster mental health programs and certifications, such as one offered by Mental Health Academy (www.mentalhealthacademy .net/cce), will continue to be offered to helping professionals. There is a credential for Disaster Mental Health Certification (www.mentalhealthacademy.net/ cce) offered online in a 31-credit-hour, self-paced course by Dr. Cirecie West-Olatunji. Opportunities for additional counseling licensure, certifications, and credentialing may be a continued trend in the future for counselors to hone in on current issues and specialty areas and topics experienced widespread throughout our world.

Tip: High-Risk Clients

The following clinical resources support counselors' work with high-risk students or clients by offering warning signs to be mindful of. As counselors, it is vitally important to practice within your scope and recognize when there is a need for a referral to mental health providers and/or additional support:

■ *Treating Suicidal Clients and Self-Harm Behaviors: Assessments, Worksheets, and Guides for Interventions and Long-Term Care* by Meagan Houston (2017).

■ *High Risk Clients: Evidenced-Based Assessments and Clinical Tools to Recognize and Effectively Respond to Mental Health Crises* by Paul Brasler (2019).

MINDFUL MOMENT

When teaching counseling courses, instructors often encourage students to consider mindfulness and self-care practices as they begin their academic journey. Beginning these self-care strategies at the onset of one's career is particularly important as these daily practices can be carried into practice and throughout a counselor's professional and personal life.

How do you take care of yourself? What do you need physically, spiritually, mentally, and holistically to optimally get through your day? How can you envision sharing and teaching these same strategies or others with your current or future clients? For example, considering self-care as a routine practice, rather than an escape from day-to-day life can be a start. The article, entitled "8 Types of Self-Care and How to Practice Them" from *Bustle* (Polish, 2020), highlights the importance of taking inventory of the multiple aspects of caring for yourself from an overall wellness perspective, not only the physical aspects but also financial, professional, environmental, and so on.

What are some realistic and simple ways you can add self-care strategies into your day? For example, we can start by assessing the space you are in at home, in your "office," or in other spaces you tend to be located frequently. Are the spaces organized or cluttered? What is your preference? Either way, how does this make you feel when you are in the space?

TECH TOOLS

Interviews, particularly early-round screenings for professional roles, are increasingly being hosted via virtual platforms. AI is being used within systems to accelerate the candidate screening process and optimize the human relations professional's time, and HireVue is one such system. HireVue's automated interviewing tool is being used by mid- and large-sized corporations across the world to evaluate candidates' competencies and behaviors (Harwell, 2019). Candidates are invited to a web-based interview and are prompted to record responses to preselected questions. It can be more challenging for candidates to demonstrate enthusiasm, manage any interview-related anxiety, and effectively communicate their qualifications without speaking to a human being.

As a counselor, familiarizing yourself with these types of tools will allow you to allay client concerns and prepare them to be their best during a digital, human-free, interview. Role-playing with a client through a mock interview provides the opportunity to counsel your client around their nonverbal behaviors as well as the content and delivery of their responses. These types of tools will continue to adapt and their influence grow as AI improves.

REFLECTION ACTIVITY

Consider the following questions related to workforce trends and your role as a counselor. Think of your personal and workforce values. What would you need in your job to feel satisfied with your career? What changes have you observed during the past few years in the workforce? What are some workplace skill sets you believe will be necessary as we move into the future? What is the difference between workplace diversity and inclusion? Why is workplace inclusion so crucial to job satisfaction and employee retention? As a counselor, why is it important to stay current with workforce trends?

END-OF-CHAPTER RESOURCES

SUMMARY

Counseling-training programs need to be prepared to provide skills training and career readiness not only for students enrolled in the programs and their own careers but also for the clients these students will be serving in the future. The current climate and historical context will remain seminal in the development of new and relevant theories, practices, techniques, and approaches related to crises, grief, disaster preparedness, advocacy, and social justice topics. There is no doubt that technology will be a driving force in any future trends in the profession for many years and decades to come. This chapter explored current and future trends to watch, including AI, remote learning, and telemental health. Effective career-counseling practice must remain responsive to the evolution of the workforce and impact of current social and political events locally, regionally, and globally.

REFERENCES

Barrero, J. M., Bloom, N., & Davis, S. J. (2021, April 22). *Working from home will stick.* https://bfi.uchicago.edu/working-paper/why-working-from-home-will-stick/

Brasler, P. (2019). *High risk clients: Evidenced-based assessments and clinical tools to recognize and effectively respond to mental health crises.* PESI Publishing & Media.

Bureau of Labor Statistics. (2022, May). *Job openings and labor turnover – March 2022.* BLS.gov. https://www.bls.gov/news.release/pdf/jolts.pdf

Bureau of Labor Statistics, U.S. Department of Labor. (n.d.-a). *Occupational outlook handbook.* School and Career Counselors and Advisors. https://www.bls.gov/ooh/community-and-social-service/school-and-career-counselors.htm

Bureau of Labor Statistics, U.S. Department of Labor. (n.d.-b). *Occupational outlook handbook.* Substance Abuse, Behavioral Disorder, and Mental Health Counselors. https://www.bls.gov/ooh/community-and-social-service/substance-abuse-behavioral-disorder-and-mental-health-counselors.htm

Bush, M. (April 13, 2021). *Why is diversity & inclusion in the workplace important?* Great Place to Work. https://www.greatplacetowork.com/resources/blog/why-is-diversity-inclusion-in-the-workplace-important

Czeisler, M. É., Lane, R. I., Petrosky, E., Wiley, J. F., Christensen, A., Njai, R., Weaver, M. D., Robbins, R., Facer-Childs, E., Barger, L. K., Czeisler, C. A., Howard, M. E., & Rajaratnam, S. M. W. (2020). Mental health, substance use, and suicidal ideation during the COVID-19 pandemic—United States, June 24–30, 2020. *Morbidity and Mortality Weekly Report, 69*(32), 1049–1057. https://doi.org/10.15585/mmwr.mm6932a1

Davis, A. E. (2021). *Invest in career-readiness training for college students. Sketching a New Conservative Education Agenda.* American Enterprise Institute.

Delfino, G. F., & van der Kolk, B. (2021). Remote working, management control changes and employee responses during the COVID-19 crisis. *Accounting, Auditing and Accountability Journal, 34*(6), 1376–1387. https://doi.org/10.1108/AAAJ-06-2020-4657

Evans, B. (2020, June 4). *The Zoom revolution: 10 eye-popping stats from tech's new super-star*. Cloud Wars. https://accelerationeconomy.com/news/the-zoom-revolution-10-eye-popping-stats-from-techs-new-superstar/

Frink, D. D., & Klimoski, R. J. (1998). Toward a theory of accountability in organizations and human resource management. In G. R. Ferris (Ed.), *Research in personnel and human resources management* (*Vol. 16*, pp. 1–51). Elsevier Science/JAI Press.

Global Talent Trends. (n.d.). *Global talent trends 2022: The reinvention of company culture*. https://business.linkedin.com/talent-solutions/global-talent-trends?trk=media+-Global-Talent-Trends-2022

Harwell, D. (2019, October 22). A face-scanning algorithm increasingly decides whether you deserve a job. *Washington Post*. https://www.washingtonpost.com/technology/2019/10/22/ai-hiring-face-scanning-algorithm-increasingly-decides-whether-you-deserve-job/

Holman, F., & Mejía, E. (2019, December 19). *Safe spaces, brave spaces and why we gon' be alright*. https://www.citybureau.org/notebook/2019/12/19/safe-spaces-brave-spaces-and-why-we-gon-be-alright

Houston, M. N. (2017) *Treating suicidal clients & self-harm behaviors: Assessments, worksheets, and guides for interventions and long-term care*. PESI Publishing & Media.

Huffman, K. (2021, January 28). *Council post: Three ways to counter workplace monitoring: Building a culture of trust*. Forbes. https://www.forbes.com/sites/forbestechcouncil/2021/01/29/three-ways-to-counter-workplace-monitoring-building-a-culture-of-trust/?sh=12c1700b658c+https%3A%2F%2Fhbr.org%2F2020%2F11%2Fhow-to-actually-encourage-employee-accountability

International Society of Automation. (n.d.). *What is automation?* https://www.isa.org/about-isa/what-is-automation

Johnson, C. (2016, September 1). *The importance of career readiness and authentic business engagement*. U.S. Chamber of Commerce Foundation. https://www.uschamberfoundation.org/blog/post/importance-career-readiness-and-authentic-business-engagement

Karl, K. A., Peluchette, J. V., & Aghakhani, N. (2022). Virtual work meetings during the COVID-19 pandemic: The good, bad, and ugly. *Small Group Research*, *53*(3), 343–365. https://doi.org/10.1177/10464964211015286

Kelly, J. (2021, September 16). The 30 fastest-growing jobs and careers for the next 10 years. *Forbes*. https://www.forbes.com/sites/jackkelly/2021/09/16/the-30-fastest-growing-jobs-and-careers-for-the-next-10-years/?sh=35da027609f0

Krumboltz, J. D. (2009). The happenstance learning theory. *Journal of Career Assessment*, *17*(2), 135–154. https://doi.org/10.1177/1069072708328861

Lorenzo, R., Voigt, N., Tsusaka, M., Krentz, M., & Abouzahr, K. (2021, December 16). *How diverse leadership teams boost innovation*. United States - EN. https://www.bcg.com/en-us/publications/2018/how-diverse-leadership-teams-boost-innovation

National Association of Colleges and Employers. (March 2021). *Competencies*. https://www.naceweb.org/career-readiness/competencies/

National Association of Colleges and Employers (n.d.). *What is career readiness?* https://www.naceweb.org/career-readiness/competencies/career-readiness-defined/#:~:text=Career%20readiness%20is%20a%20foundation,successful%20entrance%20into%20the%20workforce

O'Donovan, D. (2018). Diversity and inclusion in the workplace. In C. Machado & J. Davim (Eds.), *Organizational behaviour and human resource management* (pp. 73–108). *Management and Industrial Engineering.* Springer. https://doi.org/10.1007/978-3-319-66864-2_4

Organization for Economic Cooperation and Development. (2018). *Good jobs for all in a changing world of work: The OECD jobs strategy.* https://www.oecd.org/employment/good-jobs-for-all-in-a-changing-world-of-work-9789264308817-en.htm

Owl Labs. (n.d.). *State of remote work 2021.* https://owllabs.com/state-of-remote-work/2022

Pappas, I. O., Mikalef, P., Giannakos, M. N., Krogstie, J., & Lekakos, G. (2018). Big data and business analytics ecosystems: Paving the way towards digital transformation and sustainable societies. *Information Systems and e-Business Management, 16*(3), 479–491. https://doi.org/10.1007/s10257-018-0377-z

Peters, P. (2020. April 28). *Google's Meet teleconferencing service now adding about 3 million users per day.* The Verge. https://www.theverge. com/2020/4/28/21240434/google-meet-three-million-users-per-day-pichai-earnings

Pew Research Center, Washington, DC. (2016). *The state of American jobs.* https://www.pewresearch.org/social-trends/2016/10/06/3-how-americans-view-their-jobs/

Pew Research Center, Washington, DC. (2022, March 9). *Majority of workers who quit a job in 2021 cite low pay, no opportunities for advancement, feeling disrespected.* https://www.pewresearch.org/fact-tank/2022/03/09/majority-of-workers-who-quit-a-job-in-2021-cite-low-pay-no-opportunities-for-advancement-feeling-disrespected/

Polish, J. (2020, August 14). *8 types of self-care & how to practice them.* Bustle. https://www.bustle.com/wellness/types-of-self-care-how-to-practice-experts

Pryce-Jones, J. (2010). *Happiness at work: Maximizing your psychological capital for success.* Wiley-Blackwell.

Riffkin, R. (2021, May 7). *In U.S., 55% of workers get sense of identity from their job.* Gallup.com. https://news.gallup.com/poll/175400/workers-sense-identity-job.aspx#:~:text=In%20U.S.%2C%2055%25%20of%20Workers,of%20Identity%20From%20Their%20Job&text=Employee%20Engagement%20Create%20a%20culture,in%20their%20work%20and%20workplace

Robbins, S. P., & Judge, T. (2022). *Organizational behavior* (18th ed.). Pearson.

Sestino, A., & De Mauro, A. (2022). Leveraging artificial intelligence in business: Implications, applications and methods. *Technology Analysis & Strategic Management, 34*(1), 16–29. https://doi.org/10.1080/09537325.2021.1883583

Shabanpour, R., Golshani, N., Tayarani, M., Auld, J., & Mohammadian, A. K. (2018). Analysis of telecommuting behavior and impacts on travel demand and the environment. *Transportation Research Part D: Transport and Environment, 62,* 563–576. https://doi.org/10.1016/j.trd.2018.04.003

Shobe, K. (2018). Productivity driven by job satisfaction, physical work environment, management support and job autonomy. *Business and Economics Journal, 9*(2), 1–9. https://doi.org/10.4172/2151-6219.1000351

Soroui, S. T. (2021). Understanding the drivers and implications of remote work from the local perspective: An exploratory study into the dis/reembedding dynamics. *Technology in Society, 64,* 101328. https://doi.org/10.1016/j.techsoc.2020.101328

Standaert, W., Muylle, S., & Basu, A. (2021). How shall we meet? Understanding the importance of meeting mode capabilities for different meeting objectives. *Information & Management, 58*(1), 103393. https://doi.org/10.1016/j.im.2020.103393

Thorp-Lancaster, D. (2020, April 29). *Microsoft Teams hits 75 million daily active users, up from 44 million in March*. Windows Central. https://www.windowscentral.com/microsoft-teams-hits-75-million-daily-active-users

U.S. Census Bureau Public Information Office. (2016, May 19). *U.S. Census Bureau projections show a slower growing, older, more diverse nation a half century from now – population – newsroom – U.S. Census Bureau*. United States Census Bureau. https://www.census.gov/newsroom/releases/archives/population/cb12-243.html

Visier. (n.d.). *Workplace trends 2022 executive summary*. https://discover.visier.com/Workplace-Trends-2022?

Wigert, B. (2022, April 18). *The top 6 things employees want in their next job*. Gallup.com. https://www.gallup.com/workplace/389807/top-things-employees-next-job.aspx

Index